D1535338

SYNOPSIS

OF THE

Books of the Bible

SYNOPSIS

OF THE

Books of the Bible

By J. N. DARBY

Volume IV

ACTS—PHILIPPIANS

LOIZEAUX BROTHERS, Inc.

NEW YORK

REVISED EDITION, NOVEMBER 1942
SECOND EDITION, JANUARY 1950

PRINTED IN THE UNITED STATES OF AMERICA

CONTENTS

———

ACTS

OF THE

APOSTLES

The three divisions of the book

THE Acts of the Apostles are divided essentially into
three parts—chapters 1, 2, to 12, and 13 to the end.
Chapters 11, 12 may be termed transitional chapters
founded on the event related in chapter 10. Chapter 1
gives us that which is connected with the Lord's resurrection; chapters 2-12 that work of the Holy Ghost of which
Jerusalem and the Jews were the centre, but which
branches out into the free action of the Spirit of God,
independent of, but not separated from, the twelve, and
Jerusalem as the centre; chapter 13 and the succeeding
chapters the work of Paul, flowing from a more distinct
mission from Antioch; chapter 15 connecting the two in
order to preserve unity in the whole course. We have
indeed the admission of Gentiles in the second part, but it
is in connection with the work going on among the Jews.
These latter had rejected the witness of the Holy Ghost to
a glorified Christ, as they had rejected the Son of God in
His humiliation; and God prepared a work outside them,
in which the apostle of the Gentiles laid foundations that
annulled the distinction between Jew and Gentile, and
which unite them—as in themselves equally dead in trespasses and sins—to Christ, the Head of His Body, the
assembly, in heaven.[1]

---

[1] It is a sorrowful but instructive thing to see, in the last division
of the book, how the spiritual energy of a Paul closes, as to its effect
in work, in the shadow of a prison. Yet we see the wisdom of God in
it. The boasted apostolicism of Rome never had an apostle but as a
prisoner; and Christianity, as the Epistle to the Romans testifies, was
already planted there.

Chapter 1

The risen Lord and the apostles' position before the descent of the Holy Spirit

LET us now examine the chapters in their course. Chapter 1 supplies us with the narrative of that which relates to Jesus risen, and the actions of the apostles before the descent of the Holy Ghost. The Lord's communications present several very interesting points. Jesus, the risen Man, acts and speaks by the Holy Ghost after His resurrection as before it. Precious token of our own position, as reminding us that we shall have the Holy Ghost after our resurrection, and that, being no longer engaged in restraining and mortifying the flesh, His divine energy in us will be entirely consecrated to eternal joy and worship, and to the service committed to us by God. The risen Lord then gives His disciples commandments in connection with the new position He assumes. Their life and their service are to be formed and guided in view of His resurrection—a truth of which they had irrefragable proofs. They were still on earth, but they were pilgrims there, having Him in view who had gone before them raised from among the dead. Their relations with Him are still connected with their position on earth. He speaks to them of the kingdom, and of that which concerned the kingdom. Jerusalem was the starting-point of their ministry, even more than of His own. For He had gathered together the poor of the flock wherever He had found them, especially in Galilee;[2] but now, resurrection having made Him in power the vessel of the sure mercies of David, He calls Israel afresh to own as Prince and Saviour

[2] The mission given in Luke 24 is the one fulfilled both in Peter's and Paul's discourses in the Acts, but especially in chapters 2, 13, not that of Matthew 28 which, indeed, was only to Gentiles. Luke's was on His ascension from Bethany, Matthew's in resurrection from Galilee, where He had sought the poor of the flock. (Compare Matt. 4: 15.)

the One whom they had rejected as the living Messiah on earth. The Epistles of Peter are connected with the gospel in this point of view.

The apostles' mission in the power of the promised Holy Spirit and the foundation of their testimony

Nevertheless, to exercise this ministry, they were to wait for the accomplishment of the Father's promise, the Holy Ghost, with whom they were to be baptized, according to John's testimony, which the Lord assured them should soon take place. The mission of the Holy Ghost led them, at the same time, out of the Jewish field of purely temporal promises. The Father's promise of the Holy Ghost was a very different thing from that of the restoration of the kingdom of Israel by the power of Jehovah, the God of judgment. It was not for them to know the time and season of this restoration, the knowledge of which the Father kept in His own possession; but they should themselves receive the power of the Holy Ghost, who would come down upon them; and they should be witnesses unto Jesus (as they had known Him, and according to the manifestation of Himself after His resurrection), both in Jerusalem and in all Judea, and in Samaria, and unto the uttermost parts of the earth—thus making Jerusalem the starting-point and first object, according to the mission, Luke 24: 47. Nevertheless, their testimony was founded on their beholding their Master and their Lord caught up from their midst, and received into the clouds of heaven, which hid Him from their sight. While looking steadfastly upwards, as this took place, two messengers from heaven come and announce to them that He will return in like manner. His manifestation in this lower world, beneath the heavens, is therefore here intended. He will return to earth to be seen of the world. We have not the rapture of the assembly, nor the assembly's association with Him while absent. With the knowledge of Jesus taken up out of the world, and to come again into the world, as the termini and elements of all their teaching, they return to Jerusalem, there to wait for the Holy Ghost who was promised unto them. It is not into Galilee that they go. They are to be witnesses in Jerusalem of the heavenly rights of that Christ who had been rejected on earth by Jerusalem and the Jews.[3]

Apostolic authority exercised according to intelligence in the Word : Judas' place taken by Matthias

All this clearly shows the position in which they were placed, and the mission committed to them. But before they _eceive the Holy Ghost for its fulfilment, some other characteristic circumstances find their place in this chapter. The fact, under the guidance of Peter, according to intelligence in the Word, before they are endowed with power from on high. These two things are therefore distinct from each other.

It appears that, although Peter was not directly led of the Holy Ghost, the Spirit put His seal on that which was done in accordance with the Word in the Old Testament understood by the apostle. We have before seen that Christ, after His resurrection, opened the understanding of His disciples that they might understand the Scriptures. They now act, not having received the Holy Ghost, according to a Jewish principle. They present _the lot_ to the Lord, that He may decide. Nevertheless the lot was not all, nor was it drawn without making a distinction. Apostolic authority flowed from the nomination of Christ Himself. Intelligence of the Scriptures makes them understand that which ought to be. The object which the Lord had assigned to their service narrowed the choice to the little circle of those who could fulfil that object. Their his-

[3] In this sense it is not a continuation of Christ's mission on the earth, continued in the Matthew mission from Galilee.

tory made them capable, as Jesus had said, of being His witnesses, because they had been with Him from the beginning, and could now testify that this same Jesus, whom the Jews had rejected and crucified, was indeed risen from among the dead.

Apostolic authority is exercised in Jerusalem on the Jewish principle, before the gift of the Holy Ghost. In this there was neither research nor the exercise of the human mind. "His bishopric let another take" guided their conduct; the capacity to testify of Jesus in His life on earth, and now of His resurrection and ascension, decided on the needed qualifications; the lot of Jehovah determined the individual who was to take Judas' place. Two are chosen, according to these needful qualifications, and the lot falls upon Matthias, who is numbered with the eleven apostles. But they were still without the promised power.

Chapter 2

The descent of the Holy Spirit in power

CHAPTER 2 relates the fulfilment of this promise, in answer to the spirit of dependence manifested in their united prayers.

The Spirit comes from above, in His own power, to possess and fill the dwelling-place prepared for Him.

This event, important beyond all others with respect to man's condition here below, has here a very simple character, because there is no question of the causes of this marvellous gift, of the work on which it depends, of the glory with which it is connected and which it reveals, and of which it is the earnest: we have here only the fact of its power. The disciples "were endued with power from on high."

The form of its appearance, however, is characteristic.
On Jesus the Holy Ghost descended in the shape of a dove,
because He was not to make His voice heard in the streets,
nor break the bruised reed, nor quench the smoking flax.
But here it was the power of God in testimony, the Word;
which was like consuming fire, judging all that came before it. Nevertheless it was in grace, and was to go beyond
the narrow limits of Jewish ordinances to proclaim the
wonderful works of God to every tongue and nation under
the sun. It was that mighty wind from heaven, which
manifested itself to the disciples, and came upon them in
the form of tongues of fire, each one divided into several.
This marvel attracts the multitude; and the reality of this
divine work is proved by the fact that persons from numerous countries hear these poor Galileans proclaim to them
the wonderful works of God, each one in the language of
the country whence he came up to Jerusalem.[4] The Jews,
who did not understand these languages, mock; and Peter
declares to them in their own tongue, and according to
their own prophecies, the true character of that which
had taken place. He takes his stand upon the resurrection
of Christ, foretold by the prophet-king, and upon His exaltation by the right hand of God. This Jesus, whom they
had crucified, had there received the promise of the
Father, and shed forth that which produced the effects
that they heard and saw. They were therefore to know
assuredly, that God had made that same Jesus whom they
had rejected both Lord and Christ.

The character of Peter's testimony: the promise also to those afar off

The character of this testimony will be remarked here.
It is essentially that of Peter. It goes no farther than the

[4] The rationalistic notion that it was a kind of excited gibberish, just
as the unbelieving Jews thought, is absurd beyond conception. Think
of Paul's thanking God that he spoke more kinds of gibberish than
they all, and God giving a gift for interpreting gibberish!

affirmation of the fact, that He who had been rejected by the Jews is *made* in heaven Lord and Christ. It begins with Jesus known of the Jews on earth, and establishes the truth of His being raised again, and exalted to the position of Lord. God has done this. The apostle does not even proclaim Him as the Son of God. We shall see that, if it is not done by Peter in the Acts, Paul on the contrary does it from the first moment of his conversion. Peter states the result at that moment in power, and does not speak of the kingdom. He only reminds them that the Spirit was promised in the last days, and alludes to the terrible day of the coming judgment, which would be preceded by alarming signs and wonders. Without speaking of the fulfilment of the promise of the kingdom, the time of which the Father had kept secret, he puts the fact of the gift of the Holy Ghost in connection with the responsibility of Israel, to whom God still acted in grace, by preaching to them a glorified Christ, and by giving them proofs of His glory in the gift of the Holy Ghost, made sensible to all. This is the presence of the Holy Ghost according to John 15: 26, 27. The testimony as a whole, however, is founded on and carries out the mission of Luke 24. Only in Luke we have nothing of baptism. See Luke 24: 47-49, to which this fully corresponds. The testimony was addressed to the Jews; nevertheless it was not confined to them,[5] and it was separative. "Separate yourselves from this untoward generation." This separation was founded on a real and moral work—"repent:" the past was all to be judged, and publicly demonstrated by their reception amongst Christians by baptism, in order to receive the remission of their sins, and participate

---

[5] The testimony is in terms which, applying to Jews there and scattered abroad, yet opened the door to the Gentiles in the sovereignty of God—"All that are afar off, as many as the Lord our God shall call." God is still the God of man; but He calls whom He pleases.

in this heavenly gift of the Holy Ghost. "Repent, and be baptized every one of you in the name of Jesus Christ, for the remission of sins, and ye shall receive the gift of the Holy Ghost." This work is individual. There was judgment on all the past, the admission amongst them by baptism, and the consequent participation in the Holy Ghost, who dwelt where they came. We see at once the difference between the moral change already wrought, the repentance which their godly sorrow works, and the reception of the Holy Ghost. This was consequent on the remission of their sins to which they were brought. This gift depended in a regular way on their admission amongst Christians, the house where He dwelt, built in the name of Jesus. Afterwards the promise is declared to belong to them and to their children—to the house of Israel as such—to them and to their children after them. But it went beyond the limits of God's ancient people. The promise was also to those that were afar off; for it was fulfilled, in connection with faith in Christ, to all who through grace should come into the new house—all whom the Lord, the God of Israel, should call. The call of God characterized the blessing. Israel, with her children, was owned, but a remnant called out from among them. The Gentiles, being called, shared the blessing.

The result of the gift of the Holy Spirit

The result of this ineffable gift is related to us. It was not merely a moral change, but a power which set aside all the motives that individualized those who had received it, by uniting them as one soul and in one mind. They continued steadfastly in the apostle's doctrine; they were in communion with each other and the apostles; they broke bread; they spent their time in prayer. The sense of God's presence was powerful among them; and many

signs and wonders were wrought by the hands of the
apostles. They were united in the closest bonds; no man
called anything his own, but all divided their possessions
with those that needed. They were daily in the temple,
the public resort of Israel for religious exercises, whilst
having their own apart—breaking bread at home daily.
They ate with joy and gladness of heart, praising God and
having favor with all the people around them.

The formation of the assembly

Thus the assembly was formed; and the Lord added to
it daily the remnant of Israel, who were to be saved from
the judgments that should fall on a nation which had
rejected the Son of God, their Messiah, and, thank God,
from yet deeper ruin. God brought into the assembly—
thus owned of Him by the presence of the Holy Ghost—
those whom He spared in Israel.[6] A new order of things
had commenced, marked by the presence of the Holy
Ghost.[7] Here was found the presence and the house of
God, although the old order of things still existed until
the execution of judgment upon it.

The assembly was formed therefore by the power of the
Holy Ghost come down from heaven, on the testimony
that Jesus, who had been rejected, was raised up to
heaven, being made of God both Lord and Christ. It was
composed of the Jewish remnant who were to be spared,
with the reserve of bringing in Gentiles whenever God
should call them. It was as yet formed in connection
with Israel in the patience of God, yet apart in power,
God's dwelling-place.

[6] This is the force of *sozomenoi*.
[7] God never dwelt with man but on the ground of redemption, not
with Adam nor Abraham. Compare Exodus 29: 46.

Chapters 3, 4

God's patience and grace in virtue of Christ's death and resurrection answered by opposition and rejection

IN chapter 3 the Spirit addresses His testimony to the people by the mouth of Peter. God still acted in patience towards His foolish people, and with more than patience. He acts in grace towards them, as His people, in virtue of the death and intercession of Christ—alas, in vain! Their unbelieving leaders silenced the Word.[8]

The lame man healed: Christ preached: the return of the rejected Lord in blessing dependent on repentance

The attention of the people is attracted by a miracle that restored strength to a poor lame man, known to all who frequented the temple; and, the multitude crowding to behold him, Peter preaches Christ to them. The God of their fathers, said he, had glorified His servant Jesus, whom they had denied, when Pilate would have set Him free. They had denied the Holy One and the Just—desired a murderer—killed the Prince of Life; but God had raised Him from the dead. And His name, through faith, had healed the impotent man. Grace could esteem their act done as through ignorance, and that as to their rulers also. We here see the Holy Ghost responding to their in-

---

[8] It is striking to see the counsels of God and their accomplishment in grace, as far as they were now being fulfilled, so clearly distinguished from the responsibility of those with whom God was dealing. In chapter 2 Peter says, "Save yourselves from this untoward generation." God was gathering, according to His own knowledge of what was coming. In chapter 3 he says, "God hath sent Him to bless you in turning every one of you away from his iniquities." So He had, and patience still waited, though God acted in present grace according to the result known to Himself: so in Jeremiah often. Had they repented, God would surely have turned from judgment, as stated also in Jeremiah.

tercession of Christ: "Father, forgive them, for they
know not what they do!" Guilty of the ten thousand
talents, the great King remits it them, sending the message
of mercy which calls them to repentance. To this Peter
invites them: "Repent ye, and be converted; so[9] that the
time of refreshing may come from the presence of the
Lord, and that He may send Jesus, whom the heaven
must receive," he tells them, until the time ordained of
God for the restoration which should accomplish all that
the prophets had foretold. That is to say, he preaches
repentance to the Jews as a nation, declaring that, on
their repentance, Jesus, who had ascended up to heaven,
would return; and the fulfilment of all the blessings spoken
of by the prophets should take place on their behalf. The
return of Jesus with this object depended (and still depends) on the repentance of the Jews. Meanwhile He
remains in heaven.

Moreover Jesus was the prophet announced by Moses:
and whosoever would not hear Him should be cut off from
the people. His voice still sounded in especial grace by
the mouth of His disciples. All the prophets had spoken
of these days. They were the children of the prophets,
the natural heirs of the blessings which they had announced for Israel, as well as of the promises made to
Abraham of a seed in whom all nations should be blessed.
To them also in consequence, God, having raised up His
servant Jesus,[10] had sent Him to bless them, in turning
away every one of them from his iniquities.

The apostles imprisoned

In a word, they are invited to return by repentance, and
enjoy all the promises made to Israel. The Messiah Him-

---

[9] Not "when." There is no pretence for so translating it.

[10] This refers to the time of His life on the earth, though on His intercession there was a renewal of the mercy in testimony to a glorified
Christ, who would return on their repentance.

self should return from heaven to establish their blessing.
The whole nation is here addressed as natural heirs of
the promises made to Abraham. But, while they were
speaking, the priests, and the captain of the temple, and
the Sadducees came to lay hands on them, being grieved
that they preached the resurrection, which their unbelief
and dogmatic system did not receive. They put them in
prison, for it was evening. The hope of Israel was set
aside; the grace of God had spoken in vain, great and
patient as it was. Many, however, believed their word:
five thousand persons already confessed the Lord Jesus.

The deliberate answer of the rulers' inmost heart: the Stone rejected by the builders

We have seen the address which God, in His grace, sent
to Israel by the mouth of Peter. We shall now see, not
only the reception (already noticed) which it met with
from the rulers of the people, but the deliberate answer
of their inmost heart, as we may call it. On the morrow
the rulers, the elders, and the scribes assemble at Jerusalem, together with Annas and his kindred; and, setting
the apostles in their midst, they demand by what power
or in what name they have wrought this miracle on the
impotent man. Peter, full of the Holy Ghost, declares—
announcing it to all Israel, and with the utmost readiness
and entire boldness—that it was by Jesus, whom they had
crucified, and whom God had raised from the dead. Thus
the question between God and the rulers of Israel was very
formally stated, and that by the Spirit of God. Jesus was
the Stone rejected by them, the builders, which had become the Head of the corner. Salvation could nowhere
else be found. No carefulness not to offend, with regard
to the adversaries and the rulers; with the people, as such,
ignorant and misled, everything to win them. The council
recognized them as former companions of Christ: the
man who had been healed was there. What could they

say or do in the face of the multitude who had witnessed the miracle? They could only exhibit a will in decided opposition to the Lord and His testimony, and yield to the public opinion, which was necessary to their own importance, by which too they were governed. With threats they commanded the apostles to teach no more in the name of Jesus. We may remark here, that Satan had Sadducean instruments arrayed against the doctrine of the resurrection, as he had Pharisees as suited instruments against a living Christ. We must expect the well-ordered opposition of Satan against the truth.

God's command or man's prohibition

Now Peter and John allow of no ambiguity with respect to their course. God had commanded them to preach Christ: the prohibition of man had no weight with them. "We cannot," say they, "but speak the things which we have seen and heard." What a position for the rulers of the people! Accordingly, a testimony like this plainly demonstrates that the leaders of Israel were fallen from the place of interpreters of the will of God. The apostles do not drive them away—do not attack them: God would judge them; but they act immediately on the part of God, and disregard their authority altogether with respect to the work that God had committed to themselves. The testimony of God was with the apostles, and not with the rulers of the temple; and the presence of God was in the assembly, and not there.

The Holy Spirit's power and God's presence and guidance in the midst of the disciples

Peter and John return to their own company, for a separate people who knew each other was formed; and all, moved by the Holy Ghost (for it was there that *God* dwelt by His Spirit, not now in the temple), lift up their voice to God, the Governor of all things, to acknowledge that this opposition of the rulers was but the accomplishment of the Word and the counsels and the purposes of God. These threatenings were but the occasion of asking God to manifest His power in connection with the name of Jesus. In a word, the world (including the Jews, who formed a part of it in their opposition) had stood up against Jesus, the Servant of God, and opposed itself to the testimony rendered to Him. The Holy Ghost is the strength of this testimony, whether in the courage of those who bore witness (ver. 8), or in His presence in the assembly (ver. 31), or in the energy of service (ver. 33), or in the fruits that are again produced among the saints with a power which makes it manifest that the Holy Ghost has dominion in their hearts over all the motives that influence man, making them walk by those of which He is the source. It is the energy of the Spirit in the presence of opposition, as before it was His natural fruit in those among whom He dwelt. Fresh persons sell their goods, and lay their price at the apostles' feet; among others, a man whom the Holy Ghost takes pleasure in distinguishing—Barnabas, from the island of Cyprus.

To sum up: this chapter demonstrates, on one side, the condition of the Jews, their rejection of the testimony which was addressed to them in grace; and on the other, the power of the Holy Ghost and God's presence and guidance elsewhere, namely, in the midst of the disciples.

These three chapters (2, 3, 4) present the first forming of the assembly, and its blessed character through the Holy Spirit dwelling in it. They present to us its first beauty as formed of God, and His habitation.

Chapter 5

Ananias and Sapphira: evil in the assembly manifesting the Spirit's power and God's presence

ALAS, evil shows itself there also. If the mighty Spirit of God is there, the flesh also is there. There are some who wished to have the credit of devotedness which the Holy Ghost produces, although devoid of that faith in God, and that self-renunciation, which, showing itself in the path of love, constitutes all the value and all the truth of this devotedness. But it only gives fresh occasion to manifest the power of the Spirit of God, the presence of God within, against evil; as the preceding chapter showed His energy outside, and the precious fruits of His grace. If there be not the simple fruit and of good already described, there is the power of good against evil. The present state of the assembly, as a whole, is the power of evil over good. God cannot endure evil where He dwells; still less than where He does not dwell. However great the energy of the testimony which He sends to those who are outside, He exercises all patience until there is no remedy within. The more His presence is realized and manifested (and even in proportion as that is done), the more He shows Himself intolerant of evil. It cannot be otherwise. He judges in the midst of His saints, where He will have holiness; and that according to the measure of the manifestation of Himself. Ananias and Sapphira disregarding the presence of the Holy Ghost, whose impulse they pretended to follow, fall down dead before the God whom, in their blindness, they sought to deceive in forgetting Him. God was in the assembly.

Mighty, though painful, testimony to His presence! Fear pervades every heart, both within and outside. In fact, the presence of God is a serious thing, however great its blessing. The effect of this manifestation of the power of a God present with those whom He acknowledged as His own was very great. Multitudes joined themselves by faith to the confession of the name of the Lord—at least from among the people, for the rest dared not. The more position we have in the world, the more we fear the world which gave it to us. This miraculous testimony to the power of God was also displayed in a still more remarkable way, so that people came from far to profit by it. The apostles were constantly together in Solomon's porch.

Opposition and jealousy of the Jewish rulers: the apostles again imprisoned

But alas, the manifestation of the power of God, in connection with the despised disciples of Jesus, and working outside the beaten track in which the self-importance of the high priest and those that were with him found its path, together with the progress made by that which they rejected, and the attention drawn to the apostles by the miracles that were wrought, excite the opposition and jealousy of the rulers; and they put the apostles in prison. In this world good ever works in the presence of the power of evil.

Set free by the providence of God through angelic ministry

A power different from that of the Holy Ghost in the assembly now displays itself. The providence of God, watching over His work, and acting through the ministry of angels, frustrates all the plans of the unbelieving heads of Israel. The priests shut up the apostles in prison. An angel of the Lord opens the prison doors, and sends the apostles to pursue their accustomed work in the temple. The officers whom the council send to the prison find it shut, and everything in order; but no apostles.

God to be obeyed rather than men

Meanwhile the council are informed that they are in the temple, teaching the people. Confounded and alarmed, the council send to fetch them; but the officers bring them without violence, fearing the people. For God holds everything in check, until His testimony be rendered, when He will have it rendered. The high priest remonstrates with them on the ground of his former prohibition. Peter's reply is more concise than on the former occasion, and is rather the announcement of a settled purpose, than the rendering a testimony by reasoning with those who will not hearken, and who showed themselves to be adversaries. It is the same in substance as what he had said when previously brought before the rulers: God is to be obeyed rather than men. Opposed to God, the heads of Israel were merely *men*. In saying this, all was decided: the opposition between them and God was evident. The God of their fathers had raised up Jesus, whom the rulers of Israel had crucified. The apostles were His witnesses, and so was the Holy Ghost, whom God had given to those who obeyed Him. All was said; the position clearly announced. Peter, in the name of the apostles, formally takes it on the part of God and of Christ, and in agreement with the seal of the Holy Ghost, who, given to believers, bore witness in the Saviour's name. Nevertheless there is no pride, no self-will. He must *obey* God. He still takes his place in Israel ("the God," he says, "of our fathers"); but the place of testimony for God in Israel. The advice of Gamaliel prevails to turn aside the purposes of the council, for God has always His instruments ready, unknown perhaps to us, where we are doing His will; nevertheless they cause the apostles to be beaten, and command them not to preach, and send them away. They were at a loss what to do—only made the opposition of their will the more evident, while how simple the path when sent of God, and consciously doing His will! We must obey God.

God Himself maintains His testimony

The object of this latter part of the chapter is to show that the providential care of God, whether miraculously by means of angels, or by disposing the hearts of men to accomplish His purposes, was exercised on behalf of the assembly, even as the Spirit of God bore testimony in it and manifested in it His power. The apostles, in no wise terrified, return, full of joy at being counted worthy to suffer for the name of Jesus; and every day, in the temple, or from house to house, they cease not to teach and to preach the good news of Jesus the Christ. However weak they might be, God Himself maintains His testimony.

Chapters 6, 7

The flesh showing itself: wisdom given by the Spirit meets the difficulty

OTHER evils, unhappily, assail the Church. The flesh begins to show itself, in the midst of the power of the Holy Ghost, the trouble arising from the different circumstances of the disciples, and in those things in which grace had been especially manifested, on the side on which they were connected with the flesh. The Hellenists (Jews born in Grecian or heathen countries) murmur against the Hebrews (natives of Judea), because the widows of the latter were favored, as they imagined, in the distribution of the goods bestowed on the assembly by its wealthier members. But here the wisdom given by the Spirit meets the difficulty, profiting by the occasion to give development to the work, according to the necessities that were growing up; and seven persons are named to undertake this business, for which the apostles would not forsake their own work. We also find, in the case of Philip and Stephen, the truth of what Paul says: "Those who have used the office of a deacon well, purchase to themselves a good degree and great boldness in the faith which is in Christ Jesus."

Observe here, that the apostles put prayer before preaching in their work, their conflict with the power of evil being more especially carried on in it, as well as their realization of the power of God for the strength and wisdom they needed; and, in order that they might act directly on God's part, it was necessary that grace and unction should be maintained in their hearts.

Observe also the grace that discovers itself under the influence of the Spirit of God in this matter: all the names, as far as we can judge, are those of Hellenists.

Evil bearing witness to the efficacy of the Spirit's presence

The influence of the Word extended, and many priests were obedient to the faith. Thus, until now, the opposition from without, and the evil within, did but minister occasion to the progress of the work of God, by the manifestation of His presence in the midst of the church. Take especial notice of this fact. It is not only that the Spirit does good by His testimony, but, although evil is there without and within, yet where power displays itself, that evil does but bear witness to the efficacy of His presence. There was evil, but there was power to meet it. Still it showed there was leaven even in the Pentecostal cake.

Stephen rendering the Spirit's last testimony to the nation's heads: judgment pronounced by ·the Holy Spirit

The energy of the Spirit manifests itself especially in Stephen, who is full of grace and power. The Hellenist Jews oppose him; and, not being able to answer him, they accuse him before the council, and in particular of having announced in the name of Jesus the destruction of the temple and of the city, and the change of the customs of

their law. Here, observe, we see the free power of the
Holy Ghost, without any sending by any other to the
work, as in the apostles appointed by Christ Himself. It
is not authority in the apostles, it is not in the Jews of
Palestine. He distributes to whom He will. It is the
godly and devoted Hellenist who renders the last testimony to the heads of the nation. If priests believe on the
one side, Jews from without Judea bear testimony on the
other, and prepare the way for a still more extended testimony; but at the same time for the definitive rejection,
morally, of the Jews as the basis and centre of the testimony, and of the work of gathering together. For ; yet
Jerusalem was the centre of testimony and gathering.
Peter had testified of a glorious Christ promising His
return on their repentance, and they had stopped His
testimony. Now judgment is pronounced on them by the
Holy Ghost through the mouth of Stephen, in whom they
show themselves open adversaries to this testimony. It is
not the apostles who, by official authority, break off with
Jerusalem. The free action of the Holy Ghost anticipates
a breach, which did not take place so as to form a part of
the scripture narrative. The thing is done by the power
of God; and the taking up to heaven of the witness raised
up by the Spirit to denounce the Jews as adversaries, and
to declare their fallen condition, placed the centre of gathering in heaven according to the Spirit—that heaven to
which the faithful witness, who was filled with the Spirit,
had gone up. Already, while on earth, he had the appearance of an angel to the eyes of the council who judged
him; but the hardness of their hearts would not let them
stop in the path of hostility towards the testimony rendered to Christ—a testimony which comes out here in a
special way as the testimony of the Holy Ghost.

Stephen,[11] as far as we are told, had not known the

[11] He is the expression of the power of the Holy Ghost witnessing to
Christ glorified, who had been now thus presented to Israel, who had
already rejected Him in humiliation. From the fall to the flood, man,

Lord during His life on earth. Certainly he was not appointed, like the apostles, to be a witness of that life. He was simply the instrument of the Holy Ghost, distributing to whom He would.

The nation's history and full measure of guilt summed up

He begins therefore their history from the beginning of God's way, that is, from Abraham, called out by the revelation of the God of glory, slow indeed to obey, but at length led by the patient grace of God into Canaan. Nevertheless, he was a stranger in the promised land; and bondage was to be the portion of his descendants, until God interposed in grace. The lot, therefore, of the blessed patriarch was not that of possessing the promises, but of being a stranger; and that of his descendants was to be captives until God delivered them with a strong arm. Nothing can be more striking than the calm superiority to circumstances displayed by Stephen. He recites to the Jews a history they could not deny, a history they boasted in, yet it condemned them utterly. They were doing as their fathers had done. But two persons are specially prominent in Stephen's account, in connection with the goodness of God towards Israel at this period—Joseph and Moses. Israel had rejected them both, given up Joseph to the Gentiles, rejected Moses as judge and leader. It was, in cases which the Jews could not deny or object to, the history of Christ also, who, too, at the time ap-

though not left without witness, was otherwise left to himself. There were no special ways and institutions of God. The result was the flood, to cleanse, so to speak, the earth from its horrible pollution and violence. In the new world God began to deal with man. Government was set up in Noah. But in Abraham one was, by electing grace, called out, and God's promises given to him when the world had turned to demons. This began the history of God's people; but the question of righteousness was not raised. This the law did, claiming it from man. Then prophets came in patient grace. Then, the last appeal of God for fruits, and testimony of grace, the Son was sent. He was now rejected, and on His intercession the Holy Ghost had witnessed to His glory by Peter (Acts 3) for their repentance, and now dealt with them as to it by Stephen.

pointed of God, will indeed be the Redeemer of Israel.
This is the substance of Stephen's argument. The Jews
had always rejected those whom God had sent and in
whom the Holy Ghost had acted, and the testimony of
the same Holy Ghost in the prophets who had spoken of
the Christ whom they had now betrayed and slain. Besides this, according to Moses, they had worshipped false
gods, even from the time of their deliverance out of
Egypt[12]—a sin which, however great the long-suffering of
God, would cause them to be carried away, now that they
had filled up the measure of their iniquity, beyond the
Babylon which had already been their punishment.

It is a most striking summing up of their whole history
—the history of man with all the means of restoration
supplied. The full measure of guilt is stated. They had
received the law and had not kept it, rejected the prophets
who had testified of Christ, and betrayed and murdered
Christ Himself—always resisted the Holy Ghost. What
they did trust in, the temple, God rejected. God Himself
has been, as it were, a stranger in the land of Canaan;
and if Solomon built Him a house, it was in order that
the Holy Ghost might declare that He who had heaven for
His throne, and earth for His footstool, whose dominion
was universal, would not dwell in houses of stone, which
were the creation of His own hand. Thus we have the
complete summing up of their history, connected with the
last days of their judgment. They always resisted the
Holy Ghost, as they had always disobeyed the law.
Judaism was judged, after the long patience of God and
all His ways of grace with man as means were exhausted.
For Israel was man under the special dealings and care
of God. Man's guilt now is not only sin, but sin in spite
of all that God has done. It was the turning-point of
man's history. Law, prophets, Christ, the Holy Ghost, all

[12] Observe, too, here, that however long the patience of God had lasted,
repentance not being its result, the first sin, the first departure from
God, bears its penalty at the end.

tried, and man at enmity against God. The cross had
really proved it, but this had added the rejection of the
testimony of the Holy Ghost to a glorified Christ. All
was over with man, and began anew with the second Man
ever in connection with heaven.

Man's rejection of a glorified Christ: the heavens opened to faith: the Son of Man in the glory

Their conscience convicted, and their heart hardened,
their will unchanged, the members of the council were
filled with rage, and gnashed upon him with their teeth.
But if Stephen was to bear this definite testimony against
Israel, he was not merely to render the testimony, but
much more to place it in its true relative position, by a
living expression of that which a believer was in virtue
of the presence of the Holy Ghost here below dwelling in
Him. In their history we have man always resisting the
Holy Ghost; in Stephen, a man full of Him consequent
on redemption.

Such are the elements of this touching and striking
scene, which forms an epoch in the history of the assembly. The heads of Israel gnash their teeth with rage,
against the mighty and convincing testimony of the Holy
Ghost, with which Stephen was filled. They had rejected
a glorified Christ, as they had slain a humbled One. Let
us follow out the effect as to Stephen himself. He looks
stedfastly up to heaven; now fully opened to faith. It is
thither that the Spirit directs the mind, making it capable
of fixing itself there. He reveals to one who is thus filled
with Himself the glory of God on high, and Jesus in that
glory at the right hand of God, in the place of power—
Son of Man in the far higher place than that of Psalm
2, that of Psalm 8, though all things were not yet put
under Him. (Compare John 1: 50, 51.) Afterwards He
gives the effect of the testimony borne in the presence of
the power of Satan, the murderer.

Stephen as the first example of the state of the believer's soul after death with Christ glorified

"I see," said Stephen, "the heavens opened." Such then is the position of the true believer—heavenly upon the earth—in presence of the world that rejected Christ, the murderous world; the believer, alive in death, sees by the power of the Holy Ghost into heaven, and the Son of Man at the right hand of God. Stephen does not say "Jesus." The Spirit characterizes Him as the Son of Man! Precious testimony to man! Nor is it to the glory of God that he testifies (this was natural to heaven) but to the Son of *Man* in the glory, heaven being open to him, and then looks to Him as the Lord Jesus, to receive his spirit, the first example and full testimony of the state of the believer's soul after death with Christ glorified.

The resemblance of Stephen to his Master

With regard to the progress of the testimony, it is not now that Jesus is the Messiah, and He will return if you repent (which, however, does not cease to be true), but it is the Son of Man in heaven, which is open to the man that is filled with the Holy Ghost—that heaven to which God is about to transport the soul, as it is the hope and the testimony of those that are His. The patience of God was doubtless still acting in Israel; but the Holy Ghost opened new scenes and new hopes to the believer.[13] But

---

[13] The Holy Ghost opens heaven to our view, and enables us to contemplate that which is found there; and forms us on earth according to the character of Jesus. As to the change that took place in the progress of God's dealings, it appears to me that it was the realization by the Spirit of the effect of the veil being rent. Jesus is seen still standing; because, until the rejection by Israel of the testimony of the Holy Ghost, He did not definitely sit down, waiting for the judgment of His enemies. Rather He remained, in the position of High Priest, standing; the believer with Him on high by the Spirit, and the soul having thus far joined Him there in heaven; for now, by the blood of Christ, by that new and living way, it could enter within the veil. On the other hand, the Jews having done the same thing with regard to the testimony of the Holy Ghost that they did with regard to Jesus, having (so to speak) in Stephen sent a messenger after Him to say, "We will not have this man to reign over us," Christ definitely takes His place,

remark that Stephen, in consequence of seeing Jesus in heaven, perfectly resembles Jesus upon earth—a fact precious in grace to us: only that the glory of His Person is in all cases carefully guarded. Jesus, though heaven was opened to Him, was Himself the object to which heaven looked down, and who was publicly owned and sealed of the Father. He did not need a vision to present an object to His faith, nor did it produce any transformation into the same image by revelation of the glory. But, "Father, into Thy hands I commit My spirit," is found in "Lord Jesus, receive my spirit." And the affection for Israel which expresses itself in intercession, "Father, forgive them, for they know not what they do," is found again in "Lord, lay not this sin to their charge;" save that here the Holy Ghost does not now affirm that they are ignorant.

Stephen's position and the divine character and Person of Jesus, the Object of heaven

But it is well to dwell a moment on that which brings out more clearly the especial position of Stephen, the vessel of the Spirit's testimony, so definitively rejected by the Jews; and the divine character and Person of Jesus, even where His disciple is most like Him. Heaven is open to Jesus, the Holy Ghost descends upon Him and He is acknowledged the Son of God. Heaven opens on Jesus, and the angels descend upon the Son of Man: but He has

seated in heaven, until He shall judge the enemies who would not that He should reign over them. It is in this last position that He is viewed in the Epistle to the Hebrews; in which consequently they are exhorted to come out of the camp of Israel, following after the victim whose blood had been carried into the sanctuary; thus anticipating the judgment, which fell upon Jerusalem intermediately by means of the Romans, in order to set the nation aside, as it will be finally executed by Jesus Himself. The position of Stephen therefore resembles that of Jesus, the testimony being that of the Spirit to Jesus glorified. This makes the great principle of the Epistle to the Hebrews very plain.

The doctrine of the Church, announced by Paul after the revelation made to him on his way to Damascus, goes further than this; that is, it declares the union of Christians with Jesus in heaven, and not merely their entrance into the holy place through the rent veil, where the priest might only go in previously, behind the veil which hid God from the people.

no object presented to Him; He is Himself the Object on which heaven is gazing. Heaven will open at the end of the age, and Jesus Himself come forth on the white horse (that is, in judgment and triumph). Here, too, heaven opens, and the disciple, the Christian, full of the Holy Ghost, sees into it, and there beholds Jesus at the right hand of God. Jesus is still the Object, before of heaven, now of the believing man who is filled with the Holy Ghost; so that, as to the object of faith and the position of the believer, this scene is definitively characteristic. Jesus has no object, but is the Object of heaven when it opens; the saint has, and it is Jesus Himself in heaven when it is open. Rejected, and rejected by the Jews, like Jesus, partaking in His sufferings, and filled with His Spirit of grace, Stephen's eyes are fixed on high, on the heaven which the Holy Ghost opens to him; and he sees the Son of Man there ready to receive his spirit. The rest will come later; but it is not only Jesus, whom the heavens must receive until the times of restitution, but also the souls of His believing people until the moment of resurrection, and the whole Church, in spirit, detached from the world that rejected Him, and from Judaism that opposed the testimony of the Holy Ghost. The latter, Judaism, is no longer at all recognized; there is no longer any room for the long-suffering of God towards it. Its place is taken by heaven, and by the assembly, which, so far as it is consistent, follows her Master there in spirit, while waiting for His return.

Saul was present at Stephen's death, and consenting to it.[14]

---

[14] We may remark here, that the sanctuary, so to speak, is open to all believers. The veil indeed was rent by the death of Christ, but the grace of God was still acting towards the Jews, as such, and proposed to them the return of Jesus to the earth, that is to say, outside the veil, in the event of their repentance, so that the blessing would then have been upon the earth—the times of refreshing by the coming of Christ, which the prophets had announced. But now it is no longer a Messiah, the Son of David, but a Son of Man in heaven; and, by the Holy Ghost

The end of the first phase of the assembly of God

This is the end of the first phase of the assembly of God—its history in immediate connection with Jerusalem and the Jews, as the centre to which the work of the apostles related, "beginning at Jerusalem;" carried on, however, in a believing remnant, but inviting Israel, as such, to come into it, as being nationally the object of the love and care of God, but they would not. Some accessory events follow, which enlarge the sphere of labor and maintain the unity of the whole, previously to the revelation of the call of the Gentiles, as such, properly speaking, and of the assembly as one Body, independent of Jerusalem, and apart from the earth. These events are—the work of Philip in the conversion of Samaria and of the Ethiopian; that of Cornelius, with Peter's vision that took place after the vocation of Saul, who himself is brought in by a Jew of good report among the Jews as such; the labors of Peter in all the land of Canaan; and, finally, the connection established between the apostles at Jerusalem and the converted Gentiles at Antioch; the opposition of Herod, the false king of the Jews, and the care which God still takes of Peter, and the judgment of God upon the king. Afterwards comes the direct work among the Gentiles, having Antioch for its starting-point, already prepared by the conversion of Paul, through means and with a revelation that were quite peculiar. Let us follow the details of these chapters.

here below, an opened heaven is seen and known, and the great High Priest (standing as yet) at the right hand of God is not hidden behind a veil. All is open to the believer; the glory, and He who has entered into it for His people. And this, it appears to me, is the reason why He is seen standing. He had not definitely taken His place as seated (*eis to dienekes*) on the heavenly throne, until the testimony of the Holy Ghost to Israel of His exaltation had been definitively rejected on earth. The free testimony of the Spirit which is developed, here and afterwards, is highly interesting, without touching apostolic authority in its place, as we shall see. As to the Jews, till the High Priest comes out, they cannot know that His work is accepted for the nation; as, in the day of atonement, they had to wait till he came out that they might know it. But for us the Holy Ghost is come out while He is within, and we know it.

Chapter 8

Persecution and dispersion accomplishing God's will in sovereign judgment on Israel

AFTER the death of Stephen persecution breaks out. The victory, gained by a hatred the accomplishment of whose object was allowed by Providence, opens the floodgates to the violence of the Jewish leaders, enemies to the gospel. The barrier that restrained them once broken, the waves of passion overflow on all sides. People are often held back by a little remaining conscience, by habits, by a certain idea of the rights of others; but when the dykes are broken, hatred (the spirit of murder in the heart) satiates itself, if God permit, by actions that show what man is when left to himself. But all this hatred accomplishes the will of God, in which man would perhaps otherwise have failed, and which in some respects he could not or ought not even to have executed, that is to say, the will of God in sovereign judgment. The dispersion of the assembly was Israel's judgment—a judgment which the disciples would have found it difficult to declare and to execute by the communication of greater light to them; for whatever may be the blessing and energy in the sphere where the grace of God acts, the ways of God in directing all things are in His own hand. Our part, too, in His ways as to those without, is in grace.

The apostles' concentration at Jerusalem: its continuance as a centre of authority and influence

The whole assembly then, except the apostles, is scattered. It is questionable also, that the apostles did right in remaining, and whether a more simple faith would not have made them go away, and thus have spared the assembly many a conflict and many a difficulty in connection with the fact that Jerusalem continued to be a centre

of authority.[15] The Lord had even said with Israel in
view, "When they persecute in one city, flee into another,"
and after His resurrection He commands them to go and
disciple all nations. This last mission we do not find executed in the history of the Acts and the work among the
Gentiles, and, as we see in Galatians 2, by a special agreement entered into at Jerusalem, it fell into the hands of
Paul, being placed on an entirely new footing. The Word
tells us nothing of the accomplishment of this mission of
the twelve towards the Gentiles, unless it be the slight general intimation in the end of Mark. God is mighty in
Peter toward the circumcision and in Paul towards the
Gentiles. It may be said that the twelve were not persecuted. It is possible, and I say nothing decided on the
point; but it is certain that the passages which I have
quoted have no fulfilment in the Bible history, and that
another arrangement, another order of things, took place
in lieu of that which the Lord prescribed, and that Jewish
prejudices had in fact an influence, resulting from this
concentration at Jerusalem, from which even Peter had
the greatest difficulty to free himself.

Those who were scattered abroad preached the Word
everywhere, but only to the Jews, before some of them
arrived at Antioch. (Chap. 11: 19.)

Philip's work in Samaria: apostolic recognition

Philip however went down to Samaria, and preached
Christ to them, and wrought miracles. They all give heed
to him and are even baptized. A man who until then had

---

[15] This in no wise prevents the manifestation of the sovereign wisdom
of God. The development of the doctrine of the assembly in its oneness,
and as the Body of Christ, was but so much the more perfect and un-
mixed, as we find it taught by Paul; who was called outside of Judaism
by the revelation of a heavenly Christ. Neither do these ways of sovereign wisdom in God make any change at all in the responsibility of
man. The outward unity of the assembly was also preserved by this
means, by the connection kept up between the other places and Jerusalem, until the work among the Gentiles outside Judaism made these
connections extremely difficult and precarious. This, however, rendered
the grace and the wisdom of God but so much the more apparent.

bewitched them with sorcery, so that they had said he was the great power of God, even he also submits to the power which eclipsed his false marvels, and convinced him so much the more of its reality as he was conscious of the falseness of his own. The apostles make no difficulty with regard to Samaria. The history of Jesus must have enlightened them in that respect. Moreover the Samaritans were not Gentiles. Still it was a Hellenist who preached the gospel there.

The Holy Spirit conferred by the apostles through prayer and laying on of hands: Jerusalem set aside

A new truth comes out here in connection with the regular process of the assembly—namely, that the apostles conferred the Holy Ghost by means of prayer and the laying on of hands: a very important fact in the history of God's dealings. Moreover Samaria was a conquest which all the energy of Judaism had never been able to make. It was a new and splendid triumph for the gospel. Spiritual energy to subdue the world appertained to the assembly. Jerusalem was set aside: its day was over in that respect.

Simon the sorcerer: the true condition of his heart

The presence of the power of the Holy Ghost acting in Peter preserves the assembly as yet from the entrance of hypocrites, the instruments of Satan. The great and powerful fact that God was there manifested itself and made the darkness evident which circumstances had concealed. Carried along by the strong current, Simon had yielded, as to his intelligence, to the authority of Christ whose name was glorified by Philip's ministry. But the true condition of his heart, the desire of his own glory, the complete opposition between his moral condition and all principle—all light from God—betrays itself in presence

of the fact that a man can impart the Holy Ghost. He
desires to buy this power with money. What a thought!
It is thus that the unbelief which appears quite to pass
away, so that the things of God are outwardly received,
betrays itself by something which, to one who has the
Spirit, is so grossly contrary to God that its true character
is manifest even to a child taught by God Himself.

The free energy of the Spirit outside Jerusalem

Samaria is thus brought into connection with the centre
of the work at Jerusalem, where the apostles still were.
Already the Holy Ghost's being bestowed on the Samaritans was an immense step in the development of the
assembly. Doubtless they were circumcized, they acknowledged the law, although the temple had in a certain degree
lost its importance. The body of believers was more consolidated, and, so far as they still held to Jerusalem, it was
a positive gain; for Samaria, by receiving the gospel, entered into connection with her ancient rival, as much as
the apostles themselves were so, and submitted to her.
Probably the apostles, during that time of persecution, did
not go to the temple. God had opened a wide door to
them outside, and thus made them ample amends in their
work, for the success of the rulers of Israel who had
stopped it in Jerusalem; for the energy of the Spirit was
with them. To sum up: that which is presented here is
the free energy of the Spirit in others than the apostles,
and outside Jerusalem which had rejected it; and the relations maintained with the apostles and Jerusalem by their
central action, and the authority and power with which
they were invested.

Philip's ready obedience: the Spirit's guidance: the grace of the gospel to the Ethiopian

Having accomplished their work, and themselves evan-
gelized several villages of the Samaritans, Peter and John

return to Jerusalem. The work outside goes on, and by
other means. Philip, who presents the character of prompt
unquestioning obedience in simplicity of heart, is called
to leave his prosperous work with which all his personal
importance (if he had been seeking it) was connected, and
in which he was surrounded with respect and affection.
"Go," said the angel of the Lord, "toward the south, unto
the way that leads from Jerusalem to Gaza." It was a
desert. Philip's ready obedience does not think of the
difference between Samaria and Gaza, but of the Lord's
will: and he goes. The gospel now extends to the proselytes from among the Gentiles, and makes its way to the
centre of Abyssinia. The Queen's treasurer is admitted
among the disciples of the Lord by baptism, which sealed
his faith in the testimony of the prophet Isaiah; and he
goes on his way, rejoicing in the salvation which he had
taken a toilsome journey from a far country to seek in
legal duties and ceremonies, but with faith in God's Word,
in Jerusalem. Beautiful picture of the grace of the gospel!
He carries away with him, and to his home, that which
grace had bestowed on him in the wilderness—that which
his wearisome journey to Jerusalem had not procured
him. The poor Jews, who had driven away the testimony
from Jerusalem, are outside everything. The Spirit of the
Lord carries Philip far away, and he is found at Azotus;
for all the power of the Lord is at the service of the Son
of Man for the accomplishment of the testimony to His
glory. Philip evangelizes all the cities unto Cæsarea.

Chapter 9: 1 to 31

Saul, the apostle of Jewish hatred, called to be an apostle of the Lord of glory

A WORK and a workman of another character begin
now to dawn upon the scene.

We have seen the inveterate opposition of the heads of

Israel to the testimony of the Holy Ghost, their obstinacy
in repelling the patient grace of God. Israel rejected all
the work of the God of grace in their behalf. Saul makes
himself the apostle of their hatred to the disciples of Jesus,
to the servants of God. Not content with searching them
out at Jerusalem, he asks for letters from the high priest,
that he may go and lay hands on them in foreign cities.
When Israel is in full opposition to God, he is the ardent
missionary of their malice—in ignorance, no doubt, but
the willing slave of his Jewish prejudices.

Thus occupied, he approaches Damascus. There, in the
full career of an unbroken will, the Lord Jesus stops him.
A light from heaven shines round about him, and en-
velopes him in its dazzling brightness. He falls to the earth,
and hears a voice saying unto him, "Saul, Saul, why persecutest thou Me?" The glory which had thrown him to
the ground left no doubt—accompanied as it was by that
voice—that the authority of God was revealed in it. His
will broken, his pride overthrown, his mind subdued, he
asks, "Who art Thou, Lord?" The authority of the One
who spoke was unquestionable; Saul's heart was subject to
that authority: and it was Jesus. The career of his self-
will was ended for ever. But moreover the Lord of glory
was not only Jesus; He also acknowledged the poor disciples, whom Saul desired to carry prisoners to Jerusalem,
as being Himself.

The revelation that the rejected, despised Jesus is Lord and that His disciples are one with Him

How many things were revealed in those few words!
The Lord of glory declared Himself to be Jesus, whom
Saul persecuted. The disciples were one with Himself.
The Jews were at open war with the Lord Himself. The
whole system which they maintained, all their law, all
their official authority, all the ordinances of God, had not
prevented their being at open war with the Lord. Saul

himself, armed with their authority, found himself occupied in destroying the name of the Lord and His people from off the earth: a terrible discovery, completely overwhelming his soul, all-powerful in its effects, not leaving one moral element of his soul standing before its strength. Extenuation of the evil was fruitless; zeal for Judaism was zeal against the Lord. His own conscience had only animated that zeal. The authorities constituted of God, surrounded with the halo of centuries of honor, enhanced by the present calamities of Israel which had now nothing but her religion—these authorities had but sanctioned and favored his efforts against the Lord. The Jesus whom they rejected was the Lord. The testimony which they endeavored to suppress was *His* testimony. What a change for Saul! What a new position, even for the minds of the apostles themselves who remained at Jerusalem, when all were dispersed—faithful indeed in spite of the opposition of the rulers of Israel, but themselves in connection with the nation.

The effect of the Lord's revelation on Saul

But the work went deeper yet. Misguided no doubt, but his conscience in itself—for he thought he ought to do many things against the name of Jesus of Nazareth—left him the enemy of the Lord. Blameless righteousness according to law, as man could measure it, more than left him hardened in open opposition to the Lord. His superiors, and the authorities of the ancient religion—all his soul was based on morally as well as religiously—all was smashed within him for ever. He was broken up in the whole man before God. Nothing remained in him but discovered enmity against God, save as his own will was also broken in the process, he who an hour before was the conscientious, blameless, religious man! Compare, though the revelation of Christ carried him much farther,

Galatians 2:20; Philippians 3; 2 Corinthians 1:9; 4:10;
and a multitude of passages.

Other important points are brought out here. Saul had
not known Jesus on earth. He had not a testimony because he had known Him from the beginning, declaring
that He was made Lord and Christ. It is not a Jesus who
goes up into heaven where He is out of sight; but the Lord
who appears to him for the first time in heaven, and who
announces to him that He is Jesus. A glorious Lord is
the only one whom he knows. His gospel (as he expresses
it himself) is the gospel of the glory. If he had known
Christ after the flesh, he knows Him no more. But there
is yet another important principle found here. The Lord
of glory has His members on earth. "I am Jesus, whom
thou persecutest." It was Himself: those poor disciples
were bone of His bones and flesh of His flesh. He looked
upon them and cherished them as His own flesh. The
glory and the oneness of the saints with Jesus, their Head
in heaven, are the truths connected with the conversion of
Saul, with the revelation of Jesus to him, with the creation of faith in his heart, and that in a way which over-
threw Judaism in all its bearings in his soul; and that in
a soul in which this Judaism formed an integral part of
its existence, and gave it its whole character.

United to a glorified Christ

Another point, borrowed from his account of the vision
later in the book, which is remarkable in connection with
his career: "Separating thee," says the Lord, "from the
people and from the Gentiles, to whom I now send thee."
This moral end of Saul separated him from both—of
course from the Jews, but did not make a Gentile of him
either—and united him with a glorified Christ. He was
neither a Jew nor a Gentile in his spiritual standing. All
his life and ministry flowed from his association with a
heavenly glorified Christ.

The Lord's conversation with Ananias: Saul's baptism

Nevertheless he comes into the assembly by the usual means—like Jesus in Israel—humbly taking his place there where the truth of God was established by His power. Blind for three days and fully engrossed—as was natural—with such a discovery, he neither eats nor drinks; and afterwards, besides the fact of his blindness, which was a quiet, continual, and unequivocal proof of the truth of that which had happened to him, his faith must have been confirmed by the arrival of Ananias, who can declare to him from the Lord that which had happened to him, although he had not been out of the city—a circumstance so much the more striking because, in a vision, Saul had seen him come and restore his sight. And this Ananias does: Saul receives sight, and is baptized. He takes food and is strengthened. The conversation of Jesus with Ananias is remarkable, as showing with what distinct evidence the Lord revealed Himself in those days, and the holy liberty and confidence with which the true and faithful disciple conversed with Him. The Lord speaks as a man to his friend in details of place and circumstances, and Ananias reasons in all confiding openness with the Lord in regard to Saul; and Jesus answers him, not in harsh authority, though of course Ananias had to obey, but with gracious explanation, as with one admitted to His confidence, by declaring that Saul is a chosen vessel to bear His name before Gentiles and kings and the children of Israel; and that He will show him how great things he must suffer for His sake.

The subject of Saul's preaching

Saul makes no delay in confessing and declaring his faith; and that which he says is eminently worthy of notice. He preaches in the synagogue that Jesus is the Son of God. It is the first time that this is done. That He was exalted to the right hand of God—that He was

Lord and Christ—had been already preached; the rejected
Messiah was exalted on high. But here it is the simple
doctrine as to His personal glory; Jesus is the Son of God.

In the words of Jesus to Ananias, the children of Israel
come last.

The two great elements of blessing—the fear of God and the comfort of the Holy Spirit: persecution accomplishing God's designs

Saul does not yet begin his public ministry. It is, so to
speak, only the expression of his personal faithfulness, his
zeal, his faith, among those that surrounded him, with
whom he was naturally connected. It was not long before
opposition manifested itself, in the nation that would have
no Christ, at least according to God, and the disciples
sent him away, letting him down by the wall in a basket;
and through the agency of Barnabas (a good man, and
full of the Holy Ghost and of faith, whom grace had
taught to value the truth with regard to the new disciple)
the dreaded Saul found his place among the disciples even
at Jerusalem.[16] Wonderful triumph of the Lord! Singu-
lar position for himself there, had he not been absorbed by
the thought of Jesus. At Jerusalem he reasons with the
Hellenists. He was one of them. The Hebrews were not
his natural sphere. They seek to put him to death; the
disciples bring him down to the sea, and send him to
Tarsus, the place of his birth. The triumph of grace has,
under God's hand, silenced the adversary. The assemblies
are left in peace, and edify themselves—walking in the
fear of God and in the comfort of the Holy Ghost, the two
great elements of blessing; and their numbers increase.
Persecution accomplishes the designs of God. The peace
which He grants gives opportunity for ripening in grace
and in the knowledge of Himself. We learn the ways and

[16] This was, it would appear, later, but is noticed here to put him,
so to speak, in his place among Christians.

government of God in the midst of the imperfection of man.

Chapters 9: 32 to 11: 18

Peter's apostolic energy and work existing with the new light and work, not set aside by it

PEACE being established through the goodness of God —sole resource of those who truly wait upon Him in submission to His will—Peter passes throughout all parts of Israel. The Spirit of God relates this circumstance here, between the conversion of Saul and his apostolic work, to show us, I doubt not, the apostolic energy in Peter existing at the very time when the call of the new apostle was to bring in new light, and a work that was new in many important respects (thus sanctioning as His own work, and in its place, that which had been done before, whatever progress in accomplishment His counsels might make); and in order to show us the introduction of the Gentiles into the assembly as it was at first founded by His grace in the beginning, preserving thus its unity, and putting His seal upon this work of heavenly grace.

The assembly existed. The doctrine of her oneness, as the Body of Christ, outside the world, was not yet made known. The reception of Cornelius did not announce it, although paving its way.

Cornelius' entrance into God's house through Peter's ministry: the Holy Spirit given to Gentiles as well as to Jews

The undiminished power of Peter, his apostolic authority, in the midst of which the entrance of Cornelius into the spiritual house of God takes place, in connection with Peter's ministry, and that, after the calling of Saul, which opened a new perspective—all these facts taken together

confirmed that which went before. The original work was
in no wise set aside to bring in another. Nevertheless,
Peter's vision did not reveal the assembly as the Body of
Christ, neither did the admission of Cornelius. They only
showed that in every nation he who feared God was acceptable to Him—in a word, that the favor of God was not
limited to the Jews, and that there was no need of becoming a Jew in order to share the salvation that is in
Christ. The oneness of the Body united to its Head in
heaven was not brought out by this event; but it prepared
the way for the promulgation of that truth, since in fact
the Gentile was admitted on earth without becoming a
Jew. The thing was done on earth individually, although
the doctrine itself was not taught. Repentance unto life
eternal was granted to the Gentiles as such. The Holy
Ghost—the seal of Christian blessing among the Jews, the
fruit of redemption accomplished by Jesus—was given to
Gentiles as to Jews. The latter might be astonished at it;
but there was no resisting God. Through grace they could
praise Him for it.

The door open to Gentiles; summary of the Spirit's work in Chapters 9: 32 to 11: 18

From chapter 9: 32 to 11: 18, we find then, the power
of the Spirit of God with Peter in the midst of Israel, and
the admission of Gentiles into the earthly assembly, without their becoming Jews, or submitting to the ancient
order which was passing away; the seal of the Spirit put
upon them; and the heads of the assembly at Jerusalem,
and the most ardent of the circumcision, accepting the
fact as the will of God, and praising Him while submitting to it, in spite of their prejudices. The door then is
open to the Gentile. This was an immense step. The
precious doctrine of the assembly had yet to be announced.

Peter had proclaimed the call of the Gentiles in his first
discourse; but to realize it, and give form to its condi-

tions, in connection with that which had already existed historically, required the intervention, the authority, and the revelation of God. Progress is evident through the patient grace of God; for it was not the wisdom of man. Altogether Jewish at the commencement, the people of Jerusalem were taught that Jesus would return if they repented. This testimony of grace is rejected, and, in the person of him who maintained it, the firstfruits of the assembly go up to heaven. The Holy Ghost, in His sovereign liberty, acts in Samaria and among the proselytes. The assembly being scattered by the persecution, Saul is brought in by the revelation of a glorious Christ, and by a testimony from His mouth which implies the union of saints on earth with Himself their Head in heaven as only one body. After this a pious Gentile, converted but still a Gentile, receives faith in Christ and the Holy Ghost; so that, marked out by this testimony—this seal from God Himself to his faith—the apostle and the disciples who were the most attached to Judaism receive him; Peter by baptizing him, and the others by accepting Peter's act.

The meaning of salvation: the seal of the Spirit

Let us notice here, that salvation is not only the fact of being quickened and pious, but that of complete deliverance so as to present us to Himself in righteousness, which God grants to every one who has life through the operation of God. Cornelius was pious and earnestly so; but he hears words of a work done for him whereby he may be, and (as we know) was saved. Finally the seal of the Holy Ghost, upon believing in Jesus,[17] is the ground on which those whom God accepts are acknowledged. That is to say, it is the full evidence for man.

---

[17] If we examine closely the Scriptures in its statements and facts, we shall find, I think, as to detail, that it is faith in the work of Jesus for the remission of sins which is sealed.

Chapter 11: 19 to 30

The new order of things distinguishing Paul's ministry

CHAPTER 11: 19 begins the narration of the new order
of things by which the ministry of Paul is distinguished. Among those who were scattered abroad on the
occasion of Stephen's death, and who went as far even as
Antioch preaching the Lord Jesus, there were some who,
being men of Cyprus and Cyrene, were more habitually
connected with Greeks. They addressed the Greeks therefore in this ancient capital of the Seleucidæ, and many received their word and turned to the Lord. The assembly
at Jerusalem, already prepared through the conversion of
Cornelius, by which God had shown them the entering in
of the Gentiles, accept this event also and send Barnabas
—himself a man of Cyprus—to Antioch. A good man
and filled with the Holy Ghost, his heart is full of joy on
seeing this work of the grace of God; and much people is
added unto the Lord.

Barnabas and Saul at Antioch : a local assembly formed, composed primarily of Gentiles, distinct from but linked with Jerusalem

As yet all is linked with the work at Jerusalem, although
extending now to the Gentiles. Barnabas, apparently no
longer sufficient for the work and at all events led of God,
departs in search of Saul, who had gone to Tarsus, when
they sought to kill him at Jerusalem. And these two meet
with the assembly at Antioch, teaching much people. Still
everything takes place in connection with Jerusalem,
whence some prophets come down and announce a famine.
The links between the flock and Jerusalem as a centre
are shown and strengthened, by the sending of relief to
that religious metropolis of Judaism, and of Christianity

looked at as having its commencement in the Jewish remnant who believed in Jesus as the Christ.

Barnabas and Saul are themselves charged with this service, and go up to Jerusalem to accomplish it. This circumstance carries us back to Jerusalem, where the Spirit has still something to show us of the ways of God.

Chapter 12

Herod's persecution: God's answer to prayer

HEROD, to please the Jews, begins to persecute the assembly in that city. We may remark here, that the company of believers at Antioch are also called the assembly (Church), which is the case nowhere else as yet. All were accounted as forming a part integrally of the work at Jerusalem,[18] even as all Jews were in connection with that centre of their religious system, however numerous their synagogues or great the influence of their rabbis. Every Jew, as such, sprang from Jerusalem. Barnabas and Saul assemble with the church or assembly at Antioch. A local assembly, conscious of its existence—distinct from, while connected with, Jerusalem—has been formed; and assemblies without a metropolis begin to appear.

To return to Jerusalem. Herod, an impious king, and in certain respects a type of the adversary king at the end, begins to persecute the faithful remnant at Jerusalem. It is not only the Jews who are opposed to them. The king—whom, as Jews, they detested—unites himself to them by his hatred to the heavenly testimony, thinking to win their favor by this means. He kills James, and proceeds to take Peter and put him in prison. But God preserves His servant, and delivers him by His angel in an-

[18] There is a question of the reading in chapter 9: 31, which does not however affect the general thought, that a local assembly, distinct from Jerusalem, composed primarily of Gentiles, was now formed.

swer to the prayers of the saints. He allows some to be slain (happy witnesses to their heavenly portion in Christ), and preserves others to carry on the testimony on earth, in spite of all the power, apparently irresistible, of the enemy—a power which the Lord baffles by the manifestation of that which belongs to Him and to Him alone, and which He employs when He will and how He will. The poor saints, although praying fervently (they had prayer-meetings in those days), can hardly believe, when Peter comes to the door, that God had really granted their prayer. The desire presents itself sincerely to God; faith can scarcely reckon upon Him.

Herod's pride and sin contrasted with the power of the Word of God

Herod, confounded by the power of Him whom he resisted, condemns the instruments of his hatred to death, and goes away to the Gentile seat of his authority. There displaying his glory, and accepting the adulatory homage of the people, as though he were a god, God Himself smites him, and shows that He is the governor of this world, however great the pride of man. But the Word of God extends through His grace; and Barnabas and Saul, having fulfilled their ministry, return to Antioch, taking with them John whose surname was Mark.

Chapter 13

Paul's mission: sent forth by the Spirit from Antioch, a Greek city

WE come now to the beginning of the direct history of the work, new in some important respects, that is, connected with Paul's mission by the immediate intervention of the Holy Ghost. It is not now Christ upon

earth, who by His personal authority sends forth the
twelve, afterwards endowed with the power of the Holy
Ghost from on high to announce His exaltation to
heaven and His return, and to gather under the standard
of the cross those who should believe in Him. Paul has
seen Christ in glory, and therefore has united himself to
the assembly already gathered. But here there is no
Christ personally present to send him forth as the witness
of His presence on earth, or of His rejection as One whom
Paul had known on earth. The Holy Ghost Himself sends
him, not from Jerusalem, but from a Greek city, in which
in free and sovereign power He had converted and gathered together some Gentiles, doubtless some Jews likewise,
but forming an assembly whose existence was first marked
by the fact that the gospel had been preached to the
Greeks.

The independent action of the Spirit: the source of the ministry of Paul and Barnabas

In chapter 13 we find ourselves again in the assembly
at Antioch, and in the midst of the independent[19] action
of the Spirit of God. Certain prophets are there, Saul
among them. They fasted and were occupied with the
service of the Lord. The Holy Ghost commands them to
separate unto Him Barnabas and Saul for the work to
which He had called them. Such was the source of the
ministry of these two. Assuredly it bore testimony to Him
in whom they had believed, and whom Saul, at least, had
seen, and it was under His authority they acted; but the
positive and obvious source of their mission was the Holy
Ghost. It was the Holy Ghost who called them to the
work. They were sent forth (ver. 4) by Him—an all-
important principle as to the Lord's ways upon earth. We

---

[19] The acting of the Spirit is always independent; but here I mean
to express that it was outside the authority of the apostles. This authority
is not the source of that which is done; nor does that which is done refer
itself to it.

come out from Jerusalem, from Judaism, from the jurisdiction of the apostles nominated by the Lord while He
was on earth. Christ is no longer known after the flesh, as
Saul (when become Paul) expresses it. They have to
strive against the Judaic spirit—to show consideration for
it as far as it is sincere; but the sources of their work are
not now in connection with the system which that work
no longer knows as a starting-point. A glorious Christ in
heaven, who owns the disciples as members of His Body
as Himself on high—a mission from the Holy Ghost on
earth which only knows His energy as the source of action
and authority (bearing testimony of course to Christ)—
this is the work which now opens, and which is committed
to Barnabas and Saul.

Barnabas as the link between Judaism and the work from Christ in heaven

Barnabas, it is true, forms a link between the two. He
was himself a Hellenist of Cyprus; it was he who presented Saul to the apostles after his conversion near
Damascus. Barnabas had more largeness of heart—was
more open to the testimonies of divine grace—than even
the apostles and the others who had been nurtured in a
strict Judaism; for God in His grace provides for everything. There is always a Barnabas, as well as a Nico-
demus, a Joseph, and even a Gamaliel, whenever needed.
The actings of God in this respect are remarkable in all
this history. Would that we only trusted more entirely,
while by the Spirit doing His will, to Him who disposes
all things!

Nevertheless even this link is soon broken. It was still
in connection with the "old cloth," the "old bottles;"
blessed as the man himself was, to whom the Holy Ghost
rendered so fine a testimony, and in whom we see an ex-
quisite character. He determined to take his kinsman also
(see Col. 4: 10), Mark. Mark returns to *Jerusalem* almost

from the beginning of the work of evangelization in the Gentile regions; and Saul continues his work with such instruments as God formed under his hand, or a Silas who chose to remain at Antioch when (the particular service which had been committed to him at Jerusalem being ended) he might naturally have returned thither with Judas.

Preaching to the Jews first, and then to the Gentiles

Sent forth thus by the Holy Ghost, Barnabas and Saul, with John Mark as their ministering servant, go away to Seleucia, then to Cyprus; and being at Salamis, a town in that island, they preach the Word of God in the synagogues of the Jews. Whatever therefore might be the energy of the Holy Ghost, He acts in connection with the counsels and the promises of God, and that with perfect patience. To the end of his life, notwithstanding the opposition of the Jews, vexatious and implacable as it might be, the apostle continues—as the ways and counsels of God in Christ had commanded—to the Jews first, and then to the Gentiles. Once brought in where truth and grace were fully revealed in God's assembly, there was no difference between Jew and Gentile. God is one in His character and fully revealed, and the veil rent; sin is one in its character and is opposed to God; the foundation of truth changes not, and the oneness of the assembly is connected with the height of grace in God and comes down to the deep totality of sin, in respect of which that grace has displayed itself. But, with regard to the ways of God upon earth, the Jews had the first place, and the Spirit, who is above all, can therefore act in full liberty in recognizing all the ways of God's sovereignty; even as Christ, who made Himself a Servant in grace, submitted to them all, and now, being exalted on high, unites all these various ways and dispensations in Himself as head and centre of a glory to which the Holy Ghost bears witness, in order to accomplish it here below, as far as may be, by grace.

This does not prevent his giving a distinct and positive judgment as to the condition of the Jews when the occasion requires it.

Need met wherever found: judgment pronounced upon what withstands God's gospel

Even here, at the commencement of his ministry, the two things are presented together. We have already noticed that he begins with the Jews. Having traversed the island, he arrives at the seat of government. There the proconsul, a prudent and thoughtful man, asks to hear the gospel. Beset already by a false prophet (who took advantage of the felt need of a soul which, while ignorant, was earnestly desirous of something that could fill up the void it experienced in the nothingness of pagan ceremonies, and in its disgusting immorality), he sends for Barnabas and Saul. Elymas withstands them. This was natural. He would lose his influence with the governor if the latter received the truth that Paul preached. Now Elymas was a Jew. Saul (who is henceforth named Paul) filled with the Holy Ghost, pronounces on him the sentence, on God's part, of temporary blindness, executed at the moment by the mighty hand of God. The proconsul, struck with the power that accompanied his word, submits to the gospel of God.

I do not doubt that in this wretched Bar-jesus we see a picture of the Jews at the present time, smitten with blindness for a season, because jealous of the influence of the gospel. In order to fill up the measure of their iniquity, they withstood its being preached to the Gentiles. Their condition is judged: their history given in the mission of Paul.[20] Opposed to grace, and seeking to destroy

[20] I do not know if the change of name pointed out on this occasion—the meaning of which has excited the curiosity of etymologists—is not simply an alteration by which its Jewish form was lost, in order to assume a Roman or Gentile aspect.

its effect upon the Gentiles, they have been smitten with blindness—nevertheless only for a season.

Return to Antioch: Paul's testimony in the synagogue

Departing from Paphos, they go into Asia Minor; and now Paul definitively takes his place in the eyes of the historian of the Spirit. His whole company are only those who were with Paul, an expression in Greek which makes Paul everything (*hoi peri Paulon*). When they reached Perga, John Mark leaves them to return to Jerusalem—a milder and more moderate form of the Judaic influence, but showing that, wherever it exercised itself, if it did not produce opposition, it at least took away the vigor needful for the work of God as it was now unfolding among the Gentiles. Barnabas however goes farther, and still continues with Paul in the work. The latter, when they were come to Antioch,[21] again begins first with the Jews. He goes on the sabbath day into the synagogue, and, on the invitation of the ruler, proclaims Jesus, rejected by the Jews at Jerusalem and crucified, but by the power of God raised up again, and through whom they might be justified from all things, from which they could not be justified by the law of Moses. Here the testimony of Paul is very like that of Peter, and is very particularly allied to the beginning of the Epistle to the Hebrews, with regard to the character of the testimony: verse 33 is quite Peter's testimony in Acts 3. In verse 31 he sets the twelve distinctly in the place of testimony to Israel, as those who had personally accompanied the Lord, and who had seen Him after His resurrection. "They are," he says, "His witnesses unto the people." But Paul's testimony (which, as to the fulfilment of the promises by the coming of Christ, and the mercies of David made sure in His resurrection, returns into the order of Peter's preaching) departs from it in an important point. He says nothing of God's having made Jesus both Lord and Christ. He announces that

[21] In Pisidia.

the remission of sins is proclaimed in His name, exhorting
his hearers not to neglect this great salvation.[22]

The gospel of grace rejected by Jews — Paul and Barnabas turn boldly to the Gentiles

Many follow Paul[23] and Barnabas in consequence of
this announcement, and are exhorted by them to continue
in the grace which had been proclaimed to them. The
mass of the people come together the following sabbath to
hear the Word of God; the Gentiles having besought that
this gospel of grace might be preached to them again.
Their souls had found more truth in the doctrine of the
one only God, acknowledged by the Jews, than in the
senseless worship of the pagans, which, to an awakened
and unsatisfied mind, no longer presented any food that
could appease it—a mind that was too active to allow
the imagination to amuse itself with ceremonies which had
no charms but for ignorance, which could be captivated
by the pageantry of festivals, to which it was accustomed,
and which gratified the religious element of the flesh. Still,
the coldly acknowledged doctrine of one only true God,
although it set the mind free from all that shocked it in
the senseless and immoral mythology of Paganism, did
not at all feed the soul as did the powerful testimony of
a God acting in grace, borne by the Holy Ghost through
the mouth of messengers whom He had sent—a testimony
which, while faithful to the promises made to the Jews,
yet addressed itself as a "word of salvation" (ver. 26) to
all those who feared God. But the Jews, jealous of the
effect of the gospel which thus met the soul's need in a
way that their system could not, withstand Paul and blaspheme the doctrine of Christ. Paul therefore and Barnabas
turn boldly to the Gentiles.

[22] Both, as we have seen, follow (in the main) the commission in
Luke 24.
[23] Here Paul is placed before Barnabas; in the former chapter, Barnabas has the first place.

Old Testament prophetic declarations turned into light and authority for action when the Spirit gives their application

It was a decisive and important moment. These two messengers of the Holy Ghost quote the testimony of the Old Testament with regard to God's purpose towards the Gentiles, of whom Christ was to be the light—a purpose which they accomplished according to the intelligence in it that the Spirit gave them, and by His power. The passage is in Isaiah (chap. 49), where the opposition of Israel, that made the testimony of Christ useless to themselves, gave God occasion to declare that this work was but a small thing, and that Christ should be a light to the Gentiles, and great even to the ends of the earth.

We shall do well to observe this last circumstance, the energy in action imparted by spiritual intelligence, and the way in which prophetic declarations turn into light and authority for action, when the Spirit of God gives the true practical meaning—the application. Another might not perhaps understand it; but the spiritual man has a full guarantee for his own conscience in the Word which he has understood. He leaves the rest to God.

Gentile belief: the true character of the Jews shown as enemies of the Lord and His truth

The Gentiles rejoice at the testimony, and the election believe. The Word spreads through all the region. The Jews now show themselves in their true character of enemies to the Lord and to His truth. With regard to them Paul and Barnabas shake off the dust of their feet against them. The disciples, whatever might be their difficulties, are no hindrance to this. The position here taken by the Jews—which, moreover, we find everywhere—makes us understand what a source of grief and pain they must have been to the apostles.

Chapter 14

In Iconium : unbelieving Jews stir up the Gentiles against the work: worship offered and refused in Lystra, followed by stoning and departure

THEIR missionary labors continue in Iconium with the same opposition from the Jews who, incapable themselves of the work, stir up the Gentiles against those who are performing it. As long as it was only opposition, it was but a motive for perseverance; but, being warned in time of an assault that was planned against them, they depart to Lystra and Derbe. There, having healed a cripple, they excite the idolatrous respect of these poor pagans; but, filled with horror, they turn them from their error by the energy of the Holy Ghost—faithful to the testimony of their God. Hither also the Jews follow them. Now, if man will not ally himself with the idolatry of the heart, and accept exaltation from men, the power of his testimony, which they began by admiring as long as they thought they could elevate man and acquire importance through their flatteries being accepted, ends by exciting the hatred of their hearts. The Jews bring this hatred into action and stir up the people, who leave Paul for dead. But he rises up and re-enters the city, remaining tranquilly there another day, and on the morrow he goes with Barnabas to Derbe.

The close of the first formal mission to the Gentiles: its results

Afterwards they revisit the cities through which they had passed, and at Lystra, Iconium, and Antioch, they confirm the disciples in the faith, and teach them that they must pass through tribulation to inherit the kingdom. They choose elders for them; and passing through some other cities to the place where they had disembarked, they return to Antioch, from whence they had been commended to God for the work, causing great joy to the disciples there in that the door of faith was opened to the Gentiles. This is the first formal mission among the Gentiles where assemblies are formed, elders appointed by the apostles, and the hostility of the Jews to the grace of God, outside their nation and independently of their law, is distinctly marked. The Word assumes a positive character among the Gentiles, and the energy of the Holy Ghost displays itself to this end, constituting and forming them into assemblies, establishing local rulers in them, outside and independently of the action of the apostles and assembly at Jerusalem, and the obligation of the law which was still maintained there.

A question concerning this (that is, whether it could be allowed) is soon raised at Antioch. It is no longer the opposition of the Jews hostile to the gospel, but the bigotry of those who had embraced it, desiring to impose the law on the converted Gentiles. But the grace of God provides for this difficulty also.

Chapter 15

Jewish believers from Jerusalem seeking to impose the law's requirements on Gentiles

CHAPTER 15 contains the account of this. Certain persons come from Jerusalem, where all was still going on in connection with the requirements of the law; and they seek to impose these requirements on the Gentiles in this new centre and starting-point of the work which was formed at Antioch. It was the will of God that this matter should be settled, not by the apostolic authority of Paul, or by the action of His Spirit at Antioch only, which might

have divided the Church, but by means of conference at
Jerusalem, so as to maintain union, whatever might be
the prejudices of the Jews. The ways of God in this respect are remarkable, showing the way in which He has
maintained sovereign care in grace over the Church. In
reading the Epistle to the Galatians, we see that in reality
things were in question that touched Christianity to the
quick, that affected its very foundations, the deep principles of grace, of the rights of God, of the sinful condition
of man—principles on which the whole edifice of man's
eternal relations with God is founded. If any one was
circumcized, he was under the law; he had given up grace,
he had fallen away from Christ. Nevertheless Paul the
apostle, Paul full of faith, of energy, of burning zeal, is
obliged to go up to Jerusalem, whither he had not desired
to go, in order to arrange this matter. Paul had labored
at Antioch; but the work in that city was not his work. He
was not the apostle at Antioch as he was that of Iconium,
of Lystra, and afterwards of Macedonia and of Greece.
He went out from Antioch, from the bosom of the Church
already formed there. The question was to be settled for
the Church, apart from the apostolic authority of Paul.
The apostle must yield before God and His ways.

Paul disputes with the men from Judea, but the end is
not gained. It is determined to send some members of
the Church to Jerusalem, but with them Paul and Barnabas, so deeply interested in this question. Moreover Paul
had a revelation that he should go up. God directed his
steps. It is good however to be obliged to submit sometimes, although ever so right or so full of spiritual energy.

The wisdom of God in ordering that the matter should be settled at Jerusalem

The question then is entered upon at Jerusalem. It was
already a great thing that the subjecting of the Gentiles to
the law should be resisted at Jerusalem, and still more

that they should there decide not to do it. We see the
wisdom of God in so ordering it, that such a resolution
should have its origin at Jerusalem. Had there been no
bigotry there, the question would not have been necessary;
but alas, good has to be done in despite of all the weakness and all the traditions of men. A resolution made at
Antioch would have been a very different thing from a
resolution made at Jerusalem. The Jewish church would
not have acknowledged the truth, the apostolic authority
of the twelve would not have given its sanction to it.
The course at Antioch and of the Gentiles would have
been a course apart; and a continual struggle would have
commenced, having (at least in appearance) the authority
of the primitive and apostolic Church on the one side,
and the energy and liberty of the Spirit with Paul for its
representative on the other. The Judaizing tendency of
human nature is ever ready to abandon the high energy
of the Spirit, and return into the ways and thoughts of
the flesh. This tendency, nourished by the traditions of
an ancient faith, had already given sorrow and difficulty
enough to him who was specially laboring among the
Gentiles according to the liberty of the Spirit, without the
additional strength of having the course of the apostles
and of the church at Jerusalem to countenance it.

The apostles' declarations: James sums up the judgment of the assembly

After much discussion at Jerusalem, full liberty for
which was given, Peter, taking the lead, relates the case
of Cornelius. Afterwards Paul and Barnabas declare the
wonderful manifestation of God through the power of the
Holy Ghost which had taken place among the Gentiles.
James then sums up the judgment of the assembly, which
is assented to by all, that the Gentiles shall not be obliged
to be circumcised, or to obey the law; but only to abstain
from blood, from things strangled, from fornication, and

from meat offered to idols. We shall do well to consider
the nature and stipulations of this decree.

The principles established in James' decree

It is a direction which teaches, not that which is abstractedly good or evil, but that which was suitable to the
case presented. It was "necessary," not "righteous before
God," to avoid certain things. The things might be really
evil, but they are not here looked at in that way. There
were certain things to which the Gentiles were accustomed,
which it was proper they should renounce, in order that
the assembly might walk as it ought before God in peace.
To the other ordinances of the law they were not to be
subjected. Moses had those who preached him. That sufficed, without compelling the Gentiles to submit to his
laws, when they joined themselves, not to the Jews, but to
the Lord.

This decree therefore does not pronounce upon the
nature of the things forbidden, but upon the opportuneness—the Gentiles having in fact been in the habit of
doing all these things. We must observe that they were
not things forbidden by the law only. It was that which
was contrary to the order established by God as Creator,
or to a prohibition given to Noah when he was told to
eat flesh. Woman was only to be connected with man in
the sanctity of marriage, and this is a very great blessing.
Life belonged to God. All fellowship with idols was an
outrage against the authority of the true God. Let Moses
teach his own laws; these things were contrary to the intelligent knowledge of the true God. It is not therefore a new
law imposed by Christianity, nor an accommodation to
the prejudices of the Jews. It has not the same kind of
validity as a moral ordinance that is obligatory in itself.
It is the expression to Christian intelligence of the terms
of man's true relations with God in the things of nature,
given by the goodness of God, through the leaders at Jeru-

salem, to ignorant Christians, setting them free from the
law, and enlightening them with regard to the relations
between God and man, and to that which was proper to
man—things of which, as idolatrous Gentiles, they had
been ignorant. I have said, *addressed to Christian intelligence:* accordingly there is nothing inconsistent in eating
anything that is sold at the shambles; for I acknowledge
God who gave it, and not an idol. But if the act implies
communion with the idol, even to the conscience of another, it would be provoking God to jealousy; I sin against
Him or against my neighbor. I do not know whether an
animal is strangled or not, but if people act so as to
imply that it is indifferent whether life belongs to God or
not, I sin again; I am not defiled by the thing, but I fail
in Christian intelligence with regard to the rights of God
as Creator. With regard to fornication, this enters into
the category of Christian purity, besides being contrary
to the order of the Creator; so that it is a direct question
of good and evil, and not only of the rights of God revealed
to our intelligence. This was important as a general principle, more than in the detail of the things themselves.

In sum the principles established are these: purity by
marriage according to God's original institution; that life
belongs to God; and the unity of God as one only true
God—Godhead, life, and God's original ordinance for
man. The same thing is true of the foundations laid by
the assembly at the basis of their decree, "It seemed good
to the Holy Ghost and to us."

Apostolic authority representing that of Christ, but the whole flock acting in concert with them

The Holy Ghost had manifested Himself in the case
of Cornelius and of the conversion of the Gentiles, of
which Peter and Paul and Barnabas had given the account. On the other hand the apostles were the depositaries of the authority of Christ, those to whom the gov-

ernment of the assembly as founded in connection with
the true Jewish faith had been committed. They represented the authority of Christ ascended on high, even as
the power and will of the Holy Ghost had been shown in
the cases I have just mentioned. The authority was exercised in connection with that which, in a certain sense,
was the continuation of a Judaism enlarged by fresh revelations, and which had its centre at Jerusalem, acknowledging as Messiah the ascended Jesus rejected by the people. Christ had committed to them the authority necessary
to govern the assembly. They had also been sealed on the
day of Pentecost in order to perform it.

The spirit of grace and wisdom is truly seen in their
way of acting. They give their full sanction to Paul and
Barnabas, and they send with them persons of note in
the assembly at Jerusalem, who could not be suspected
of bringing an answer in support of their own pretensions,
as might have been supposed in the case of Paul and
Barnabas.

The apostles and elders assemble for deliberation; but
the whole flock acts in concert with them.

The decision at Jerusalem that the law was not binding on the Gentiles sent by Judas and Silas to Antioch

Thus Jerusalem has decided that the law was not binding on the Gentiles. These, sincere in their desire of walking with Christ, rejoice greatly at their freedom from this
yoke. Judas and Silas, being prophets, exhort and confirm them, and afterwards are dismissed in peace. But
Silas thinks it good to remain on his own account, influenced by the Spirit. He prefers the work among the
Gentiles to Jerusalem. Judas returns from it to Jerusalem.

The work continues at Antioch by means of Paul and
Barnabas and others. At Antioch we again see the full
liberty of the Holy Ghost.

Paul's second visit to the assemblies in Asia Minor: contention with and separation from Barnabas

Paul proposes to Barnabas that they should go and visit the assemblies already formed by their means in Asia Minor. Barnabas consents, but he determines to take John who had formerly forsaken them. Paul wishes for some one who had not drawn back from the work, nor abandoned for his own home the place of a stranger for the work's sake. Barnabas insists; and these two precious servants of God separate. Barnabas takes Mark and goes to Cyprus. Now Mark was his kinsman, and Cyprus his own country. Paul takes Silas, who had preferred the work to Jerusalem instead of Jerusalem to the work, and departs. From his name we may believe that Silas was a Hellenist.

It is happy to find that, after this, Paul speaks of Barnabas with entire affection, and desires that Mark should come to him, having found him profitable for the ministry.

The title given to Paul and Barnabas conferred by their work

Moreover Paul is commended by the brethren to the grace of God in his work. The title given to Paul and Barnabas by the apostles shows the difference between the apostolic authority, established by Christ in person, and that which was constituted such by the power of the Holy Ghost—sent by Christ Himself, no doubt, but in point of fact going forth by the direction of the Holy Ghost, and their mission warranted by His power. With the apostles, Paul and Barnabas have no title except their work—"Men that have hazarded their lives for the name of our Lord Jesus Christ." They are that which the Holy Ghost has made them. The apostles are the twelve.

Chapter 16

Paul characterized by the Spirit's liberty and power

THE liberty and the power of the Spirit characterize
Paul. He is that which the Spirit makes him. If Jesus
had appeared to him, although Ananias can testify it, he
must in reality prove it by the power of his ministry. The
effects of this ministry are related as well as its character
in chapters 16 to 20. The action and the liberty of the
Holy Ghost are there displayed in a remarkable manner.

The circumcision of Timothy

There is perhaps no example of this more remarkable
than that which Paul does with regard to Timothy. He
uses circumcision in all liberty to set aside Jewish prej-
udice. It is very doubtful whether, according to the law,
he ought to have been circumcized. Ezra and Nehemiah
show us the strange wives sent away; but here, the mother
being a Jewess, Paul causes the child of this mixed marriage to follow the rule of the Jews and submit to that
rite. Liberty fully recognizes the law in its place, although
itself exempt from it, and distinctly states, for the assurance of the Gentiles, the absence of all pretension, on the
part of the Judæan Christians, to impose the law upon
Gentiles. Paul circumcizes Timothy, and does not give
subjection for an hour to those who would have compelled
Titus to be circumcized. He would become a Jew to the
Jews from love; but the Jews themselves must renounce
all pretension to impose the law on others. The decrees
given at Jerusalem are left with the churches—a plain
answer to every Jew who desired to subject the Gentiles to
Judaism. The decrees, we may remark, were those of
the apostles and the elders.

The Holy Spirit's direction: called into Macedonia

It is the Holy Ghost alone who directs the apostle. He forbids him to preach in Asia (the province), and will not suffer him to go into Bithynia. By a vision in the night they are called to go into Macedonia. Here the historian meets them. It is the Lord who calls them into Macedonia. It is well to note here that, while the gospel is sent under Paul's ministry to the whole creation under heaven, yet there is specific direction as to where we are to go.

At Philippi: the work of the Spirit and that of Satan by an evil spirit

Here the apostle goes first to the Jews, even when it was only a few women who came together by the river side— a place, as it appears, usually chosen where there was no synagogue. A Greek woman, who worshipped the God of Israel, is converted by grace. Thus the door is opened, and others also believe (ver. 14). Here Satan tries to tamper with the work by bearing a testimony to the ministers of the word. Not that this spirit acknowledged Jesus—he would not then have been an evil spirit, he would not have thus possessed the damsel. He speaks of the agents, in order to have a share of the glory, and of the most high God—compelled perhaps by the presence of the Spirit to speak, as had been the case with others by the presence of Jesus, when His power was before their eyes. The testimony of Satan could not go so far as to own Him Lord; and if Paul had not been faithful, it would have mixed up the work of the enemy with that of the Lord. But it was not a testimony to Paul that Paul sought, nor a testimony rendered by an evil spirit, whatever might be the appearance of its testimony. The proof which the evil spirit had to give that the power of God was present, was to submit to it by being driven away. It could not be a support to the work of God. We see in this circumstance the disinterestedness of the apostle, his spir-

itual discernment, the power of God with him, and the
faith which will have no other support than that of God.
It would have been useful to have a testimony rendered to
his ministry: the reasonings of the flesh might have said,
"I did not seek it." Persecution would have been avoided.
But God will have no other testimony than that which He
bears to Himself. No other can be a testimony from Him,
for He reveals Himself where He is not known; faith waits
only on Him to render it. Paul went on without troubling
himself about this malicious attempt of the enemy's, and
possibly in wisdom avoiding conflict where there was no
fruit for the Lord, until by its persistency the apostle was
forced to attend to it. The Spirit of God does not tolerate
the presence of an evil spirit when it makes itself actively
manifest before Him. He does not lend Himself to its
devices by giving it importance through a voluntary inter-
position; for He has His own work, and He does not turn
away from it to occupy Himself about the enemy. He is
occupied, in love, about souls. But if Satan comes in His
way, so as to perplex these souls, the Spirit reveals Himself in His energy, and the enemy flees before Him.

Satan's resources: God's use of apparent evil for the jailer's blessing and the gathering out of an assembly

But Satan is not without resources. The power which
he cannot exercise in a direct way, he employs in exciting
the passions and lusts of men in opposition to that power
against which he cannot himself stand, and which will
neither unite itself to him nor recognize him. Even as the
Gadarenes desired Jesus to depart, when He had healed
Legion, so the Philippians rise up tumultuously against
Paul and his companions at the instigation of the men
who had lost their dishonest gains. But God makes use
of all this to direct the progress of His own work, and
give it the form He pleases. There is the jailer to be con-

verted, and the magistrates themselves are to confess their
wrong with respect to the messengers of God. The assembly is gathered out, a flock (as the epistle addressed to
them bear witness) full of love and affection. The apostle
goes to labor elsewhere. We see a more active, a more
energetic, testimony here than in the similar case that
happened to Peter. The intervention of God is more striking in Peter's case. It is the old Jerusalem, worn out in
everything except hatred, and God faithful to the one
who trusted in Him. The hatred is disappointed. Paul
and Silas sing, instead of quietly sleeping; the doors burst
suddenly open; and the jailer himself is converted, and
his family. The magistrates are obliged to come as sup-
pliants to Paul. Such is the result of the tumult. The
enemy was mistaken here. If he stopped their work at
Philippi, he sent the apostles to preach elsewhere according to the will of God.

Chapter 17

Energetic testimony to the Christian faith: the enemy's power and persecution

WE must not pass over in silence this energy which
embraced whole houses, and subdued them to the
Christian faith. We only see it, however, when it is a
question of bringing in the Gentiles.[24] But Cornelius,
Lydia, the jailer of Philippi, are all witnesses to this power.

In the last case it was the power exercised by the enemy
over the passions of the Gentiles that caused the persecution of the apostles: at Thessalonica we again find the old

[24] We see however, in the case of Lydda and Saron, what is more analogous to the introduction of a people. They heard of the miracle done to
Æneas; and the town and neighborhood turned to the Lord. Saron is a
district along the coast.

and universal enmity of the Jews. Nevertheless many
Jews and proselytes received the gospel. After a tumult
there also, the apostles go away to Berea. There the Jews
are more noble; what they hear, they examine by the
Word of God. Through this a great number among them
believed. Nevertheless the Jews of Thessalonica, jealous
of the progress the gospel made, go over to Berea. Paul
leaves the city and passes on to Athens. Silas and Timothy remain for the moment at Berea, Paul being the
special object of the Jews' pursuit. At Athens, although he
resorted to the synagogue, yet, his spirit stirred at the
sight of the universal idolatry in that idle city, he disputes daily in public with their philosophers; consequent
on these interviews, he proclaims the true God to the chief
men of that intellectual capital. He had sent word to Silas
and Timothy to join him there.

Universal idolatry at Athens: intellectual cultivation without God: Paul's preaching of Jesus and the resurrection

With a people like the Athenians—such is the effect of
intellectual cultivation without God—he has to come down
to the lowest step in the ladder of truth. He sets forth
the oneness of God, the Creator, and the relationship of
man to Him, declaring also that Jesus will judge the
world, of which God had given proof by raising Him up
from the dead. With the exception of the judgment of
this world being put in place of the promises respecting
the return of Jesus, we might think it was Peter addressing the Jews. We must not imagine that the historian relates everything that Paul said. What is given is his
defence, not his preaching. The Holy Ghost gives us that
which characterized the manner in which the apostle met
the circumstances of those he addressed. That which remained on the minds of his first hearers was that he
preached Jesus and the resurrection. It appears even that

some took the resurrection, as well as Jesus, to be a God.
It is, indeed, the basis of Christianity, which is founded
on Jesus personally, and the fact of His resurrection; but
it is only the basis.

The appropriateness of the preaching of Peter and Paul

I have said that we are reminded here of Peter's preaching. I mean as to the degree of height in his doctrine with
regard to Christ. We shall observe, at the same time, the
appropriateness of the application of facts in either case
to the persons addressed. Peter set forth the rejected
Christ ascended on high, ready to return on the repentance
of the Jews, and who would establish at His coming all
things of which the prophets had spoken. Here the judgment of the world—sanction of the truth to the natural
conscience—is presented to the learned men, and to the
inquisitive people; nothing that could interest their philosophic minds, but a plain and convincing testimony to the
folly of their idolatry, according even to that which the
natural conscience of their own poets had acknowledged.

Chapters 18: 1 to 19: 7

The power of the gospel

THE dishonest gain, to which Satan ministered opportunity, met the gospel at Philippi; the hardness and
moral indifference of knowledge that flattered human vanity, at Athens; at Thessalonica, the efforts of Jewish jealousy. The gospel goes on its way, victorious over the one,
yielding to the effect of another, and, after laying bare
to the learned Athenians all that their condition tolerated,
leaving them, and finding, amid the luxury and the depraved manners of the wealthy city of Corinth, a nu-

merous people to bring into the assembly. Such are the
ways of God, and the exercises of His devoted servant led
by the Holy Ghost.

We may notice, that this energy, which seeks the Gentiles, never loses sight of the favor of God towards His
elect people—a favor that sought them until they rejected it.

The apostle's support: his bold and decisive course as led of God: turning to the Gentiles

At Thessalonica Paul twice received succor from
Philippi; at Corinth, where money and commerce abounded, he does not take it, but quietly works with two of his
countrymen of the same trade as himself. He again begins
with the Jews, who oppose his doctrine and blaspheme.
The apostle takes his course with the boldness and decision
of a man truly led of God, calmly and wittingly, so
as not to be turned aside. He shakes his garments in
token of being pure of their blood, and declares that now
he turns to the Gentiles according to Isaiah 49, taking
that prophecy as a command from God.

Paul's labors in Corinth: his desire to go to Jerusalem

In Corinth God had "much people." He therefore uses
the unbelieving indifference of Gallio to defeat the projects
and malice of the Jews, jealous as ever of a religion that
eclipsed their importance, whatever might be its grace
towards them. Paul, after laboring there a long time, goes
away in peace. His Jewish friends, Priscilla and Aquila,
go with him. He was going himself to Jerusalem. He was
also under a vow. The opposition of the Jews does not
take away his attachment to his nation—his faithfulness
in preaching the gospel to them first—in recognizing everything that belonged to them in grace before God. He even
submits to Jewish ordinances. Possibly habit had some
influence over him, which was not of the Spirit; but ac-

cording to the Spirit he had no thought of disallowing that which the patient grace of God granted to the people. He addresses himself to the Jews at Ephesus. They are inclined to hear him, but he desires to keep the feast at Jerusalem. Here he is still a Jew with his feasts and vows. The Spirit has evidently introduced these circumstances to give us a true and complete picture of the relationship that existed between the two systems—the degree of freedom from the influence of the one, as well as the energy that established the other. The first remains often to a certain degree, where energy to do the other is in a very high degree. The liberty that condescends to the prejudices and habits is not the same thing as subjection to these prejudices in one's own person. In our feebleness the two mingle together; but they are in fact opposed to each other. To respect that which God respects, even when the system has lost all real force and value, if called to act in connection with this system when it is really nothing more than a superstition and a weakness, is a very different thing from putting oneself under the yoke of superstition and weakness. The first is the effect of the Spirit; the last, of the flesh. In us, alas, the one is often confounded with the other. Charity becomes weakness, giving uncertainty to the testimony.

Paul as a Jew

Paul takes his journey; goes up to Jerusalem, and salutes the assembly; goes down to Antioch, and visits again all the first assemblies he had formed, thus binding all his work together—Antioch and Jerusalem. How far his old habits influenced him in his ways of acting, I leave the reader to judge. He was a Jew. The Holy Ghost would have us see that he was as far as possible from any contempt for the ancient people of God, for whom divine favor will never change. This feeling was surely right. It appears elsewhere that he went beyond the limits of the

Spirit and of spirituality. Here we have only the facts. He may have had some private reason that was valid in consequence of the position in which he stood. One may be in circumstances which contradict the liberty of the Spirit, and which, nevertheless, when we are in them, have a certain right over us, or exercise an influence which necessarily weakens in the soul the energy of that liberty. We may have done wrong in putting ourselves into those circumstances, but, being in them, the influence is exercised, the rights assert their claim. A man called to serve God, driven out from his father's house, walks in the liberty of the Spirit. Without any change in his father, he goes into the paternal house: the rights of his father revive—where is his liberty? Or a man possessed of much clearer spiritual intelligence places himself in the midst of friends who are spiritually altogether below him: it is almost impossible for him to retain a spiritual judgment. However it may have been here, the link is now formed voluntarily on the part of him who stood in the place of liberty and grace, and the Christians in Jerusalem remain at the level of their former prejudices, and claim patience and indulgence from him who was the vessel and the witness of the liberty of the Spirit of God.

This, with the supplement of his work at Ephesus, forms the circle of the active labors of the apostle in the gospel, to show us in him the ways of the Spirit with men.

Apollos enlightened by Aquila and Priscilla

From verse 24 of chapter 18 to verse 7 of chapter 19 we have a kind of summary of the progress made by the doctrine of Christ, and of the power that accompanied it. Apollos knew only of the teaching of John; but, upright in heart, he publicly confessed and preached that which he knew. It was the faith of a regenerate soul. Aquila and Priscilla enlighten him fully with regard to the facts of the gospel, and the doctrine of a dead and glorified Christ.

At Corinth he becomes a powerful teacher of the gospel, of the Lord among the Jews, thus confirming the faith of the disciples. The energy of the Holy Ghost manifests itself in him without any intervention of the apostle or of the twelve. He acts independently; that is, the Spirit acts independently in him. People could say, "I am of Apollos." It is interesting to see these different manifestations of the power and liberty of the Spirit, and to remember that the Lord is above all, and that, if He acts greatly by a Paul, He acts also in whom He will.

At Ephesus: John's baptism and Christianity

In that which follows we find, on another side, the progress of the divine revelation in union with Paul's apostolic power made very prominent by the capability of communicating the Holy Ghost. Twelve persons had believed, but with no other instruction than that of John: their baptism had been in reference to it. It was a Christ to come, and a Holy Ghost whom He would communicate, that they looked for. Now John's baptism required repentance, but in no way came out of the Jewish pale; although it opened a perspective of something different, according to the sovereignty of God, and as the effect of Christ's coming. But it was a baptism unto repentance for man on the earth, and not Christ's death and resurrection. Grace acted in a remnant, but of whom Jesus was a companion on earth. Now Christianity (for man's sin has been fully manifested) in founded on death and resurrection; first, that of Christ, thus accomplishing redemption, and then on our death and resurrection with Him so as to place us in Him and as Him before God is sinless life, life of His life, and washed in His blood from all our sins. But John's baptism, in fact, only taught repentance here below in order to receive Christ; Christianity taught the efficacy of the death and resurrection of a rejected Christ, in virtue of which the Holy Ghost, the Paraclete come down from heaven, should be received.

These twelve men (although John had announced that
the baptism of the Holy Ghost should be the result of
Christ's intervention) did not know whether there was yet
any Holy Ghost[25]—a plain proof that they had not come
into the house of God in which He dwelt. Paul explains
this to them, and they are baptized in the name of Jesus.
Paul, in his apostolic capacity, lays his hands on them;
and they receive the Holy Ghost. They speak with
tongues, and they prophesy.

Chapter 19: 8 to 41

In Asia: Paul as the founder of what was according to God: the disciples separated: God's presence and power

THIS power, and he who was its instrument, were now
to be brought out into distinct relief. The capital city
of Asia (that is, of the Roman province so named) is the
theatre on which this was to be effected. We shall see a
power displayed in this locality, which acts independently
of all traditional forms, and which governs all that surrounds it, whether man, conscience, or the enemy—an
organizing power, which forms of itself and for itself the
institutions and the body that suit it, and which governs
the whole position. The power of active grace has been
displayed in the work of Paul, beginning with Antioch;
and had shown itself in different ways. Here we have
some details of its formal establishment in a great centre.

During three months of patience he preaches Christ in
the synagogue, and reasons with the Jews, conscious of

---

[25] Literally whether the Holy Ghost was. The expression, which is the
same as in John 7, is a very striking testimony to the distinctness and
importance of the Holy Ghost's presence down here on earth. It is called
"the Holy Ghost," though we all know He had ever been. But what is
called the Holy Ghost, that is, His presence down here—this had never
been.

divine strength and of the truth. He grants precedence, as the sphere of testimony, to that which had been the instrument and the people of God: "To the Jews first." It is no longer said, "Salvation is of the Jews," but it is preached to them first.

But this work having had its development, and many taking the place of adversaries, Paul acts as the founder of that which was according to God and on the part of God. He separates the disciples, and discourses upon Christianity in the hall of a Greek who had a public class. This went on for two years: so that the doctrine was spread through all the country among both the Jews and the Greeks. God did not fail to bear testimony to the Word of His grace, and His power was displayed in a remarkable manner in connection with the person of the apostle who bore the testimony. The manifestations of the enemy's power disappear before the action of this liberative power of the Lord, and the name of Jesus was glorified. Now the reality of this action was demonstrated in a striking way, that is, its source in the personal, positive, and real action of the Lord on the one side, and on the other, the mission of Paul, and faith as the instrument by which this supernatural power wrought. Certain Jews desired to avail themselves of it for their own self-interest; and devoid of faith, they use the name of "Jesus whom Paul preached" as though it had been a kind of charm. But the evil spirit, whose power was as true and real in its way as that of the Lord which he was forced to acknowledge when it was in exercise, knew very well that here it was not so, that there was neither faith nor power. "Jesus I know," said he, "and who Paul is I know; but who are ye?" And the man who was possessed attacked and wounded them. Striking testimony to the action of the enemy, but at the same time to that superior force, to the reality of that intervention of God, which was carried into effect by means of Paul. Now, when God shows Himself, conscience always shows itself; and the power of the

enemy over it is manifested and ceases. The Jews and
Greeks are filled with fear, and many who became Christians brought the proofs of their sorceries.

The mighty action of the Spirit showed itself by the
decision it produced, by the immediate and unhesitating
acting out of the thoughts and resolutions produced in
the heart. There were no long inward arguments; the
presence and the power of God produced their natural
effects.

The power of the enemy among the Gentiles used by the Jews: Demetrius and "Diana of the Ephesians"

The enemy's resources were, however, not exhausted.
The work of God was done, in the sense of the establishment of the testimony through apostolic labor; and God
was sending His servant elsewhere. The enemy, as usual,
excites a tumult, stirring up the passions of men against
the instruments of the testimony of God. Paul had already
intended to go away, but a little later; he had therefore
sent Timothy and Erastus before him into Macedonia, pur-
posing to visit Macedonia, Achaia, and Jerusalem, and
afterwards to go to Rome; and he still remains some time
in Asia. But after the departure of these two brethren,
Demetrius excites the people against the Christians. Inveterate against the gospel, which shook the whole system
in connection with which he made his fortune, and which
was linked with all that gave him importance, this agent
of the enemy knew how to act on the passions of the work-
men who had the same occupation as himself; for he made
little portable shrines to Diana in silver. His employment
was connected with that which all the world admired,
with that which had possession of men's minds—a great
comfort to man who feels the need of something sure—
with that which had long given its hue to their religious
habits. A great part of the influence exercised was, not
"Great is Diana!" but "Great is Diana of the Ephesians!"

It was, in short, the power of the enemy among the Gentiles. The Jews apparently sought to avail themselves of this by putting one Alexander forward—the same possibly who had withstood Paul, and who they supposed would therefore be listened to by the people. But it was the evil spirit of idolatry that agitated them; and the Jews were foiled in their hope. Paul was prevented, both by the brethren and by some of the Asiarchs,[26] from showing himself in the theatre. The assembly was dissolved by the town authorities; and Paul, when he had seen the disciples, went away in peace.[27]

His work there was finished, and the gospel planted in the capital of the province of Asia, and even in the whole province: Greece and Macedonia had already received it.

The gospel in Rome as the apostle's desire: Paul's free and active life ended

There was yet Rome. In what manner should he go thither? This is now the remaining question. His free and active life ended with the events which now occupy us, as far as it is given us by the Holy Ghost. A life blessed with an almost unequalled faith, with an energy

---

[26] Honorary magistrates from among the notables, who presided over the celebration of religious festivals.

[27] It may perhaps interest the reader and help him to understand this part of the New Testament history, if I point out the time at which Paul wrote some of his epistles. He wrote the First to the Corinthians from Ephesus, and sent it by Titus. Timothy he sent by way of Macedonia. The latter might perhaps go into Greece; "If he come," the apostle says to the Corinthians. Then came the tumult, and just at this moment, or about the same time, his life was endangered; he did not even suppose that he should save it. He had purposed going by Greece into Macedonia, and then returning to Greece; but the state Corinth was in prevented it, and he went first into Macedonia. On his way he goes to Troas, but does not stay there; in Macedonia he is much exercised in mind, and has no rest, because Titus had not brought him tidings of the Corinthians. There, however, Titus found him, and the apostle was comforted in his trouble by the good news of the return of the Corinthians to a right mind. Upon this he writes the second letter to them, and, after having visited the assemblies, he pursues his journey to Corinth, whence he wrote his Epistle to the Romans. I only speak here of that which relates to this part of the apostle's history, and throws light upon his labors.

that surpassed anything that has been seen in men, and which, through the divine power that wrought in it, produced its effects in spite of obstacles apparently insurmountable, in spite of every kind of opposition, in contempt and destitution, and which stamped its character on the assembly by giving it, instrumentally, its existence; and that, not only in spite of two hostile religions which divided the civilized world between them, but in spite of a religious system which possessed the truth, but which ever sought to confine it within the boundary of traditions that granted some place to the flesh—a system that had the plea of priority, and was sanctioned by the habits of those apostles who were nominated by the Lord Himself.

The path of traditions and forms is never power

The assembly indeed, as Paul foresaw, soon returned to its Judaic ways, when the energy of the apostle was absent. It requires the power of the Holy Ghost to rise above the religiousness of the flesh. Piety does not necessarily do this; and power is never a tradition—it is itself, and thereby independent of men and of their traditions, even when bearing with them in love. The flesh therefore always returns to the path of traditions and forms; because it is never *power* in the things of God, although it can recognize duty. It does not therefore rise to heaven; it does not understand grace; it can see what man ought to be for God (without however perceiving the consequences of this, if God is revealed), but it cannot see what God in His sovereign grace is for man. It will perhaps retain it as orthodoxy, where the Spirit has wrought; but it will never bring the soul into it. This it was, more than the violence of the pagans or the hatred of the Jews, which wrung the heart and caused the anguish of the faithful and blessed apostle, who by grace had a character, or rather a position, more like that of Christ than any other on earth.

Paul's remarkable position as used by the Holy Spirit

These conflicts will be unfolded to us in the Epistles, as well as that ardent heart which—while embracing in its thoughts all the revealed counsels of God, and putting each part in its place, and embracing in its affections the whole of the work and of the assembly of God—could equally concentrate its whole energy of thought on a single important point, and of affection on a poor slave whom grace had given to him in his chains. The vessel of the Spirit, Paul shines with a heavenly light throughout the whole work of the gospel. He condescends at Jerusalem, thunders in Galatia when souls were being perverted, leads the apostles to decide for the liberty of the Gentiles, and uses all liberty himself to be as a Jew to the Jews, and as without law to those that had no law, as not under law, but always subject to Christ. Yet how difficult to maintain the height of life and of spiritual revelation, in the midst of so many opposing tendencies! He was also "void of offence." Nothing within hindered his communion with God, whence he drew his strength to be faithful among men. He could say, and none but he, "Be ye imitators of me, as I am of Christ." Thus also he could say, "'I endure all things for the elect's sake, that they may obtain the salvation which is in Christ Jesus with eternal glory," words which would not be improper in the Lord's mouth—in a more exalted sense doubtless, because He endured for Paul himself the wrath that would have been his eternal condemnation—yet words which bring out the remarkable position of this man of God. as the vessel of the Holy Ghost by whom he was used. "I fill up," said he, "that which is lacking[28] of the sufferings

---

[28] The reader must distinguish between the Lord's sufferings for sin from God in righteousness, and those which He endured from sinful men for righteousness' sake. We partake in the latter, while Christ has saved us from the former, in which there is no question at all of participation, but of His substitution for us when we have deserved the condemnation due to sin.

of Christ for His Body's sake, which is the assembly; whereof I am made a minister to complete the Word of God."

Paul's part in what John maintained

John (through his intimate knowledge of the Person of Christ, born on earth and Son of God) was able to maintain this essential and individually vital truth, in the same field in which Paul labored; but it was Paul's part to be the active instrument for propagating the truth which saves the soul, and brings ruined man into connection with God by faith, by communicating all His counsels of grace.

The intrinsic power of Judaism if a man takes his place below grace

Still Paul was a man, although a man wonderfully blest. The intrinsic power of Judaism in connection with its relationship to the flesh is marvellous. As to the result indeed, if man takes his place below grace, that is, below God, it is better in a certain sense that he should be man under law than man without law. He will be the one or the other; but in taking up the exclusive idea of duty he forgets God as He is—for He is love; and too often forgets also man as he is—for he is sin. If he unites the idea of duty and of sin, it is continual bondage, and this is what Christianity in general is reduced to; with the addition of ordinances to ease the burdened conscience, of forms to create piety where communion is absent; clothing it all with the name of Christ, and with the authority of the Church, so named, the very existence of which in its reality is identified with the principle of sovereign grace, and characterized by subjection.[29]

But let us return to the history of Paul.

---

[29] See Ephesians 5: 24.

Chapter 20

In Macedonia and Greece; Paul's long address at Troas: Eutychus' death and revival

AFTER the uproar has ceased he sends for the disciples, embraces them, and departs for Macedonia; he visits that whole country, and comes into Greece. The beginning of the Second Epistle to the Corinthians gives the details of this part of his history. In Greece he remains three months; and when the Jews lay wait for him, he goes round by Macedonia, instead of sailing straight to Syria. At Troas (where a door had been opened to him on his way into Greece, but where his affection for the Corinthians had not allowed him to remain) he spends his Sunday, and even the whole week, in order to see the brethren. We perceive the usual object of their assembly: they "came together to break bread;" and the ordinary occasion of holding it—"the first day of the week." Paul avails himself of this to speak to them all night; but it was an extraordinary occasion. The presence and the exhortations of an apostle failed in keeping them all awake. It was not however an assembly held in secret or in the dark. There were many lamps to light the upper chamber in which they met. By the place in which they came together we see that the assemblies were not composed of very many persons. The upper room in Jerusalem received, *perhaps*, one hundred and twenty. It appears by different salutations, that they met in private houses— probably in several, if the number of believers required it; but there was only one assembly.

Eutychus pays the penalty of his inattention; but God bears testimony to His own goodness, and to the power with which He had endued the apostle, by raising him from a state of death. Paul says that his soul was yet in him: he had only to renew the connection between it and his physical organization. In other cases the soul had been recalled.

Paul the centre of energy in his labors only as filled with the Spirit

Paul chose to go alone from Troas to Assos. We see all through the history, that he arranged, by the power that the Spirit gave him over them, the willing services of his companions—not, doubtless, as their master, yet more absolutely than if he had been so. He is (under Christ) the centre of the system in which he labors, the centre of energy. Christ alone can be by right the centre of salvation and of faith. It was only as filled with the Spirit of God that Paul was the centre even of that energy; and it was, as we have seen, by not grieving Him, and by exercising himself to have a conscience void of offence both towards God and towards men.

Paul does not stop at Ephesus, because in so central a place he must have stayed some time. It is necessary to avoid that which has a certain moral claim upon us, if we would not and ought not to be detained by the obligation it imposes upon us.

Paul's address to the Ephesian elders: how and what he had preached: this ministry ended; their responsibility

It was no want of affection for the beloved Ephesians, nor any thought of neglecting them. He sends for the elders, and addresses a discourse to them, which we must examine a little, as setting before us the position of the assembly at that time, and the work of the gospel among the nations.

The assemblies were consolidated over a pretty large extent of country, and in divers places at least had taken the form of a regularly ordered institution. Elders were

established and recognized. The apostle could send for
them to come to him. His authority also was acknowledged on their part. He speaks of his ministry as a past
thing—solemn thought!—but he takes them to witness not
only that he had preached the truth to them, but a truth
that spoke to their conscience; setting them before God
on the one hand, and on the other presenting to them Him
in whom God made Himself known, and in whom He
communicated all the fulness of grace on their behalf—
Jesus, the object of their faith, the Saviour of their souls.
He had done this through trouble and through difficulty,
in face of the unprincipled opposition of the Jews who
had rejected the Anointed One, but in accordance with the
grace that rose above all this evil and declared salvation
to the Jews, and going beyond these limits (because it was
grace) addressed itself to the Gentiles, to all men, as sinners and responsible to God. Paul had done this, not
with the pride of a teacher, but with the humility and the
perseverance of love. He desired also to finish his ministry, and to fail in nothing that Jesus had committed to
him. And now he was going to Jerusalem, feeling bound
in spirit to do so, not knowing what would befall him, but
warned by the Holy Ghost that bonds and afflictions
awaited him. With regard to themselves, he knew his
ministry was ended, and that he should see their face no
more. Henceforth responsibility would specially rest upon
them.

Apostolic labors having ended, the assembly was re-sponsible to stand fast: dangers and difficulties would complicate the work of the elders

Thus what the Holy Ghost here sets before us is, that
now, when the detail of his work among the Gentiles to
plant the gospel is related as one entire scene among Jews
and Gentiles, he bids adieu to the work; in order to leave
those whom he had gathered together in a new position,

and in a certain sense to themselves.[30] It is a discourse
which marks the cessation of one phase of the assembly—
that of apostolic labors—and the entrance into another—
its responsibility to stand fast now that those labors had
ceased, the service of the elders whom "the Holy Ghost
had made overseers," and at the same time the dangers
and difficulties that would attend the cessation of apostolic
labor, and complicate the work of the elders on whom the
responsibility would now more especially devolve.

Apostolic succession entirely denied

The first remark that flows from the consideration of
this discourse is, that apostolic succession is entirely denied by it. Owing to the absence of the apostle various
difficulties would arise, and there would be no one in his
place to meet or to prevent these difficulties. Successor
therefore he had none. In the second place the fact appears that, this energy which bridled the spirit of evil
once away, devouring wolves from without, and teachers
of perverse things from within, would lift up their heads
and attack the simplicity and the happiness of the assembly, which would be harassed by the efforts of Satan
without possessing apostolic energy to withstand them.

The elders' duty to care for, shepherd, and watch over the flock and themselves: their commendation to God and the Word of His grace

This testimony of Paul's is of the highest importance
with regard to the whole ecclesiastical system. The attention of the elders who are left in charge is directed elsewhere than to present apostolical care (as having no

---

[30] If Paul was ever set free and restored to these parts (not necessarily
to Ephesus) as Philippians and Philemon and perhaps 2 Timothy would
lead us to suppose, we have no scriptural account of it.

longer this resource, or anything that officially replaced
it), in order that the assembly might be kept in peace and
sheltered from evil. It was their part to care for the
assembly in these circumstances. In the next place, that
which was principally to be done for the hindrance of evil
was to shepherd the flock, and to watch whether over
themselves or over the flock for that purpose. He reminds
them how he had himself exhorted them night and day
with tears. Let them therefore watch. He then commends
them, neither to Timothy nor to a bishop, but—in a way
that sets aside all official resource—to God, and to the
Word of His grace which was able to build them up and
assure them of the inheritance. This was where he left
the assembly; that which it did afterwards is not my subject here. If John came later to work in these parts, it
was a great favor from God, but it changed nothing in the
position officially. His labors (with the exception of the
warnings to the seven assemblies in the Apocalypse, where
judgment is in question) regarded the individual life, its
character, and that which sustained it.

Paul's affection shown by his parting from the Ephesian assembly

With deep and touching affection Paul parts from the
assembly at Ephesus. Who filled the gap? At the same
time he appealed to their consciences for the uprightness
of his walk. The free labors of the apostle of the Gentiles
were ended. Solemn and affecting thought! He had been
the instrument chosen of God to communicate to the
world His counsels respecting the assembly, and to establish in the midst of the world this precious object of His
affections united to Christ at His right hand. What would
become of it down here?

Chapter 21

The apostle's personal testimony in suffering

AFTER this time the apostle has to give account of himself, and to accomplish in a striking manner the predictions of the Lord. Brought before tribunals by the malice of the Jews, given up through their hatred into the hands of the Gentiles, it was all to turn to a testimony. Kings and rulers shall hear the gospel, but the love of many will grow cold. This in general is his position; but there were details personal to himself.

The development in the Acts of the Jews' enmity and antagonism

We may remark here a leading feature in this book which has been little noticed; that is, the development of the enmity of the Jews, bringing on their final rejection, such as they were. The Acts ends with the last case presented; the work in the midst of that people is left in oblivion, and that of Paul occupies the whole scene in the historical narrative given by the Spirit. The antagonism of the Jews to the manifestation of the assembly, which took their place and blotted out the distinction between them and the Gentiles, by bringing in heaven and full sovereign grace in contrast with law, which while universal in its direction was given to a distinct people (grace of which the sinner availed himself by faith)—this antagonism, presenting itself at every step in the career of the apostle, although he acted with all possible circumspection, is aroused in its full intensity at Jerusalem, its natural centre, and manifests itself by violence and by efforts made with the Gentiles for the purpose of cutting off Paul from the earth. This rendered the apostle's position very serious with regard to the Gentiles at Jerusalem—a city

the more jealous of its religious importance from having
in fact under Roman bondage lost the reality of it, through
its being transformed into a spirit of rebellion against the
authority which crippled it.

Paul in three different positions

After the history of Christianity, viewed as connected
with Judaism (in reference to the promises and their fulfilment in the Messiah), we find Paul in three different
positions. First, condescending, for the purpose of con-
ciliation, to take account of that which still existed at
Jerusalem, and even addressing the Jews everywhere in
their synagogues, as having administratively the first
right to hear the gospel ("To the Jew first and then to
the Greek") for Jesus was the minister of the circumcision
for the truth of God, to fulfil the promises made to the
fathers. In this respect he never failed, and he establishes
these principles clearly and dogmatically in the Epistle to
the Romans. We next find him, in all the liberty of the
full truth of grace and of the purposes of God, in his own
especial work from which he condescended in grace. This
is recorded in the Epistle to the Ephesians. In both these
cases he acts under the guidance of the Holy Ghost, fulfilling the Lord's will. Afterwards, in the third place, we
see him in conflict with the hostility of legal Judaism, the
emissaries of which he met continually, and into the very
focus of which he at length threw himself by going to
Jerusalem, in that part of his history which we are now
considering. How much was of God—how much was the
consequence of his own steps—is matter for consideration
in this narrative. That the hand of God was in it for the
good of the assembly, and in conducting His beloved servant for his own good in the end, is beyond all doubt.
We have only to search out how far the will and the mind
of Paul came in, as means which God used to bring about
the result He intended, whether for the assembly or for

His servant, or for the Jews. These thoughts are of the deepest interest, and require humble examination of that which God has set before us to instruct us on this point in the history which the Spirit Himself has given us of these things.

Paul forbidden by the Spirit to go to Jerusalem: something impelled him thither

The first thing which strikes us at the beginning of this history is that the Holy Ghost tells him not to go to Jerusalem. (Chap. 21: 4.) This word has evident importance. Paul felt himself bound: there was something in his own mind which impelled him thither, a feeling that forced him in that direction; but the Spirit, in His positive and outward testimony, forbade his going.

Paul's intention to go to Rome: his love for his own nation

The apostle's intention had been to go to Rome. The apostle of the Gentiles sent forth to preach the gospel to every creature, there was nothing of self in this project that was not according to grace. (Rom. 1: 13-15.) Nevertheless God had not allowed him to go thither. He was obliged to write his Epistle to them without seeing them. Heaven is the metropolis of Christianity. Rome and Jerusalem must have no place with Paul, except as to bearing with the one in affection, and being ready, when he might, to evangelize the other. Acts 19: 21, which is translated, "in the spirit," only means the spirit of Paul. He purposed, in his own mind, saying, "When I have been there, I must also see Rome." Afterwards he charged himself with the offerings of the saints in Achaia and Macedonia. He wished to prove his affection for the poor of his own people (Gal. 2: 10). This was all well. I do not know if it was a function suited to an apostle. It was an evidently Jewish feeling, which set peculiar value on the poor of Jerusalem, and so far on Jerusalem itself. A Jew would rather be poor at Jerusalem than rich among the Gentiles. Poor Christians were there no doubt from the time of their conversion, but that was the origin of this system. (Compare Neh. 11: 2 and Acts 24: 17.) All this belonged to relationship with Judaism (Rom. 15: 25-28). Paul loved the nation to which he belonged after the flesh, and which had been the people beloved of God and was still His people although rejected for a time, the remnant having now to enter the kingdom of God through Christianity. This attachment of Paul to them (which had its right and deeply affecting side, but which on another side had to do with the flesh) led him into the centre of Judaism. He was the messenger of the heavenly glory, which brought out the doctrine of the assembly composed of Jews and Gentiles, united without distinction in the one body of Christ, thus blotting out Judaism; but his love for his nation carried him, I repeat, into the very centre of hostile Judaism—Judaism enraged against this spiritual equality. His testimony, the Lord had told him, they would not receive.

Paul as a beloved and faithful servant, but still a man

Nevertheless the hand of God was doubtless in it. Paul individually found his level.

As the instrument of God's revelation, he proclaims in all its extent and all its force the purpose of the sovereign grace of God. The wine is not adulterated; it flows out as pure as he had received it. And he walked in a remarkable way at the height of the revelation committed to him. Still Paul individually is a man; he must be exercised and manifested, and in those exercises to which God has subjected us. Where the flesh has found its pleasure, the sphere in which it has gratified itself, it is there that, when God acts, it finds its sorrow. Yet, if God saw fit to prove His servant and manifest him to himself, He stood by him, and blessed him even through the trial itself—turned it into testimony, and refreshed the heart of His beloved and faithful servant. The manifestation of that in him which is not according to the Spirit, or to the height of his calling, was in love for his blessing and for that of the assembly. Blessed is he who can walk as faithfully and maintain his standing to the same degree through grace in the path of grace! Nevertheless Christ is the only model. I see no one who (in another career) so much resembled Him in His public life as Paul.

The more we search into the apostle's walk the more we shall see this resemblance, Only that Christ was the model of perfection in obedience; in His precious servant there was the flesh. Paul would have been the first to acknowledge that perfection may be ascribed to Jesus only.

The over-ruling hand of God

I believe then that the hand of God was in this journey of Paul's; that in His sovereign wisdom He willed that His servant should undertake it, and also have blessing in it; but that the means employed to lead him into it according to that sovereign wisdom, was the apostle's human affection for the people who were his kinsmen after the flesh; and that he was not led into it by the Holy Ghost acting on the part of Christ in the assembly. This attachment to his people, this human affection, met with that among the people which put it in its place. Humanly speaking, it was an amiable feeling; but it was not the power of the Holy Ghost founded on the death and resurrection of Christ. Here there was no longer Jew nor Gentile. In the living Christ it was right. Christ went on in it to the end in order that He might die; for this purpose He came.

Paul's affection was good in itself, but as a spring of action it did not come up to the height of the work of the

Spirit, who on Christ's part had sent him afar from Jerusalem to the Gentiles in order to reveal the assembly as
His Body united to Him in heaven. Thus the Jews hearkened to him till it came to that word, and then they cried
out and raised the tumult which caused Paul to be made
prisoner.[31] He suffered for the truth, but where that truth
had no access according to Christ's own testimony: "They
will not receive thy testimony concerning Me." It was
necessary however that the Jews should manifest their
hatred to the gospel, and give this final proof of their inveterate opposition to the ways of God in grace.

The apostolic mission to the Gentiles as to the foundation of the assembly concluded

At the same time, whatever may have been the subsequent labors of the apostle (if there were any the Holy
Ghost does not make mention of them: Paul sees the Jews
in his own house, and receives all who come to him; but)
the page of the Spirit's history closes here. This history
is ended. The apostolic mission to the Gentiles in connection with the founding of the assembly is concluded. Rome
is but the prison of the apostle of the truth, to whom the
truth had been committed. Jerusalem rejects him, Rome
imprisons him and puts him to death, as it had done to
Jesus, whom the blessed apostle had to resemble in this
also according to his desire in Philippians 3; for Christ
and conformity to Him was his only object. It was given
him to find this conformity in his service, as it was so
strongly in his heart and soul, with the necessary difference between a ministry which was not to break the
bruised reed nor lift up its voice in the street, and one

---

[31] And this circumstance is worthy of note, that it was Christ's declaration that he should go to the Gentiles; to which we may add that this at
the time was accompanied by the declaration, "Get thee quickly out of
Jerusalem, for they will not receive the testimony concerning Me." So
that what declared his testimony was of no avail in Jerusalem was the
occasion of his being seized. On Christ's word and his own showing, his
apostolic service was not there but elsewhere.

which in testimony was to bring forth judgment to the
Gentiles.

Man's universal failure: the assembly remaining the object of faith until manifested in glory as the heavenly Jerusalem

The mission of the twelve to the Gentiles, going out from
Jerusalem (Matt. 28), never took place, so far as any
record of it by the Holy Ghost goes.[32] Jerusalem detained
them. They did not even go over the cities of Israel. The
ministry of the circumcision was given to Peter, that of
the Gentiles to Paul in connection with the doctrine of the
assembly and of a glorious Christ—a Christ whom he no
longer knew after the flesh. Jerusalem, to which the apostle was drawn by his affection, rejected both him and his
mission. His ministry to the Gentiles, so far as the free
effect of the power of the Spirit, ended likewise. Ecclesiastical history may perhaps tell us more; nevertheless God
has taken care to bury it in profound darkness. Nothing
farther is owned by the Spirit. We hear no more of the
apostles at Jerusalem; and Rome, as we have seen, had
none, so far as the Holy Ghost informs us, excepting that
the apostle of the Gentiles was a prisoner there and finally
put to death. Man has failed everywhere on earth. The
religious and political centres of the world—centres, according to God, as to the earth—have rejected the testimony, and put the testifier to death; but the result has
been that Heaven has maintained its rights inviolate and
in their absolute purity. The assembly, the true heavenly
and eternal metropolis of glory and of the ways of God—
the assembly which had its place in the counsels of God
before the world was—the assembly which answers to His

[32] Mark 16: 20 is the only passage which may be supposed to allude to
what would fulfil it; and even not so as such, for that and Colossians 1: 6
refer to all the world, and are founded on ascension, not a mission to the
Gentiles only founded on resurrection.

heart in grace as united to Christ in glory—remains the
object of faith. It is revealed according to the mind of
God, and perfectly such as it is in His mind, until, as the
heavenly Jerusalem, it shall be manifested in glory, in
connection with the accomplishment of the ways of God
on the earth, in the re-establishment of Jerusalem as the
centre of His earthly dealings in grace, His throne, His
metropolis in the midst even of the Gentiles, and in the
disappearance even of Gentile power, the seat and centre
of which was Rome.

Christianity in Rome before any apostle planted it there

Let us now examine the thoughts of the apostle, and
that which took place historically. Paul wrote from
Corinth to Rome, when he had this journey in view.
Christianity had flowed towards that centre of the world,
without any apostle whatsoever having planted it there.
Paul follows it. Rome is, as it were, a part of his apostolic domain which escapes him (Rom. 1:13-15). He returns to the subject in chapter 15. If he might not come
(for God will not begin with the capital of the world—
compare the destruction of Hazor in Canaan, Joshua
11:11), he will at least write to them on the ground of his
universal apostleship to the Gentiles. Some Christians
were already established there: so God would have it. But
they were in some sort, of his province. Many of them
had been personally in connection with him. See the
number and character of the salutations at the end of the
epistle, which have a peculiar stamp, making the Roman
Christians in great part the children of Paul.

Jerusalem or Rome and Spain

In Romans 15:14-29 he develops his apostolic position with respect to the Romans and others. He desired
also to go into Spain when he had seen the brethren at

Rome a little. He wishes to impart spiritual gifts to them, but to be comforted by their mutual faith, to enjoy a little of their company. They are in connection with him; but they have their place as Christians at Rome without his ever having been there. When therefore he had seen them a little, he would go into Spain. But he was disappointed with regards to these projects. All that we are told by the Holy Ghost is that he was a prisoner at Rome. Profound silence as to Spain. Instead of going farther when he had seen them and imparted gifts, he remains two years a prisoner at Rome. It is not known whether he was set free or not. Some say yes, others no; the Word says nothing.

It is here, when he had laid open his intentions and the character of his relationships in the Spirit with Rome, and when a large field opens before him in the west, that his old affection for his people and for Jerusalem intervenes—"But now I go unto Jerusalem to carry help to the saints" (Rom. 15: 25-28). Why not go to Rome according to the energy of the Spirit, his work being finished in Greece? (ver. 23). God, no doubt, ordained that those things should happen at Jerusalem, and that Rome and the Romans should have this sad place with respect to the testimony of a glorified Christ and of the assembly, which the apostle rendered before the world. But as to Paul, why put rebellious Jerusalem between his evangelical desire and his work? The affection was good, and the service good—for a deacon, or a messenger of the churches: but for Paul, who had the whole west open before his evangelizing thought!

For the moment Jerusalem intercepted his view. Accordingly, as we have seen, the Holy Ghost warned him on his way. He foresaw himself also the danger he was running into (Rom. 15: 30-32). He was sure (ver. 29) of coming in the fulness of the blessing of the gospel of Christ; but he was not sure that he should come with joy. The thing for which he asked their prayers turned

out quite otherwise than he desired. He was delivered,
but as a prisoner. He took courage when he saw the
brethren at Appii Forum and the Three Taverns. There
was no journey into Spain either.

The Lord standing by His servant in trial but giving needful discipline

All this to me is very solemn. The Lord, full of grace
and tenderness, was with His poor but beloved servant.
In the case of such an one as Paul, it is a most affecting
history, and the Lord's ways adorable and perfect in goodness. The reality of faith is there in full: the ways of
grace perfect, and perfect in tenderness also, in the Lord.
He stands by His servant in the trial in which he finds
himself, to encourage and strengthen him. At the same
time, with regard to the desire of going to Jerusalem, he
is warned by the Spirit, and its consequences are set before him; and, not turning back, he undergoes the needful
discipline, which brings his soul into its place, and a full
place of blessing before God. His walk finds its level as
to spiritual power. He feels the power outwardly of that
whereof he had felt the moral power seeking to hinder his
ministry; and a chain upon his flesh answers to the liberty
he had allowed it. There was justice in God's dealings.
His servant was too precious for it to be otherwise. At
the same time, as to result and testimony, God ordered
everything for His own glory, and with perfect wisdom
as to the future welfare of the assembly. Jerusalem, as
we have seen, rejects the testimony to the Gentiles, in a
word the ways of God in the assembly (compare 1 Thess.
2: 14-16); and Rome becomes the prison of that testimony; while according to the Lord's promise the testimony is carried before rulers and kings, and before Cæsar
himself.

Paul put in Christ's position as given up to the Gentiles by Jewish hatred

I have said that grace put Paul into the position of Christ given up to the Gentiles by the hatred of the Jews. It was a great favor. The difference—besides the infinite love of the Lord who gave Himself up—was that Jesus was there in His true place before God. He had come to the Jews: that He should be delivered up was the crowning act of His devotedness and His service. It was in fact the offering Himself by the Eternal Spirit. It was the sphere of His service as sent of God. Paul re-entered it: the energy of the Holy Ghost had placed him outside— "Delivering thee," said the Lord, "from the people and from the Gentiles, to whom I now send thee to open their eyes," &c. (Acts 26: 17). Jesus had taken him out from them both, to exercise a ministry that united the two in one Body in Christ in heaven who had thus sent him. In his service Paul knew no one after the flesh; in Christ Jesus there was neither Jew nor Greek.

Warned by the Holy Spirit, but unpersuaded

Let us resume his history. He is warned by the Holy Ghost not to go up (chap. 21: 4). Nevertheless he continues his journey to Cæsarea. A prophet named Agabus comes down from Judea, and announces that Paul shall be bound and given up to the Gentiles. It might be said that this did not forbid his going. It is true; yet, coming after the other, it strengthened the warning already given. When he walked in the liberty of the Spirit, warned of danger, he fled from it, while braving every peril if the testimony required it. At Ephesus he allowed himself to be persuaded not to go into the theatre.

The Holy Ghost does not usually warn of danger. He leads in the path of the Lord, and if persecution comes, He gives strength to endure it. Here Paul was continually warned. His friends entreat him not to go up. He will

not be persuaded. They hold their peace, little satisfied,
saying, "The will of the Lord be done." And, I doubt
not, it was His will, but for the accomplishment of purposes that Paul knew not by the intelligence given of the
Holy Ghost. Only he felt pressed in spirit to go, and
ready to suffer all things for the Lord.

Seeking to please the believing Jews, Paul finds him-self in the hands of the adversaries to the gospel

He departs therefore to Jerusalem; and when there, he
goes to the house of James, and all the elders assemble.
Paul relates to them the work of God among the Gentiles.
They turn to their Judaism, of which the multitude were
full, and, while rejoicing in the good that was wrought of
God by the Spirit, they wish Paul to show himself obedient to the law. The believers in Jerusalem must needs
come together on the arrival of Paul, and their prejudices
with regard to the law must be satisfied. Paul has brought
himself into the presence of man's exigencies: to refuse
compliance with them would be to say that their thoughts
about him were true; to act according to their desire was
to make a rule, not of the guidance of the Spirit in all
liberty of love, but of the ignorant and prejudiced condition of these Jewish believers. It is that Paul was there,
not according to the Spirit as an apostle, but according to
his attachment to these former things. One must be above
prejudices of others, and free from their influence, to be
able to condescend to them in love.

Being there, Paul can hardly do other than satisfy their
demands. But the hand of God is in it. This act throws
him into the power of his enemies. Seeking to please the
believing Jews, he finds himself in the lion's mouth, in the
hands of the Jews who were adversaries to the gospel. It
may be added that we hear nothing more of the Christians of Jerusalem. They had done their work. I have
no doubt that they accepted the alms of the Gentiles.

Chapter 22

Rescued by Roman soldiers: permitted to speak to the people

THE whole city being moved and the temple shut, the
commander of the band comes to rescue Paul from
the Jews who wished to kill him taking him however into
custody himself, for the Romans were used to these tu-
mults, and heartily despised this nation beloved of God
but proud and degraded in their own condition. Nevertheless Paul commands the respect of the captain of the
band by his manner of addressing him, and he permits
him to speak to the people. To the chief captain Paul
had spoken in Greek; but, always ready to win by the
attentions of love, and especially when the loved though
rebellious people were in question, he speaks to them in
Hebrew (that is, in their ordinary language called Hebrew). He does not enlarge upon what the Lord said
revealing Himself to him, but he gives them a particular
account of his subsequent interview with Ananias, a faithful Jew and esteemed of all. He then enters on the point
which necessarily characterized his position and his defence. Christ had appeared to him, saying, "They will
not receive thy testimony at Jerusalem. I will send thee
far hence unto the Gentiles." Blessed be God, it is the
truth; but why tell it to those very persons who, according to his own words, would not receive his testimony?
The only thing which gave authority to such a mission
was the Person of Jesus, and they did not believe in it.

The effect of his discourse: brought before the Sanhedrin

In his testimony to the people the apostle laid stress in
vain upon the Jewish piety of Ananias: genuine as it
might be, it was but a broken reed. Nevertheless it was

all, except his own. His discourse had but one effect—to bring out the violent and incorrigible hatred of this unhappy nation to every thought of grace in God, and the unbounded pride which indeed went before the fall that crushed them. The chief captain, seeing the violence of the people, and not at all understanding what was going on, with the haughty contempt of a Roman, orders Paul to be bound and scourged to make him confess what it meant. Now Paul was himself a Roman citizen, and born such, while the chief captain had purchased that freedom. Paul quietly makes this fact known, and they who were about to scourge him withdraw. The chief captain was afraid because he had bound him; but, as his authority was concerned in it, he leaves him bound. The next day he looses him and brings him before the council, or Sanhedrin of the Jews. The people, not merely their rulers, had rejected grace.

Chapter 23

Paul's address to the council: its result: sent as a prisoner to Cæsarea

PAUL addresses the council with the gravity and dignity of an upright man accustomed to walk with God. It is not a testimony borne them for their good; but the appeal of a good conscience to their conscience, if they had any. The immediate answer is an outrage on the part of the judge or chief of the council. Paul, roused by this procedure, denounces judgment on him from God; but, warned that he was the high priest (who was not so clothed as to be recognized), he excuses himself by his ignorance of the fact, quoting the formal prohibition of the law to speak evil of the ruler of the people. All this was right and in place with regard to men; but the Holy Ghost could not say, "I wist not." It is not the activity of the Spirit performing the work of grace and of testimony. But it is the means of the final judgment of God upon the people. It is in this character, as regards the Jews, that Paul appears here. Paul makes a much better appearance than his judges, who thoroughly disgrace themselves and manifest their dreadful condition; but he does not appear for God before them. Afterwards he avails himself of the different parties of which the council were composed to throw complete disorder into it, by declaring himself to be a Pharisee, the son of a Pharisee, and called in question for a dogma of that sect. This was true; but it was below the height of his own word, "That which was gain I counted loss for Christ's sake." The Jews however fully manifest themselves. That which Paul said raises a tumult, and the chief captain takes him from among them. God has all things at his disposal. A nephew of Paul's, never mentioned elsewhere, hears of an ambush laid for him and warns him of it. Paul sends him to the chief captain, who expedites the departure of Paul under a guard to Cæsarea. God watched over him, but all is on the level of human and providential ways. There is not the angel as in Peter's case, nor the earthquake as at Philippi. We are sensibly on different ground.

Chapters 24, 25

Before the governors

PAUL appears before the governors in succession—the Sanhedrin, Felix, Festus, Agrippa, and afterwards Cæsar. And here, when occasion offers, we have striking appeals to conscience; when his defence is in question, the manly and honest declarations of a good conscience, that rose above the passions and interests that surrounded him. I pass over in silence the worldly egotism which betrays itself in Lysias and Festus, by their assumption of all sorts of good qualities and good conduct; the mixture of awakened conscience and absence of principle in the governors; the desire to please the Jews for their own importance or to facilitate their government of a rebellious people; and the contempt felt by those who were not as responsible as Lysias for the public tranquillity. The position of Agrippa and all the details of the history have a remarkable stamp of truth, and present the various characters in so living a style that we seem to be in the scenes described. We see the persons moving in it. This moreover strikingly characterizes the writings of Luke.

Paul's appeal to Cæsar

Other circumstances claim our attention. Festus, in order to please the Jews, proposed to take Paul to Jerusalem. But Rome was to have its share in the rejection of the gospel of grace, of the testimony to the assembly; and Paul appeals to Cæsar. Festus must therefore send him thither, although embarrassed to know what crime he is to charge him with in sending him. Sad picture of man's injustice! But everything accomplishes the purposes of God. In the use of the means Paul succeeds no better than in his attempt to satisfy the Jews. It was perhaps to the eye of man his only resource under the circumstances; but the Holy Ghost is careful to inform us that he might have been set at liberty if he had not appealed to Cæsar.

Chapter 26

King Agrippa's conscience aroused

IN Agrippa there was, I believe, more curiosity than conscience, though there may have been some desire to profit by the occasion to know what the doctrine was which had so stirred up people's minds, a disposition to inquire which was more than curiosity. In general his words are taken as if he was not far from being convinced that Christianity was true: perhaps he would have been so if his passions had not stood in the way. But it may be questioned whether this is the force of the Greek, as generally supposed, and not, rather, "In a little you are going to make a Christian of me," covering his uneasiness at the appeal to his professed Judaism before Festus, by an affected and slighting remark. And such I believe to be the case. The notion of an "almost Christian" is quite a mistake, though a man's mind may be under influences which ought to lead him to it, and yet reject it. He would have been glad for Paul to be set free. He expresses his conviction that it might have been done if he had not appealed to Cæsar. He gives his opinion to Festus as a wise and reasonable man; but his words were in reality dictated by his conscience—words that he could venture to utter when Festus and all the rest were agreed that Paul had done nothing worthy of death or of bonds.

God would have the innocence of his beloved servant proved in the face of the world. His discourse tends to this. He goes farther, but his object is to give account of his conduct. His miraculous conversion is related in order to justify his subsequent career; but it is so related as to act upon the conscience of Agrippa, who was acquainted with Jewish things, and evidently desired to hear something of Christianity, which he suspected to be the truth. Accordingly he lays hold with eagerness of the opportunity that presents itself to hear the apostle explain it. But he remains much where he was. His condition of soul opens however the mouth of Paul, and he addresses himself directly and particularly to the king; who moreover, evidently engrossed by the subject, had called on him to speak. To Festus it was all rhapsody.

A missionary from God before the Gentiles

The dignity of Paul's manner before all these governors is perfect. He addresses himself to the conscience with a forgetfulness of self that showed a man in whom communion with God, and the sense of his relationship with God, carried the mind above all effect of circumstances. He was acting for God; and, with a perfect deference for the position of those he addressed, we see that which was morally altogether superior to them. The more humiliating his circumstances, the more beauty there is in this superiority. Before the Gentiles he is a missionary from God. He is again (blessed be God!) in his right place. All that he said to the Jews was right and deserved; but why was he, who had been delivered from the people, subjected to their total want of conscience and their blind passions which gave no place for testimony? Nevertheless, as we have seen, it was to be so in order that the Jews might in every way fill up the measure of their iniquity, and indeed that the blessed apostle might follow the steps of his Master.

Paul's address to Agrippa: his personal history: the conduct of the Jews put in the clearest light

Paul's address to king Agrippa furnishes us with the most complete picture of the entire position of the apostle, as he himself looked at it when his long service and the light of the Holy Ghost illuminated his backward glance.

He does not speak of the assembly—that was a doctrine for instruction, and not a part of his history. But everything that related to his personal history, in connection with his ministry, he gives in detail. He had been a strict Pharisee; and here he connects the doctrine of Christ with the hopes of the Jews. He was in bonds "for the hope of the promise made unto the fathers." No doubt resurrection entered into it. Why should the king think resurrection impossible, that God was not able to raise

the dead? This brings him to another point. He had
verily thought with himself that he ought to do many
things against Jesus of Nazareth, and had carried them
out with all the energy of his character, and with the
bigotry of a devout Jew. His present condition, as a witness among the Gentiles, depended on the change wrought
in him by the revelation of the Lord when he was engaged
in seeking to destroy His name. Near Damascus a light
brighter than the sun struck them all to the earth, and
he alone heard the voice of the Righteous One, so that he
knew from His own mouth that it was Jesus, and that He
looked upon those who believed in Him as Himself. He
could not resist such a testimony. But as this was the
great grievance to the Jews, he shows that his own position was formally marked out by the Lord Himself. He
was called to give ocular evidence of the glory which he
had seen, that is, of Jesus in that glory; and of other
things also, for the manifestation of which Jesus would
again appear to him. A glorious Christ known (personally) only in heaven was the subject of the testimony
committed to him. For this purpose He had set Paul
apart from the Jews as much as from the Gentiles, his
mission belonging immediately to heaven, having its origin
there; and he was sent formally by the Lord of glory to
the Gentiles, to change their position with respect to God
through faith in this glorious Jesus, opening their eyes,
bringing them out of darkness into light, from the power
of Satan to God, and giving them an inheritance among
the sanctified. This was a definite work. The apostle was
not disobedient to the heavenly vision, and he had taught
the Gentiles to turn to God, and to act as those who had
done so. For this cause the Jews sought to kill him.

Nothing more simple, more truthful, than this history.
It put the case of Paul and the conduct of the Jews in the
clearest light. When called to order by Festus, who naturally thought it nothing more than irrational enthusiasm,
he appeals with perfect dignity and quick discernment to

Agrippa's knowledge of the fact upon which all this was based: for the thing had not been done in a corner.

The king and the poor prisoner, rich in God

Agrippa was not far from being convinced; but his heart was unchanged. The wish that Paul expresses brings the matter back to its moral reality. The meeting is dissolved. The king resumes his kingly place in courtesy and condescension, and the disciple that of a prisoner; but, whatever might be the apostle's position, we see in him a heart thoroughly happy and filled with the Spirit and love of God. Two years of prison had brought him no depression of heart or faith, but had only set him free from his harassing connection with the Jews, to give him moments spent with God.

Agrippa, surprised and carried away by Paul's clear and straightforward narrative,[33] relieves himself from the pressure of Paul's personal address by saying, "In a little you are going to make a Christian of me." Charity might have said, "Would to God that thou wert!" But there is a spring in the heart of Paul that does not stop there. "Would to God," says he, "that not only thou, but *all* those that hear me, were . . . . *altogether such as I am,* except these bonds!" What happiness and what love (and in God these two things go together) are expressed in these words! A poor prisoner, aged and rejected, at the end of his career he is rich in God. Blessed years that he had spent in prison! He could give himself as a model of happiness; for it filled his heart. There are conditions of soul which unmistakably declare themselves. And why should he not be happy? His fatigues ended, his work in a certain sense finished, he possessed Christ and in Him all things. The glorious Jesus, who had brought him into

---

[33] It is hardly to be read "almost." Relieving himself, Agrippa says, "You'll soon be making a Christian of me," covering his feelings, as I have said, by a slighting speech. But I have no doubt his mind was greatly wrought upon.

the pains and labor of the testimony, was now his possession and his crown. Such is ever the case. The cross and service—by virtue of what Christ is—is the enjoyment of all that He is, when the service is ended; and in some sort is the measure of that enjoyment. This was the case with Christ Himself, in *all its fulness;* it is ours, in our measure, according to the sovereign grace of God. Only Paul's expression supposes the Holy Ghost acting fully in the heart in order that it may be free to enjoy, and that the Spirit is not grieved.

The glorious Object of Paul's heart and faith

A glorious Jesus—a Jesus who loved him, a Jesus who put the seal of His approbation and love upon his service, a Jesus who would take him to Himself in glory, and with whom he was one (and that known according to the abundant power of the Holy Ghost, according to divine righteousness), a Jesus who revealed the Father, and through whom he had the place of adoption—was the infinite source of joy to Paul, the glorious object of his heart and of his faith; and, being known in love, filled his heart with that love overflowing towards all men. What could he wish them better than to be as he was except his bonds? How, filled with this love, could he not wish it, or not be full of this large affection? Jesus was its measure.

The servant eclipsed before Christ

His innocence fully established and acknowledged by his judges, the purposes of God must still be accomplished. His appeal to Cæsar must carry him to Rome, that he may bear testimony there also. In his position here he again resembles Jesus. But at the same time, if we compare them, the servant, blessed as he is, grows dim, and is eclipsed before Christ, so that we could no longer think of him. Jesus offered Himself up in grace; He appealed to God only; He answered but to bear testimony to the truth—that truth was the glory of His Person, His own rights, humbled as He was. His Person shines out through all the dark clouds of human violence, which could have had no power over Him had it not been the moment for thus fulfilling the will of God. For that purpose He yields to power given them from above. Paul appeals to Cæsar. He is a Roman—a human dignity conferred by man, and available before men; he uses it for himself, God thus accomplishing His purposes. The one is blessed, and his services; the other is perfect, the perfect subject of the testimony itself.

The prisoner filled with liberty and joy; the Lord's gracious encouragement

Nevertheless, if there is no longer the free service of the Holy Ghost for Paul, and if he is a prisoner in the hands of the Romans, his soul at least is filled with the Spirit. Between him and God all is liberty and joy. All this shall turn to his salvation, that is, to his definite victory in his contest with Satan. How blessed! Through the communications of the Spirit of Jesus Christ the Word of God shall not be bound. Others shall gain strength and liberty in view of his bonds, even although, in the low state of the Church, some take advantage of them. But Christ will be preached and magnified, and with that Paul is content. Oh how true this is, and the perfect joy of the heart, come what may! We are the subjects of grace (God be praised!), as well as instruments of grace in service. Christ alone is its object, and God secures *His* glory—nothing more is needed: this itself is our portion and our perfect joy.

It will be remarked in this interesting history, that at the moment when Paul might have been the most troubled, when his course was perhaps the least evidently according to the power of the Spirit, when he brought disorder into the council by using arguments which afterwards

he hesitates himself entirely to justify — it is then
that the Lord, full of grace, appears to him to encourage
and strengthen him. The Lord, who formerly had told
him at Jerusalem to go away because they would not
receive his testimony, who had sent him warnings not to
go thither, but who accomplished His own purposes of
grace in the infirmity and through the human affections
of His servant, by their means even, exercising at the
same time His wholesome discipline in His divine wisdom by these same means—Jesus appears to him to tell
him that, as he had testified of Him at Jerusalem, so
should he bear witness at Rome also. This is the way that
the Lord interprets in grace the whole history, at the
moment when His servant might have felt all that was
painful in his position, perhaps have been overwhelmed
by it, remembering that the Spirit had forbidden him to
go up; for, when in trial, a doubt is torment. The faithful
and gracious Saviour intervenes therefore to encourage
Paul, and to put His own interpretation on the position
of His poor servant, and to mark the character of His
love for him. If it was necessary to exercise discipline
for his good on account of his condition and to perfect
him, Jesus was with him in the discipline. Nothing more
touching than the tenderness, the opportuneness, of this
grace. Moreover, as we have said, it all accomplished the
purposes of God with regard to the Jews, to the Gentiles,
to the world. For God can unite in one dispensation the
most various ends.

Chapter 27

Paul as master of the position on the voyage to Rome

AND now, restored, reanimated by grace, Paul shows
himself in his journey to be master of the position.
It is he who counsels, according to the communication he

receives from God, he who encourages, he who acts, in
every way, on God's part, in the midst of the scene around
him. The description, full of life and reality, which Luke
his companion gives of this voyage, needs no comment.
It is admirable as a living picture of the whole scene. Our
concern is to see what Paul was amid the false confidence
or the distress of the whole company.

Chapter 28

Shipwrecked at Melita: God with him

A T Melita we find him again exercising his accustomed
  power among that barbarous people. One sees that
God is with him. Evangelization does not, however, appear in the account of his sojourn there or of his journey.

In Rome as a prisoner: the Jews sent for: Esaias' judgment solemnly declared upon their rejection of Jesus and the testimony of the Holy Spirit

Landed in Italy, we see him depressed: the love of the
brethren encourages and reanimates him; and he goes on
to Rome, where he dwells two years in a house that he
hires, a soldier being with him as a guard. Probably those
who carried him to Rome had been given to understand
that it was only a matter of Jewish jealousy, for all
through the journey they treated him with all possible
respect. Besides he was a Roman.

Arrived at Rome, he sends for the Jews; and here, for
the last time, their condition is set before us, and the judgment which had been hanging over their heads ever since
the utterance of the prophecy (which was especially connected with the house of David and with Judah)—the
judgment pronounced by Esaias, which the Lord Jesus
declared should come upon them because of His rejection,

the execution of which was suspended by the long-suffering of God, until the testimony of the Holy Ghost was also rejected—this judgment is here brought to mind by Paul at the end of the historical part of the New Testament. It is their definitive condition solemnly declared by the minister of sovereign grace, and which should continue until God interposed in power to give them repentance, and to deliver them, and to glorify Himself in them by grace.

The setting aside of the Jews a characteristic of the Acts: the assembly, the One Body, put in their place by God as His house

We have already marked this characteristic of the Acts, which comes out here in a clear and striking manner—the setting aside of the Jews. That is to say, they set themselves aside by the rejection of the testimony of God, of the work of God. They put themselves outside that which God was setting up. They will not follow Him in His progress of grace. And thus they are altogether left behind, without God and without present communication with Him. His word abides for ever, and His mercy; but others take the place of positive and present relationship with Him. Individuals from among them enter into another sphere on other grounds; but Israel disappears and is blotted out for a time from the sight of God.

It is this which is presented in the book of Acts. The patience of God is exercised towards the Jews themselves in the preaching of the gospel and the apostolic mission at the beginning. Their hostility develops itself by degrees and reaches its height in the case of Stephen. Paul is raised up, a witness of grace towards them as an elect remnant, for he was himself of Israel; but introducing, in connection with a heavenly Christ, something entirely new as doctrine—the assembly, the Body of Christ in heaven; and the setting aside of all distinction between Jew and

Gentile as sinners, and in the oneness of that Body. This
is linked historically with that which had been established
at Jerusalem, in order to maintain unity and the connection of the promises; but in itself, as a doctrine, it was a
thing hidden in God in all the ages, having been in His
purposes of grace before the world was. The enmity of
the Jews to this truth never abated. They used every
means to excite the Gentiles against those who taught the
doctrine, and to prevent the formation of the assembly itself. God, having acted with perfect patience and grace
unto the end, puts the assembly into the place of the Jews,
as His house, and the vessel of His promises on earth, by
making it His habitation by the Spirit. The Jews were
set aside (alas, their spirit soon took possession of the
assembly itself); and the assembly, and the clear and positive doctrine of no difference between Jew and Gentile (by
nature alike the children of wrath) and of their common
and equal privileges as members of one only Body, has
been fully declared and made the basis of all relationship
between God and every soul possessed of faith. This is
the doctrine of the apostle in the Epistles to the Romans
and Ephesians.[34] At the same time the gift of eternal life,
as promised before the world was, has been made manifest
by being born again[35] (the commencement of a new existence with a divine character), and partaking of divine
righteousness; these two things being united in our resurrection with Christ, by which, our sins being forgiven, we
are placed before God as Christ, who is at once our life
and our righteousness. This life manifests itself by conformity to the life of Christ on earth, who left us an
example that we should follow His steps. It is the divine

[34] In Romans in their personal position, in Ephesians in the corporate

[35] The word "regeneration" is not applied in Scripture to our being
born again; it is a change of position in us connected with our having
died with Him and resurrection. It is found twice; once in Matthew 19
it is Christ's coming kingdom; and in Titus it is the washing of baptism,
as typically bringing out of the old Adam state and into the Christian,
but distinguished from the renewing of the Holy Ghost.

life manifested in man—in Christ as the object, in us as testimony.

The cross of Christ the basis of all relationship with God

The cross of Christ is the basis, the fundamental centre, of all these truths,—the relations between God and man as he was, his responsibility; grace; expiation; the end of life, as to sin, the law, and the world; the putting away of sin through the death of Christ, and its consequences in us. Everything is established there, and gives place to the power of life that was in Christ, who there perfectly glorified God—to that new existence into which He entered as Man into the presence of the Father; by whose glory, as well as by His own divine power and by the energy of the Holy Ghost, He was raised from the dead.

God's ways in government with the Jews on earth, with Gentiles and the world in judgment, and warnings for the assembly

This does not prevent God's resuming His ways in government with the Jews on earth, when the Church is complete and manifested on high; and which He will do according to His promises and the declarations of prophecy. The apostle explains this also in the Epistle to the Romans; but it belongs to the study of that epistle. The ways of God in judgment with regard to the Gentiles also at the same period will be shown us in the Apocalypse, as well as in prophetic passages of the Epistles, in connection with the coming of Christ, and even with His government of the world in general from the beginning to the end; together with the warnings necessary for the assembly, when the days of deception begin to dawn and to be developed morally in the ruin of the assembly, viewed as God's witness in the world.

Paul's history ended: Rome's history in connection with the gospel begun

Our apostle, when brought to Rome, declares (upon the manifestation of unbelief among the Jews, which we have pointed out) that the salvation of God is sent to the Gentiles; and he dwells two whole years in the house he had hired, receiving those who came to him (for he had not liberty to go to them) preaching the kingdom of God and those things which concerned the Lord Jesus with all boldness, no man forbidding him. And here the history is ended of this precious servant of God, beloved and honored by his Master, a prisoner in that Rome which, as head of the fourth empire, was to be the seat of opposition among the Gentiles as Jerusalem of opposition among the Jews, to the kingdom and to the glory of Christ. The time for the full manifestation of that opposition was not yet come; but the minister of the assembly and of the gospel of glory is a prisoner there. It is thus that Rome begins its history in connection with the gospel that the apostle preached. Nevertheless God was with him.

THE EPISTLES

INTRODUCTION

The Epistles as the exposition of the result of Christ's work: His death, resurrection and exaltation the centre of their teaching

IN the Epistles, we find the exposition of the result of that glorious work of grace, by which man is placed on entirely new ground with God, in reconciliation with Him; as well as the development of the counsels of God in Christ, according to which this new world is established and ordered. In giving this exposition of the ways of God in connection with the work which is their basis, the perfect efficacy of the work itself, and the order of our relations with God, are plainly set forth; so that the whole system, the whole plan of God, and the way in which it was put in execution, are presented. And in doing this, that which man is, that which God is, that which eternal life is, are clearly put before us.

The death and resurrection of Christ, as well as His exaltation to the right hand of God, form the centre of all this instruction.

The three great divisions of the Epistles and their character

There are three great divisions in this instruction, which are connected in general with the instrument used of God in the communication of each part. 1st. The counsels of God, which are developed by Paul in connection with the revelation of true righteousness before God, the ground on which a man can be truly righteous before God—God's righteousness, man being a sinner. 2nd. The life of God, eternal life manifested and imparted. This is in John's

Epistle.[1] 3rd. Christian life on the earth, in following a risen Christ. This we find in the Epistle of Peter, in connection with God's government of the world as such: the Christian is a pilgrim. There are also James and Jude. The first presents moral life—the life of faith on earth— as the true demonstration to men of our faith, and, in particular, of practical faith in Christ as well as in God, who answers our requests and our wants. On this account, while clearly and distinctly recognizing faith in Christ, and our being begotten by the mighty grace of God through His Word, this epistle scarcely rises in fact above such life as could have manifested and developed itself at any period whatsoever in a believer; only that it was the Christian, born of God, who now exemplified it, and that thus it was the law of liberty, because the new nature and the will of God ran together, and both were fully revealed in Christ. Thus the Epistle of James is linked with the synagogue, and with Christians still in connection with Judaism, as we have seen them historically at Jerusalem with James at their head. The Epistle does not go beyond that position. It is the last testimony rendered to Israel looked at as the people of God, while at the same time distinguishing the quickened remnant who had faith in Christ, although they were not yet separated from the nation. Our habits of thought, founded not on imposed law without reason, but upon a much more complete development of Christianity (a development which was the manifestation of counsels much more ancient than the Jewish nation, for they were the eternal counsels of God),

[1] Paul's writings present man to God in and through Christ. John's Gospel presents God to man in Christ; the Epistles unfold divine life in Christ communicated to the believer; though Paul of course speaks of life, and John of man as in Christ before God. We must add for John's Gospel the coming of the Comforter. The reader will remark also that John's Gospel presents to us the new thing taking the place of Judaism, especially from chapter 4. Election runs all through it, very strongly expressed. The synoptical Gospels present Christ to the Jews, to man, to be received; but the world and the Jews are judged in John 1: 10, 11. From that, our grace and the elect remnant, the sheep alone, are recognized, and the Jews treated as reprobate.

make it difficult for us to apprehend this form of the truth—a form in which it is connected with that which, because of the promises made to Israel, was historically its cradle here below.

If we have rightly understood the history of the Acts, it will make the position of believers, as we find it in the Epistle of James, much more intelligible to us. The Epistle is a correction of profession without life, and most valuable in this respect.

Jude has a very different character. It is not the cradle of Christianity or of the assembly on earth: it is its decay and its death here below. It does not keep its first estate. This Epistle resembles a part of the second by Peter; but the latter speaks of the judgment brought in by the general government of God; Jude, of the fall of that which has had its existence since Pentecost under the eye of God, as responsible for the maintenance of the glory of His grace on the earth—a fall which, with regard to the present state of things, brings on the judgment of which Peter speaks, and which he carries on even to the dissolution of the earth and its elements. The evil that had already begun in its earliest germs gave rise to this development in Jude, and to the distinction of the true assembly, or at least of its members, who would be presented in glory before the presence of the Lord in heaven. The Epistle to the Hebrews views the saint on earth, perfected as to acceptance by the work of Christ, and as having thus boldness to enter into the holiest, but as walking in weakness here on the earth, not united to Christ in heaven; hence it sets forth the priesthood of Christ as obtaining grace to help in time of need, while He appears always in the presence of God for us. It is not intercession in respect of sins (we have no more conscience of sins), but grace and help for us, such as we are. Christ's Person as God and Man also is very fully brought out.

A more complete and more precise development will be found in studying the Epistles themselves.

Paul's Epistles as throwing light on that of the others

We will begin with the Epistles of Paul. In the historical character of their doctrine James and Peter should precede them; this is to say, in the progress of the manifestations of God's counsels in their whole extent. But as developing the foundations of truth, and laying open its range as a whole, the Epistles of Paul have evidently the first place and throw light on that of the others. The Epistle to the Romans especially establishes the grand foundations of divine truth, and individual relationship with God, in the most plain and complete manner, so that we have no motive for deviating from the order in which we find them habitually placed. There is nothing in that order which, as to its details, is connected with any moral or chronological reason: it differs also in different countries and in different versions; but it is most convenient to take that order which the reader will find in his ordinary Bible. We may notice that which will be interesting in this respect as we study each epistle. It is probable that among the epistles of Paul that to the Thessalonians was the first. The date of the Epistle to the Galatians is less certain, but it was written after several years of labor; the two to the Corinthians, and that to the Romans, at Ephesus, Macedonia, and Corinth, respectively, during his journey round the Archipelago after his long sojourn at Ephesus; those to the Ephesians, Philippians, and Colossians, during his captivity. I reserve the others, Hebrews included, for the study of those epistles, pointing out only that which it may be useful to know in those of which the date is pretty certain.

John's First Epistle and the catholic Epistles

The First Epistle of John, we may add, hardly belongs to any particular period, save that (in setting forth the nature and character of the life of God, the touchstone of all profession, and safeguard against all error, against all that does not bear its stamp, and against all the pretensions which, being devoid of it, betray themselves by that very fact) this epistle supposes the entrance of these errors, and thus the latter days of the apostolic age. And this indeed is more or less the case with the epistles called catholic, from not being addressed to any particular assembly, as Paul's, the master-builder's, were. In these we find prophecies of the evil from the very first, and the fact that the mystery of iniquity was at work already. But the catholic epistles take that ground. Jude speaks of corruption entering in, John of apostates going out.

The diversified character of Paul's Epistles

Let us now consider a little the epistles of Paul himself. They have more than one character, whilst all displaying that spirit gifted from on high, which expatiates in the wide range of the thoughts of God, and in its wonderful energy can enter at the same time into every detail, even into those of individual life; that knows how to place itself exactly in the relations of a fugitive slave with his master, in view of grace, and to set forth with divine clearness all the counsels by which the Father glorifies His Son, by making Him the centre of all His purposes, of the system which results from the exercises of all His power.

The care of the assemblies, the development of the counsels of God, the exercise of brotherly affection, have each their place in his thoughts and his labors; while he is often forced to develop the truth in striving against errors which rend his heart, whether he thinks of the Christ whom they dishonor, and of the truth—the instrument of salvation—which they undermine; or whether he remembers the dear redeemed ones of Christ who are troubled by these errors, perhaps turned aside from the true path by them.

ROMANS

The special place and scope of the Epistle

THE Epistle to the Romans is well placed at the head of all the others, as laying the foundations, in a systematic way, of the relations of man with God; reconciling at the same time this universal truth of man's position, first in responsibility, and secondly in grace, with the special promises made to the Jews. It also establishes the great principles of Christian practice, the morality, not of man, but that which is the fruit of the light and revelation given by Christianity. It is important to see that it always views the Christian as in this world. He is justified and has life in Christ, but is here, and not viewed as risen with Him.

The arrangement, divisions and contents of the book

The following is, I believe, the arrangement of the epistle. After some introductory verses, which open his subject, several of which are of the deepest importance and furnish the key to the whole teaching of the epistle and man's real state with God (chap. 1: 1-17), the apostle (to the end of chap 3, verse 20[1]) shows man to be utterly corrupt and lost, in all the circumstances in which he stands. Without law, it was unbridled sin; with philosophy, it was judging evil and committing it; under law, it was breaking the law, while boasting of its possession, and dishonoring the name of Him with whose glory those

[1] After the introduction till the end of chapter 3 we find the evil, and the remedy which God has granted in the blood of Jesus Christ: and afterwards, in chapter 4, the resurrection of Christ (after being delivered for our offences) for our justification, and thus peace with God, our present standing in favor, and hope of glory, with all its blessed consequences in the love of God. Abraham and David, the great roots of promise, confirmed this principle of grace and justification without works. This part closes with chapter 5: 11, which divides the epistle into two distinct parts, as to its main doctrine of justification, and our standing before God. Of this farther on.

who possessed it were (so to say) identified, by having received from Him that law as His people. From chapter 3: 21 to the end of chapter 8 we find the remedy plainly set forth in two parts. In chapter 3: 21 to the end of the chapter, in a general way, through faith the blood of Christ is the answer to all the sin which the apostle has just been describing; afterwards, in chapter 4, resurrection, the seal of Christ's work, and the witness of its efficacy for our justification. All this meets the responsibility of the child of Adam, which the law only aggravated, according to the full grace unfolded in chapter 5: 1-11. But in chapter 8 they are assumed to be in Christ who is on high, placing him who had part in it (that is, every believer) in a new position before God in Christ, who thus gave him liberty and life—the liberty in which Christ Himself was, and the life which He Himself lived. It is this last which inseparably unites justification and holiness in life.

But there is connected with this another point, which gives occasion to notice a division yet more important of the subjects of the epistle. From chapter 3: 21 to the end of verse 11 of chapter 5, the apostle treats the subject of our sins—individual guilt is met by the blood of Christ who (in chap. 4), delivered for our offences, is raised for our justification. But from chapter 5: 12 the question of sin is treated—not a future judgment met, but deliverance from a present state.[2] One ends in the blessing of chapters 5: 1-11, the other in that of chapter 8.

In chapters 9-11 the apostle reconciles these truths of the same salvation, common to every believing man without distinction, with the promise made to the Jews, bringing out the marvellous wisdom of God, and the way in which these things were foreseen, and revealed in the Word.

---

[2] This, while the subject is sin in the flesh and death to it, involves the question of law—the means of discovering it when its spirituality is known.

He afterwards sets forth (in chap. 12 *et seq.*) the practical Christian spirit. In this last part, he alludes to the assembly as a Body. Otherwise, it is in general man, the individual, before a God of righteousness; and the work of Christ, which places him there individually in peace. For the same reason, save in one passage in chapter 8 to bring in intercession, the ascension is not spoken of in Romans. It treats of death, and Christ's resurrection as the ground of a new status for man before God.[3]

The Epistle as the revelation of God in the Person of Christ: awakening man's need and bringing what meets it

Let us now examine the line of thought given by the Holy Ghost in this epistle. We find in it the answer to the solemn question of Job, angry at finding himself without resource in the presence of the judgment of God: "I know it is so of a truth, but how should man be just with God?" Nevertheless that is not the first thought which presents itself to the apostle. *That* is man's necessity; but the gospel comes first revealing and bringing Christ. It is grace and Jesus which it brings in its hands; it speaks of God in love. This awakens the sense of need,[4] while bringing that which meets it; and gives its measure in the grace that sets before us all the fulness of the love of God in Christ. It is a revelation of God in the Person of Christ. It puts man in his place before God, in the presence of Him who is revealed—both in himself, and in grace in Christ. All the promises are also accomplished in the Person of Him who is revealed. But it is important to note that it begins with the Person of Christ, not forgiveness of righteousness, though this is fully developed afterwards from verse 17.

[3] See what has just been said on the division at chapter 5: 11, and the fuller development of the division of the epistle farther on.

[4] The heart and the conscience are both brought in. Law can show man's guilt, and even, when spiritually known, man's ruined state, to the conscience; a sense of need proves that the heart also is brought into action.

Chapter 1: 1 to 17

Paul's apostleship as called and set apart

THERE is no epistle in which the apostle places his apostleship on more positive and formal ground than in this; for at Rome he had no claim in virtue of his labors. He had never seen the Romans. He was none the less their apostle; for he was that of the Gentiles. He was a debtor to the Gentiles. He writes to them because he had received a mission from the Lord Himself towards all the Gentiles. They were in his allotted sphere of service as being Gentiles. It was his office to present them as an offering sanctified by the Holy Ghost (chap. 15: 16). This was his commission. God was mighty in Peter towards the Jews; the mission of Paul was to the Gentiles. It was to him this mission was entrusted. The twelve moreover acknowledged it. If God had ordained that Paul should accomplish his mission in direct connection with heaven and outside the secular influence of the capital, and if Rome was to be a persecutor of the gospel, that city was not the less Gentile on this account. It belonged to Paul with reference to the gospel. According to the Holy Ghost Peter addresses the Jews in the exercise of his apostleship; Paul, the Gentiles.

This was the administrative order according to God; let us now come to the substance of his position. Paul was the servant of Christ—that was his character, his life. But others were, more or less, that. He was more than that. He was an apostle by the call of the Lord, a "called apostle;" and not only that, and laborious as occasion presented itself, he was nothing *but* that in life here below. He was set apart for the glad tidings of God.

These two last characters are very definitely warranted by the revelation of the Lord to Paul in the way to Damascus—his call, and his mission to the Gentiles on that occasion; and by setting apart by the Holy Ghost at Antioch, when he went forth to fulfil his mission.

The Source and Author of the gospel

He calls the gospel to which he was set apart the gospel or glad tidings "of God:" the Holy Ghost presents it in its source. It is not that which man ought to be for God, nor yet the means merely by which man can approach Him on His throne. It is the thoughts of God, and His acts, we may add, towards man—His thoughts in goodness, the revelation of Him in Christ His Son. He approaches man according to that which He is and that which He wills in grace. God comes to him; it is the gospel of *God*. This is the true aspect: the gospel is never rightly understood until it is to us the gospel of *God*, the activity and revelation of His nature, and of His will in grace towards man.

The connection of the Old Testament with the gospel

Having pointed out the source, the Author of the gospel, the One whom it thus reveals in His grace, the apostle presents the connection between this gospel and the dealings of God which historically preceded it—its promulgation here below, and at the same time its own proper object; that is to say, its subject properly so called, and the place held with regard to it by that which preceded it (the order of things which those to whom they belonged sought to maintain as a substantive and independent system by rejecting the gospel). He here introduces that which preceded, not as a subject of controversy but in its true character, to enforce the testimony of the gospel (anticipating objections, which are thus solved beforehand).

To the Gentile it was the revelation of the truth, and of God, in grace; to the Jews it was indeed that, while also putting everything that regarded him in its right place.

The connection of the Old Testament with the gospel is this: the gospel of God had been announced beforehand by His prophets in holy writings. Observe here, that in these Holy Scriptures the gospel of God was not *come*, nor was it then addressed to men: but promised or announced beforehand, as to be sent. The assembly was not even announced: the gospel was announced, but as being yet to come.

Its primary subject—the One presented as Son of David and the Son of God in power over death and evil

Moreover, the subject of this gospel is, first of all, the Son of God. He has accomplished a work: but it is Himself who is the true subject of the gospel. Now He is presented in a twofold aspect: 1st, the object of the promises, Son of David according to the flesh; 2nd, the Son of God in power, who, in the midst of sin, walked by the Spirit in divine and absolute holiness (resurrection being the illustrious and victorious proof of who He was, walking in this character). That is to say, resurrection is a public manifestation of that power by which He walked in absolute holiness during His life—a manifestation that He is the Son of God in power. He is clearly shown forth as Son of God in power by this means. Here it was no question of promise, but of power, of Him who could enter into conflict with the death in which man lay, and overcome it completely; and that, in connection with the holiness which bore testimony during His life to the power of that Spirit by which He walked, and in which He guarded Himself from being touched by sin. It was in the same power by which He was holy in life absolutely that He was raised from the dead.

In the ways of God on the earth He was the object and the fulfilment of the promises. With regard to the condition of man under sin and death, He was completely conqueror of all that stood in His way, whether living or in resurrection. It was the Son of God who was there, made known by resurrection according to the power that was in Him, a power that displayed itself according to the Spirit by the holiness in which He lived.[5]

What marvellous grace to see the whole power of evil—that dreadful door of death which closed upon the sinful life of man, leaving him to the inevitable judgment that he deserved—broken, destroyed, by Him, who was willing to enter into the gloomy chamber it shut in, and take upon Himself all the weakness of man in death, and thus completely and absolutely deliver him whose penalty He had borne in submitting to death! This victory over death, this deliverance of man from its dominion, by the power of the Son of God become Man, when He had undergone it, and that as a sacrifice for sin, is the only ground of hope for mortal and sinful man. It sets aside all that sin and death have to say. It destroys, for him who has a portion in Christ, the seal of judgment upon sin, which is in death; and a new man, a new life, begins for him who had been held under it outside the whole scene, the whole effect of his former misery—a life founded on all the value of that which the Son of God had there accomplished.

The Source, object and extent of the apostle's mission

In fine, we have, as the subject of the gospel, the Son of God, made of the seed of David after the flesh; and, in the bosom of humanity and of death, declared to be the Son of God in power by resurrection,[6] Jesus Christ our Lord. The gospel was the gospel of God Himself; but it is by Jesus Christ the Lord that the apostle received his mission. *He* was the head of the work, and sent forth the laborers into the harvest which they were to reap in the

---

[5] This puts us, since it is for us, in connection with a holiness (as does the revelation of righteousness farther on, but there more openly) which implies connection with God as He is in Himself fully revealed—not like the Jews outside the veil.

[6] It is not said "by His resurrection," but "by resurrection" abstractly. His own was the great proof; but that of every man is a proof likewise.

world. The object of his mission, and its extent, was the obedience of faith (not obedience to the law) among *all* nations, establishing the authority and the value of the name of Christ. It was this name which should prevail and be acknowledged.

The message of grace to all men carried by grace and as grace

The apostle's mission was not only his service; the being trusted with it was at the same time the personal grace and favor of Him whose testimony he bore. I am not speaking of salvation, although in Paul's case the two things were identified—a fact that gave a remarkable color and energy to his mission; but there was grace and favor in the commission itself, and it is important to remember it. It gives character to the mission and to its execution. An angel performs a providential mission; a Moses details a law in the spirit of the law; a Jonah, a John the Baptist, preaches repentance, withdraws from the grace that appeared to falsify his threatenings against the wicked Gentiles, or in the wilderness lays the axe to the root of the unfruitful trees in God's garden. But by Jesus, Paul, the bearer of the glad tidings of God, receives grace and apostleship. He carries, by grace and as grace, the message of grace to men wherever they may be, the grace which comes in all the largeness of the rights of God over men, and in Himself as sovereign, and in which He exercises His rights. Among these Gentiles, the believing Romans also were the called of Jesus Christ.

"Grace and peace" to assemblies: the addition of "mercy" to individuals

Paul therefore addresses all the believers in that great city. They were beloved of God, and saints by calling.[7]

[7] The reader must take notice that, in verses 1 and 7, it is not "called to be an apostle," nor "called to be saints," but apostle by call, saints by call. They *were* the thing declared, and they were so by the call of God. A Jew was not holy by call; he was born holy, relatively to the Gentiles. These were the called of Jesus Christ; but they were not simply called to be holy, they were so by call.

He wishes them (as in all his epistles) grace and peace
from God the Father and from the Lord Jesus Christ, on
whose part he delivered his message. The perfect grace of
God by Christ, the perfect peace of man, and that with
God; it was this which he brought in the gospel and in
his heart. These are the true conditions of God's relationship with man, and that of man with God, by the gospel—
the ground on which Christianity places man. When an
individual is addressed, another consideration comes in,
namely, that of his own weaknesses and infirmities: therefore "mercy" is added to the wish of the sacred writers in
the case of individuals. (See the Epistles to Timothy and
Titus, and the Second Epistle of John.)[8]

The objects of grace and the work in them

If the love of God is in the heart, if He has His place
there, it is before God that one is occupied with the objects of grace; and then, the work of God in them, the
grace that has been displayed, is the first thing that comes
into the mind, whether in love or in thankfulness. The
faith of the Romans ascends in thanksgivings from the
heart of the apostle, whom the report of it had reached.

The apostle as the servant of the Gentiles

He then expresses his desire to see them, a desire that
often occupied his mind. Here he brings out his apostolic
relationship towards them, with all the tenderness and all
the delicacy that belong to the grace and the love which
had formed this relationship and which constituted its
strength. He is apostle by right to all the Gentiles, even
although he may not have seen them; but in heart he is
their servant; and with the most true and ardent broth-

---

[8] The Epistle to Philemon might appear at first to be an exception;
but it confirms this remark, for it will be seen that the assembly in his
house is included in the wish. This makes the address of Jude the more
remarkable. There is however a question of a various reading in
Titus 1: 4.

erly love, flowing from the grace that had made him apostle, he desires to see them, that he might impart to them some spiritual gift, which his apostleship put him in a position to communicate. What he had in his heart in this was, that he might enjoy the faith which was common to him and to them—faith strengthened by these gifts—for their mutual comfort. Often he had purposed coming, that he might have some fruit in this part also of the field which God had committed to him; but he had been hindered until now.

He then declares himself a debtor to all the Gentiles, and ready, as far as in him lay, to preach the gospel to those of Rome also. The way in which the apostle claims the whole field of the Gentiles as his own, and in which he was prevented by God from going to Rome until he arrived there at the end of his career (and then only as a prisoner), is worthy of all attention.

The value and character of the gospel of God

However it might be, he was ready, and that because of the value of the gospel—a point which leads him to state both the value and the character of this gospel. For, he says, he was not ashamed of it. It was the power of God to salvation. Observe here the way in which the apostle presents everything as coming from God. It is the gospel of God, the power of God to salvation, the righteousness of God, and even the wrath of God, and that from heaven—a different thing from earthly chastisement. This is the key to everything. The apostle lays stress upon it, putting it forward from the commencement of the epistle; for man ever inclines to have confidence in himself, to boast of himself, to seek for some merit—some righteousness, in himself, to Judaize, to be occupied with himself, as though he could do something. It was the apostle's joy to put his God forward.

The salvation of God entirely His own work

Thus, in the gospel, God intervened, accomplishing a salvation which was entirely His own work—a salvation of which He was the source and power, and which He Himself had wrought. Man came into it by faith: it was the believer who shared it; but to have part in it by faith was exactly the way to share it without adding anything whatsoever to it, and to leave it wholly the salvation of God. God be praised that it is so, whether for righteousness or for power, or for the whole result; for thus it is perfect, divine. God has come in, in His almighty power and in His love, to deliver the wretched, according to His own might. The gospel is the expression of this: one believes it and one shares it.

The power of God in salvation: a righteousness of God—not of man—revealed

But there is an especial reason why it is the power of God in salvation. Man had departed from God by sin. Righteousness alone could bring him back into the presence of God, and make him such that he could be there in peace. A sinner, he had no righteousness but quite the contrary; and if man were to come before God as a sinner, judgment necessarily awaits him: righteousness would be displayed in this way. But, in the gospel, God reveals a positive righteousness on His part. If man has none, God has a righteousness which belongs to Him, which is His own, perfect like Himself, according to His own heart. Such a righteousness as this is revealed in the gospel. Human righteousness there was none: a righteousness *of God* is revealed. It is all-perfect in itself, divine and complete. To be revealed, it must be so. The gospel proclaims it to us.

The righteousness of God on the principle of faith— to every believer

The principle on which it is announced is faith, because it exists, and it is divine. If man wrought at it, or performed a part of it, or if his heart had any share in carrying it out, it would not be the righteousness *of God;* but it is entirely and absolutely His. We believe in the gospel that reveals it. But if it is the believer who participates in it, every one who has faith has part in it. This righteousness is on the principle of faith. It is revealed, and consequently to faith, wherever that faith exists.

This is the force of the expression which is translated "from faith to faith"—on the principle of faith unto faith. Now the importance of this principle is evident here. It admits every believing Gentile on the same footing as the Jew, who has no other right of entrance than he. They both have faith: the gospel recognizes no other means of participating in it. The righteousness is that of God; the Jew is nothing more in it than the Gentile. As it is written, "The just shall live by faith." The Scriptures of the Jews testified to the truth of the apostle's principle.

The grand theme of what follows the revelation of the Person of Christ

This is what the gospel announced on God's part to man. The primary subject was the Person of Christ, son of David according to flesh (accomplishment of promise); and the Son of God with power according to the Spirit of holiness. But the righteousness of God (not of man) was revealed in it. This is the grand theme of all that follows. The apostle had indeed reason not to be ashamed of it, despised as it was by men.

God's wrath from heaven against ungodliness

But this doctrine was confirmed by another consideration, and was based on the great truth contained in it. God, in presenting Himself, could not look at things according to the partial communications adapted to the ignorance of men, and to the temporary dispensations by which He governed them. Wrath was not merely His intervention in government, as by the Assyrian or Babylonish captivity. It was "wrath from heaven." The essential opposition of His nature to evil, and penal rejection of it wherever it was found, was manifested. Now God manifested Himself in the gospel. Thus divine wrath does not break forth indeed (for grace proclaimed the righteousness of God in salvation for sinners who should believe), but it is revealed (not exactly in the gospel—that is the revelation of righteousness; but it is revealed) from heaven against ungodliness—all that does not respect the presence of God—against all that does not comport with the presence of God, and against all unrighteousness or iniquity in those who possessed the truth but still dishonored God; that is to say, against all men, Gentile or otherwise, and particularly the Jews who had the knowledge of God according to the law; and, again (for the principle is universal, and flows from that which God is, when He reveals Himself), against every one who professes Christianity, when he walks in the evil that God hates.

The gospel's opportuneness and necessity demonstrated by man's sin and God's righteousness

This wrath, divine wrath, according to God's nature as in heaven, against man as a sinner, made *God's* righteousness necessary. Man was now to meet God fully revealed as He is. This showed him wholly a sinner, but paved the way in grace for a far more excellent place and standing —one based on the righteousness of God. The gospel reveals the righteousness: its opportuneness and necessity are demonstrated by the state of sin in which all men are, and by occasion of which wrath was revealed from heaven. Man was not merely to be governed by God, and find governmental wrath, but to appear before God. How could we stand there? The answer is the revelation of

God's righteousness by the gospel. Hence, too, even in speaking of resurrection Christ is declared to be the Son of God according to the Spirit of holiness. God has to be met such as He is. The revelation of God Himself in His holy nature went necessarily farther than mere Jews. It was against the thing sin, wherever it was, wherever it met sin, to make good what God is. It is a glorious truth; and how blessed that thus divine righteousness in sovereign grace should be revealed! And, God being love, we can say that it could not be otherwise; but how glorious to have God thus revealed!

Chapters I: 18 to 3: 20

The Epistle's thesis: what proved its need — the condition of all men: God's answer in grace

THE thesis of the epistle then is in verse 17, that which proved its need in verse 18. From verse 19 to the end of verse 20 in chapter 3, the condition of men, Jews and Gentiles, to whom this truth applies, is given in detail, in order to show in what way this wrath was deserved, and all were shut up in sin (vers. 19 and 21 of this chapter giving the leading principles of the evil as regards the Gentiles). From verse 21 to 31 of chapter 3, the answer in grace by the righteousness of God, through the blood of Christ, is briefly but powerfully declared. For we first get the answer by Christ's blood to the old state, and then the introduction, by death and life through Christ, into the new.

The apostle begins with the Gentiles—"All ungodliness" of men. I say the Gentiles (it is evident that if a Jew falls into it, this guilt attaches to him; but the condition described, as far as chapter 2: 17, is that of Gentiles); afterwards that of the Jews, to chapter 3: 20.

The ground of God's wrath: the Gentiles without excuse through the witness of creation and conscience

Chapter 1: 18 is the thesis of the whole argument from verse 19 to chapter 3: 20, this part of the epistle showing the ground of that wrath.

The Gentiles are without excuse on two accounts. First, that which may be known of God has been manifested by creation—His power and His Godhead. This proof has existed since the creation of the world. Secondly, that, having the knowledge of God as Noah had it, they had not glorified Him as God, but in the vanity of their imaginations, reasoning upon their own thoughts on this subject and the ideas it produced in their own minds, they became fools while professing themselves to be wise, and fell into idolatry, and that of the grossest kind. Now God has judged this. If they would not retain a just thought of the glory of God, they should not even retain a just idea of the natural honor of man. They should dishonor themselves as they had dishonored God. It is the exact description, in a few strong and energetic words, of the whole pagan mythology. They had not discernment, moral taste, to retain God in their knowledge: God gave them up to a spirit void of discernment, to boast themselves in depraved tastes, in things unbecoming nature itself. The natural conscience knew that God judged such things to be worthy of death according to the just exigencies of His nature. Nevertheless they not only did them, but they took pleasure in those who did them, when their own lusts did not carry them away. And this left no excuse for those who judged the evil (and there were such), for they committed it while judging it. Man then by judging condemned himself doubly: for by judging he showed that he knew it to be evil, and yet he did it. But the judgment of God is according to truth against those who commit such things: they who acquired credit by judging them should not escape it.

God's sure judgment of evil and His mercy to the evil-doer

Two things are presented here with respect to God; His judgment against evil—the evil-doer shall not escape (the real difference of right and wrong would be maintained by judgment); and His mercy, patience, and long-suffering with regard to the evil-doer—His goodness inviting him to repentance. He who continued in evil deceived himself by trying to forget the sure judgment of God and by despising His goodness. The consequences, both of a life opposed to God and to His truth on the one hand, and of the search after that which is pleasing to Him, and thereby for eternal life on the other, were sure—tribulation and anguish in the one case, in the other glory and honor; and that without more respect to the Jews than to the Gentiles.

The character of God's omniscient judgment of the individual

God judged things according to their true moral character, and according to the advantages which the guilty one had enjoyed.[9] Those who had sinned without law should perish without law, and those who had sinned under the law should be judged according to the law, in the day when God should judge the secrets of the heart according to the gospel which Paul preached. This character of the judgment is very important. It is not the government of the world by an earthly and outward judgment, as the Jew understood it, but that of the individual according to God's knowledge of the heart.

[9] How strikingly this also brings out what so breaks everywhere through the doctrine of this epistle—that everything is according to its reality before God, God being revealed through Christ and the cross. All must take its true character and result according to what He was. Note moreover that the terms suppose gospel knowledge—"seek for glory, honor, and incorruptibility." These are known by Christianity.

Reality before God required

Also God would have realities. The Gentile who fulfilled the law was better than a Jew who broke it. If he
called himself a Jew and acted ill (chap. 2: 17), he only
dishonored God, and caused His name to be blasphemed
among the Gentiles whilst boasting in his privileges. He
then enlarges on the point that God requires moral reality,
and that a Gentile who did that which the law demanded
was better worth than a Jew who disobeyed it, and that
the real Jew was he who had the law in his heart, being
circumcized also in the spirit, and not he who had only
outward circumcision. This was a condition which God
could praise, and not man only.

The position of the Jews: their possession of the law: its judgment of them and all men as sinners

Having established the great truth that God required
real moral goodness, he considers the position of the Jews.
Could they not plead special divine favor? Was there no
advantage in Judaism? Surely there was, especially in
that they possessed the oracles of God. The ways of God
were full of blessing in themselves, although that did not
change the immutable truths of His nature. And if many
among them had been unbelieving, this did not alter the
faithfulness of God; and the fact that the unbelief of
many did but the more demonstrate the faithfulness of
God, who remained the same whatever they might be,
took nothing from the claims of righteousness. Unbelievers should be punished according to what they were; it
would but magnify the unfailing faithfulness of God, which
never failed, however unavailing it might be for the mass
of the nation. Otherwise He could judge no one, not even
the world (which the Jew was willing to see judged); for
the condition of the world also enhanced and put in
evidence the faithfulness of God towards His people. If

then the Jew had advantages, was he therefore better? In no wise: all were shut up under sin, whether Jew or Gentile, as God had already declared.[10]

The apostle now cites the Old Testament to prove this with regard to the Jews, who did not deny it with regard to the Gentiles which he had already also shown. The law, says he, belongs to you. You boast that it refers to you exclusively. Be it so: hear then what it says of the people, of yourselves. It speaks to you, as you acknowledge. There is not then one righteous man among you on whom God can look down from heaven. He quotes Psalm 14: 2, 3; Isaiah 59: 7, 8, to set forth the judgment pronounced on them by those oracles of which they boasted. Thus every mouth was shut, and all the world guilty before God. Therefore it is that no flesh can be justified before God by the law; for if the world in the midst of darkness wallowed in sin, by means of the law sin was known.

Chapter 3: 21 to 31

A righteousness of God manifested

BUT now, without law, apart from all law, a righteousness that is of God has been manifested, the law and the prophets bearing witness to it.

The whole question between man and God with regard to sin and righteousness settled

Hence then we find not only the condition of the Gentiles and of the Jews set forth, together with the great immutable principles of good and evil, whatever might be the dealings of God, but the effect of the law itself, and

[10] Note here a very important principle, that there are positive advantages of position, where there is no intrinsic change. Compare chapter 11: 17, and 1 Corinthians 10.

that which was introduced by Christianity as regarded righteousness, altogether outside the law, although the law and the prophets bore witness to it. In a word, the eternal truth as to sin and as to the responsibility of man, the effect of the law, the connection of the Old Testament with Christianity, the true character of the latter in that which relates to righteousness (namely, that it is a thing entirely new and independent), the righteousness of God Himself—the whole question between man and God, with regard to sin and righteousness, is settled, as to its foundation, in these few words. The manner of its accomplishment is now to be treated of.[11]

How the question is settled: justified by faith through the redemption that is in Christ Jesus: the range of God's righteousness "unto all"

It is the righteousness of God by faith in Jesus Christ. Man has not accomplished it, man has not procured it. It is of God, it is His righteousness; by believing in Jesus Christ participation in it is obtained. Had it been a human righteousness, it would have been by the law which is the rule of that righteousness—a law given to the Jews only. But being the righteousness of God Himself, it had reference to all; its range embraced not the one more than the other. It was the righteousness of God "unto all." A Jew was not more in relation with the righteousness *of God* than a Gentile. It was in fact universal in its aspect and in its applicability. A righteousness of God for man, because no man had any for God, it was applied to all those who believed in Jesus. Wherever there was faith, there it was applied. The believer possessed it. It was *towards all,* and *upon* all those who believed in Jesus. For there was no difference: all had sinned, and outside the

---

[11] Chapter 3: 21 reverts in fact to chapter 1: 17; what comes between is the demonstration of the ground of chapter 1: 18, which made the righteousness of verse 17 imperatively necessary.

glory of God,[12] deprived of that glory, were justified freely by His grace, through the redemption that is in Christ Jesus. Whether a Jew or a Gentile, it was a sinful man: the righteousness was the righteousness of God; the goodness of God was that which bestowed it, redemption in Christ Jesus the divine means of having part in it.[13]

Christ the propitiatory: redemption by His blood

Before the accomplishment of this redemption, God in view of it had in patience borne with the faithful, and His righteousness in forgiving them was now clearly manifested. But, further, the righteousness itself was manifested: we come to Christ as a propitiatory that God has set forth before men, and we find on it the blood which gives us free access to God in righteousness,—God whose glory is satisfied in the work that Christ Jesus had accomplished, His blood upon the mercy-seat bearing witness thereof. It is no longer "forbearance"—righteousness is manifested, so that God is seen to be righteous and just in justifying him who is of faith in Jesus. Where then is boasting? For the Jews boasted much in reference to the Gentiles—self-righteousness always boasts: it is not a law of works that can shut it out. Man justifying himself by his works would have something to boast in. It is this

[12] Remark here how, God being revealed, sin is measured by the glory of God. We are so used to read this that we overlook its force. How strange to say, "And come short of the glory of God!" Man might say, Why, of course we have; but, morally speaking, this law been revealed, and if one cannot stand before it, according to it, we cannot subsist before God at all. Of course it is not of His essential glory—all creatures are short of that, of course—but of that which was fitting for, according to, could stand in, His presence. If we cannot stand there, fitly "walk in the light as God is in the light," we cannot be with God at all. There is no veil now.

[13] To show how complete is this instruction of Paul's, I give here a summary of its elements. In itself it is the righteousness of God, without law, the law and the prophets bearing witness to it; as to its application, the righteousness of God by faith in Christ Jesus unto all, and upon all them that believe. Christ is proposed as the propitiatory by faith in His blood, to show forth this righteousness by the remission of past sins (of the Abrahams, &c.) according to the forbearance of God; but to show it forth in the present time, in order that He may be just, and justify those who believe in Jesus.

law of faith, this divine principle on which we are placed, which shuts it out: for it is by the work of another, without works of law, that we through grace have part in divine righteousness, having none of our own.

Men justified by faith, whether Jew or Gentile

And is God a limited God[14]—the God of the Jews only? No, He is also the God of the Gentiles. And how? In grace: in that it is one God who justifies the Jews (who seek after righteousness) on the principle of faith, and —since justification is on the principle of faith—the believing Gentiles also by faith. Men are justified by faith; the believing Gentile then is justified. With regard to the Jew, it is the principle which is established (for they were seeking the righteousness). With regard to the Gentile, since faith existed in the case supposed, he was justified, for justification was on that principle.

The law's demands: faith's full establishment of its authority

Is it then that faith overturned the authority of law? By no means. It established completely the authority of law; but it made man participate in divine righteousness, while acknowledging his just and total condemnation by the law when under it—a condemnation which made another righteousness necessary, since according to the law man had none—had none of his own. The law demanded righteousness, but it showed sin was there. If righteousness which it demanded had not been necessary, when it failed to produce it in man, there was no need of another. Now faith affirmed this need and the validity of man's condemnation under law, by making the believer participate in this other righteousness, which is that of God.

[14] See here again how God is brought out in Himself. Compare Matthew 15: 19-28.

That which the law demanded it did not give; and even,
because it demanded it, man failed to produce it. To have
given it would have effaced the obligation. God acts in
grace, when the obligation of the law is fully maintained
in condemnation. He gives righteousness, because it must
be had. He does not efface the obligation of the law,
according to which man is totally condemned;[15] but, while
recognizing and affirming the justice of that condemnation,
He glorifies Himself in grace by granting a divine righteousness to man, when he had no human righteousness to
present before God in connection with the obligations imposed on him by the law. Nothing ever put divine sanction on the law like the death of Christ, who bore its
curse, but did not leave us under it. Faith does not then
annul law; it fully establishes its authority. It shows man
righteously condemned under it, and maintains the authority of the law in that condemnation, for it holds all
who are under it to be under the curse.[16]

The blood of Christ making forgiveness of sins a righteous thing

The reader will remark that what is distinctly set forth
to the end of this third chapter is the blood of Christ as
applying itself to the sins of the old man, hence making
forgiving a righteous thing, and the believer clear from
sins, because cleared by Christ's blood. This met all the
guilt of the old man.

[15] The law is the perfect rule of right and wrong for every child of
Adam in itself, though only given to the Jews. But it was not arbitrary.
It took up all the relationships in which men stood, gave a perfect rule
as to them, and the sanction of God's authority to them, with a penal
sanction. But now we have something much higher, not what man
ought to be, but God Himself glorified.

[16] Hence those who put Christians under law do not maintain its
authority; for they hold them exempt from its curse, though they break it.

Chapter 4

Abraham justified by faith, not by works

WE now enter on another aspect of that which justifies, but still proves sins; not yet, however, putting
us in a new place—that of resurrection, in connection with,
and consequent on, this.

In dealing with the Jews, and even in dealing with the
question of righteousness, there was, besides the law, another consideration of great weight both with the Jews
themselves and in the dealings of God. What of Abraham,
called of God to be the parent-stock, the father of the
faithful? The apostle, therefore, after having set forth
the relation in which faith stood towards the law by the
introduction of the righteousness of God, takes up the
question of the ground on which Abraham was placed as
well-pleasing to God in righteousness. For the Jew might
have admitted his personal failure under the law, and
pleaded the enjoyment of privilege under Abraham. If
we consider him then thus according to the flesh (that is,
in connection with the privileges that descended from him
as inheritance for his children) and take our place under
him in the line of succession to enjoy those privileges, on
what principle does this set us? On the same principle of
faith. He would have had something to boast of if he
was justified by works; but before God it was not so. For
the scriptures say, "Abraham believed God, and it was
counted unto him for righteousness. Now to him that
worketh is the reward not counted of grace, but of debt.
But to him that worketh not, but believeth on him who
justifieth the ungodly, his faith is counted for righteousness." For thereby, in fact, he glorifies God in the way
that God desires to be glorified, and according to the
revelation He has made of Himself in Christ.

David's testimony that unrighteous sinners are pardoned

Thus the testimony borne by Abraham's case is to justification by faith. David also supports this testimony and speaks of the blessedness of the man to whom righteousness is imputed without works. He whose iniquities are pardoned, whose sins are covered, to whom the Lord does not impute sin—he is the man whom David calls blessed. But this supposed man to be a sinner and not righteous in himself. It was a question of what God was in grace to such a one, and not of what he was to God, or rather when he was a sinner. His blessedness was that God did not impute to him the sins he had committed, not that he was righteous in himself before God. Righteousness for man was found in the grace of God. Here it is identified with non-imputation of sins to man, guilty through committing them. No sin is imputed.

Abraham counted righteous and received promises through faith

Was then this righteousness for the circumcision only? Now our thesis is, that God counted Abraham to be righteous by faith. But was he circumcised when this took place? Not so; he was uncircumcised. Righteousness then is by faith, and for the uncircumcised through faith—a testimony that was overwhelming to a Jew, because Abraham was the *beau idéal* to which all his ideas of excellence and of privilege referred. Circumcision was only a seal to the righteousness by faith which Abraham possessed in uncircumcision, that he might be the father of all believers who were in the same state of uncircumcision, that righteousness might be imputed to them also; and the father of circumcision—that is, the first model of a people truly set apart for God—not only with regard to the circumcised, but to all those who should walk in the steps of his faith when uncircumcised. For, after all, the promise that he should be heir of the world was not made to Abraham nor to his seed in connection with the law, but with righteousness by faith. For if they who are on the principle of law are heirs, the faith by which Abraham received it is vain, and the promise made of none effect; [17] for, on the contrary, the law produces wrath—and that is a very different thing from bringing into the enjoyment of a promise—for where there is no law there is no transgression. Observe, he does not say there is no sin; but where there is no commandment, there is none to violate. Now, the law being given to a sinner, wrath is necessarily the consequence of its imposition.

This is the negative side of the subject. The apostle shows that with regard to the Jews themselves, the inheritance could not be on the principle of law without setting Abraham aside, for to him the inheritance had been given by promise, and this implied that it was by faith: for we believe in a promise, we do not ourselves fulfil a promise that has been made to us. Accordingly the righteousness of Abraham was—according to Scripture—through this same faith. It was imputed to him for righteousness.

The principle of righteousness by faith admitting Gentiles as well as Jews

This principle admitted the Gentiles; but here it is established with regard to the Jews themselves or rather with regard to the ways of God, in such a manner as to exclude the law as a means of obtaining the inheritance of God. The consequence with regard to Gentiles believing the gospel is stated in verse 16, "Therefore it is of faith, that it might be by grace, to the end that the prom-

[17] The careful reader of St. Paul's epistles must attend to the use of this word "for." In very many cases it does not express an inference, but turns to some collateral subject which, in the apostle's mind, would lead to the same conclusion, or some deeper general principle, which lay at the groundwork of the argument, enlarging the sphere of vision in things connected with it.

ise might be sure to all the seed" of Abraham to whom
the promise was made; not to that only which was under
the law, but to all that had the faith of Abraham, who
is the father of us all before God, as it is written, "I have
made thee a father of many nations."

The great principle established: righteousness by faith, justification by faith

Thus we have the great principle established. It is
by faith, before and without law; [18] and the promise is
made to a man in uncircumcision, and he is justified by
believing it.

Faith in God who raised up Jesus from among the dead embraces the whole extent of His work for our sakes

Another element is now introduced. Humanly speaking,
the fulfilment of the promise was impossible, for in that
respect both Abraham and Sarah were as dead, and the
promise must be believed in against all hope, resting on
the almighty power of Him who raises the dead and calls
things that are not as though they were. This was
Abraham's faith. He believed the promise that he should
be the father of many nations, because God had spoken,
counting on the power of God, thus glorifying Him, without calling in question anything that He had said by
looking at circumstances; therefore this also was counted
to him for righteousness. He glorified God according to
what God was. Now, this was not written for his sake
alone: the same faith shall be imputed to us also for
righteousness—faith in God as having raised up Jesus
from the dead. It is not here faith in Jesus, but in Him
who came in power into the domain of death, where Jesus
lay because of our sins, and brought Him forth by His
power, the mighty activity of the love of God who brought

[18] *Choris nomou,* "apart from law," which had nothing to do with it.

Him—who had already borne all the punishment of our
sins—out from under all their consequences; so that, by
believing God who has done this, we embrace the whole
extent of His work, the grace and the power displayed in
it; and we thus know God. Our God is the God who has
done this. He has Himself raised up Jesus from among
the dead, who was delivered for our offences and raised
again for our justification. Our sins were already upon
Him. The active intervention of God delivered Him who
lay in death because He had borne them. It is not only
a resurrection of the dead, but from among the dead—
the intervention of God to bring forth in righteousness
the One who had glorified Him. By believing in such a
God we understand that it is Himself who, in raising
Christ from among the dead, has delivered us Himself
from all that our sins had subjected us to; because He has
brought back in delivering power Him who underwent it
for our sakes.

Chapter 5: I to II

Peace with God: the difference between Abraham's faith and ours: what God has done

THUS, being justified by faith, we have peace with God.
Remark here also the difference of Abraham's faith
and ours. He believed God could perform what He
promised. We are called to believe He has performed.
Faith in God's Word, believing God, and this faith laying
hold on His power in resurrection, is faith that this has
lifted us out [19] of the whole effect of our sins. It reposes
in God's power as having wrought this deliverance for
us, and justified us therein. Christ has been delivered
for our offences and raised again for our justification.[20]

[19] Not that the body of course is yet renewed.
[20] I reject entirely the interpretation "because we have been justified."
It is not the force of the Greek, and by excluding faith from our being
justified contradicts the beginning of chapter 5.

The effect of these glorious truths received by faith: the enjoyment of God's present favor

The apostle had established the great principles. He comes now to the source and application of all (that is to say, their application to the condition of the soul in its own feelings). He sets before us the effect of these truths when received by faith through the power of the Holy Ghost. The work is done; the believer has part in it, and is justified. Having been justified, we have peace with God, we stand in divine favor, and rejoice in hope of the glory of God. We believe in a God who has intervened in power to raise Him from the dead who had borne our offences, and who, being raised, is the eternal witness that our sins are put away, and that the only true God is He who has done it in love. I have then peace with Him; all my sins are blotted out—annulled—by the work of Christ; my unburdened heart knows the Saviour God. I stand as a present thing in that grace or favor, God's blessed present favor resting on me, which is better than life. Through Christ, entered into His presence, I am even now in the enjoyment of His favor, in *present* grace. All the fruits of the old man are cancelled before God by the death of Christ. There cannot be a question as to my sins between me and God. He has nothing to impute to me—that has been all settled in Christ's death and resurrection. As to the present time, I am brought into His presence in the enjoyment of His favor. Grace characterizes my present relationship with God. Further, all my sins having been put away according to the requirements of God's glory, and Christ being risen from the dead, having met all that glory, I rejoice in the hope of the glory of God. It is a full well-grounded hope of. being in it, not a coming short of it. All is connected with God Himself, with, and according to, His perfections, the favor of God, and His glory for our hope. All is connected with *His* power in resurrection—peace with God already settled, the present favor of God, and the hope of glory.

Justification as distinct from peace: the efficacy of God's grace

Remark here that justification is distinct from peace. "Having been justified, we have peace." Justification is my true state before God, by virtue of the work of Christ, of His death, and of resurrection. Faith, thus knowing God, is at peace with God; but this is a result, like the present enjoyment of the grace wherein we stand. Faith believes in the God who has done this, and who—exercising His power in love and in righteousness—has raised from the dead the One who bore my sins, having entirely abolished them, and having perfectly glorified God in so doing. On this ground, too, "by Him" we have found access into the full favor of God in which we stand. And what is the result? It is glory; we rejoice in the hope of the glory of God. It is God who is the root and the accomplisher of all. It is the gospel of God, the power of God in salvation, the righteousness of God, and it is into the glory of God that we are introduced in hope. Such is the efficacy of this grace with regard to us; it is peace, grace or favor, glory. One would say, This is all we can have: the past, present, and future are provided for.

Joy and glory in tribulation: practical experience working hope because we have the key to all in God's love

Nevertheless there is more. First, practical experience. We pass in fact through tribulations; but we rejoice in this, because it exercises the heart, detaches us from the world, subdues the will, the natural working of the heart, purifies it from those things which dim our hope by filling it with present things, in order that we may refer more to God in all things, which, after all, are entirely directed by Him whose faithful grace ministered all this to us. We learn better that the scene in which we move passes away and changes, and is but a place of exercise and not the proper sphere of life. Thus hope, founded on the work of Christ, becomes more clear, more disentangled from the mixture of that which is of man here below; we discern more clearly that which is unseen and eternal, and the links of the soul are more complete and entire with that which is on before us. Experience, which might have discouraged nature, works hope, because, come what may, we have the key to all, because the love of God who has given us this hope, made clearer by these exercises, is shed abroad in our hearts by the Holy Ghost who is given to us, who is the God of love dwelling in us.

What God has done outside us: His love peculiar to Himself: the proof and time of display of it

Nevertheless, while giving this inward foundation of joy, the Spirit is careful to refer it to God, and to what He has done outside us, as regards the proof we have of it, in order that the soul may be built upon that which is in Him, and not on that which is in ourselves. This love is indeed in us; it sweetly explains all; but the love which is there through the presence of the Holy Ghost is the love *of God*, proved, namely, in that when we were destitute of all strength, in due time Christ died for the ungodly. The due time was when man had been demonstrated to be ungodly, and without strength to come out of this condition, although God, under the law, showed him the way. Man can devote himself when he has an adequate motive; God has displayed the love that was *peculiar* [21] *to Himself*, in that, when there was no motive for Him in us, when we were nothing but sinners, Christ died for us! The source was in Himself, or rather was Himself. What a joy to know that it is in Him and of Him that we have all these things!

[21] The word is emphatic in the original, *heautou*.

The love of God with regard to our past, present and future

God, then, having reconciled us to Himself according to the prompting of His own heart, when we were enemies, will much more, now that we are justified, go on to the end; and we shall be saved from wrath through Christ. Accordingly he adds, speaking of the means, "If we were reconciled to God by the death of His Son," by that which was, so to speak, His weakness, "much more shall we be saved by His life," the mighty energy in which He lives eternally. Thus the love of God makes peace with regard to that which we were, and gives us security with regard to our future, making us happy withal in the present. And it is that which God is that secures to us all these blessings. He is love—full of consideration for us, full of wisdom.

The second "not only": joy and glory in God

But there is a second "not only," after our state—peace, grace, and glory—what seemed complete and is complete salvation, had been established. "Not only" do we joy in tribulation, but we joy in God. We glory in Himself. This is the second part of the Christian's blessed experience of the joy which results from our knowledge of God's love in Christ, and our reconciliation by Him. The first was that he gloried in tribulation because of its effect, divine love being known. The second is the love of God Himself in man. This known, we glory, not only in our salvation, and even in tribulation, but, knowing such a Saviour God (a God who has raised up Jesus from the dead, and has saved us in His love), we glory *in Him*. Higher joy than this we cannot have.

Chapter 5: 12 to 21

Christ's glorious work: the question of sin settled: the present state of man

THIS closes this section of the epistle, in which, through the propitiation made by Christ, the putting away of our sins, and the love of God Himself, has been fully made good and revealed: peace, grace possessed, and glory in hope; and that by the pure love of God Himself known in Christ's dying for sinners. It is purely of God and thus divinely perfect. It was no matter of experience, whatever joy flowed from it, but God's own acting from Himself, and so revealing Himself in what He is. Up to this, sins and personal guilt are treated of; now, sin and the state of the race. The pure favor of God towards us, beginning with us as sinners, is wonderfully brought out, going on to our rejoicing in Himself who has been, and is, such to us.

Having given the foundation and the source of salvation, and the confidence and enjoyment that flow from it, having based all on God, who had to do with those who were nothing but sinners devoid of all strength, and that by the death of Christ, the question of our sins was settled—that for which each man would have had to be judged according to what each had respectively done. Lawless, or under law, all were guilty; a propitiatory, or mercy-seat, was set forth in the precious blood of Christ, peace made for the guilty, and God revealed in love. But this has carried us up higher. We have to do with God, and man as he is as a present thing. It is a question of sinful man; *the Jew* had no privilege here, he had nothing to boast of. He could not say, sin came in by us and by the law. It is man, sin, and grace that are in question. The apostle takes up this fundamental and essential question—not sins and guilt to be judged of hereafter if not repented of, but the present state of man.

The condition of the race, not merely the acts of the individual

Man had nothing to boast of either. The God of grace is before our eyes, acting with regard to sin, when there was nothing else, save that law had aggravated the case by transgressions. Now sin came in by one man, and by sin death. This brings us to the condition of the race, not merely the acts of the individuals. That condition was exclusion from God, and an evil nature. All were alike in it, though surely each had added his own personal sins and guilt. Sin had come in by one, and death by sin. And thus death passed upon all men, for that all have sinned. For sin was in the world before the law. Nor did the law add much to the advantage of man's condition; it definitely imputed[22] his sin to him by giving him knowledge of it and forbidding it. Nevertheless, although there had been no imputation according to the government of God in virtue of an imposed and known rule, yet death reigned—a constant proof of sin (moreover, the history of Genesis made all this incontestable, even to the Jew—over those who had not broken a covenant founded on a known commandment, as Adam[23] had done; and the Jews also, after the law was given. Men, between Adam and Moses, when there was no question of a law, as there was both before and after that interval, died just the same—sin reigned.

The two heads: Adam's one sin and the abundance of grace by Jesus Christ

We must observe here that from the end of verse 12 to that of 17 is a parenthesis: only the idea is developed, as in similar cases. In the parenthesis the apostle, after hav-

---

[22] The word "imputed" in this passage (chap. 5: 13) is not the same as righteousness imputed, or faith imputed for righteousness. It means an act (or sum) put to the account of another, not esteeming the person to be such or such.

[23] This is a quotation from Hosea 6: 7 according to its true sense, which accuses Israel of having done the same thing as Adam. "But they, like Adam, have transgressed the covenant."

ing presented Adam as the figure of Him who was to come—of Christ, argues that the character of the gift cannot be inferior to that of the evil. If the sin of the one first man was not confined in its effects to him who committed it, but extended to all those who as a race were connected with him, with much greater reason shall the grace which is by one, Christ Jesus, not end in Him, but embrace the many under Him also. And with regard to the thing, as well as to the person—and here the law is in view—one single offence brought in death, but grace remits a multitude of offences. Thus it could suffice for that which the law had made necessary. And, as to the effect, death has reigned; but by grace, not only shall life reign, but we shall reign in life by One according to the abundance of grace—by Jesus Christ.

The act of the individual affecting many others

In verse 18 the general argument is resumed in a very abstract way. "By one offence," he says, "towards all for condemnation, even so by one accomplished righteousness (or act of righteousness) towards all men, for justification of life." One offence bore—in its bearing, so to speak, referred to all; and so it was with the one act of righteousness. This is the scope of the action in itself. Now for the application: for as by the disobedience of one man (only) many are constituted sinners, so by the obedience of one (only) many are constituted righteous. It is still the thought that the act of the individual is not confined, as to its effects, within the limits of his own person. It affects many others, bringing them under the consequences of that act. It is said "all," when the scope of the action[24]

[24] The same distinction, with the same difference in the preposition, is found in connection with the righteousness of God, when the apostle speaks of the efficacy of the blood: only he points out who the *many* are, because the object of faith is presented rather than the efficacy of the work, although this is supposed, chapter 3: 22, *dikaiosune de Theou dia pisteos Jesou Christou eis pantas, kai epi pantas tous pisteuontas,* the righteousness of God by faith of Jesus Christ unto all, and upon all believers. So here it was by one offence *eis pantas,* and then the many connected with Christ are constituted righteous by His obedience.

is spoken of; "the many," when it is the definitive effect with regard to men (that is, the "many" who were in connection with him who accomplished the act).

Adam's disobedience: sins distinguished from sin: sin's reign and that of grace through righteousness by Jesus Christ

This then was outside the law, though the law might aggravate the evil. It was a question of the effect of the acts of Adam and of Christ, and not of the conduct of individuals, to which evidently the law related. It is by one man's disobedience the many (all men) were made sinners, not by their own sins. Of sins each has his own: here it is a state of sin common to all. Of what use then was the law? It came in, as it were, exceptionally, and accessory to the chief fact, "that the offence[25] might abound." But not only where the offence, but where sin abounded—for under the law and without the law it has abounded—grace has super-abounded; in order that, as sin has reigned in death, grace should reign through righteousness in eternal life by Jesus Christ our Lord. If where sin reigns righteousness had reigned, it would have been to condemn the whole world. It is grace that reigns—the sovereign love of God. Righteousness is on a level with the evil, when it deals with evil, by the fact that it is righteousness; but God is above it, and acts, and can act—has a right to act—according to His own nature; and He is love. Is it that He sanctions unrighteousness and sin? No; in His love He brings about the accomplishment of divine righteousness by Jesus Christ. He has accomplished in Him that divine righteousness in raising Him to His right hand. But this is in virtue of a work wrought for us, in which He has glorified God. Thus He is our righteousness, we the righteousness of God in Him. It is the

---

[25] Not sin. Sin was already there; the law made each of its motions a positive offence.

righteousness of faith, for we have it by believing in Him.
It is love which—taking the character of grace when sin
is in question—reigns, and gives eternal life above and
beyond death—life that comes from above and ascends
thither again; and that in divine righteousness, and in
connection with that righteousness, magnifying it and
manifesting it through the work of Jesus Christ, in whom
we have this life, when He had wrought what brought out
divine righteousness, in order that we might possess eternal
life and glory according to it. If grace reigns, it is God
who reigns. That righteousness should be maintained is
that which His nature required. But it is more than maintained according to the measure of the claim God had on
man as such. Christ was perfect surely as Man; but He
has glorified what God is Himself, and, He being raised
from the dead by the glory of the Father, God has glorified His righteousness by setting Him at His right hand,
as He did His love in giving Him. It is now righteousness
in salvation given by grace to those who possessed none—
given in Jesus, who by His work laid the full ground for it
in glorifying God with regard even to sin, in the place
where in this respect all that God is has been displayed.

God glorified: grace accounting the sinner righteous and introducing him into Christ's glory

The fulfilment of the law would have been man's righteousness: man might have gloried in it. Christ has glorified *God*—a most weighty point in connection with righteousness, connecting it withal with glory. And grace imparts this to the sinner by imputation, accounting him
righteous according to it, introducing him into the glory
which Christ merited by His work—the glory in which He
was as Son before the world began.

Chapter 6

Dead to sin, and buried with Christ by baptism

BUT alas, in this glorious redemption accomplished by
grace, which substitutes the righteousness of God and
the person of the second Adam for the sin and the person
of the first, the perversity of the flesh can find occasion
for the sin which it loves, or at least to charge the doctrine
with it. If it is by the obedience of One that I am constituted righteous, and because grace superabounds, let us
sin that it may abound: that does not touch this righteousness, and only glorifies this superabundance of grace. Is
this the apostle's doctrine? Or a legitimate consequence
of his doctrine? In no wise. The doctrine is, that we are
brought into God's presence through death, in virtue of
the work which Christ therein accomplished, and by having a part in that death. Can we live in the sin to which
we are dead? It is to contradict oneself in one's own
words. But, being baptized unto Christ (in His name, to
have part with Him, according to the truth contained in
the revelation we have of Him), I am baptized to have
part in His death, for through this it is that I have this
righteousness in which He appears before God, and I in
Him. But it is to sin that He has died. He has done
with it for ever. When He died, He who knew no sin
came out of that condition of life in flesh and blood, to
which in us sin attached, in which we were sinners; and
in which He the sinless One, in the likeness of sinful flesh
and a sacrifice for sin, was made sin for us.[26] We have

[26] This does not refer simply to bearing our sins: that is the subject of
the first part of the epistle. The condition in which we were, as a whole
race, was that of fallen, sinful Adam. Christ the sinless One came and
stood for us and God's glory substitutively; that is, as a sacrifice in that
place, He was made sin, underwent the forsaking of God, and, glorifying
God, died in and to the place, to the whole condition of being, in which
we were, and in which, as made sin, He stood for us before God. This
work, though done as and for man, I doubt not, goes farther than our
salvation. He appeared to put away sin by the sacrifice of Himself. He
takes away, as God's Lamb, the sin of the world. His sacrifice is the
basis of the condition of that new heavens and new earth wherein
dwelleth righteousness.

then been buried with Him by baptism for death (ver 4), having part in it, entering into it by baptism which represents it, in order that, as Christ was raised up from among the dead by the glory of the Father, we also should walk in newness of life. In a word I am brought into the participation of this divine and perfect righteousness by having part in death unto sin; it is impossible therefore that it should be to live in it. Here it is not duty that is spoken of, but the nature of the thing. I cannot die to a thing in order to live in it. The doctrine itself refutes as absolute nonsense the argument of the flesh, which under the pretence of righteousness will not recognize our need of grace.[27]

The resurrection of Christ: the character of the new life through Christ

The character of this new life, into which the resurrection of Christ has brought us, is presented here in a striking way. Christ had perfectly glorified God in dying; also even in dying was He the Son of the living God. It is not all, therefore, that He could not be holden of it, true as that is because of His Person; His resurrection was also a necessity of the glory of God the Father. All that was in God was compelled to do it by His glory itself (even as Christ had glorified all), His justice, His love, His truth, His power; His glory, in that He could not allow death to have the victory over the One who was faithful; His relationship as Father, who ought not, could not, leave His Son in bondage to the fruit of sin and to the power of the enemy. It was due to Christ on the part of God due to His own glory as God and Father, necessary also, in order to show the reflex of His own glory, to manifest it according to His counsels, and that in man. Christ was raised from the dead by the glory of the Father. All that

[27] Note, we are not here viewed as risen with Christ; the believer being always viewed here, as I have said, as being on the earth, though alive in Christ and justified, it is used as a ground for practice and walk here.

the Father is came into it, engaged to give Jesus the triumph of resurrection, of victory over death, and to give resurrection the brightness of His own glory. Having entered, as the fruit of the operation of His glory, into this new position, this is the model—the character—of that life in which we live before God.[28]

Without this manifestation in Christ, God, although acting and giving testimonies of His power and of His goodness, remained veiled and hidden. In Christ glorified, the centre of all the counsels of God, we see the glory of the Lord with unveiled face, and every mouth confesses Him Lord to the glory of God the Father.

Our life ought to be the practical reflection of this glory of the Lord in heaven. The power that brings us into association with Him in this place, and still works in us, is shown at the end of the first chapter of the Ephesians.[29] But there it is to introduce our resurrection with Christ. Here it is Christ's own resurrection, the doctrine, or the thing in itself, and its consequences and moral import with regard to the individual living here below, in view of his relationship with God as a responsible man. It is an altogether new life. We are alive unto God through Him.

The consequence of death with Christ is resurrection

Identified thus with Him in the likeness of His death, we shall also enter into that of His resurrection. We see here that resurrection is a consequence which he deduces as a fact, not a mystical participation in the thing; knowing this first (as the great foundation of everything), that our old man—that in us which pleads for sin as the fruit of the perfect grace of God—is crucified with Christ, in order that the whole body of sin should be destroyed so that we should no more serve sin. He takes the totality

[28] Indeed Father, Son, and Holy Ghost were all engaged in the resurrection of Christ. He raised the temple of His body in three days, was quickened by the Spirit, and raised by the glory of the Father.
[29] To which we may add in full effect the end of the third. Details are found elsewhere.

and the system of sin in a man, as a body which is nullified by death; its will is judged and no longer masters us. For he who is dead is justified[30] from sin. Sin can no longer be laid to his charge as a thing that exists in a living and responsible man. Therefore, being thus dead with Christ—professedly by baptism, really by having Him for our life who died—we believe that we shall live with Him; we belong to that other world where He lives in resurrection. The energy of the life in which He lives is our portion: we believe this, knowing that Christ, being raised from among the dead, dieth no more. His victory over death is complete and final; death has no more dominion over Him. Therefore it is that we are sure of resurrection, namely, on account of this complete victory over death, into which He entered for us in grace. By faith we have entered into it with Him, having our part in it according to His therein. It is the power of the life of love that brought Him there. Dying, He died *unto* sin. He went down even to death rather than fail in maintaining the glory of God. Until death, and even in death, He had to do with sin, though there were none in Him, and with temptation; but there He has done with it all for ever. We die unto sin by participating in His death. The consequence—by the glory of the Father—is resurrection. Now, therefore, "in that He died, He died unto sin once for all; in that He liveth, He liveth unto God."

Alive unto God through Him who is risen

Thus He has nothing more to do with sin. He lives, only perfectly, without reference in His life to anything else, unto God. In that He lives, His life is in relationship

[30] The word is "justified." And here we see distinctly the important difference between sin and sins: you cannot charge a dead man with sin. He has no perverse will, no evil lusts. He may have committed many sins while alive, he may or may not be justified from them. But you cannot accuse him of sin. And, as we have seen, from chapter 5: 12, we are treating of sin—of man's state—not of sins.

to God only.[31] We also then ought to reckon—for it is by faith—that we are dead to sin and alive to God, having no other object of life than God, in Christ Jesus. I ought to *consider* myself dead, I have a right to do so, because Christ has died for me; and being alive now for ever unto God, I ought to consider myself as come out, by the life which I live through Him, from the sin to which I died. For this is the Christ I know; not a Christ living on the earth in connection with me according to the nature in which I live here below. In that nature I am proved to be a sinner, and incapable of true relationship with Him. He has died for me as living of that life, and entered, through resurrection, into a new state of life outside the former. It is there that as a believer I know Him. I have part in death, and in life through Him who is risen. I have righteousness by faith, but righteousness as having part with Christ dead and raised again, as being therefore by faith dead unto sin.

Reckoning oneself dead and its consequences

And this is the essential difference of this part of the epistle. It is not that Christ has shed His blood for our sins, but that we have died with Him. There is an end for faith to our state and standing in flesh. The Christ who is become our life did die, and, as alive through Him, what He has done is mine; and I have to say I died. I reckon myself dead.[32] The apostle deduces the evident consequence: "Let not sin, therefore, reign in your mortal body." Do not yield your members as instruments to the

[31] This is a wonderful expression. As to faithfulness His life was spent for God, He lived to God. But now His life knows nothing but God.

[32] Note here, the Epistle to the Romans does not go on to say we are risen *with* Christ. That leads on necessarily to union, and is Ephesian ground. Only we must remark that death and resurrection never go on to the heavenly state; they are the subjective experimental state. In Ephesians, when dead in sins, we are taken, quickened, and put into Christ, as Christ was raised and put into glory above the heavens: simply God's work. Here it is individual: we are alive in Him. We *shall* have part in His resurrection, walking in newness of life. It is personal and practical: man, as we have seen, alive on earth.

sin to which you are dead by Christ; but as alive, as
awakened up from amongst the dead, yield members as
instruments of righteousness to God unto whom you live.
The body is now the mere instrument of divine life; and
we are free to use it for God as such. For in fact sin shall
not have dominion over us, because we are not under the
law but under grace. Here it is not the principle but the
power that is spoken of. In principle we are dead to sin,
according to faith; in practice it has no power over us.
Observe that the source of practical power to conquer sin
is not in the law, but in grace.

Practical righteousness: set free from sin and become servants to God in the liberty of grace

Now it is true that, not being under the law, the rule
under which we are placed is not that of imputation but
of non-imputation. Is this a reason why we should sin?
No! There is a reality in these things. We are slaves to
that which we obey. Sin leads to death; obedience to practical righteousness. We are upon the wider principle of a
new nature and grace; not the application of an external
rule to a nature which was not, and could not be subject
to it. And, in truth, having been in the former case, the
disciples in Rome had given proof of the justice of the
apostle's argument by walking in the truth. Set free from
the slavery of sin, they had become (to use human language) the slaves of righteousness, and this did not end
in itself; practical righteousness developed itself by the
setting apart of the whole being for God with ever-grow-
ing intelligence. They were obedient in such-and-such
things; but the fruit was sanctification, a spiritual capacity,
in that they were separated from evil, unto a deeper knowledge of God.[33] Sin produced no fruit, it ended in death;
but set free from sin and become servants to God—the
true righteousness of obedience, like that of Christ Himself

[33] Compare Exodus 33: 13.

—they had their fruit already in holiness, and the end should be eternal life. For the wages of sin was death, the gift of God was eternal life through Jesus Christ our Lord. Now this life was living unto God, and this is not sin; nevertheless it is grace. Here the apostle, whose subject is judicial righteousness before God, approximates to John, and connects his doctrine with that of the First Epistle of John, who there, on the other hand, enters upon the doctrine of propitiation and acceptance when speaking of the impartation of life. The appeal is very beautiful to a man in true liberty—the liberty of grace, being dead to sin. He is set wholly free by death. To whom is he now going to yield himself? For now he is free; is he going to give himself up to sin? It is a noble appeal.[34]

Chapter 7

The position of the believer with regard to the law

WE have considered the effect of the death and resurrection of Christ with reference to justification and to practical life. In the early part of the epistle (to chap. 5: 11) He has died for our sins. From chapter 5: 12, He having died, we reckon ourselves dead to sin and alive to God through Him. Our state as under the two heads, Adam and Christ, has been discussed. Another point remained to be treated of by the apostle—the effect of this last doctrine upon the question of the law. The Christian, or, to say better, the believer, has part in Christ as a Christ who has died, and lives to God, Christ being raised from the dead through Him. What is the force of this truth with regard to the law (for the law has only power over a man so long as he lives)? Being then dead, it has no longer any hold upon him. This is our position with

---

[34] It is not, note, an appeal to sinners as sometimes used, but to those already set free.

regard to the law. Does that weaken its authority? No. For we say that Christ has died, and so have we therefore; but the law no longer applies to one that is dead.

The law of marriage used as an example: the two husbands

In bringing out the effect of this truth, the apostle uses the example of the law of marriage. The woman would be an adulteress if she were to be to another while her husband was alive; but when her husband is dead she is free. The application of this rule changes the form of the truth. It is certain that one cannot be under the authority of two husbands at once. One excludes the other. The law, and Christ risen, cannot be associated in their authority over the soul. But in our case the law does not lose its force (that is, its rights over us) by its dying, but by our dying. It reigns over us only while we live. It is with this destruction of the bond by death the apostle began. The husband died, but in application it is annulled by *our* dying. We are then dead to the law by the body of Christ (for we have to do with a Christ risen after His death), that we should be to Him who is raised from the dead, in order that we should bear fruit for God; but we cannot belong to the two at once.

Those dead in Christ are dead to the law: belonging to the new husband, Christ risen

When we were in the flesh—when, as man, any one was held to be walking in the responsibility of a man living in the life of nature, as a child of Adam, the law to him was the rule and perfect measure of that responsibility, and the representative of the authority of God. The passions which impelled to sin acted in that nature, and, meeting with this barrier of the law, found in it that which, by resisting it, excited the will, and suggested, even by the prohibition itself, the evil which the flesh loved and which the law forbade; and thus these passions acted in the members to produce fruit which brought in death. But now he was outside its authority, he had disappeared from its pursuit,[35] being dead in that law to the authority of which we had been subjected. Now to have died *under* the law would have been also condemnation; but it is Christ who went through this and took the condemnation, while we have the deliverance from the old man which is in death. Our old man is crucified with Him, so that it is our deliverance to die *to* the law. It did but condemn us, but its authority ends with the life of him who was under that authority. And being dead in Christ, the law can no longer reach those who had been under it: we belong to the new husband, to Christ risen, in order that we should serve in newness of spirit, the goodwill of grace in our new life, and—as the apostle will afterwards explain, by the Holy Ghost[36]—not in the bondage of the letter.

Sin, the law, and conscience

This is the doctrine. Now for the conclusions that may be deduced from it. Is the law, then, sin, that we are withdrawn from its authority? By no means. But it gave the knowledge of sin, and imputed it. For the apostle says,

[35] It is thus, I doubt not, that this passage should be read. My reader may perhaps find "the law being dead." The expression, "dead to that wherein we were held," alludes to verse 4, where it is said, "ye died to the law." Christ under the law died under its curse. To be in the flesh is to live under the responsibility of a man in his natural life—a child of fallen Adam. In that life (unless it is lawless) the law is the rule of human righteousness. We must not confound the flesh being in the Christian with a man being in the flesh. The principle of the old life is still there, but it is in no way the principle of his relationship to God. When I am in the flesh, it is the principle of my relationship with God; but, its will being sinful, it is impossible that I should please God. I may seek for righteousness in it—it will be on the ground of law. But the Christian is dead by Christ to all that state of things—does not live of that life; his life is in Christ, and he has received the Holy Ghost. The flesh is no longer the principle of his relationship with God: on that ground he has owned himself lost. Elsewhere we learn that he is in Christ on the ground upon which Christ is before God. The Holy Ghost, as we shall see, places him there in power by faith, Christ being his life.

[36] He does not say here by the Spirit, because he has not yet spoken of the gift of the Holy Ghost in virtue of the work of Christ. He only speaks of the manner, the character, of the service rendered.

that he would not have understood that the mere impulse of his nature was sin, if the law had not said, Thou shalt not covet. But the commandment gave sin occasion to attack the soul. Sin, that evil principle of our nature,[37] making use of the commandment to provoke the soul to the sin that is forbidden (but which it took occasion to suggest by the interdiction itself, acting also on the will which resisted the interdiction), produced all manner of concupiscence. For, without the law, sin could not plunge the soul into this conflict, and give the sentence of death in it, by making it responsible in conscience for the sin which, without this law, it would not have known. Under the law lust acted, with the conscience of sin in the heart; and the result was death in the conscience, without any deliverance for the heart from the power of concupiscence.

Man's will awakened by the barrier of the law

Without the law, sin did not thus agitate a will which refused submission to that which checked it. For a barrier to the will awakens and excites the will: and the conscience of sin, in the presence of God's prohibition, is a conscience under sentence of death. Thus the commandment, which in itself was unto life, became in fact unto death. "Do this and live" became death, by showing the exigencies of God to a sinful nature whose will rejected them, and to a conscience which could not but accept the just condemnation.

The effect of the good and holy law

A man walks in quiet indifference, doing his own will, without knowledge of God, or consequently any sense of sin or rebellion. The law comes, and he dies under its just judgment, which forbids everything that he desires. Lust was an evil thing, but it did not reveal the judgment

---

[37] It will be remembered that all through this part of the epistle (that is, from chapter 5: 12) we have to do with sin, not with sins.

of God; on the contrary, it forgot it. But when the law was come, sin (it is looked at here as an enemy that attacks some person or place), knowing that the will would persist and the conscience condemn, seized the opportunity of the law, impelled the man in the direction contrary to the law, and slew him, in the conscience of sin which the law, forbade on the part of God. Death to the man, on God's part in judgment, was the result. The law then was good and holy, since it forbade the sin, but in condemning the sinner.

Sin personified as someone who seeks to kill the soul

Was death then brought in by that which was good?[38] No. But sin, in order that it might be seen in its true light, employed that which was good to bring death upon the soul; and thus, by the commandment, became exceedingly sinful. In all this, sin is personified as some one who seeks to kill the soul.

Such then was the effect of the law, that first husband, seeing sin existed in man. To bring this out more plainly, the apostle communicates his spiritual apprehension of the experience of a soul under the law.

Power to do what is good lacking

We must remark here, that the subject treated of is not the fact of the conflict between the two natures, but the effect of the law, supposing the will to be renewed, and the law to have obtained the suffrage of the conscience and to be the object of the heart's affections—a heart which recognizes the spirituality of the law. This is neither the

---

[38] Sin and death are correlative. The law is introduced in order to make manifest through the offence what they both are. The apostle first asks, "Is the law sin?" since its result was death to man. God forbid. but it gave the knowledge of sin, and wrote death upon the soul through judgment, man being a sinner. The second question is, "The law being thus good in itself, has it become death to me?" No. It is sin which (in order that it might appear in all its enormity) has slain me, using the law as a means, in my conscience. It found in man's condition the means of perverting this good thing, and making it death to him.

knowledge of grace, nor of the Saviour Christ, nor of the Spirit.[39] The chief point here is not condemnation (although the law does indeed leave the soul under judgment), but the entire want of strength to fulfil it, that it may not condemn us. The law is spiritual; but I, as man, am carnal, the slave of sin, whatever the judgment of my inward man may be: for I allow not that which I do. That which I would I do not; and that which I hate I practice. Thus loving and thus hating, I consent to the law that it is good. It is not that I do the evil as to moral intent of the will, for I would not the evil which I do; on the contrary I hate it. It is the sin then that dwells in me, for in fact in me (that is, in my flesh—the whole natural man as he is) there exists no good, for even where there is the will, I do not find the way to perform any good. Power is totally wanting.

The two warring principles: the present working of sin and the want of power to get rid of it

In verse 20 the apostle, having this explanation, lays stress upon the *I* and *me*. "If that which I myself would" (we should read), and, "Is it no longer *myself* that does it, but the sin that dwelleth in me." I find then evil present with the *myself* which would do good; for, as to the inward man, I delight in the law of God. But there is in me another constant principle which wars against the law of my mind, which brings me into captivity to this law of sin in my members. So that, whatever my desires may be, the better even that they are, I am myself a miserable man. Being man, and such a man, I cannot but be mis-

[39] There is also conflict, when the Holy Ghost dwells in us. Galatians 5 speaks of this: "The flesh lusteth against the Spirit," &c. But then we are not under the law, as the apostle goes on to say, "If ye are led by the Spirit, ye are not under the law." Here the person spoken of is under the law: everything is in connection with the law. The law is spiritual; we consent to the law, we delight in the law. Neither Christ nor the Spirit is mentioned until the question of deliverance comes in.

erable. But, having come to this, an immense step has
been taken.

The evil here spoken of is the evil that is in our nature,
and the want of power to get rid of it. The forgiveness of
sins had been fully taught. What distresses here is the
present working of sin which we cannot get rid of. The
sense of this is often a more painful thing than past sins,
which the believer can understand as put away by the
blood of Christ. But here we have the conscience of sin
still in us, though we may hate it, and the question of
deliverance is mixed up with our experience, at least till
we have learned what is taught us in this part of the
epistle, to judge the old man as sin in us, not ourselves,
and reckon ourselves dead. Christ, through whom we now
live, having died, and being a sacrifice for sin, our condemnation is impossible, while sin is condemned and we
free through "the law of the Spirit of life in him." It is
not forgiveness, but deliverance, sin in the flesh being condemned in the cross.

Deliverance in Christ: want of strength discovered, grace is our only resource

Under divine grace the renewed man learned three
things. First, he has come to the discovery that in him,
that is, in his flesh, there is no good thing; but, secondly,
he has learned to distinguish between himself, who wills
good, anu sin which dwells in him; but, further, that when
he wills good, sin is too many for him. Having thus acquired knowledge of himself, he does not seek to be better
in the flesh, but deliverance, and he has it in Christ. Power
comes after. He is come to the discovery and to the confession that he has no power. He throws himself upon
another. He does not say, How can *I?* or, How shall *I?*
but, *Who* shall deliver me? Now it was when we were
devoid of all strength that Christ died for the ungodly.
This want of strength is discovered; and we find grace at

the end, when with regard to what we are, and to all hope of amelioration in ourselves, grace is our only resource.

The question answered: deliverance already accomplished

But happily, when we cast ourselves upon grace, there is nothing but grace before us. Deliverance is accomplished by our not being alive in the flesh at all: we have died away from it, and from under the law, which held us in bondage and condemnation, and we are married to another, Christ raised from the dead; and as soon as the distressed soul has said, "Who shall deliver me?" the answer is ready, "I thank *God* through Jesus Christ our Lord." The answer is not, He *will* deliver. Deliverance is already accomplished: he gives thanks.

The man was wretched in conflict under law, without knowledge of redemption. But he has died in the death of Christ out of the nature which made him so; he has quite done with himself. The deliverance of God is complete. The two natures are still opposed to each other, but the deliverance is not imperfect. This deliverance wrought of God, and the progress of its manifestations, are developed in the next chapter.

The flesh under law: the soul taken up with self

We may here remark that the apostle does not say, "We know that the law is spiritual, and *we* are carnal." Had he done so, it would have been to speak of Christians, as such, in their proper and normal condition. It is the personal experience of what the flesh is under law, when the man is quickened, and not the state of a Christian as such before God. Observe, also, that the law is looked at from the point of view of Christian knowledge—"we know"—when we are no longer under it, and when we are capable of judging concerning its whole import, according to the spirituality of him who judges: and who sees also, being spiritual, what the flesh is; because he is now not in the flesh, but in the Spirit.[40]

Literally, this passage is not the condition of anyone at all; but principles opposed to each other, the result of which is laid open by supporting a man under the law: the will always right, but good never done, evil always. Nevertheless to the conscience this is the practical condition of every renewed man under the law. We may remark one other important principle. Man in this condition is entirely taken up with himself; *he* desires good, *he* does not perform it, *he* does that which *he* would not. Neither Christ nor the Holy Ghost is named. In the normal condition of a Christian, he is occupied with Christ. But what is expressed in this seventh chapter is the natural and necessary result of the law, when the conscience is awakened and the will renewed. For to will is present with him. But he is under *law*, sees its spirituality, consents to it, delights in it after the inner man, and cannot perform what is good. Sin has dominion over him. The sense of unanswered responsibility, and the absence of peace, cause the soul necessarily to turn in upon itself. It is taken up entirely with self, which is spoken of nearly forty times from verse 14. It is well to be so, rather than to be insensible. It is not peace.

This peace is found elsewhere, and it is in this; when reduced to the consciousness of one's own inability to do

[40] This gives the key to this—alas, because souls are not free!—much spoken-of passage. It is not the present experience of any one, but a *delivered* person describing the state of an undelivered one. An undelivered person could not speak exactly thus, because he is uneasy as to the result for himself. A man in a morass does not quietly describe how a man sinks into it, because he fears to sink and stay there; when he is out, he describes how a man sinks there. The end of Romans 7 is a man out of the morass showing in peace the principle and manner in which one sinks in it. All this part of the epistle is more complicated than what precedes chapter 5: 12, because our own experience is in conflict with what faith teaches us to say. If through grace I am forgiven and justified, there is no contradiction in my experience. It is what God has done for me outside myself. My debt is paid. But if I am to say, I am dead to sin, my experience contradicts it. Hence we have no rest in this respect, till we give up self or flesh as wholly bad and irremediable, and learn that, consequent on redemption, we are not in the flesh at all. Compare chapters 7 and 8.

good towards God, one finds that God has done for us the good which we need. We are not only forgiven but delivered, and are in Christ, not in the flesh at all.

Full deliverance found only when there is conviction of powerlessness and of sin in the nature

The conflict goes on, the opposition between the two natures continues, but we give thanks to God through our Lord Jesus Christ.[41] Remark here that deliverance is only found when there is the full conviction of our incapacity and want of power, as well as of our sins. It is much more difficult to arrive at this conviction of incapacity than at that of having sinned. But the sin of our nature —its irremediable perversity, its resistance to good, the law of sin in our members—is only known in its legal gravity by experience of the uselessness of our efforts to do well. Under the law the usefulness of these efforts leaves the conscience in distress and bondage, and produces the sense of its being impossible to be with God. Under grace the efforts are not useless, and the evil nature shows itself to us (either in communion with God, or by downfalls if we neglect communion) in all its deformity in presence of that grace. But in this chapter the experience of sin in the nature is presented as acquired under the law, in order that man may know himself in this position—may know what he is as regards his flesh, and that in fact he cannot succeed in this way in coming before God with a good conscience. He is under the first husband; death had not yet severed the bond as to the state of the soul.

Why Chapter 7 is introduced parenthetically

We must now remember that this experience of the soul under the law is introduced parenthetically, to show the

[41] The last verse of chapter 7 speaks of the abstract mind and character of the opposed natures; one the mind, however, and purpose of heart in the renewed man; the other, the fact of flesh being there; one *"I myself,"* the other *"my flesh."* So the "I" is right; only it is not considered *under t*he law or the contrary.

sinful condition to which grace applies and the effect of
the law. Our subject is that the believer has part in the
death of Christ and has died, and is alive through Him
who is risen; that Christ, having by grace gone under
death, having been made sin, has for ever done with that
state in which He had to do with sin and death in the
likeness of sinful flesh; and having for ever done with all
that was connected with it, has entered by resurrection
into a new order of things—a new condition before God,
totally beyond the reach of all that to which He had subjected Himself for us, which in us was connected with our
natural life, and beyond reach of the law which bound sin
upon the conscience on God's part. In Christ we are in
this new order of things.

Chapter 8

"No condemnation": a new position in Christ Jesus: the power of a new life

"THERE is therefore now no condemnation to those
which are in Christ Jesus." He does not here speak
of the efficacy of the blood in putting away sins (all-es-
sential as that blood is, and the basis of all the rest), but
of the new position entirely beyond the reach of everything to which the judgment of God applied. Christ had
indeed been under the effect of the condemnation in our
stead; but when risen He appears before God. Could there
be a question there of sin, or of wrath, or of condemnation,
or of imputation? Impossible! It was all settled before
He ascended thither. He was there because it was settled.
And that is the position of the Christian in Christ. Still,
inasmuch as it is by resurrection, it is a real deliverance.
It is the power of a new life, in which Christ is raised from
the dead, and of which we live in Him. It is—as to this
life of the saint—the power, efficacious and continued, and

therefore called a law, by which Christ was raised from the dead—the law of the Spirit of life in Christ Jesus; and it has delivered me from the law of sin and death which previously reigned in my members, producing fruit unto death. It is our connection with Christ in resurrection, witness of the power of life which is in Him, and that by the Holy Ghost, which links the "no condemnation" of our position with the energy of a new life, in which we are no longer subject to the law of sin, having died to it in His death, or to the law, whose claims have ceased also necessarily for him who has died, for it has power over a man as long as he lives. Christ, in bearing its curse, has fully magnified it withal. We see, at the end of Ephesians 1, that it is the power of God Himself which delivers; and assuredly it had need be so—that power which wrought the glorious change—to us this new creation.

Deliverance a divine operation known by faith: experience clashing with the truth that I am dead with Christ

This deliverance from the law of sin and death is not a mere experience (it will produce precious experiences); it is a divine operation, known by faith in His operation who raised up Christ from the dead, known in all its power by its accomplishment in Jesus, in the efficacy of which we participate by faith. The difficulty of receiving it is that we find our experience clashing with it. That Christ has put away my sins, and that God has loved me, is a matter of simple faith through grace. That I am dead is apt to find itself contradicted in my heart. The process of chapter 7 must be gone through, and the condemnation of sin in the flesh seen in Christ's sacrifice for sin, and I alive by Him judging sin as a distinct thing (an enemy I have to deal with, not I), in order to have solid peace. It is not all that Christ has put away our sins. I live by Him risen, and am linked with this husband, and He being my life—the true "I" in me, I can

say that I have died because He has. "I am crucified with
Christ, nevertheless I live, yet not I, but Christ liveth in
me." If so, I have died, for He has; as one taken into
partnership has the advantages belonging to that acquired,
before he was taken into it. That this is so is evident
according to verse 3. God has done it in Christ, the apostle
says; he does not say "in us." The result in us is found in
verse 4. The efficacious operation, by which we reckon
ourselves dead, was in Christ a sacrifice for sin. There
sin in the flesh was condemned. *God has done it,* for it is
always God, and God who has wrought, whom he brings
forward in order to develop the gospel of God. The thing
to condemn is indeed in us; the work which put an end
to it for our true conscious state before God, has been
accomplished in Christ, who has been pleased in grace, as
we shall see, to put Himself into the position necessary
for its accomplishment. Nevertheless, through participation in the life that is in Him, it becomes a practical
reality to us: only this realization has to contend with
the opposition of the flesh; but not so as that we should
walk in it.

The new life setting free: the old nature condemned

One other point remains to be noticed here. In verse 2,
we have the new life in its power in Christ, which sets us
free from the law of sin and death. In verse 3, we have
the old nature, sin in the flesh, dealt with, condemned, but
in the sacrifice for sin in which Christ suffered and died,
so that it is done with for faith. This completes the deliverance and the knowledge of it.

The new position of being alive in Christ the key to the doctrine: holy practice united with absolute grace and eternal deliverance from condemnation

They key to all this doctrine of the apostle's, and that
which unites holy practice, the Christian life, with abso-

lute grace and eternal deliverance from condemnation, is the new position entirely apart from sin, which death gives to us, being alive in Christ now before God. The power of God, the glory of the Father, the operation of the Spirit, are found acting in the resurrection of Christ, and placing Him, who had borne our sins and been made sin for us, in a new position beyond sin and death before God. And by faith I have part in His death, I participate in this life.

It is not only satisfaction made by Christ for sins committed, and glorifying God in His work—the basis, indeed, of all—but the deliverance of the person who was in sin, even as when Israel was brought out of Egypt. The blood had stayed the hand of God in judgment; the hand of God in power delivered them for ever at the Red Sea. Whatever they may have been, they were for that time with God who had guided them to His holy habitation.

The summing up of the result of God's work

Moreover, the first verses of this chapter sum up the result of God's work with regard to this subject in chapters 5: 12 to the end, 6, 7: no condemnation for those who are in Christ; the law of the Spirit of life in Him delivering from this law of sin and death; and that which the law could not do God has done.

Absolute and complete deliverance from the law of sin and death: the secret of it—Christ's coming down among us

It will be remarked that the deliverance is from the *law* of sin and death: in this respect the deliverance is absolute and complete. Sin *is no longer at all* a law. This deliverance, to one who loves holiness, who loves God, is a profound and immense subject of joy. The passage does not say that the flesh is changed—quite the contrary; one would not speak of the law of a thing which no

longer existed. We have to contend with it, but it is no
more a law; neither can it bring us under death in our
conscience.

The law could not work this deliverance. It could condemn the sinner, but not the sin while delivering the sinner. But that which the law could not do—inasmuch as
it required strength in man, while on the contrary he had
only strength for sin—*God has done*. Now it is here that
Christ's coming down among us, and even unto death, is
set before us in all its importance—His coming down without sin unto us and unto death. This is the secret of our
deliverance. God, the God of all grace and of glory, has
sent Him who was the eternal Object of His delight, His
own Son, in whom was all the energy and divine power
of the Son of God Himself, to partake of flesh and blood
in the midst of men, in the position in which we all are;
ever in Himself without sin, but—to go down to the
depth of the position in which we were, even to death—
emptying Himself of His glory to be a Man, "in the likeness of sinful flesh," and being a Man humbling Himself
unto death, in order that the whole question of sin with
God should be decided in the Person of Christ, He being
considered as in our position;[42] when in the likeness of
sinful flesh He was made sin for us—"for sin," as it is
expressed (that is, sacrifice for sin). He undertook to
glorify God by suffering for that which man was. He
accomplished it, making Himself a sacrifice for sin; and
thus, not only our sins have been put away, but sin in the
flesh (it was the state of man, the state of his being; and
Christ was treated on the cross as though He were in it)
has been condemned, in that which was a sacrifice of propitiation for the sinner.

---

[42] The reader will understand that Jesus could take this position and
be made sin, precisely because He was Himself absolutely exempt in
every way from it. The power of resurrection in Christ dead was the
power of holiness in Christ living. It was also the power of that love
which He displayed while living, and which we know in perfection in
His death. He was the just Object of divine delight.

The sinless One made sin for us: sins put away and sin in the flesh totally condemned

The Son of God—sent of God in love—has come, and not only has He borne our sins, but (He having offered Himself up freely to accomplish His will, whose will He was come to do, a spotless victim) God made Him who knew no sin to be sin for us. He has placed Himself, ever without sin (in Him it was grace and obedience), in the place in which our failure in our responsibility here below had set man, and, made in the likeness of men, died to glorify God in respect of sin, so that we are discharged by the cross from the burden on the conscience of the sin that dwells in us. He takes on Himself before God the whole charge of sin (but according to the power of eternal life and the Holy Ghost that was in Him)—offers Himself as a victim for it. Thus placed, He is made sin; and in His death, which He undergoes in grace, sin in the flesh is totally condemned by the just judgment of God, and the condemnation itself is the abolition of that sin by His act of sacrifice—an act which is valid for every one that believes in Jesus who accomplished it. We have died with Him and are alive through Him. We have put off the body of the flesh, the old man; we have become dead to the law by the body of Christ, our old man crucified with Him, that the body of sin might be annulled. I have no doubt that the full result will be the putting of sin out of the whole scene of heaven and earth, in that new heavens and new earth, wherein dwelleth righteousness. But here I speak of the state of conscience in respect of the glory of God.

The moral perfection of the cross

What a marvellous deliverance! What a work for the glory of God! The moral import of the cross for the glory of God is a subject which, as we study it, becomes ever more and more magnificent—a never-ending study.

It is, by its moral perfection, a motive for the love of the Father Himself with regard to Jesus. "Therefore doth My Father love Me, because I lay down My life, that I may take it again."

The distinct subjects of Chapters 3 and 7

What a perfect work for putting away sin from the sight of God (setting before Him in its stead that perfect work itself which removed the sin) and for delivering the sinner, placing him before God according to the perfect abolition of the sin and the value of that work in His sight! It is possible we may have known the forgiveness of sins before we go through Romans 7, and some have said that chapter 3 comes before chapter 7. But the subjects are quite distinct. In the first part we have God dealing in grace with the sinner as guilty for his justification, and that part is complete in itself: "we joy in God." The second part takes up what we are, and experiences connected with it; but the work of chapter 7 is always essentially legal, the judgment of what we are, only hence in respect of what is in us, not of what we have done—struggle, not guilt. The form of experience will be modified. The soul will say, I hope I have not deceived myself, and the like. But it is always law, and so the apostle gives it its proper character in itself.

The fulfilment of the law

The practical result is stated in verse 4: "In order that the righteousness of the law," its just requirement, "might be fulfilled in us who walk not after the flesh but after the Spirit." We are perfect before God in Christ without any righteousness by the law; but, walking according to the Spirit, the law is fulfilled in us, although we are not subject to it. He who loves has fulfilled the law. The apostle does not go farther in fruits of righteousness here, because the question was that of subjection to the law and man's fulfilling it. Grace produces more than this as in Ephesians, Colossians, and elsewhere, reproduces the character of God, not merely what man should be for God, but what Christ was. But here he meets the question of law, and shows that in walking by the Spirit we so fulfil it.

The new nature: the acknowledged fact of the Spirit's presence and the development of His energy in the life

In this new nature, in the life of resurrection and of faith, that which the law demands is accomplished in us because we are not under it, for we walk according to the Spirit, and not according to the flesh. The things now in opposition are the flesh and the Spirit. In fact the rule, from the yoke of which as a system we are set free, is accomplished in us. Under the law sin had the mastery; being set free from the law, that law is fulfilled in us.[43] But it is the Spirit working in us and leading us which characterizes our position. Now this character (for it is thus the apostle presents it) is the result of the presence, the indwelling of the Holy Ghost in us. The apostle supposes this great truth here. That is to say, writing to Christians, the fact (for it was a fact that is in question here) of the presence of the Holy Ghost, the Comforter, is treated as a well known fact. It publicly distinguished the Christian as the seal and mark of his profession. The individual knew it for himself; he knew it with regard to the assembly. But in the latter aspect, we leave it aside here, for Christians individually are the subject. They had the Spirit; the apostle everywhere appeals to their consciousness of this fact: "After that ye believed ye

[43] Abstracting the flesh, the life by which we live is in fact Christ. He is our life, and, as to *life*, what we are before God is that by which we live here. Our life is hid with Christ in God, and Christ is our life down here. And therefore it is that John—who had displayed Christ as being this life—can say, "He that is born of God cannot sin, because he is born of God." It is the same Christ in us and in heaven. Practically this life is developed in the midst of the opposition of the flesh. Our weakness—guilty weakness—comes in, and it is quite another thing.

were sealed;" "Received ye the Spirit by the works of the
law or by the hearing of faith?" &c. It is the individual
moral effect, extending, however, to the resurrection of the
body, which is here spoken of. The two things are connected: the acknowledged fact of the presence of the Holy
Ghost; and the development of His energy in the life, and
afterwards in the resurrection of the believer. This had
been seen in Christ; resurrection itself was according to
the Spirit of holiness.

The practical effect of the realization of the Holy Spirit's indwelling

We come then now into the practical effect, in the Christian on earth, of the doctrine of death with, and life
through, Christ, realized by the dwelling in us of the Holy
Ghost who has been given us. He is distinct, for He is the
Spirit, the Spirit of God; nevertheless He acts in the life,
so that it is practically ourselves in that which is of the
life of Christ in us.

In the flesh, and walking after the flesh

We will examine the apostle's teaching briefly on this
subject.

He introduces it abruptly, as characterizing the Christian—"Us, who walk not after the flesh, but after the
Spirit." Those who are after the flesh desire the things
of the flesh; those after the Spirit, the things of the Spirit.
It is not a question here of duty, but of the sure action
of the nature according to which a person subsists; and
this tendency, this affection of the nature, has its unfailing result—that of the flesh is death, that of the Spirit is
life and peace. Because the affection of the flesh is enmity against God. It has its own will, its own lusts; and
the fact that it has them makes it not subject to the law
of God—which, on the contrary, has its own authority—

and the flesh cannot indeed be subject; it would cease to exist if it could be so, for it has a will of its own which seeks independency, not the authority of God over it—a will which does not delight either in what the law requires. Therefore those who are in the flesh, and who have their relationship with God as living of this nature, of this natural life, cannot please God. Such is the verdict on man, living his natural life, according to the very nature of that life. The law did not bring him out thence: he was still in the flesh as before. It had a rule for man, such as he is as man before God, which gave the measure of his responsibility *in* that position, but which evidently did not bring him out of the position to which it applied. So that man being in the flesh, the workings of sin were, by means of the law itself, acting to produce death.

The Holy Spirit constituting the believer's link with God but distinct from the person indwelt

But the principle of the believer's relationship with God is not the flesh but the Spirit, if the Spirit of God dwells in us. It is that which characterizes our position before God. In His sight, and before Him, we are not in the flesh. This, indeed, supposes the existence of the flesh, but having received the Holy Ghost, and having life of the Holy Ghost, it is *He* who constitutes our link with God. Our moral existence before God is in the Spirit, not in the flesh or natural man.

Observe here, that the apostle is not speaking of gifts or manifestations of power, acting outside us upon others, but of the vital energy of the Spirit, as it was manifested in the resurrection of Jesus and even in His life in holiness. Our old man is reckoned dead; we live unto God by the Spirit. Accordingly this presence of the Spirit—all real as it is—is spoken of in a manner which has the force rather of character than of distinct and personal presence, although that character could not exist unless He were personally there. "Ye are in Spirit, if so be that Spirit God dwell in you."[44] The emphasis is on the word "God," and in the Greek there is no article before "Spirit." Nevertheless it plainly refers to the Spirit personally, for it is said, "dwell in you," so that He is distinct from the person He dwells in.

The Spirit of God and His work in man: the Christian's standing before God

But the force of the thing is this: there is nothing in man that can resist the flesh or bring man out of it; it is himself. The law cannot go beyond this boundary (namely, that of man to whom it is addressed), nor ought it, for it deals with his responsibility. There must be something which is not man, and yet which acts in man, that he may be delivered. No creature could do anything in this: he is responsible in his own place.

It must be God. The Spirit of God coming into man does not cease to be God, and does not make the man cease to be man; but He produces divinely in the man, a life, a character, a moral condition of being, a new man; in this sense, a new being, and in virtue of the cleansing by Christ's blood. He dwells—Christ having accomplished the work of deliverance, of which this is the power in us —in the man, and the man is in Christ and Christ in the man. But having thus really a new life, which has its own moral character, the man is, as such, before God; and in His sight, what he is in this new nature inseparably from its source, as the stream from the fountain; the believer is in the Spirit, the Holy Ghost being in consequence of Christ's work active in, and the power of, the life He has

[44] Note here, we are said to be in Christ in the beginning of the chapter, and in the Spirit here: so to have the Spirit of Christ, and then "If Christ be in you;" because it is by the Spirit we are in Christ. He that is joined to the Lord is one spirit. (Compare John 14.) And this gives its true character to our life and place before God. In Christ and Christ in us constitutes, in many places in Scripture, the Christian position, known too by the Holy Ghost dwelling in us. (Compare John 14.)

given. This is the Christian's standing before God. We are no longer in the flesh, but in the Spirit, if so be that the Spirit of God dwell in us. There is no other means. And it is indeed the Spirit of Christ—He in the power of whom Christ acted, lived, offered Himself; by whom also He was raised from the dead. His whole life was the expression of the operation of the Spirit—of the Spirit in man. "Now, if any man have not the Spirit of Christ, he is none of His." It is the true and only link, the eternal reality, of the new life in which we live in God.

The new life

We have to do with reality. Christianity has its realization in us in a conformity of nature to God, with which God cannot dispense, and without which we cannot enjoy or be in communion with Him. He Himself gives it. How indeed can we be born of God, unless God acts to communicate life to us? We are His workmanship, created in Jesus Christ unto good works. But it is the Spirit who is its source and its strength. If any one has not the Spirit of Christ, if the energy of this spiritual life which was manifested in Him, which is by the power of the Spirit, is not in us, we are not of Him, we have no part in Christ, for it is thus that one participates in Him. But if Christ is in us, the energy of this spiritual life is in Him who is our life, and the body is reckoned dead; for if it have a will as being alive, it is nothing but sin. The Spirit is life, the Spirit by whom Christ actively lived; Christ in Spirit in us is life—the source of thought, action, judgment, everything that constitutes the man, speaking morally, in order that there may be righteousness; for that is the only practical righteousness possible, the flesh cannot produce any. We live only as having Christ as our life; for righteousness is in Him, and in Him only, before God. Elsewhere there is nothing but sin. Therefore to live is Christ. There is no other life; everything else is death.

Our mortal bodies to be raised

But the Spirit has yet another character. He is the Spirit of *Him* who raised up Jesus from among the dead. This God did with regard to the Christ. If the Spirit dwells in us, God will accomplish in us that which He accomplished in the Christ,[45] because of this same Spirit. He will raise up our mortal bodies. This is the final deliverance, the full answer to the question, "Who shall deliver me from this body of death?"

The threefold designation of the Spirit

Observe here, that the Spirit is designated in three ways: the Spirit of God, in contrast with sinful flesh, with the natural man; the Spirit of Christ, the formal character of the life which is the expression of His power (this is the Spirit acting in man according to the perfection of the divine thoughts); the Spirit of Him that raised up the Man Christ from among the dead. Here it is the perfect and final deliverance of the body itself by the power of God acting through His Spirit. Thus then we have got the full answer to the question, "Who shall deliver me?" We see that Christian life in its true character—that of the Spirit, depends on redemption. It is by virtue of redemption that the Spirit is present with us.

The Christian's life as dependent and imparted

In verses 10, 11, we have present death to flesh and sin, and actual resurrection; only, since there is nothing but sin if we live of our own natural life, Christ being in us, our life, we reckon even now, while still living, our body to be dead. This being the case, we have that which was seen in Christ (chap. 1: 4)—the Spirit of holiness and resurrection from the dead. We should observe how (thus

[45] Observe here, that Jesus is the personal name of Christ. Christ though it became so, is properly a name of position and office—the Anointed. He who raised up the Christ will quicken the bodies of those connected with Him.

far according to the force of the expression, "the Spirit is life") the Person of the Spirit is linked with the state of the soul here, with the real life of the Christian. A little lower down we find Him distinct from it. We understand this: for the Spirit is truly the divine Person, but He acts in us in the life which He has imparted. "That which is born of the Spirit is spirit." Thus it is indeed the Spirit who produces practical righteousness, good thoughts; but He produces them in me so that they are mine. Nevertheless I am entirely dependent, and indebted to God for these things. The life is of the same nature as its source according to John 3, but it is dependent; the whole power is in the Spirit. Through Him we are dependent on God. Christ Himself lived thus. Only the life *was* in Him, and no sin in the flesh to resist it: whereas, if God has given us life, it remains always true that this life is in His Son. "He that hath the Son hath life." And we know the flesh lusts against the Spirit, even when we have it.

The Christian's strength to live after the Spirit

But to proceed with our chapter. The apostle concludes this exposition of the spiritual life, which gives liberty to the soul, by presenting the Christian as being thus a debtor, not to the flesh, which has now no longer any right over us. Yet he will not say directly that we are debtors to the Spirit. It is indeed our duty to live after the Spirit; but if we said that we are debtors, it would be putting man under a higher law, the fulfilment of which would thereby be yet more impossible to him. The Spirit was the strength to live, and that through the affections which He imparts—not the obligation to have them. If we live after the flesh, we are going to die; but if by the Spirit we mortify the deeds of the body, we shall live. The evil is there, but strength is there to overcome it. This is the effect according to the nature of God and of the flesh. But there is another side of the subject—the relationship which this presence and operation of the Spirit gives us towards God. Instead then of saying "legal debtors to the Spirit," the Spirit Himself is our power, by which we mortify the flesh and thus are sure of living with God; and we are the sons of God, being led of the Spirit. For we have not received a spirit of bondage to be again in fear (that was the condition of the faithful under the law), but a Spirit that answers to our adoption to be sons of God, and this is its power—a Spirit by which we cry, "Abba, Father."

The Spirit of adoption: the relationship of believers as sons known by the Spirit

The apostle again connects the Spirit of God in the closest union with the character, the spirit, which He produces in us, according to the relationship in which we are placed by His grace in Christ, and of which we are conscious, and which in fact we realize by the presence of the Holy Ghost in us: He is in us a Spirit of adoption. For He sets us in the truth, according to the mind of God. Now as to the power for this, as to its moral reality in us, it is by the presence of the Holy Ghost alone that it takes place. We are only delivered from the law and the spirit of bondage in that the Spirit dwells in us, although the work and the position of Christ are the cause. This position is neither known nor realized except by the Spirit, whom Jesus sent down when He had Himself entered into it in glory on high as Man.[46] But this Spirit dwells in us, acts in us, and brings us in effect into this relationship which has been acquired for us by Christ, through that work which He accomplished for us, entering into it Himself (that is, as man risen).

[46] Though ever walking as Son down here of course, and that not merely when publicly entering on His ministry and proclaimed such, as we know from what happened in the temple when He was about twelve years old. Indeed we are sons before we receive the Spirit of adoption. It is because we are sons the Spirit of the Son is sent into our hearts. (Gal. 4.) But Christ, entering into the full place of glory as Man, according to the purpose of God through His work, received (Acts 2) the Spirit so as to confer it on us and associate us with Him there.

The Spirit as characterizing our moral existence but carefully distinguished as a distinct Person

The apostle, we have seen, speaks of the Spirit in us as of a certain character, a condition in which we are, because He instils Himself into our whole moral being—our thoughts, affections, object, action; or, rather, He creates them; He is their source; He acts by producing them. Thus He is practically a Spirit of adoption, because He produces in our souls all that appertains to this relationship. If He acts, our thoughts, our affections, act also; we are in the enjoyment of this relationship by virtue of this action. But having thus identified (and it could not be otherwise) the Holy Ghost with all that He produces in us, for it is thus that the Christian knows Him (the world does not receive Him because it does not see Him, nor know Him; but ye know Him because He is with you, and dwells in you: precious state!) —when the Holy Ghost Himself is the source of our being and of our thoughts, according to the counsels of God in Christ and the position which Christ has acquired for us —the apostle, I repeat, having spoken of the Spirit as characterizing our moral existence, is careful to distinguish Him as a Person, a really distinct existence. The Spirit Himself bears witness with our spirit that we are the children of God. The two things are equally precious:[47] participation in the Spirit, as the power of life by which we are capable of enjoying God, and the relationship of children to Him; and the presence and authority of the Spirit to assure us of it.

Position as sons: relationship as children: the position and condition of the child: the Holy Spirit's work of grace and sympathy

Our position is that of *sons*, our proper relationship that of *children*. The word *son* is in contrast with the

---

[47] We shall see, farther on, that the Epistle to the Colossians speaks only of life: the Ephesians, of the Holy Ghost.

position under the law, which was that of servants; it is the state of privilege in its widest extent. To say the *child* of such an one, implies the intimacy and the reality of the relationship. Now there are two things which the apostle lays open—the position of child and its consequences, and the condition of the creature in connection with which the child is found. This gives occasion for two operations of the Spirit—the communication of the assurance of being children with all its glorious consequences; and His work of sympathy and grace in connection with the sorrows and infirmities in which the child is found here below.

The certainty, power and blessing of God's grace: God for us

Having thus completed the exposition of the child's condition, he ends this account of his position in Christ with a statement of the certainty of the grace—outside himself—in God, which secures him in this position, and guards him, by the power of God in grace, from everything that could rob him of his blessing—his happiness. It is God who gives it him, and who is its Author. It is God who will bring to a good end the one whom He has placed in it. This last point is treated in verses 31-33. Thus in verses 1-11, we have the Spirit in life; in verses 12-30, the Spirit as a power acting in the saint; in verses 31-33, God acting *for*, not *in*, us to ensure our blessing. Hence, in the last part, he does not speak of sanctification.

The Holy Spirit's witness that we are children of God

The first point then we have to touch on in this second part is, that the Spirit Himself bears witness with our spirit that we are the children of the family of God. That is to say, that as the Holy Ghost (acting in us in life, as we have seen) has produced the affections of a child, and by these affections, the consciousness of being a child of God, so He does not separate Himself from this, but, by His powerful presence, He bears witness Himself that we are children. We have this testimony in our hearts in our relationship with God; but the Holy Ghost Himself, as distinct from us, bears this testimony to us in whom He dwells. The true freed Christian knows that his heart recognizes God as Father, but he knows also that the Holy Ghost Himself bears His testimony to him. That which is founded on the Word is realized and verified in the heart.

The consequences of being children of God and possessing a moral nature totally opposed to the world

And, if we are children, we are heirs—heirs of God and joint-heirs with Christ. Glorious position in which we are placed with Christ! And the witness of this is the first part of the Spirit's personal office; but this has its consequences here, it has its character here. If the Spirit of Christ is in us, He will be the source in us of the sentiments of Christ. Now in this world of sin and of misery Christ necessarily suffered—suffered also because of righteousness, and because of His love. Morally this feeling of sorrow is the necessary consequence of possessing a moral nature totally opposed to everything that is in the world. Love, holiness, veneration for God, love for man, everything is essential suffering here below; an active testimony leads to outward suffering. Co-heirs, co-sufferers, co-glorified—this is the order of Christian life and hope; and, observe, inasmuch as possessors of the whole inheritance of God, this suffering is by virtue of the glorious position into which we are brought, and of our participation in the life of Christ Himself. And the sufferings are not worthy to be compared with the glory that shall be revealed in us.

Creation's groans while waiting for the manifestation of the sons of God

For the creature waits for the manifestation of the sons of God. Then shall its deliverance come. For, if we suffer, it is in love, because all is suffering around us. The apostle then explains it. It is our connection with the creature which brings us into this suffering, for the creature is subjected to misery and vanity. We know it, we who have the Spirit, that all creation groans in its estrangement from God, as in travail, yet in hope. When the glory shall set the children free, the creature will share their liberty: it cannot participate in the grace; this is a thing which concerns the soul. But glory being the fruit of God's power in outward things, even the creature shall be delivered from the bondage of corruption and partake in the liberty of the glory. For it is not the will of the creature which made it subject (it has none in that respect); but it was on account of him who subjected it, on account of man.

Waiting for the redemption of the body

Now the Spirit, who makes us know that we are children and heirs of glory, teaches us by the same means to understand all the misery of the creature; and through our bodies we are in connection with it, so that there is sympathy. Thus we also wait for the adoption, that is, the redemption of the body. For as to possession of the full result, it is in hope that we are saved; so that meanwhile we groan, as well as understand, according to the Spirit and our new nature, that all creation groans. There are the intelligence of the Spirit, and the affections of the divine nature on the one side; and the link with fallen creation by the body, on the other.[48] Here then also the

---

[48] In this how much more perfect (all in Him was absolute) was the sympathy of Christ! For though capable of sympathy as truly a man, He was not linked in His own state with the fallen creation, as we are. He felt for it, a true man, but as man born of the Holy Ghost; we, as above the flesh and by faith not in it, still in fact are linked with it in the earthen vessel we are in.

operation of the Holy Ghost has its place, as well as bearing witness that we are children and heirs of God with Christ.

The Holy Spirit taking part in the sorrow and sense of the misery brought in by sin expressed in us by groans

It is not therefore creation only which groans, being in bondage to corruption in consequence of the sin of man; but we ourselves, who have the first-fruits of the Spirit—which God has given in anticipation of the accomplishment of His promises in the last days, and which connects us with heaven—we also groan, while waiting for the redemption of our body to take possession of the glory prepared for us. But it is because the Holy Ghost who is in us takes part in our sorrow and helps us in our infirmities; dwelling in us, He pleads in the midst of this misery by groans, which do not express themselves in words. The sense of the evil that oppresses us and all around us is there; and the more conscious we are of the blessing and of the liberty of the glory, the more sensible are we of the weight of the misery brought in by sin. We do not know what to ask for as a remedy; but the heart expresses its sorrow as Jesus did at the grave of Lazarus—at least in our little measure. Now this is not the selfishness of the flesh which does not like to suffer; it is the affection of the Spirit.

We have here a striking proof of the way in which the Spirit and the life in us are identified in practice: God searches the *hearts*—ours; He finds the affection of the Spirit, for He, the Spirit, intercedes. So that it is my heart—it is a spiritual affection, but it is the Spirit Himself who intercedes. United to the creature by the body, to heaven by the Spirit, the sense which I have of the affliction is not the selfishness of the flesh, but the sympathy of the Spirit, who feels it according to[49] God.

[49] "The will of" should not be inserted here.

The attentive ear of God to groans that are divine as well as human in character: their value

What a sweet and strengthening thought, that when God searches the heart, even if we are burdened with a sense of the misery in the midst of which the heart is working, He finds there, not the flesh, but the affection of the Spirit; and that the Spirit Himself is occupied in us, in grace, with all our infirmities. What an attentive ear must God lend to such groans!

The Spirit, then, is the witness in us that we are children, and thereby heirs; and He takes part in the sorrowful experience that we are linked with creation by our bodies, and becomes the source of affections in us, which express themselves in groans that are divine in their character as well as human, and which have the value of His own intercession. And this grace shows itself in connection with our ignorance and weakness. Moreover, if after all we know not what to ask for, we know that everything works together under God's own hand for our greatest good.[50] (ver. 28).

God's counsels, purposes, acts, and operations to bless and secure us

This brings in, thirdly, another side of the truth—that which God does, and that which God is for us, outside ourselves, to assure us of all blessing. The Holy Ghost is life in us; He bears witness to our glorious position; He acts in divine sympathy in us, according to our actual position of infirmity in this poor body and this suffering creation. He becames, and makes us, the voice of this suffering before God. All this takes place in us; but God maintains all our privileges by that which He is in Himself. This is the last part of the chapter, from verse 28 or 31 to the end. God orders all things in favor of those who

---

[50] Here read in the text, "but we know." "We know not what to ask for as we ought, but we do know that everything works together for our good."

are called according to His purpose. For that is the source
of all good and of all happiness in us and for us.

Therefore it is, that in this beautiful and precious cli-
max, sanctification and the life in us are omitted. The
Spirit had instructed our souls on these points at the beginning of the chapter. The Spirit is life, the body dead,
if Christ be in us; and now He presents the counsels, the
purposes, the acts, the operation of God Himself, which
bless and secure us, but are not the life in us. The inward
reality has been developed in the previous part; here, the
certainty, the security, in virtue of what God is and of
His counsels. He has foreknown His children, He has
predestinated them to a certain glory, a certain marvellous
blessing, namely, to be conformed to the image of His Son.
He has called them, He has justified them, He has glorified them. God has done all this. It is perfect and stable,
as He is who willed it, and who has done it. No link in
the chain is wanting of all that was needful in order to
bind their souls to glory according to the counsels of God.

Conformed to the image of His Son: blessed with Jesus as well as by Him

And what a glory! What a position—poor creatures as
the saved are—to be conformed to the image of the Son
of God Himself! This, in fact, is the thought of grace,
not to bless us only by Jesus, but to bless us with Him.
He came down even to us, sinless, in love and in righteousness, to associate us with Himself in the fruit of His
glorious work. It was this which His love purposed, that
we should have one and the same portion with Himself:
and this the counsels of the Father (blessed be His name
for it!) had determined also.

God is for us

The result of all for the soul is, that God is for us.
Sweet and glorious conclusion, which gives the heart a

peace that is ineffable, and rest that depends on the power and stability of God—a rest that shuts out all anxiety as to anything that could trouble it; for if God be for us who can be against us? And the way of it shuts out all thought as to any limit to the liberality of God. He who had given His Son, how should He not with Him give us all things? Moreover, with regard to our righteousness before God, or to charges which might be brought against the saints, as well as with regard to all the difficulties of the way, God *Himself* has justified: who shall condemn? Christ has died, He has risen, and is at the right hand of God, and intercedes for us: who shall separate us from His love? The enemies? He has already conquered them. Height? He is there for us. Depth? He has been there; it is the proof of His love. Difficulties? We are more than conquerors: they are the immediate occasion of the display of His love and faithfulness, making us feel where our portion is, what our strength is. Trial does but assure the heart, which knows His love, that nothing can separate us from the love of God which is in Jesus. Everything else is the creature, and cannot separate us from the love of God—a love of God, which has entered also into this misery of the creature, and gained the victory for us over all. Thus the deliverance, and liberty, and security of the saints by grace and power are fully brought out.

God for us in giving, justifying and no possible separation

We have thus in three ways God's being for us unfolded: in giving, justifying, and no possible separation. Two triumphant questions settle the last two points, on which the heart might easily raise questions. But the two questions are put—Who shall condemn? Who shall separate? Who shall condemn when God Himself justifies? It is not said justified before God. God is for us. The second is answered by the precious fact that in all that might seem to do so, we have seen, on the contrary, His love proved. Besides it is the creature which might tend to separate, and the love is the love of God. The beginning of verse 34 should be read with 33.

The Christian's place in Christ before God shown in Chapter 8

We have advanced here to a fuller experimental state than in chapter 5, following on what unfolds the exercises of a soul learning what it is in itself, and the operation of the law, and what it is to be dead with Christ, and to be alive through and associated with Him, and coming out, as in Him before God, with the consciousness of God for it. But there is in chapter 5 more of the simple grace of God, what He is in His own blessed nature and thoughts, as above sin, towards the sinner. We have the Christian's place more fully with God here, but what God is simply in grace more fully in chapter 5. Chapter 5 is more what God is thus known through the work of Christ; chapter 8 more our place in Christ before Him. Blessed to have both!

Chapter 9

How the common salvation is to be reconciled with God's special promises to the Jews

THERE remained one important question to be considered, namely, how this salvation, common to Jew and Gentile, both alienated from God—this doctrine that there was no difference—was to be reconciled with the special promises made to the Jews. The proof of their guilt and ruin under the law did not touch the promises of a faithful God. Was the apostle going to do away with these to place the Gentiles on the same footing? They did not fail also to accuse the apostle of having despised his nation and its privileges. Chapters 9, 10 and 11 reply to this question; and, with rare and admirable perfection, set forth the position of Israel with respect to God and to the gospel. This reply opens, in itself, a wide door to intelligence in the ways of God.

God's sovereignty proved in Abraham's family

The apostle begins by affirming his deep interest in the blessing of Israel. Their condition was a source of constant grief to him. Far from despising them, he loved them as much as Moses had done. He had wished to be anathema from Christ for them.[51] He acknowledged that all the privileges granted by God until then, belonged to them. But he does not allow that the Word of God had failed; and he develops proof of the free sovereignty of God, conformably to which, without trenching upon the promises made to the Jews, He could admit the Gentiles according to His election.

In the first place, this truth displayed itself in the bosom of Abraham's own family. The Jews alleged their exclusive right to the promises in virtue of their descent from him, and to have their promises by right, and exclusively, because they were descended from him, but they are not all Israel which are of Israel. Neither because they were of the seed of Abraham were they therefore all children. For in that case Ishmael must have been received; and the Jews would by no means hear of that. God then was sovereign. But it might be alleged that Hagar was a slave. But Esau's case excluded even this saving thought. The same mother bore both sons of one father, and God had chosen Jacob and rejected Esau. It was thus on the principle of sovereignty and election, that God had decided that the seed should be called in the family of Isaac. And before Esau and Jacob were born, God declared that the elder should serve the younger. The Jews must then admit God's sovereignty on this point.

[51] Read, "I have wished." Moses, in his anguish, had said, "Blot me out of Thy book." Paul had not been behind him in his love.

Sovereignty exercised in mercy toward Israel and in judgment on Pharaoh

Was God then unrighteous? He plainly declared His sovereignty for good to Moses as a principle. It is the first of all rights. But in what case had He exercised this right? In a case that concerned that right of Israel to blessing, of which the Jews sought to avail themselves. All Israel would have been cut off, if God had dealt in righteousness; there was nothing but the sovereignty of God which could be a door of escape. God retreated into His sovereignty in order to spare whom He would, and so had spared Israel (justice would have condemned them all alike, gathered round the golden calf which they set up to worship)—this, on the side of mercy; on that of judgment, Pharaoh served for an example. The enemy of God, and of His people, he had treated the claims of God with contempt, exalting himself proudly against Him— "Who is Jehovah, that I should obey Him? I will not let His people go." Pharaoh being in this state, Jehovah uses him to give an example of His wrath and judgment. So that He shows mercy to whom He will, and hardens whom He will. Man complains of it, as he does of the grace that justifies freely.

God's rights established—the power to do all things, His endurance with and wrath against the wicked; His glory displayed in vessels of mercy

As to rights, compare those of God and those of the creature who has sinned against Him. How can man, who is made of clay, dare to reply against God? The potter *has power* to do as he will with the lump. No one can say to God, What doest thou? God's sovereignty is the first of all rights, the foundation of all rights, the foundation of all morality. If God is not God, what will He be? The root of the question is this; is God to judge man, or man God? God can do whatsoever He pleases. He is not the object for judgment. Such is His title: but when in fact the apostle presents the two cases, wrath and grace, He puts the case of God showing *longsuffering* towards one already fitted for wrath, in order to give at last an example to men of His wrath in the execution of His justice; and then of God displaying His glory in vessels of mercy whom *He* has prepared for glory. There are then these three points established with marvellous exactitude; the power to do all things, no one having the right to say a word; wonderful endurance with the wicked, in whom at length His wrath is manifested; demonstration of His glory in vessels, whom He has Himself prepared by mercy for glory, and whom He has called, whether from among the Jews or Gentiles, according to the declaration of Hosea.

God's sovereignty in derogation of the Jews' pretensions of exclusive enjoyment of all His promises

The doctrine established, then, is the sovereignty of God in derogation of the pretensions of the Jews to the exclusive enjoyment of all the promises, as being descended from Abraham; for, among his descendants, more than one had been excluded by the exercise of this sovereignty; and it was nothing less than its exercise which, on the occasion of the golden calf, had spared those who pretended to the right of descent. It was necessary therefore that the Jew should recognize it, or else that he should admit the Idumeans in full right, as well as the Ishmaelites, and renounce it himself, the families of Moses and Joshua alone perhaps excepted. But if such was the sovereignty of God, He would now exercise it in favor of the Gentiles, as well as Jews. He called whom He would.

Peter's and Paul's quotations from the prophets

If we look closely into these quotations from Hosea, we shall find that Peter, who writes to converted Jews alone, takes only the passage at the end of chapter 2, where Lo-ammi and Lo-ruhamah become Ammi and Ruhamah. Paul quotes that also, which is at the end of chapter 1, where it is written, "In the place where it was said unto them, Ye are not My people, there shall they be called— not 'My people,' but—'the children of the living God.' " It is this last passage which he applies to the Gentiles called by grace.

But further passages from the prophets amply confirm the judgment which the apostle pronounces by the Spirit on the Jews. Isaiah declared formally that, if God had not left them a little remnant, they would have been as Sodom and Gomorrah; numerous as the people were, a little remnant only should be saved; for God was cutting the work short in judgment on the earth. And here was the state of things morally: the Gentiles had obtained the righteousness which they had not sought, had obtained it by faith; and Israel, seeking to obtain it by the fulfilment of a law, had not attained to righteousness. Why? Because they sought it not by faith, but by works of law. For they had stumbled at the stumbling-stone (that is, at Christ), as it is written, "I lay in Sion a stumbling-stone and rock of offence: and whosoever believeth in Him shall not be ashamed."

Chapter 10

The apostle's love for his nation: their own righteousness opposed to that of God

HAVING touched on this subject, the apostle, who deeply loved his nation as the people of God, pours out his heart with respect of the doctrine which was a stumbling-stone to them. His desire, the aim of his heart's affection, was their salvation. The object of his affections, they were clothed in his eyes with their zeal for God, ignorant as it was; ignorant, alas, on the side of that which God taught. Being ignorant of God's righteousness, they sought in their zeal to establish their own righteousness, and did not submit themselves to that of God. For Christ is the end of law for righteousness to every believer. There was found the righteousness of God, there the stumbling-stone to Israel.

The remarkable significance of Paul's quotation of Deut. 30

Nevertheless the apostle establishes his argument clearly and firmly. He establishes it on his own part; but Deuteronomy supplies him with an unexpected proof of the great principle. He quotes a passage from that book which speaks on the subject of Israel's condition, when they should have broken the law and be suffering its consequences. "Secret things," the lawgiver had said, "belong to our God; but those that are revealed" are for the people. That is to say, the law was given as a condition to the enjoyment of the blessing, plainly and positively; what God might do in grace, when Israel should be under the consequences of the broken law, remained in the secrecy of His supreme will. Upon this, however, another *principle* is distinctly revealed, namely, that when the fulfilment of the law was impossible, and when Israel had been driven out of their land for having broken it, if then their heart turned to God in that far country, He would accept them. It was all over with the law as a condition of relationship with God. Israel was driven out according to the chapter we are looking at (Deut. 30)—was Lo-ammi, no longer the people of God. The testimony of God was nevertheless addressed to them: they might turn to Him in spirit, and by faith. It was no longer the law, it was faith. But, says the apostle, if so, it is Christ who is its object. No Jew would have denied that the testimony of God was the hope of every true Israelite when all was ruined.

This passage then in Deuteronomy—when Moses has done with the law, and has supposed other counsels of God, and on them founds the principle of turning in heart to God when all is over with regard to the law, and Israel is in a place where it would be impossible to keep it, being in captivity among the Gentiles—this passage has remarkable significance in the argument of the apostle; and its being quoted is an extraordinary proof, that in his reasonings it is the Holy Ghost who acts. It is the apostle who introduces Christ; but the combination of the truths of the different positions of Israel, of the law, and of the return in heart when they were lost under the law—a combination of which Christ was the key-stone and alone could be—exhibits a comprehensive view of the oneness of all God's ways, morally and in His dispensations, of which the Spirit of God alone is capable, and which evidently expresses His thoughts. See Deuteronomy 29 (at the end), and 30.

The Word of faith believed in the heart

The Word of faith then set forth as being the hope of Israel, was that which the apostle announced—that if any one confessed with his mouth the Lord Jesus, and believed in his heart that God had raised Him from the dead, he should be saved. Precious, simple, and positive assertion! And borne out, if that were needed, by the testimony of the Old Testament: "Whosoever believeth in Him shall not be ashamed." The words *heart* and *mouth* are in contrast with the law. In the case Deuteronomy supposes, Israel could not fulfil the law; the Word of their God, Moses told them, could be in their heart and in their mouth. Thus now for the Jew (as for every one) it was the belief of the heart.

Observe, it does not say, If you love in your heart, or, If your heart is what it ought to be towards God; but, If you *believe* in your heart. A man believes with his heart, when he really believes with a heart interested in the thing.

His affections being engaged in the truth, he desires, when grace is spoken of, that that which is told him should be the truth. He desires the thing, and at the same time he does not doubt it. It is not in his having part in it that he believes, but in the truth of the thing itself, being concerned in it as important to himself. It is not the state of his affections (a very serious consideration, however, *in its place*) that is the subject here, but the importance and the truth of that which is presented by the Word— its importance to himself, as needing it for his salvation, a salvation that he is conscious of needing, that he cannot do without—a truth of which he is assured, as a testimony from God Himself. God affirms to such a one that salvation belongs to him, but it is not *that* which he has to believe in as the object of faith; it is that of which God assures every one who does believe.

The faith of the heart manifested by the confession of the mouth

Moreover this faith is manifested by the proof it gives of its sincerity—by confession of the name of Christ. If some one were convinced that Jesus is the Christ, and refused to confess Him, his conviction would evidently be his greater condemnation. The faith of the heart produces the confession of the mouth; the confession of the mouth is the counterproof of the sincerity of the faith, and of honesty, in the sense of the claim which the Lord has upon us in grace. It is the testimony which God requires at the outset. It is to sound the trumpet on earth in face of the enemy. It is to say that Christ has conquered, and that everything belongs in right to Him. It is a confession which brings in God in answer to the name of Jesus. It is not that which brings in righteousness, but it is the public acknowledgment of Christ, and thus gives expression to the faith by which there is participation in the righteousness of God, so that it may be said, "He believes in Christ unto salvation; he has the faith that justifies."

"He first loved us": God's favor not dependent on the soul's affections: the perfection of Christ's work

I have entered here a little more into detail, because this is a point on which the human heart perplexes itself; and perplexes itself so much the more because it is sincere, as long as there is any unbelief and *self-righteousness* remaining. It is impossible that an awakened soul should not feel the necessity of having the heart set right and turned to God; and hence, not submitting to the righteousness of God, he thinks to make the favor of God depend on the state of his own affections, whereas God loves us while we are yet sinners. The state of our affections is of all importance; but it supposes a relationship already existing, according to which we love. We love too because we are loved of God. Now His love has done something—has done something according to our necessities, and according to the divine glory. It has given Jesus; and Jesus has accomplished what was required, in order that we may participate in divine righteousness; and thus He has placed every one who (acknowledging that he is a lost sinner) believes in Him, in the secure relationship of a child and of a justified soul before God, according to the perfection of the work of Christ. Salvation belongs to this soul according to the declaration of God Himself. Loved with such love, saved by such grace, enjoying such favor, let it cultivate affections suitable to the gift of Jesus, and to the knowledge it has of Him and of His goodness.

"No difference" in the ruin of sinners and "No difference" in the richness of mercy

It is evident that, if it is "whosoever" believes in Jesus, the Gentile comes in as well as the Jew. There is no difference; the same Lord is rich unto all that call upon Him. It is beautiful to see this form of expression, "There is no difference," repeated here. The apostle had used it before with the addition "for all have sinned." Sin puts all men on a level in ruin before God. But there is also no difference, "for the same Lord over all is rich unto all," for every one who calls upon His name shall be saved.

The true and living God proclaimed to the Gentiles: the Gentiles received: Israel, perverse and disobedient, at enmity

On this declaration, the apostle founds another argument; and by it he justifies the ways of God that were accomplished in his ministry. The Jewish Scriptures declared that every one who called upon the name of the Lord should be saved. Now, the Jews acknowledged that the Gentiles did not know the name of the true and living God. It was needful therefore to proclaim Him, in order that they might call upon Him, and the whole ministry of the apostle was justified. Accordingly it was written, "How beautiful are the feet of those who preach the gospel of peace." For, in dealing with these questions among the Jews, he naturally rests on the authority of their own Scriptures.

But he applies this principle for evangelization to the Jews as well as to the Gentiles (for the law was not the announcement of good news). He quotes Isaiah to the same purpose. It was in a proclamation—a truth thus publicly preached—that Israel had not believed; so that there ought to be faith in a truth thus preached, in the word proclaimed. Verse 18 presents some difficulty. It is certain that the apostle intends to explain that a proclamation of the truth on God's part had taken place. Israel was without excuse, for the report had even gone out everywhere, the words which announced God unto the ends of the earth. The testimony then was not confined to the Jews. The Gentiles had heard it everywhere. This is plain. But does the apostle merely borrow the words (which in the passage quoted apply to the testimony of creation), or does he mean to speak of the testimony of nature itself? I believe that he uses the passage to show that God had the Gentiles in view in His testimonies; that he wishes quietly to suggest this to the Jews by a quotation from their own Scriptures, that not only have they, the Jews, heard, but that the testimony has gone everywhere, and that this was in the mind of God. Paul does not quote the passage as a prophecy of that which was taking place; he borrows the words, without that form of speech, to show that this universal testimony was in the mind of God, whatever might be the means employed. And then, stating the thing with more precision for the Jew, he adds, Did not Israel know? Was not the nation apprised of this extension to the Gentiles, of the testimony of this proclamation of grace to them, of the reception of the testimony by the Gentiles, so as to bring them into relationship with God? Yes; Moses had already said, that God would provoke Israel to jealousy by a people without knowledge. And Isaiah had spoken boldly, formally declaring that God should be found by a nation that sought Him not; and to Israel, that all day long He had stretched forth His hands to a rebellious and gainsaying people; in a word, that the Gentiles should find Him, and Israel be perverse and disobedient. Thus, the testimony borne to their relative positions—although the apostle approaches it gradually and quietly—is distinct and formal: the Gentiles received; Israel at enmity.

Chapter 11

Three proofs that God has not rejected His people

HEREUPON the question is immediately raised, has God then rejected His people? To this chapter 11 is the answer. The apostle gives three proofs that it is by no means the case. First, he is himself an Israelite; there is a remnant whom God has reserved, as in the days of Elias—a proof of the constant favor of the Lord, of the interest He takes in His people, even when they are unfaithful; so that when the prophet, the most faithful and energetic among them, knew not where to find one who was true to God besides himself, God had His eyes upon the remnant who had not bowed the knee to Baal. Secondly, the call of the Gentiles, and their substitution for Israel, was not the definitive rejection of the latter in the counsels of God; for God had done it to provoke Israel to jealousy. It was not, then, for their rejection. Thirdly, the Lord would come forth out of Sion, and turn away the iniquities of Jacob.

That which the apostle, or rather which the Holy Ghost, says on this point requires to be looked at in more detail.

The election of sovereign grace in Elias' time

The apostle, in quoting the case of Elias, shows that when Israel was in such a state that even Elias pleaded against them, yet God had not rejected them, He had reserved for Himself seven thousand men. This was the election of sovereign grace. It was the same thing now. But it was by grace, and not by works. The election then, has obtained the blessing, and the rest were blinded. Even as it was written, "God hath given them the spirit of slumber," &c.

Israel provoked to jealousy by God's favor to Gentiles in grafting them into the olive-tree

Had they then stumbled that they should fall? No! But through their fall salvation is come to the Gentiles to provoke Israel to jealousy—a second proof that it was not for their rejection. But if their diminishing and fall was a blessing to the Gentiles, what should not the fruit be of their restoration? If the first-fruits are holy, so is the lump; if the root, the tree also. Now, as to the continued chain of those who enjoy the promises in this world, Abraham was the root, and not the Gentiles; Israel, the natural stock and branches. And here is that which happened in the good olive-tree of promise in this world, of which Abraham was the root (God Himself the source of leaf and fruit), and Israel the stem and the tree. There had been some bad branches, and they had been cut off; and others from the Gentiles grafted in, in their place, who thus enjoyed the richness natural to the tree of promise. But it was on the principle of faith that they, being of the wild olive-tree, had been grafted in. Many of the Israelite branches, the natural heirs of the promises, had been cut off because of their unbelief; for when the fulfilment of the promises was offered them, they rejected it. They rested on their own righteousness, and despised the goodness of God. Thus the Gentiles, made partakers of the promises, stood on the principle of faith. But if they abandoned this principle, they should lose their place in the tree of promise, even as the unbelieving Jews had lost theirs. Goodness was to be their portion in this dispensation of God's government, with regard to those who had part in the enjoyment of His promises, if they continued in this goodness; if not, cutting off. This had happened to the Jews; it should be the same with the Gentiles if they did not continue in that goodness. Such is the government of God, with regard to that which stood as His tree *on the earth*. But there was a positive counsel of God accomplished in that which took place, namely, the partial blinding of Israel (for they were not rejected) until all the Gentiles who were to have part in the blessing of these days should have come in. After this Israel should be saved as a whole; it should not be individuals spared and added to the assembly, in which Israel had no longer any place as a nation; they should be saved as a whole, as Israel. Christ shall come forth from Sion as the seat of His power, and shall turn away iniquity from Jacob, God pardoning them all transgressions.

God's unchangeable counsels and promises fulfilled in mercy to the Jews: the tree of promise on the earth

This is the third proof that Israel was not rejected. For while enemies, as concerning the gospel at the present time, they are still beloved for the fathers' sakes. For that which God has once chosen and called He never casts off. He does not repent of His counsels, nor of the call which gives them effect. But if the counsel of God remains unchangeable, the way in which it is accomplished brings out the marvellous wisdom of God. The Gentiles had long continued in the disobedience of unbelief. God comes in in grace. The Jews opposed themselves to the actings of grace. They lose all *right* to the promises through this unbelief, so that they must receive the effect of the promise on the footing of pure mercy and the sovereign grace of God,[52] in the same way as the poor Gentile. For He had shut them all up in unbelief, that it might be pure mercy to all. Therefore it is that the apostle exclaims, O depth of wisdom and knowledge! The promises are fulfilled, and the pretension to human righteousness annihilated; the Jews who have lost everything receive all on the true ground of the goodness of God. Their apparent loss of all is but the means of their receiving all from sovereign grace, instead of having it by virtue of human righteousness, or an unforfeited promise. All is grace; yet God is ever faithful, and that in spite of man's unfaithfulness. Man is blessed; the Jew receives the effect of the promise; but both the one and the other have to attribute it to the pure mercy of God. There is nothing about the assembly

---

[52] Verse 31 should be translated, "Even so these [the Jews] have now been unbelieving with regard to your mercy, in order that they should receive mercy" (or that they should be the objects of mercy)—"your mercy," that is to say, the grace in Christ which extended to the Gentiles. Thus the Jews were the objects of *mercy*, having forfeited all *right* to enjoy the effect of the promise. God would not fail to fulfil it. He bestows it on them in mercy at the end, when He has brought in the fulness of the Gentiles.

here: it is the tree of promise, and those who in virtue of their position have part successively in the enjoyment of the promises of earth. The unbelieving Jews were never cut off from the Church, they were never in it. They had been in the position of natural heirs of the right to the promises. The assembly is not the Jews' own olive-tree according to nature, so that they should be grafted into it again. Nothing can be plainer: the chain of those who had a right to the promises from Abraham was Israel; some of the branches were then cut off. The tree of promise remains on the earth: the Gentiles are grafted into it in place of the Jews, they also become unfaithful (that is to say, the case is supɩosed), and they would in their turn be cut off, and the Jews be reinstated in the old olive-tree, according to the promises and in order to enjoy them; but it is in pure mercy. It is clearly not by the gospel they get the blessing; for, as touching the gospel, they are enemies for the Gentiles' sake; as touching election, beloved for the fathers' sake.

The privileges and responsibility of the place of blessing

Remark further here an important principle: the enjoyment of privileges by position makes us responsible for them, without saying the individual was born again. The Jewish branch was in the tree of promise and broken off: so the Gentile. There was nothing vital or real; but they were in the place of blessing, "partakers of the root and fatness of the olive tree," by being grafted in.

These communications of the mind of God end this portion of the book, namely, that in which the apostle reconciles sovereign grace shown to sinners (putting all on a level in the common ruin of sin) with the especial privileges of the people of Israel, founded on the faithfulness of God. They had lost everything as to right. God-would fulfil His promises in grace and by mercy.

Chapters 12, 13

The ground of all Christian morality laid on God's mercy and saving grace

THE apostle resumes the thread of his instructions, by taking up—as he does in all his epistles—the moral consequences of his doctrine. He places the believer at the outset on the ground of God's mercy, which he had fully developed already. The principle of grace that saves had been established as the basis of salvation. The ground of all Christian morality is now laid in this fundamental principle:—to present our bodies as a sacrifice, living, holy, acceptable to God—an intelligent service, not that of the hands, not consisting in ceremonies which the body could perform—a simple but deep-reaching and all-efficacious principle. This was for man personally. As to his outward relationships, he was not to be conformed to the world. Neither was this to be an outside mechanical nonconformity, but the result of being renewed in mind, so as to seek for and discern the will of God, good and acceptable and perfect (the life being thus transformed).

This connects itself with the end of chapter 6. It is not those sitting in heavenly places, imitators of God as dear children, but men on earth set free by the delivering power of redemption and grace, yielding themselves up to God to do His will. The exhortation follows the character we have seen to be that of the epistle.

The Christian's walk and life characterized by devotedness, obedience, humility and dependence

Thus the Christian walk was characterized by devotedness and obedience. It was a life subjected to the will of another, namely, to the will of God; and therefore stamped with humility and dependence. But there was absolute devotedness of heart in self-sacrifice. For there was a danger, flowing from the power that acted in it, of the flesh coming in and availing itself of it. With regard to this, every one was to have a spirit of wisdom and moderation, and to act within the limits of the gift which God had dispensed to him, occupying himself with it according to the will of God; even as each member has its own place in the body, and should accomplish the function which God has ascribed to it. The apostle passes on insensibly to all the forms which duty assumes in the Christian, according to the various positions in which he stands, and to the spirit in which he ought to walk in every relationship.

The Christian's relationship with the authorities under which he is placed

It is in chapter 12 only that the idea of the assembly as a Body is thus found in this epistle; and that, in connection with the duties of the members individually—duties that flowed from their position as such. Otherwise it is the position of man in his individual responsibility before God, and this met by grace, and then the delivered man, that is set before us in the Epistle to the Romans. The directions given by the apostle extend to the Christian's relationship with the authorities under which he is placed. He recognizes them as accomplishing the service of God, and as armed with authority from Him, so that resisting them would be resisting that which God had established. Conscience therefore, and not merely force, constrained the Christian to obey. In fine he was to render to every man that which was due to him in virtue of his position; to leave nothing owing to any one, be it of whatever character it might—excepting love—a debt which never can be liquidated.

Christians among themselves as to those of high or low degree

Among themselves Christians are exhorted not to seek the high things of this world, but to walk as brethren with those of low degree: a precept too much forgotten in the assembly of God—to her loss. If the Christian of high degree requires that honor according to the flesh should be paid him, let it be done with good will. Happy he who, according to the example of the King of kings and to the precept of our apostle, knows how to walk in company with those of low degree in their journey through the wilderness. Now love is the fulfilling of the law; for love works no ill to his neighbor, and so fulfils the law.

Admonition to walk as children of the day, which is at hand

Another principle acts also on the spirit of the Christian. It is time to awake. The deliverance from this present evil age, which the Lord will accomplish for us, draws nigh. The night is far spent, the day is at hand—God knows the moment. The characteristics which marked its approach in the days of the apostle have ripened in a very different way since then, although God, with a view to those whom He is gathering in, is still even now restraining them. Let us then walk as children of the day, casting off the works of darkness. We belong to the day, of which Christ Himself will be the light. Let our walk be in accordance with that day, putting on Christ Himself, and not being studious of that which is in accordance with the will and the lusts of the flesh.

Chapters 14: 1 to 15: 7

Conscientious weakness of others as to days and meats and being conscientious ourselves: three directions given in this respect

FROM the beginning of chapter 14 to the end of verse 7 in chapter 15 another point is taken up, to which the different positions of the Jew and Gentile gave rise. It was difficult for a Jew to rid himself of the sense of difference between days and between meats. A Gentile, having abandoned his whole religious system as idolatrous, held to nothing. Human nature is liable in this respect to sin on both sides—a want of conscience, an unbridled will; and a ceremonial conscience. Christianity recognizes neither of these things. It delivers from the question of days and meats by making us heavenly with Christ. But it teaches us to bear with conscientious weakness, and to be conscientious ourselves. Conscience cannot—has not a right to—prescribe a new thing to us as a duty, but it may, through ignorance, hold to a traditional thing as obligatory. In reality we have entire liberty, but we ought to bear with weakness of faith in another, and not put a stumbling-block in his way. The apostle gives three directions in this respect: 1st, to receive the weak, but not for the discussion of questions that have to be settled; 2ndly, not to judge our brother, since he is Christ's servant, not ours; and every one must give account of himself to God; 3rdly, to bear the infirmities of the weak, and not to please ourselves; to walk in the spirit of love, and, if we are in a higher state, to show it by receiving one another, as Christ has received us, to the glory of God, which eclipses man and his petty superiorities, and which kindles charity and makes it ardent, earnest in seeking the good of others —taking us so out of self, and beyond little things, that we are able to adapt ourselves to others, where the will of God and His glory are not in question.

Individual responsibility to the Lord in regard to ourselves and our brethren

Many important principles are brought forward in these exhortations. Every one shall give account of himself to God. Every one, in these cases, should be fully persuaded in his own mind, and should not judge another. If any one has faith that delivers him from traditional observances, and he sees them to be absolutely nothing—as indeed they are—let him have his faith for God, and not cause his brother to stumble.

No one lives to himself, and no one dies to himself; we are the Lord's. The weak then regard the day for the Lord's sake; the others do not regard it because of the Lord. This is the reason therefore for not judging. He whom I judge is the Lord's. Therefore also I should seek to please my brother for his edification—he is the Lord's; and I should receive him, as I have been received, to share in the glory of God which has been conferred on him. We serve Christ in these things by thinking of the good of our brother. As to the energy of a man's faith, let him have it between himself and God. Love is the rule for the use of his liberty, if it *is* liberty, and not the bondage of disregarding. For the converse of this principle, when these observances are used to destroy liberty in Christ, see Galatians 4, where the apostle shows that, if the observance is taught as a principle, it is really turning back to Paganism.

Chapters 15: 8 to 16: 27

THESE instructions close the epistle. From chapter 15: 8, it is the exordium, the personal circumstances of the apostle, and salutations.

Paul's thought of God's dealings with Jew and Gentile in the advent of Jesus

Verses 8 *et seqq.*, he sums up his thought respecting God's dealings with the Jew and the Gentile in the advent of Jesus. He was a minister of the circumcision for the *truth* of God, to accomplish the promises made to the fathers. For to the Jews God had made promises; but none to the Gentiles. To the latter it was not *truth* that was in question: but by *grace* they might through Jesus glorify God for His mercy. For them the apostle quotes passages from Deuteronomy (that is to say, from the Law), from the Psalms, and from the Prophets.

Paul's desires for the Roman Christians and his present service for Jews

In verse 13, he turns affectionately to the Romans to express his desires for them, and his confidence in the blessing they had received from God, which enabled them mutually to exhort one another, while expressing at the same time his boldness in some sort, because of the grace God had given him, to be the minister of Jesus Christ to the Gentiles by fulfilling a public function with regard to them; being, as it were, a priest to offer up the Gentiles as an offering acceptable to God, because sanctified by the Holy Ghost. (See Num. 8: 11.) This was his glory before God. This sanctification by the Holy Ghost was that which took the place of sanctification by birth, and it was well worth it.

Moreover he had accomplished his task from Jerusalem round about Illyricum; not where Christ had been preached before, but where they had not yet heard of Him. This had prevented his coming to Rome. But now that there was no more place for him, according to the Holy Ghost—nothing more in those parts for him to do, and having long desired to see them, he thought to visit them on his way to Spain. For the moment he was going to Jerusalem with the collection made in Macedonia and Achaia for the saints.

We see that his heart turns to the Jews; they occupied his thoughts; and while desiring to put the seal of performance on the grace which this collection betokened, he was pre-occupied with them as Jews, as those who had a claim: a mingled feeling perhaps of one who was anxious to show that he did not forget them; for, in fact, he loved his nation. We have to learn whether, in executing this

service (properly that of a *deacon*), pleasing as it might
be, he was at the height of his mission as apostle. However that might be, the hand of God was in it to make
all things work for the good of His beloved servant and
child, as well as for His own glory. Paul had a presenti-
ment that it would not perhaps turn out well, and he
asks the prayers of the saints at Rome, that he might be
delivered from the hands of the wicked, and see their
face with joy. We know how it ended: the subject was
spoken of when we were considering the Acts. He saw
them indeed at Rome; he was delivered, but as a prisoner;
and we do not know if he ever went to Spain. The ways
of God are according to His eternal counsels, and according to His grace, and according to His perfect wisdom.

Personal salutations and loving remembrance of service for the Lord

Never having known the Roman Christians as an assembly, Paul sends many personal salutations. This was
the link which subsisted. We see how touchingly his heart
dwells upon all the details of service which attached him
to those who had rendered it. He who by grace had
searched into all the counsels of God, who had been admitted to see that which could not be made known to
man here below, remembered all that these humble Chris-
tions—these devoted women—had done for him and for
the Lord. This is love; it is the real proof of the power
of the Spirit of God; it is the bond of charity.

A precious and perfect rule for the Christian walk

We have also here a precious and most perfect rule for
our walk, namely, to be simple concerning evil, and wise
unto that which is good. Christianity alone could have
given such a rule; for it provides a walk that is positively
good, and wisdom to walk in it. As Christians we may
be simple concerning evil. What a deliverance! While the

man of the world must needs acquaint himself with evil, in order to avoid it in this world of snares and of artifice, he must corrupt his mind, accustom himself to think of evil, in order not to be entrapped by it. But soon there should be entire deliverance—soon should Satan be trodden under their feet.

The apostle's letters, the prophetic writings

We see also that the apostle did not write his letters himself, but employed a brother to do it. Here it was one named Tertius (ver. 22). Deeply concerned at the condition of the Galatians, he wrote himself the letter addressed to them; but the salutation at the end of this, as of other epistles, was in his own hand in order to verify the contents of the epistle.   (1 Corinthians 16: 21; 2 Thessalonians 3: 17, in which the feigned epistle alluded to in 2 Thessalonians 2 gave occasion to state this proof, which he always gave, that an epistle was truly his.) We see likewise, by this little circumstance, that he attached a solemn and authoritative character to his epistles, that they were not merely the effusions of a spiritual heart, but that in writing them he knew and would have others understand, that they were worthy of consideration and of being preserved as authorities, as the expression and exercise of his apostolic mission, and were to be received as such; that is to say, as possessing the Lord's authority, with which he was furnished by the power of the Holy Ghost. They were letters from the Lord by his means, even as his words had also been. (1 Thess. 2: 13, and 1 Cor. 14: 37.)

The doxology of the last verses suggesting truths linking this Epistle with Paul's writings in general

We have yet to observe, with regard to the three verses at the end of the epistle, that they are, as it were, de-

tached from all the rest, introducing, in the form of a
doxology, the suggestion of a truth, the communication of
which distinguished the apostle's teaching. He does not
develop it here. The task which the Holy Ghost accomplished in this epistle, was the presentation of the soul
individually before God according to the divine thoughts.
Nevertheless this connects itself immediately with the
position of the Body; and the doctrine respecting the
Body, the assembly, cannot be separated from it. Now
the apostle informs us distinctly, that the mystery, the
assembly, and the gathering together in one of all things
under Christ, had been entirely unknown: God had been
silent on that subject in the times which were defined by
the word *"ages,"* the assembly not forming a part of that
course of events, and of the ways of God on earth. But
the mystery was now revealed and communicated to the
Gentiles by prophetic writings—not "the writings of the
prophets." The epistles addressed to the Gentiles possessed this character; they were prophetic writings—a
fresh proof of the character of the epistles in the New
Testament.

The significance of the postscript: the scope of the Epistle

He who has understood the doctrine of this epistle, and
of the writings of Paul in general, will readily apprehend
the significance of this postscript. The epistle itself develops with divine perfection and fulness how a soul can
stand before God in this world, and the grace and righteousness of God, maintaining withal His counsels as to
Israel.

1 CORINTHIANS

The occasion for and circumstances surrounding the Epistle

THE Epistle to the Corinthians presents very different subjects from those which occupied us in the one addressed to the Romans. We find in it moral details, and the interior order of an assembly, with regard to which the Spirit of God here displays His wisdom in a direct way. There is no mention of elders or of other functionaries of the assembly. Through the labors of the apostle a numerous assembly had been formed (for God had much people in that city) in the midst of a very corrupt population, where riches and luxury were united with a moral disorder which had made the city a proverb. At the same time, here as elsewhere, false teachers (in general, Jews) sought to undermine the influence of the apostle. The spirit of philosophy did not fail also to exercise its baneful influence, although Corinth was not, like Athens, its principal seat. Morality and the authority of the apostle were compromised together; and the state of things was most critical. The Epistle was written from Ephesus, where the tidings of the sad state of the flock at Corinth had reached the apostle, almost at the moment when he had determined to visit them on his way into Macedonia (instead of passing along the coast of Asia Minor as he did), then returning to pay them a second visit on his way back. These tidings prevented his doing so, and, instead of visiting them to pour out his heart among them, he wrote this letter. The second Epistle was written in Macedonia, when Titus had brought him word of the happy effect of the first.

The subjects and divisions of the Epistle

The subjects of this first epistle are very easily divided into their natural order. In the first place, before he blames the Christians at Corinth to whom he writes, the apostle acknowledges all the grace which God had already bestowed on them, and would still impart. Chapter 1: 1-9. From verse 10 to chapter 4: 21 the subject of divisions, schools of doctrine and human wisdom, is spoken of in contrast with revelation and divine wisdom. Chapter 5, the corruption of morals, and discipline, whether by power, or in the responsibility of the assembly. Chapter 6, temporal affairs, law-suits; and again the subject of fornication which was of primary importance for the Christians of this city. Chapter 7, marriage is considered. Ought people to marry? The obligation of those who had already married; and the case of a converted husband or of a converted wife, whose wife or whose husband was not converted. Chapter 8, should they eat things offered to idols? Chapter 9, his apostleship. Chapter 10, their condition in general, their danger of being seduced, whether by fornication, or by idolatry, and idolatrous feasts, with the principles relating thereto, which introduces the Lord's supper. Chapter 11, questions connected with their behavior in religious matters individually or (ver. 17) in the assembly. Afterwards, chapter 12, the exercise of gifts, and their true value, and the object of their use, magnifying (chap. 13) the comparative value of charity; to the end of chapter 14, ordering the exercise of gifts also, with which it is compared. Chapter 15, the resurrection, which some denied, and specially that of the saints; and chapter 16, the collections for the poor in Judea, with some salutations, and the principles of subordination to those whom God has raised up for service, even where there were no elders. It is of great value to have these directions immediately from the Lord, independent of a formal organization, so that individual conscience and that of the Body as a whole should be engaged.

But there are some other considerations as to the character and structure of the epistle which I must not pass by.

The character of the Epistle as addressed to the professing Church and recognizing a local assembly as representing it

The reader may remark a difference in the address in the Corinthians and Ephesians. In the Corinthians, "To the Church of God," &c., "with all that in every place call on the name of the Lord Jesus." It is the professing Church, the members being assumed to be faithful, at any rate in character such till put out, and with that, every one that owned Jesus as Lord,—the house; hence chapter 10: 1-5. In Ephesians it is "holy and faithful brethren," and we have the proper privileges of the Body. This character of the Epistle, as embracing the professing Church, and recognizing a local assembly as representing it in the locality, gives the epistle great importance. Further, I think it will be found that the outward professing assembly is dealt with to the middle of chapter 10 (and there the nature of the Lord's Supper introduces the one Body of Christ, which is treated of as to the gifts of the Spirit in chapter 12); comeliness in woman's activities in the first verses of chapter 11; and afterwards from verse 17 what befits the coming together in the assembly, and the Lord's Supper, with the government of God. Verses 1-16 do not apply to the assembly. Still, order in the local assembly is everywhere the subject; only, from chapter 1 to chapter 10: 14, the professing multitude is in view, supposed however sincere, but possibly not so. From chapter 10: 15 to the end of chapter 12 the Body is in view.

Chapter 1

Paul's apostolic authority as called by God: Christians called to holiness by relationship which reposes on God's faithfulness

I WILL now turn back to take up the thread of the contents of this epistle from the beginning. Paul was an apostle by the will of God. That was his authority, however it might be with others. Moreover the same call that made those of Corinth Christians had made him an apostle. He addresses the assembly of God at Corinth, adding a character (the application of which is evident when we consider the contents of the epistle)— "sanctified in Christ Jesus." Afterwards the universality of the application of the doctrine and instructions of the epistle, and of its authority over all Christians, wherever they might be, is brought forward in this address. Happily, whatever sorrow he felt at the state of the Corinthians, the apostle could fall back upon the grace of God, and thus recognize all the grace which He had bestowed on them. But the placing them thus in relationship to God brought all the effects of His holiness to bear upon their consciences, while giving the apostle's heart the encouragement of the perfect grace of God towards them. And this grace itself became a powerful lever for the Word in the hearts of the Corinthians. In the presence of such grace they ought to be ashamed of sin. Nor can there be a more remarkable testimony than is here found of reckoning on the faithfulness of God towards His people. The relationship does claim holiness: in holiness alone it is enjoyed; but it reposes on the faithfulness of God. The Corinthians were walking, as we know, badly. The apostle lets none of the evil pass; but still he declares that God was faithful and would confirm them to the end

that they might be—not safe, but—blameless in the day
of our Lord Jesus Christ, and then proceeds to blame
them. What a wonderful testimony!

God's grace a powerful lever for the Word in the heart

Paul (the Spirit Himself) thus linked the Corinthians
with God; and that which He was in this connection with
them had all its force upon their hearts and consciences.
At the same time the use of this weapon opened their
heart to all that the apostle had to say. One must be very
near the Lord to be able in practice thus to look at Christians who are walking badly. It is not to spare their sins
—the apostle is very far from doing that; but it is grace
which brings their own consciences to be occupied with it,
as having a relationship with God that was too precious
to allow them to continue in sin or to permit it.

The Epistle to the Galatians supplies us with a remarkable instance of the confidence thus inspired. Compare
chapters 4: 20; 5: 10.

God's testimony confirmed by His gifts

The Corinthians were enriched by God with His gifts,
and His testimony was thus confirmed among them, so
that they came behind in no gift, waiting for the revelation of the Lord, the fulfilment of all things. Solemn day!
for which God, who had called them, confirmed them in
His faithfulness, that they might be without reproach in
that day, called as they were to the fellowship and communion of His Son Jesus Christ. Short but precious exposition of the grace and faithfulness of God, serving as
a basis (if their condition did not allow the apostle to
develop it as he did to the Ephesians) to all the exhortations and instructions which he addressed to the Corinthians in order to strengthen them and direct their waver-
ing steps.

Man's wisdom and strength set aside: the preaching of the cross the power of God

The apostle first takes up the folly of the Corinthians in making the chief Christian ministers and Christ Himself heads of schools. Christ was not divided. They had not been baptized unto the name of Paul. He had indeed, on occasion, baptized a few; but his mission was to preach, not to baptize.[1] It was in virtue of, and according to, Acts 26: 17, and 13: 2, *seqq.*, and not Matthew 28: 19. Moreover, all this human wisdom was but foolishness, which God brought to nothing: the preaching of the cross was the power of God; and God had chosen the weak things, the things of nought, foolish things according to the world, to annihilate the wisdom and strength of the world, in order that the gospel should be evidently the power of God. The Jews asked for a sign, the Greeks sought for wisdom; but God caused Christ crucified to be preached, a scandal to the Jews, foolishness to the Greeks, but to them which are called the power of God. By things that are not He brought to nought things that are, because His weakness is stronger than the strength of the world; His foolishness wiser than the wisdom of the age. The flesh shall not glory *in His presence*. God dealt with conscience, though in grace, according to the true position of responsible man, and did not subject Himself to the judgment and reasonings of man's mind, wholly incompetent thereto, and which put him out of his place as if he could judge of God. But, besides this, the Christian was more even than the object of God's instruction; he was himself of God in Christ Jesus; of God he had his life, his being, his position as a Christian. And Christ was unto him, from God, wisdom, righteousness, sanctification, and redemption—all in contrast with the pretensions of the

---

[1] This statement is the more remarkable, as he had a special revelation as to the Lord's Supper. But that ordinance has reference to the unity of the Body, which was specially the testimony of the apostle. The twelve were sent to baptize the nations (Matt. 28).

human mind, with the false righteousness of the Jew under
the law, with the means and the measure of the sanctification it supplied, and with the weakness of man, the last
trace of which God will remove in the deliverance He will
accomplish by His power in Christ when He shall complete the work of His grace. Thus we are of God, and
Christ is everything for us on God's part, in order that he
who glories may glory in the Lord: a brief but mighty
testimony to what Christianity is in its elements.

Chapter 2

The power of God the solid foundation for faith

IT was in this spirit that Paul had come among them at
first; he would know nothing but Christ,[2] and Christ in
His humiliation and abasement, object of contempt to
senseless men. His speech was not attractive with the carnal persuasiveness of a factitious eloquence: but it was
the expression of the presence and action of the Spirit,
and of the power which accompanied that presence. Thus
their faith rested, not on the fair words of man, which
another more eloquent or more subtle might upset, but
on the power of God—a solid foundation for our feeble
souls—blessed be His name for it!

The wisdom of God: the way in which it is communicated and its reception

Nevertheless, when once the soul was taught and established in the doctrine of salvation in Christ, there was

[2] Take notice here, that Paul does not say he would know nothing but
the cross, as some persons—and even Christians—wrongly apply it. He
would know nothing but *Christ* in contrast with philosophy among these
Pagans, and Christ in the most humbled form, in order to overturn the
pride of man. He goes on to inform us, that among those who were
initiated into Christianity he taught wisdom, but it was the wisdom of
God, revealed by Him who searches *the deep things* of God Himself. It is
a very grievous abuse that is often made of this passage (incorrectly
quoted besides).

a wisdom of which the apostle spoke; not the wisdom of this present age, nor of the princes of this age, which perish, wisdom and all, but the wisdom of God in a mystery, a secret counsel of God (revealed now by the Spirit), ordained in His settled purpose unto our glory before the world was—a counsel which, with all their wisdom, none of the princes of this world knew. Had they known it, they would not have crucified the One in whose Person it was all to be accomplished.

The apostle does not touch the subject of the mystery, because he had to feed them as babes, and only in order to put it in contrast with the false wisdom of the world; but the way in which this wisdom was communicated is important. That which had never entered into the heart of man[3] God had revealed by His Spirit, for the Spirit searches all things, even the deep things of God. It is only the spirit of a man which is in him that knows the things which he has not communicated. So no one knows the things of God save the Spirit of God. Now it is the Spirit of God which the apostle and the other vessels of revelation had received, that they might know the things which are freely given of God. This is the knowledge of the things themselves in the vessels of revelation. Afterwards this instrument of God was to communicate them. He did so, not in words which the art of man taught, but which the Spirit — which God — taught, communicating spiritual things by a spiritual medium.[4] The communication was by the Spirit as well as the thing communicated. There was yet one thing wanting that this revelation might be possessed by others—the reception of these communications. This also required the action of the

[3] The passage is often quoted to show the things are so great one cannot know them. Whereas it is a quotation from Isaiah to show that what could not *then* be known (when the evil was there, the man was dealt with according to what he was) is now revealed, now that man is in glory in the Person of Christ, and the Holy Ghost come down to show us what is there. Christianity is not Judaism.

[4] I have no doubt that this is the meaning of the passage. The means were of the same nature as the thing for which they were employed (ver. 13).

Spirit. The natural man did not receive them; and they are spiritually discerned.

A good remedy for philosophic pride

The source, the medium of communication, the reception, all was of the Spirit. Thus the spiritual man judges all things; he is judged of no man. The power of the Spirit in him makes his judgment true and just, but gives him motives and a walk that are unintelligible to one who has not the Spirit. Very simple as to that which is said—nothing can be more important than that which is here taught. Alas, the Corinthians, whether when the apostle was at Corinth, or at the time of writing this letter, were not in a condition to have the mystery communicated to them—a grievous humiliation to their philosophic pride, but therefore a good remedy for it.

Chapter 3

The assembly viewed as God's building: its sure foundation: man's building on it and his responsibility

THEY were not natural men; but they were carnal (not spiritual) men, so that the apostle had to feed them with milk and not with meat, which was only fit for those that were of full age. That with which they nourished their pride was a proof of this—their divisions into schools of doctrine. Paul, no doubt, had planted; Apollos watered. It was well. But it was God alone who gave the increase. Moreover the apostle had laid the foundation of this building of God, the assembly at Corinth; others had built since—had carried on the work of the edification of souls. Let every one take heed. There was but one foundation; it was laid. But in connection with it, they might

teach things solid or worthless and form souls by one or
the other—perhaps even introduce souls won by such vain
doctrines among the saints. The work would be proved,
sooner or later, by some day of trial. If they had wrought
in the work of God, with solid materials, the *work* would
stand; if not, it would come to nothing. The effect, the
fruit of labor, would be ·destroyed—the man who had
wrought be saved, because he had built on the foundation
—had true faith in Christ. Yet the shaking, caused by
the failure of all that he had thought genuine,[5] would be
apt, for himself, to shake the consciousness of his connection with, and confidence in, the foundation. He
should be saved as through the fire. He who had wrought
according to God should receive the fruit of his labor. If
any one corrupted the temple of God—introduced that
which destroyed fundamental truths, he should be destroyed himself.

The workmen and their work

The subject then is ministerial labor, carried on by
means of certain doctrines, either good, worthless, or sub-
versive of the truth; and the fruits which this labor would
produce. And there are three cases: the work good as
well as the workman; the work vain, but the workman
saved; the corrupter of God's temple—here the workman
would be destroyed.

---

[5] Remark here, the very important instruction as to the assembly
viewed as God's building. In Matthew 16 we have Christ's building, and
Satan's power cannot prevail against it. This building will go on till
complete at the end. Hence in 1 Peter 2 and Ephesians 2 we have no
workman, and the stones come, and the building grows. It is Christ's
own work: He builds, and the building is not yet complete. Here it is
God's building; but there is a builder, and man's responsibility comes in.
There is a wise master-builder, or it may be those who build with wood,
hay, and stubble—yea, even those who corrupt. In Ephesians 2 there is
also a present building, but it is the fact viewed abstractedly. Here the
responsibility is formally stated. The confusion of Christ's building (not
yet finished) and man's building, the applying the promise made to one
to the other which rests on man's responsibility and is a present building on earth, is one grand source of Popish and Puseyite errors. Against
Christ's work nothing can prevail. Man may build with wood and hay
and stubble, and his work be destroyed, as it will.

True wisdom

Finally, if any one desired to be wise in this world, let him become unintelligent in order to be wise. God counted the wisdom of the wise as foolishness, and would take them in their own craftiness. But in this the saints were below their privileges. All things were theirs, since they were the children of God. "All things are yours"—Paul, Apollos, all things—you are Christ's, and Christ is God's.

Chapter 4

Stewards employed by the Lord, furnished and judged by Him

AS for the apostle and the laborers, they were to consider them as stewards employed by the Lord. And it was to Him that Paul committed the judgment of his conduct. He cared little for the judgment man might form respecting him. He was not conscious of anything wrong, but that did not justify him. He who judged (examined) him was the Lord. And, after all, who was it that gave to the one or to the other that which he could use in service?

The sufferings of Paul and his companions as God's witnesses

Paul had thought well, in treating this subject, to use names that they were using in their carnal divisions, and those, especially himself and Apollos, which could not be used to pretend he was getting rid of others to set up himself; but what was the real state of the case? They had despised the apostle. Yes, he says, we have been put to shame, despised, persecuted, in distress; you have been at ease, like kings—a reproach in accordance with their own pretensions, their own reproaches—a reproach that touched them to the quick, if they had any feeling left. Paul and his companions had been as the offscouring of the earth for Christ's sake, while the Corinthians were reposing in the lap of luxury and ease. Even while writing to them, this was still his position. "Would to God," he says, "ye did reign" (that the day of Christ were come) "in order that we might reign with you." He felt his sufferings, although he bore them joyfully. They, the apostles, were set forth on God's part as though to be the last great spectacle in those marvellous games of which this world was the amphitheatre; and as His witnesses they were exposed to the fury of a brutal world. Patience and meekness were their only weapons.

The Holy Spirit's work of affection in the assembly to bind all together

Nevertheless he did. not say these things to put them to shame, he warned them as his beloved sons; for his sons they were. Though they might have ten thousand teachers, he had begotten them all by the gospel. Let them then follow him. In all this there is the deep working of the affection of a noble heart, wounded to the utmost, but wounded in order to bring out an affection that rose above his grief. It is this which so strikingly distinguishes the work of the Spirit in the New Testament, as in Christ Himself. The Spirit has come into the bosom of the assembly, takes part in her afflictions—her difficulties. He fills the soul of one who cares for the assembly,[6] making him feel that which is going on—feel it according to God, but with a really human heart. Who could cause all this to be felt for strangers, except the Spirit of God? Who would enter into these things with all the perfection of the wisdom of God, in order to act upon the heart, to deliver the conscience, to form the understanding, and to set it free, except the Spirit of God? Still the apostolic individual bond was to be formed, to be strengthened. It was

[6] *Sunantilambanei tais astheneiais hemon.*

the essence of the work of the Holy Ghost in the assembly
to bind all together in this way. We see the man: otherwise it would not have been Paul and his dear brethren.
We see the Holy Ghost, whom the latter had grieved, no
doubt, and who acts in the former with divine wisdom, to
guide them in the right way with all the affection of their
father in Christ. Timothy, his son in the faith and in
heart, might meet the case. Paul had sent him; Paul himself would soon be there. Some said, No, he would not,
and took occasion to magnify themselves in the absence
of the apostle; but he would come himself and put everything to the test; for the kingdom of God was not in word,
but in power. Did they wish him to come with a rod or
in love?

Here this part of the epistle ends. Admirable specimen
of tenderness and of authority!—of authority sure enough
of itself on the part of God, to be able to act with perfect
tenderness towards those who were thoroughly dear to
him, in the hope of not being forced to exercise itself in
another way. The most powerful truths are unfolded in
so doing.

Chapter 5

Unreserved condemnation of evil: the purpose of needed discipline

HE begins to treat the details of conduct and of discipline; and, first of all, the carnal defilement carried on
in their midst to the last degree of hardness of conscience.
Those who sought their own personal influence as teachers
allowed them to go on in it. He condemns it without
reservation. Discipline follows; for Christ had been offered
up as the Paschal Lamb, and they were to keep the feast
without leaven, keeping themselves from the old leaven;

in order that they might be in fact, what they were before God—an unleavened lump. As to discipline, it was this: before they knew that it was their duty to cut off the wicked person, and that God had given them the power and imposed on them the obligation to do so, a moral sense of evil ought, at least, to have led them to humble themselves before God, and to pray that He would take him away. On the contrary, they were puffed up with pride. But now the apostle teaches them what must be done, and enforces it with all his apostolic authority. He was among them in spirit if not in body, and with the power of the Lord Jesus Christ, they being gathered together, to deliver such a one to Satan; but as a brother for the destruction of the flesh, that his spirit might be saved in the day of Christ.

The adversary's enmity used for the saint's Spiritual blessing: the assembly's duty in discipline

Here all the power of the assembly in its normal condition, united to and led by the apostolic energy, is displayed. Its members; the apostle, vessel and channel of the power of the Spirit; and the power of the Lord Jesus Himself, the Head of the Body. Now the world is the theatre of Satan's power; the assembly, delivered from his power, is the habitation of God by the Spirit. If the enemy had succeeded in drawing aside by the flesh a member of Christ, so that he dishonors the Lord by walking after the flesh as men of the world do, he is put outside, and by the power of the Spirit, as then exercised in their midst by the apostle, delivered up to the enemy, who is in spite of himself the servant of the purposes of God (as in the case of Job), in order that the flesh of the Christian (which, from his not being able to reckon it dead, had brought him morally under the power of Satan) should be physically destroyed and broken down. Thus would he be set free from the illusions in which the flesh held him captive. His mind would learn how to discern the difference between good and evil, to know what sin was. The judgment of God would be realized within him, and would not be executed upon him at that day when it would be definitive for the condemnation of those who should undergo it. This was a great blessing, although its form was terrible. Marvellous example of the government of God, which uses the adversary's enmity against the saints as an instrument for their spiritual blessing! We have such a case fully set before us in the history of Job. Only we have here, in addition, the proof that in its normal state, apostolic power[7] being there, the assembly exercised this judgment herself, having discernment by the Spirit and the authority of Christ to do it. Moreover, whatever may be the spiritual capacity of the assembly to wield this sword of the Lord (for this is power), her positive and ordinary duty is stated at the end of the chapter.

The assembly viewed collectively as an unleavened lump: its consequent responsibility to judge those within

The assembly was an unleavened lump, looked at in the Spirit as an assembly, and not individually. It is thus that we must view it, for it is only in the Spirit that it is so. The assembly is seen of God as being before Him in the new nature in Christ. Such she ought to be in practice by the power of the Spirit, in spite of the existence of the flesh, which by faith she ought to count as dead, and allow nothing in her walk that is contrary to this state. The assembly ought to be a "new lump," and was not if evil was allowed, and, consequently, ought to purge herself from the old leaven, because she *is* unleavened in God's

---

[7] The apostle (1 Tim. 1: 20) exercises this power alone as to certain blasphemers. It is power, not mere duty, and it is important clearly to distinguish the two: though the apostle here did it in and with the gathered assembly, yet he says, "I have judged already to deliver such an one to Satan." In verse 13 we have the positive duty of the assembly without the question of special power.

thoughts. Such is her position before God. For Christ our
Passover has been sacrificed for us: therefore we ought to
keep the feast with the unleavened bread of sincerity and
truth. They did wrong therefore in boasting while this
evil was in their midst, however great their gifts might
be. A little leaven leavens the whole lump. The evil did
not attach to that man alone who was personally guilty of
it. The assembly was not clear till the evil was put out
(2 Cor. 7: 11). They could not dissociate themselves in
the intercourse of ordinary life from all those who, in the
world, walked corruptly, for in that case they would have
to go out of the world. But if any one called himself a
brother and walked in this corruption, with such an one
they ought not even to eat. God judges those who are
outside. The assembly must herself judge those that are
within, and put out whatever must be called "wicked."

Chapter 6

Wrongs: an unchangeable morality and ecclesiastical order and discipline

CHAPTER 6: 1-11 treats the subject of wrongs. It was
shameful that those who were to judge the world and
the angels should be incapable of judging the paltry affairs
of this world. Let the least esteemed in the assembly be
employed in this service. Rather should they bear the
wrong, whereas they did wrong themselves. But the wicked
and the unrighteous would assuredly not inherit the kingdom. What a wonderful mixture we have here of astonishing revelations, of a morality that is unchangeable
whatever may be the divine supremacy of grace, and of
ecclesiastical order and discipline! The assembly is united
to Christ. When He shall judge the world and pronounce
the doom of the angels, she will be associated with Him
and take part in His judgment, for she has His Spirit and

His mind. Nothing however that is unrighteous shall enter into that kingdom, for in effect how could evil be judged by any that took pleasure in it? Christians should not go to a worldly tribunal for justice, but have recourse to the arbitration of the brethren—a service which, as entering so little into Christian spirituality, was suited to the weakest among them. Moreover the proper thing was rather to suffer the wrong. Be it as it might, the unrighteous shall not inherit the kingdom.

The two threatening dangers at Corinth: true liberty as to meats

Judaism, which took pleasure in a carnal sanctity of outward regulations, and the spirit of the world with conformity to its ways, were the two dangers that threatened the assembly at Corinth—dangers, indeed, which exist for the heart of man at all times and in all places. With regard to meats the rule is simple: perfect liberty, since all is allowed—true liberty, in that we are in bondage to none of these things. Meats and the belly, as in relationship to each other, should both perish; the body has a higher destiny—it is for the Lord, and the Lord for it. God has raised up Christ from the dead, and He will raise us up again by His power. The body belongs to this and not to meats.

The Christian's body for Christ: the two mighty motives for holiness

But the doctrine that the body is for Christ decided another question, to which the depraved habits of the Corinthians gave rise. All fornication is forbidden. To us, with our present Christian habits of mind, it is a thing of course—to Pagans, new; but the doctrine exalts every subject. Our bodies are the members of Christ. Another truth connected with this is of great importance: if (by union according to the flesh) two were one body, he who is united to the Lord is one spirit. The Spirit whose fulness is in Christ is the same Spirit who dwells in me and unites me to Him. Our bodies are His temples. What a mighty truth when we think of it!

Moreover we are not our own, but were bought with a price—the blood of Christ offered for us. Therefore we ought to glorify God in our bodies, which are His—powerful and universal motive, governing the whole conduct without exception. Our true liberty is to belong to God. All that is for oneself is stolen from the rights of Him who has bought us for His own. All that a slave was or gained was the property of his master; he was not the owner of himself. Thus it was with the Christian. Outside that, he is the wretched slave of sin and of Satan—selfishness his rule, and eternal banishment from the source of love his end. Horrible thought! In Christ we are the special objects and the vessels of that love. We have here two mighty motives for holiness: the value of Christ's blood, at which we are purchased; also the fact that we are the temples of the Holy Ghost.

Chapter 7

Christian marriage: the counsel of experience and the commandment of the Lord

THE apostle proceeds by answering a question in connection with the subject he had been treating—the will of God with regard to the relationship between man and woman. They do well who remain outside this relationship in order to walk with the Lord according to the Spirit, and not to yield in anything to their nature. God had instituted marriage—woe to him who should speak ill of it!—but sin has come in, and all that is of nature, of the creature, is marred. God has introduced a power altogether above and outside nature—that of the Spirit. To walk according to that power is the best thing; it is to walk outside the sphere in which sin acts. But it is rare; and positive sins are for the most part the effect of standing apart from that which God has ordained according to nature. In general then for this reason, every man should have his own wife: and the union once formed, he had no longer power over himself. As to the body, the husband belonged to his wife, the wife to her husband. If, by mutual consent, they separated for awhile that they might give themselves to prayer and to spiritual exercises, the bond was to be immediately acknowledged again, lest the heart, not governing itself, should give Satan occasion to come in and distress the soul, and destroy its confidence in God and in His love—lest he should tempt by distressing doubts (it is *for*, not *by* incontinency) a heart that aimed at too much, and failed in it.

This permission, however, and this direction which recommended Christians to marry, was not a commandment from the Lord, given by inspiration, but the fruit of the apostle's experience—an experience to which the presence of the Holy Ghost was not wanting.[8] He would rather that every one were like himself; but every one had, in this respect, his gift from God. To the unmarried and the widows, it is good, he says, to abide as he himself was; but if they could not subdue their nature and remain in calm purity, it was better to marry. Unsubduedness of desire was more hurtful than the bond of marriage. But as to marriage itself, there was no longer room for the counsel of experience, the commandment of the Lord was positive. The woman was not to separate from the man, nor the man from the woman; and if they separated, the bond was not broken; they must remain unmarried or else be reconciled.

[8] Note here, we have formally distinguished, what infidels of the modern school have sought to confound, spiritual thoughts as a man, and inspiration. The apostle gives his thoughts and judgment as a spiritual man, his mind animated and guided by the Spirit, and contrasts it with inspiration and what the Lord said. How wonderfully the Lord has provided in Scripture for everything! Compare verse 25.

The unbelieving husband or wife

But there was a case more complicated, when the man was converted and the wife unconverted, or *vice versa*. According to the law a man who had married a woman of the Gentiles (and was consequently profane or unclean) defiled himself, and was compelled to send her away; and their children had no right to Jewish privileges; they were rejected as unclean. (See Ezra 10: 3.) But under grace it was quite the contrary. The converted husband sanctified the wife, and *vice versa*, and their children were reckoned clean before God; they had part in the ecclesiastical right of their parent. This is the sense of the word "holy," in connection with the question of order and of outward relationship towards God, which was suggested by the obligation under the law to send away wife and children in a similar case. Thus the believer was not to send away his wife, nor to forsake an unbelieving husband. If the unbeliever forsook the believer definitively, the latter (man or woman) was free—"let him depart." The brother was no longer bound to consider the one who had forsaken him as his wife, nor the sister the man who had forsook her as her husband. But they were called to peace, and not to seek this separation; for how did the believer know if he should not be the means of the unbeliever's conversion? For we are under grace. Moreover every one was to walk as God had distributed to him.

The Christian's occupation and position in this world

As regarded occupations and positions in this world, the general rule was that everyone should continue in the state wherein he was called; but it must be "with God"— doing nothing that would not be to His glory. If the state was in itself of a nature contrary to His will, it was sin; clearly he could not remain in it with God. But the general rule was to remain and glorify God in it.

The apostle's judgment as to those unmarried

The apostle had spoken of marriage, of the unmarried and of widows; he had been questioned also with respect to those who had never entered into any relationship with woman. On this point he had no commandment from the Lord. He could only give his judgment as one who had received mercy of the Lord to be faithful. It was good to remain in that condition, seeing what the world was and the difficulties of a Christian life. If they were bound to a wife, let them not seek to be loosed. If free, they would do well to remain so. Thus if they married, they did well; not marrying, they did better. He who had not known a woman did not sin if he married, but he should have trouble after the flesh in his life here below. (It will be observed, that it is not the daughter of a Christian that is here spoken of, but his own personal condition.) If he stood firm, and had power over his own will, it was the better way; if he married, he still did well; if he did not marry, it was better. It was the same with a woman; and if the apostle said that according to his judgment it was better, he had the Spirit of God. His experience—if he had no commandment—had not been gained without the Spirit, but it was that of a man who could say (if any one had a right to say it) that he had the Spirit of God.

Serving the Lord without distraction

Moreover the time was short: the married were to be as having no wives; buyers, as having no possession; they who used the world, not using it as though it were theirs. Only the apostle would have them without carefulness or distraction, that they might serve the Lord. If by reckoning themselves dead to nature this effect was not produced, they gained nothing, they lost by it. When married they were preoccupied with things below, in order to please their wives and to provide for their children. But they enjoyed a repose of mind, in which nature did not claim her rights with a will that they had failed to silence, and holiness of walk and of heart was maintained. If the will of nature was subjugated and silenced, they served the Lord without distraction, they lived according to the Spirit and not according to nature, even in those things which God had ordained as good with respect to nature.

Directions to slaves: exceptions to the general rule to continue in the state wherein we are called

As to the slave, he might console himself as being the Lord's free-man; but (seeing the difficulty of reconciling the will of a pagan or even an unspiritual master with the will of God) if he could be made free, he should embrace the opportunity.

A new energy above nature: inspiration and the apostle's own spiritual experience accurately distinguished

Two things strike us here in passing: the holiness which all these directions breathe with regard to that which touches so closely the desires of the flesh. The institutions of God, formed for man when innocent, are maintained in all their integrity, in all their authority, a safeguard now against the sin to which man is incited by his flesh. The Spirit introduces a new energy above nature, which in no wise weakens the authority of the institution. If any one can live above nature in order to serve the Lord in freedom, it is a gift of God—a grace which he does well to profit by. A second very important principle flows from this chapter. The apostle distinguishes accurately between that which he has by inspiration, and his own spiritual experience—that which the Spirit gave him in connection with the exercises of his individual life—spiritual wisdom, however exalted it might be. On certain points he had no commandment from the Lord. He gave the conclusion at which he had arrived, through the help of the Spirit of

God, in a life of remarkable faithfulness, and aided by the Spirit whom he but little grieved. But it was not a commandment of the Lord. On other points that which he did not except in this manner was to be received as the commandment of the Lord. (Compare chap. 14:37.) That is to say, he affirms the inspiration, properly so called, of his writings—they were to be received as emanating from the Lord Himself—distinguishing this inspiration from his own spiritual competency, a principle of all importance.

Chapter 8

Meats offered to idols: the value of true Christian knowledge

AFTER this the apostle answers (chap. 8) the question respecting meats offered to idols, which gives occasion to a few words on the value of knowledge. Simply as knowledge, it is worth nothing. If we look at it as knowledge that *we possess*, it does but puff us up; it is something in *me*, *my knowledge*. Thus Christian knowledge unfolded something in God. By means of that which is revealed, God, better known, became greater to the soul. It was in Him the thing known, and not a knowledge in me by which I made myself greater. He who loves God is *known of Him*. As to the question itself, love decided it. Since such a question had arisen, it was evident that all consciences were not brought into full light by spiritual intelligency. Now undoubtedly the idol was nothing: there was but one God, the Father; and one Lord, Jesus Christ. But if he who was strong sat at meat in the idol's temple, another who had not full light would be encouraged to do the same, and his conscience would be unfaithful and defiled. Thus I lead into sin, and, as far as depends on me, I ruin a brother for whom Christ died. I sin against

Christ Himself in so doing. Thus, if meat causes a
brother to stumble, let me altogether abstain from it
rather than be a snare to him. Here the apostle treats
the question as rising among the brethren, so as that
which regards the conscience of each, choosing to maintain in all its force that in fact an idol was nothing but a
piece of wood or stone. It was important to set the question on this ground. The prophets had done so before.
But this was not all that there was to say. There was
the working of Satan and of wicked spirits to explain, and
this he does further on.

The supreme position of God and our Lord con-
trasted with the many heathen gods: considering the weak in eating meats offered to idols

We may remark in passing the expression, "To us there
is but one God, the Father, and one Lord, Jesus Christ."
The apostle does not here treat the abstract question of
the Lord's divinity, but the connection of men with that
which was above them in certain relationships. Pagans
had many gods, and many lords, intermediate beings.
Not so Christians. For them is the Father abiding in the
absoluteness of the divinity, and Christ who, become Man,
has taken the place and the relationship of Lord towards
us. The position, and not the nature, is the subject. It is
the same thing in chapter 12: 2-6, where the contrast is
with the multitude of spirits whom the Pagans knew, and
the number of gods and lords. Nevertheless every one was
not, in fact, thus delivered from the influence of false gods
on his imagination. They were still perhaps, in spite of
himself, something to him. He had conscience of the idol,
and if he ate that which had been offered to it, it was not
to him simply that which God had given for food. The
idea of the existence of a real and powerful Being had a
place in his heart, and thus his conscience was defiled.
Now they were not better in God's sight for having eaten,

and by eating they had put a stumbling-block in their brother's way, and, so far as the act of those who had full light was concerned, had ruined him by defiling his conscience and estranging him from God in unfaithfulness. This was sinning against Christ, who had died for that precious soul. If God intervened to shield him from the result of this unfaithfulness, that in nowise diminished the sin of him who led the weak one to act against his conscience. In itself that which separates us from God ruins us in that which regards our responsibility. Thus he who has the love of Christ in his heart would rather never eat meat than do that which would make a brother unfaithful, and tend to ruin a soul which Christ has redeemed.

Chapter 9

Paul's ministry and liberty: servant of all for the gospel's sake

THE apostle was exposed to the accusations of false teachers, who asserted that he carried on his evangelization and his labors from interested motives, and that he took the property of Christians, availing himself of their devotedness. He speaks therefore of his ministry. He declares openly that he is an apostle, an eye-witness of the glory of Christ, having seen the Lord. Moreover, if he was not an apostle to others, doubtless he was to the Corinthians, for he had been the means of their conversion. Now the will of the Lord was that they who preached the gospel should live of the gospel. He had a right to take with him a sister as his wife, even as Peter did, and the brethren of the Lord. Nevertheless he had not used this right. Obliged by the call of the Lord to preach the gospel, woe unto him if he failed to do it! His glory was to do it gratuitously, so as to take away all occasion from those who sought it. For, being free from all, he had made himself the servant of all, that he might win as many as he could. Observe that this was in his service; it was not accommodating himself to the world, in order to escape the offence of the cross. He put this plainly forward (chap. 2: 2); but in preaching it, he adapted himself to the religious capacity and to the modes of thought belonging to the one and to the other, in order to gain access for the truth into their minds; and he did the same in his manner of conduct among them. It was the power of charity which denied itself in all things, in order to be the servant of all, and not the sel- fishness which indulged itself under the pretence of gain- ing others. He did so *in every respect* for the sake of the gospel, desiring, as he said, to be a partaker with it, for he personifies it as doing the work of God's love in the world.

The apostle's course as a Christian first of all, then a preacher: warning and distinction between par- ticipation in Christian ordinances and salvation

It was thus they should run; and, in order to run thus, one must deny oneself. In this way the apostle acted. He did not run with uncertain steps, as one who did not see the true end, or who did not pursue it seriously as a known thing. He knew well what he was pursuing, and he pursued it really, evidently, according to its nature. Every one could judge by his walk. He did not trifle as a man who beats the air—easy prowess. In seeking that which was holy and glorious, he knew the difficulties he resisted in the personal conflict with the evil that sought to obstruct his victory. As a vigorous wrestler, he kept under his body, which would have hindered him. There was reality in his pursuit of heaven: he would tolerate nothing that opposed it. Preaching to others was not all. He might do that, and it might be, as regards himself, labor in vain; he might lose everything—be re-

jected afterwards himself, if not personally a Christian.
He was a Christian first of all, then a preacher, and a
good preacher, because he was a Christian first. Thus,
also (for the beginning of chapter 10 connects itself with
the close of chapter 9), others might make a profession,
partake of the initiatory and other ordinances, as he
might be a preacher, and after all not be owned of God.
This warning is a testimony to the condition to which, in
part at least, the assembly of God was already reduced:
a warning always useful, but which supposes that those
who bear the name of Christian, and have partaken of
the ordinances of the Church, no longer inspire that confidence which would receive them without question as the
true sheep of Christ. The passage distinguishes between
participation in Christian ordinances and the possession
of salvation: a distinction always true, but which it is
not necessary to make when Christian life is bright in
those who have part in the outward privileges of the
assembly.

Chapter 10

God's ways with Israel given for our instruction

THE apostle then gives the Corinthians the ways of
God with Israel in the wilderness, as instruction with
regard to His ways with us, declaring that the things
which happened to them were types or figures which serve
as patterns for us: an important principle, and one which
ought to be clearly apprehended, in order to profit by it.
It is not Israel who is the figure, but that which happened
to Israel—the ways of God with Israel. The things themselves happened to Israel; they were written for our instruction who find ourselves at the close of God's dispensations. That which shall follow will be the judgment of
God, when these examples will no longer serve for the life
of faith.

Christian responsibility: God's faithfulness

Two principles are next established which also have great practical importance: "Let him that thinketh he standeth take heed lest he fall." This is our responsibility. On the other side we have the faithfulness of God. He does not permit us to be tempted beyond our strength, but provides a way of escape in order that we may not stumble.

Idolatry: association and communion: the Lord's Supper and the table of demons

He enjoins, with regard to idolatry, that holy fear which avoids the occasion of doing evil, the occasion of falling. There is association and communion through the table of which we partake with that which is on it; and we Christians, being many, are but one bread and one Body,[9] inasmuch as we share the same bread at the Lord's Supper. Those in Israel who ate of the sacrifices were partakers of the altar—were identified with it. So those who ate of idol's meat as such were identified with the idol it was offered to. Was this to say that the idol was anything? No. But as it is written (Deut. 32), "The things which the Gentiles offered, they offered to demons and not to God." Should a Christian then, partake of the table of demons? The table was the table of demons, the cup the cup of demons—an important principle for the assembly of God. Would one provoke the Lord by putting Him on a level with demons? Allusion is again made to Deuteronomy 32: 21. The apostle repeats his principle already established, that he had liberty in every respect, but that on the one hand he would not put himself under the power of anything; on the other, being free, he would use

[9] It is here the apostle comes to the inner circle of the Body of Christ, the true assembly of God united together by the Holy Ghost, of which the Lord's Supper is the expression.

his liberty for the spiritual good of all. To follow out this rule, these are his instructions: Whatsoever was sold in the market they should eat without question of conscience. If any man said, "This was sacrificed to idols," it was a proof that he had conscience of an idol. They should then not eat of it, because of *his* conscience. For as to him who was free, his liberty could not be judged by the conscience of the other; for, as to doctrine, and where there was knowledge, the apostle recognizes it as a truth that the idol was nothing. The creature was simply the creature of God. Communion with that which was false I ought to avoid for myself, especially in that which relates to communion with God Himself. I should deny myself the liberty which the truth gave me, rather than wound the weak conscience of others.

Doing all to the glory of God

Moreover in all things, even in eating or drinking, we ought to see the glory of God, and do all to His glory; giving no offence by using our liberty, either to Jew or Gentile, or the assembly of God; following the apostle's example, who, denying himself, sought to please all for their edification.

Chapter 11

The Holy Spirit's presence and action: proper conduct in the assemblies

HAVING given these rules in answer to questions of detail, he turns to that which regarded the presence and action of the Holy Ghost; which also introduces the subject of the conduct proper for them in their assemblies.

Observe here the way in which the apostle grounded his replies with regard to details on the highest and fundamental principles. This is the manner of Christianity. (Compare Titus 2: 10-14.) He introduces God and charity, putting man in connection with God Himself. In that which follows, we have also a striking example of this. The subject is a direction for women.

Direction for women: the woman's covered head in prayer: the order of creation

They were not to pray without having their heads covered. To decide this question, simply of what was decent and becoming, the apostle lays open the relationship and the order of the relationship subsisting between the depositories of God's glory and Himself,[10] and brings in the angels, to whom Christians, as a spectacle set before them, should present that of order according to the mind of God. The head of the woman is the man; that of man is Christ; of Christ, God. This is the order of power, ascending to Him who is supreme. And then, with respect to their relationship to each other, he adds, the man was not created for the woman, but the woman for the man. And as to their relations with other creatures, intelligent and conscious of the order of the ways of God, they were to be covered because of the angels, who are spectators of the ways of God in the dispensation of redemption, and of the effect which this marvellous intervention was to produce. Elsewhere (see preceding note) it is added, in reference to the history of that which took place, the man was not deceived; but the woman, being deceived, transgressed first. Let us add—from the passage we are considering—that, as to creation, the man was not taken from the woman, but the woman from the man. Nevertheless the man is not without the woman, nor the woman without the man, in the Lord; but all things are of God;

[10] In 1 Timothy 2: 11-15 the moral effect of the circumstances of the fall is introduced, as giving the woman her true place in the assembly with regard to man.

—and all this to regulate a question of modesty as to women, when in praying they were before the eyes of others.[11] The result—in that which concerns the details— is that the man was to have his head uncovered, because he represented authority, and in this respect was invested (as to his position) with the glory of God, of whom he was the image. The woman was to have her head covered, as a token that she was subject to the man (her covering being a token of the power to which she was subject). Man however could not do without woman, nor woman without man. Finally the apostle appeals to the order of creation, according to which a woman's hair, her glory and ornament, showed, in contrast with the hair of man, that she was not made to present herself with the boldness of man before all. Given as a veil, her hair showed that modesty, submission—a covered head that hid itself, as it were, in that submission and in that modesty—was her true position, her distinctive glory. Moreover, if any one contested the point, it was a custom which neither the apostle nor the assemblies allowed.

Divine order in creation the expression of God's mind: men a spectacle to angels

Observe also here that, however man may have fallen, divine order in creation never loses its value as the expression of the mind of God. Thus also in James, man is said to be created in the image of God. As to his moral condition, he needs (now that he has knowledge of good and of evil) to be born again, created in righteousness and in true holiness, that he may be the image of God as now revealed through Christ; but his position in the world, as the head and centre of all things—which no angel has been—is the idea of God Himself, as well as the position of the woman, the companion of his glory but subject to

---

[11] We are not as yet come to the order in the assembly. That commences with verse 17.

him: an idea which will be gloriously accomplished in Christ, and with respect to the woman in the assembly; but which is true in itself, being the constituted order of God, and always right as such: for the ordinance of God creates order, although, no doubt, His wisdom and His perfection are displayed in it.

The reader will remark, that this order in creation, as well as that which is established in the counsels of God in respect of the woman, of the man, of Christ, and of God Himself, and the fact that men—at least Christians under redemption—are a spectacle to angels (compare chap. 4: 9), subjects which here I can only indicate, have the highest interest.[12]

A spirit of division in the assemblies

The apostle afterwards touches upon the subject of their assemblies. In verse 2 he had praised them; but on this point he could not do so (ver. 17). Their assemblies manifested a spirit of division. This division concerned the distinction between the rich and the poor, but, as it seems, gave rise to others: at least others were necessary to make manifest those who were really approved of God. Now these divisions had the character of sects; that is to say, particular opinions divided Christians of the same assembly, of the assembly of God, into schools; they were hostile to each other, although they took the Lord's Supper together—if indeed it could be said that they took it together. Jealousies that had arisen between the rich and the poor tended to foster the sectarian division. If, I observed, it could be said that they broke bread together; for each one took care to eat his own supper before the others did so, and some were hungry while others took their fill. This was not really eating the Lord's Supper.

[12] The first chapter of Genesis gives us man in his place in creation as from God the Creator; the second, his own relationship with Jehovah God, where he was placed in connection with Him, and the woman's with himself.

The nature and import of the Lord's Supper: its special revelation to Paul

The apostle, guided by the Holy Ghost, seizes the opportunity to declare to them the nature and the import of this ordinance. We may notice here, that the Lord had taught it him by an especial revelation—proof of the interest that belongs to it,[13] and that it is a part of the Lord's mind in the entire Christian walk, to which He attaches importance in view of our moral condition, and of the state of our spiritual affections individually, as well as those of the assembly. In the joy of Christian liberty, amid the powerful effects of the presence of the Holy Ghost—of the gifts by which He manifested Himself in the assembly, the Lord's death, His broken body, was brought to mind, and, as it were, made present to faith as the basis and foundation of everything. This act of love, this simple and solemn deed, weak and empty in appearance, preserved all its importance. The Lord's body had been offered for us! to which the Holy Ghost Himself was to bear witness, and which was to maintain all its importance in the Christian's heart, and to be the foundation and centre of the edifice of the assembly. Whatever might be the power that shone forth in the assembly, the heart was brought back to this. The body of the Lord Himself had been offered,[14] the lips of Jesus had claimed our remembrance. This moral equilibrium is very important to saints. Power, and the exercise of gifts do not necessarily act upon the conscience and the heart of those to whom they are committed, nor of those always who enjoy their display. And, although God is present (and when we are in a good state, that is felt), still it is a man who speaks and who acts upon others; he is promi-

[13] This connects itself too with the fact that it is the expression of the unity of the Body—truth specially committed to the apostle. On the other hand, he was not sent to baptize. That was mere admission to the house already formed, and to which the apostle had been admitted like others.

[14] I do not say "broken," the best MSS omitting it; but it is the memorial of Christ slain, and His precious blood poured out.

nent. In the Lord's Supper the heart is brought back to
a point in which it is entirely dependent, in which man
is nothing, in which Christ and His love are everything,
in which the heart is exercised, and the conscience remembers that it has needed cleansing, and that it has been
cleansed by the work of Christ—that we depend absolutely on this grace. The affections also are in the fullest
exercise. It is important to remember this. The consequences that followed forgetfulness of the import of this
ordinance confirmed its importance and the Lord's earnest
desire that they should take heed to it. The apostle is
going to speak of the power of the Holy Ghost manifested
in His gifts, and of the regulations necessary to maintain
order and provide for edification where they were exercised in the assembly; but, before doing so, he places the
Lord's Supper as the moral centre, the object of the assembly. Let us remark some of the thoughts of the Spirit
in connection with this ordinance.

The affections linked with what Christ did: a remembrance of Him in what He was on the cross

First. He links the affections with it in the strongest
way. It was the same night on which Jesus was betrayed
that He left this memorial of His sufferings and of His
love. As the paschal lamb brought to mind the deliverance
which the sacrifice offered in Egypt had procured for
Israel, thus the Lord's Supper called to mind the sacrifice
of Christ. He is in the glory, the Spirit is given; but they
were to remember Him. His offered body was the object
before their hearts in this memorial. Take notice of this
word "Remember." It is not a Christ as He now exists,
it is not the realization of what *He is:* that is not a remembrance—His body is now glorified. It is a remembrance of what He was on the cross. It is a body slain,
and blood shed, not a glorified body. It is remembered,
though, by those who are now united to Him in the glory

into which He is entered. As risen and associated with Him in glory, they look back to that blessed work of love, and His love in it which gave them a place there. They drink also of the cup in remembrance of Him. In a word, it is Christ looked at as dead: there is not such a Christ now.

Remembrance of Christ Himself, the Lord: His death to be celebrated till He come

It is the remembrance of Christ Himself. It is that which attaches to Himself, it is not only the value of His sacrifice, but attachment to Himself, the remembrance of Himself. The apostle then shows us, if it is a dead Christ, who it is that died. Impossible to find two words, the bringing together of which has so important a meaning, The *death* of the *Lord*. How many things are comprised in that He who is called the Lord had died! What love! What purposes! What efficacy! What results! The Lord Himself gave Himself up for us. We celebrate His death. At the same time, it is the end of God's relations with the world on the ground of man's responsibility, except the judgment. This death has broken every link—has proved the impossibility of any. We show forth this death until the rejected Lord shall return, to establish new bonds of association by receiving us to Himself to have part in them. It is this which we proclaim in the ordinance when we keep it. Besides this, it is in itself a declaration that the blood on which the new covenant is founded has been already shed; it was established in this blood. I do not go beyond that which the passage presents; the object of the Spirit of God here, is to set before us, not the efficacy of the death of Christ, but that which attaches the heart to Him in remembering His death, and the meaning of the ordinance itself. It is a dead, betrayed Christ whom we remember. The offered body was, as it were, before their eyes at this Supper. The shed blood of the Saviour claimed the affections of their heart for Him. They were guilty of despising these precious things, if they took part in the supper unworthily. The Lord Himself fixed our thoughts there in this ordinance, and in the most affecting way, at the very moment of His betrayal.

Discipline solemnly exercised in connection with the ordinance; the Lord judges His own house: the purpose of chastisement

But if Christ attracted the heart thus to fix its attention there, discipline was also solemnly exercised in connection with this ordinance. If they despised the broken body and the blood of the Lord by taking part in it lightly, chastisement was inflicted. Many had become sick and weak, and many had fallen asleep, that is, had died. It is not the being worthy to partake that is spoken of, but the partaking in an unworthy manner. Every Christian, unless some sin had excluded him, was worthy to partake because he was a Christian. But a Christian might come to it without judging himself, or appreciating as he ought that which the supper brought to his mind, and which Christ had connected with it. He did not discern the Lord's body; and he did not discern, did not judge, the evil in himself. God cannot leave us thus careless. If the believer judges himself, the Lord will not judge him; if we do not judge ourselves, the Lord judges; but when the Christian is judged, he is chastened of the Lord that he may not be condemned with the world. It is the government of God in the hands of the Lord who judges His own house: an important and too much forgotten truth. No doubt the result of all is according to the counsels of God, who displays in it all His wisdom, His patience, and the righteousness of His ways; but this government is real. He desires the good of His people in the end; but He will have holiness, a heart whose condition answers to that which He has revealed (and He has revealed Himself), a walk which is its expression.

The normal state of a Christian is communion, according to the power of that which has been revealed. Is there failure in this—communion is lost, and with it the power to glorify God, a power found nowhere else. But if one judges oneself, there is restoration: the heart being cleansed from the evil by judging it, communion is restored. If one does not judge oneself, God must interpose and correct and cleanse us by discipline—discipline which may even be unto death. (See Job 33, 36; 1 John 5: 16; James 5: 14, 15.)

Discerning our own condition: judging the state of heart, not only the action

There are yet one or two remarks to be made. To "judge" oneself, is not the same word as to be "judged" of the Lord. It is the same that is used in chapter 11: 29, "*discerning* the Lord's body." Thus, what we have to do is not only to judge an evil committed, it is to discern one's condition, as it is manifested in the light—even as God Himself is in the light—by walking in it. This prevents our falling into evil either in act or thought. But if we have fallen, it is not enough to judge the action; it is ourselves we must judge, and the state of heart, the tendency, the neglect, which occasioned our falling into the evil—in a word, that which is not communion with God or that which hinders it. It was thus the Lord dealt with Peter. He did not reproach him for his fault, He judged its root.

Moreover the assembly ought to have power to discern these things. God acts in this way, as we have seen in Job; but the saints have the mind of Christ by the Spirit of Christ, and ought to discern their own condition.

The Christian's position towards Christ in the Lord's Supper: His death the divine negation of sin

The foundation and centre of all this, is the position in

which we stand towards Christ in the Lord's Supper, as the visible centre of communion and the expression of His death; in which sin, all sin, is judged. Now we are in connection with this holy judgment of sin as our portion. We cannot mingle the death of Christ with sin. It is, as to its nature and efficacy, of which the full result will in the end be manifested, the total putting away of sin. It is the divine negation of sin. He died to sin, and that in love to us. It is the absolute holiness of God made sensible and expressed to us in that which took place with regard to sin. It is absolute devotedness to God for His glory in this respect. To bring sin or carelessness into it, is to profane the death of Christ, who died rather than allow sin to subsist before God. We cannot be condemned with the world, because He has died and has put away sin for us; but to bring sin to that which represents this very death in which He suffered for sin is a thing which cannot be borne. God vindicates that which is due to the holiness and the love of a Christ who gave up His life to put away sin. One cannot say, I will not go to the table (that is, I will accept the sin and give up the confession of the value of that death). We examine ourselves, and we go; we re-establish the rights of His death in our conscience—for all is pardoned and expiated as to guilt, and we go to acknowledge these rights as the proof of infinite grace.

The condemnation of the world: why there is "no condemnation" for the believer

The world is condemned. Sin in the Christian is judged, it escapes neither the eye nor the judgment of God. He never permits it; He cleanses the believer from it by chastening him, although He does not condemn, because Christ has borne his sins, and been made sin for him. The death of Christ forms then the centre of communion in the assembly, and the touchstone of conscience, and that, with respect to the assembly, in the Lord's Supper.

Chapter 12

The distinctive marks of the Spirit: the enemy's power and imitative means of deception

THE other branch of the truth, in reference to the assembly of God in general and to the assemblies, is the presence and the gifts of the Holy Ghost. These, as well as the Lord's Supper, are in connection with unity[15] (the individual being responsible in each). It is the subject of spiritual manifestations which the apostle takes up in chapter 12. The first point was to establish the distinctive marks of the Spirit of God. There were evil spirits, who sought to creep in among the Christians, and to speak or act pretending to be the Spirit of God, and thus to confound everything. Christians of the present day hardly believe in such efforts of the enemy as these. Spiritual manifestations are, no doubt, less striking now than at the time of which the apostle speaks; but the enemy adapts his means of deception to the circumstances in which man and the work of God are found. As Peter says in a similar case, "As there were false prophets among you." The enemy does not cease to act. "Forbidding to marry," &c., was the doctrine of devils. In the last days his power will be manifested still more. God can restrain him by the energy of His Spirit, and by the power of the truth; but if he is not bridled, he still acts, deceiving men, and that by such things as one would suppose it impossible (if not deceived oneself) that a man of sober sense could believe. But it is surprising what a man can believe when he is left to himself, without being kept by God, when the power of the enemy is there. We talk of common sense, of reason (very precious they are); but history tells us that God alone gives them or preserves them to us.

[15] We have seen this with regard to the Supper, in chapter 10: 17. Here, chapter 12: 13, we see it with regard to the Holy Ghost.

Here the Spirit of God manifested Himself by the effects of His power, which broke forth in the midst of the assembly, attracting the attention even of the world. The enemy imitated them. The greater part of the Christians at Corinth having been poor Gentiles, without discernment, and stupidly led by the delusions of the enemy, they were the more in danger of being again deceived by this means. When a man is not filled with the Spirit of God, who gives force to the truth in his heart, and clearness to his moral vision, the seductive power of the enemy dazzles his imagination. He loves the marvellous, unbelieving as he may be with regard to the truth. He lacks holy discernment, because he is ignorant of the holiness and character of God, and has not the stability of a soul that possesses the knowledge of God (God Himself, we may say) as his treasure—of a soul which knows that it has all in Him, so that it needs no other marvels. If a man is not thus established by the knowledge of God, the power of the enemy strikes him—pre-occupies him; he cannot shake it off, he cannot account for it. He is a victim to the influence which this power exercises over his mind; the flesh is pleased with it, for in one shape or another the result is always liberty to the flesh.

Long led blindly by the power of evil spirits, the converted Gentiles were hardly in a state to discern and judge them. Strange to say, this demoniac power exercised such an influence that they forgot the importance even of the name of Jesus, or at least forgot that His name was not acknowledged by it. The enemy transforms himself into an angel of light, but he never really owns Jesus Christ as Lord. He will speak of Paul and Silvanus, and would have his part with Christians, but Christ is not acknowledged; and at last it is the breaking up and ruin of those who follow him. An unclean *spirit* would not say, "Lord Jesus," and the Spirit of God could not say "Anathema" to Jesus. But it is a question here of spirits, and not of conversion nor of the necessity of grace working in the heart for the true confession of the name of Jesus— a very true thing, as we know, but not the subject here.

The Holy Spirit here as the link between the assembly and Christ, as well as between the Christian and Christ, to maintain communion

We come now to positive instructions. Nothing more important, more distinctive, more marvellous, than the presence of the Holy Ghost here below in the midst of Christians; the fruit to us, of the perfect work of Christ, but in itself the manifestation of the presence of God among men on the earth. The providence of God manifests His power in the works of creation, and His government which directs all things; but the Holy Ghost is His presence in this world, the testimony that He bears of Himself, of His character.[16]   He is among men to display Himself, not yet in glory, but in power and in testimony of what He is. Christ having accomplished redemption, and having presented the efficacy of His work to God, Sovereign and Judge, the assembly, being ransomed and cleansed by His blood, and united to Him as His Body, became also the vessel of this power which acts in His members. Thus she ought to display this power in holiness—she is responsible to do so. But in this way, as to its exercise, man becomes in fact individually the vessel of this spiritual energy. It is a treasure committed to him. Now the Spirit is, in the first place, the link between the assembly and Christ, as well as between the Christian and Christ. It is by the Spirit that communion is realized and maintained, it is the primary function of the Spirit; and man must be in communion in order to realize the character and discern the will of God, and

[16] It is a very striking truth that God's dwelling with men is the fruit of redemption. He did not dwell with Adam innocent; He could walk in the garden, but did not dwell there. He did not dwell with Abraham.

that, according to the testimony intended to be borne by
the Spirit come down to earth.

The assembly responsible to maintain communion with God, or strength, joy, and spiritual intelligence are lost

But if the assembly does not maintain this communion,
she loses her strength as the responsible witness of God
on earth, and in fact her joy and her spiritual intelligence
also.   God is ever sovereign to act as He chooses, and
Christ cannot fail in His faithfulness to His body; but the
testimony committed to the assembly is no longer so
rendered as to make it felt that God is present on the
earth.   The assembly is not, perhaps, aware of the
estrangement, because she retains for a time much of that
which God has given, which is far beyond all that was
according to nature; and in losing strength she has also
lost the discernment of what she ought to be.   But God
is never mistaken as to the assembly's condition—"Thou
hast left thy first love."   "Except thou repent," says He,
"and do the first works, I will take away thy candlestick"
—a solemn consideration for the assembly, as to her
responsibility, when we reflect on the grace that has been
shown her, on the fruits that have been—and those that
ought to have been—manifested, and on the power given
her to produce them.

The purposes and ways of God

The *purposes* of God for the assembly have their end
and aim in heaven.   They will be accomplished without
the possibility of the least thing failing.   All that is
needful to bring her members there according to His
counsels, Christ will do.   They are redeemed by His blood
to be His.

The *ways* of God are accomplished and unfolded on
the earth for our instruction, both in the assembly and
in individuals.

The distinct presence of the Spirit known and realized as dwelling here below

It is not only in His gifts that the presence of the Spirit of God is manifested. There were prophecies and miracles, men moved by the Holy Ghost, before the day of Pentecost. That which is attributed to faith in Hebrews 11 is often ascribed to the Spirit in the Old Testament. But the Spirit was *promised* in a special way in the Old Testament. He was never at that period the presence of God in the midst of the people, as He dwelt in the assembly. The glory came to take possession of the tabernacle or temple. His Spirit acted in sovereignty outside the order of His house, and could be with them when that glory was gone. But the Holy Ghost sent down from heaven to dwell in the disciples and in the assembly on earth, was the manifestation of the presence of God in His house, of God who was there by the Spirit. And this presence of the Spirit is so distinct, and so plainly noted as a thing known and realized by the first Christians, which demonstrated instead of being demonstrated, that it is spoken of in the Word as being the Holy Ghost Himself. In John 7 it is said, "The Holy Ghost was not yet." In Acts 19 the twelve men say to Paul, "We have not so much as heard whether the Holy Ghost is." It was not a question whether there was a Holy Ghost (every orthodox Jew believed it), but whether this presence of the Holy Ghost Himself dwelling here below, the new Comforter and Guide of the disciples, of which John the Baptist had spoken, had yet taken place. When come down, it was the presence of God in His spiritual temple on earth. The place in which the disciples were gathered together was shaken to show that God was there. Ananias and Sapphira fell down dead before the apostles for having lied to God. Philip is caught away by His power from the presence of the man who had received the knowledge of Jesus by his means.

Manifestations of the Spirit's presence: one Spirit but diversity of gifts

Such was the presence of the Holy Ghost. In our chapter, the apostle speaks of the manifestation of His presence in the gifts which were exercised by the instrumentality of members of the Body, whether for the calling out and edification of the assembly, or in testimony to those outside. Before entering on this subject, he gives the Corinthians—whom the enemy would have deeply deceived—that which would enable them to distinguish between the manifestation of the Holy Ghost and the actings of an evil spirit. He then speaks of gifts.

Now there were not divers spirits, as in the case of demons; there was only one and the same Spirit, but diversity of gifts. This gives occasion to bring in the different relationship (for he speaks of the order of the relations of man with God—the practical energy of which is in the Holy Ghost) in which men, moved by the Holy Ghost, are placed with regard to God and to Christ. The Spirit, one and the same Spirit, acts in them by various manifestations. But in the exercise of these different gifts they were administrators, and there was one Lord, that is, Christ. It was not therefore in them an independent and voluntary power: whatever might be the energy of the Spirit in them, they did not cease to be servants and stewards of Christ, and they were to act in this character, acknowledging in their service the Lordship of Christ. Nevertheless, although it was power in a man, and that it was man who acted, so that he was a servant (and a Man who was Head and who was served, although He was Son of God and Lord of all), yet it was God who wrought, one and the same God who wrought all in all. It is not the Trinity, properly speaking, that is presented here in its own character, but one only Spirit acting in Christians, Jesus Lord, and God acting in the gifts.

Gifts, as manifestations of the Spirit's energy, committed to men under Christ the Lord: the Spirit's distribution according to His will

The gifts are manifestations of the energy of the Spirit thus committed to men, under Christ who is Head and Lord; men were to use them as serving the Lord. Now Christ thought of what was profitable to His people, to those that were His; and the manifestation of the Spirit was given for the profit of souls, of the assembly in general. The apostle notices several of these gifts; but he reminds us again that it is the same Spirit who works in each case, distributing to every one according to His own will. Let the reader remark this passage. The apostle had said that God wrought all these things, and had spoken of the gifts as being manifestations of the Spirit. It might have been supposed that the Spirit was some vague influence, and that one must attribute everything to God without recognizing a personal Spirit. But these operations, which were attributed to God in verse 6, are here attributed to the Spirit; and it is added, that He, the Spirit, distributes to each as He will. It is not therefore an inferior Spirit. Where He works, it is God who works; but these operations in men are gifts distributed according to the will of the Spirit, the Spirit being thus presented as acting personally in this distribution and according to *His* will.

Wisdom, knowledge, faith, and discerning of spirits among the gifts of the Spirit

Some of the gifts may require a short observation. *Wisdom* is the application of divine light to right and wrong, and to all the circumstances through which we pass—an expression which has a wide extent, because it applies to everything with regard to which we have to form a judgment. The Holy Ghost furnishes some in a peculiar way with this wisdom, with a wisdom according to God—a perception of the true nature of things, and of their relationship to each other, and of conduct with regard to both, which, coming from God, guides us through the difficulties of the way, and enables us to avoid that which would place us in a false position towards God and man.

Knowledge is intelligence in the mind of God as it is revealed to us. *Faith* is not here simple faith in the gospel (that is not a distinctive gift which one believer may possess and another not). This is evident. It is the faith, the energy, given by God, which overcomes difficulties, which rises above dangers, which confronts them without being alarmed by them. The *discerning of spirits* is not that of a man's condition of soul—it has nothing to do with it. It is the knowing how to discern, by the mighty energy of the Spirit of God, the actings of evil spirits, and to bring them to light if necessary, in contrast with the action of the Spirit of God.

The Spirit as the centre and living power of unity of the Body

The other gifts require no comment. We must now return to the unity of the Spirit, with which is connected that which the apostle says after having spoken of the gifts. The Spirit was one, he had said, working diversely in the members according to His will. The importance of His personality, and the immense import of His divinity (if we reflect that it is He who works in and by man) is very evident when we observe that He is the centre and the living power of the unity of the whole Body, so that the individuals, in the exercise of their gifts, are but the members of the one and the same Body divinely formed by the power and the presence of the Spirit. This point the apostle develops largely, in connection with the oneness of the body, the mutual dependence of the members, and the relationship of each one to the Body as a whole.

The oneness of the Body: its Producer: its expression

The practical instructions are easily understood, but there are some important points in the general principles. The oneness of the Body is produced by the baptism of the Holy Ghost, and the connection of the members depends upon it. By one Spirit we have all been baptized to be one Body. The Lord's Supper is the expression of this oneness; the Spirit is He who produces it, and who is its strength. The distinctive character of Jew and Gentile—and all other distinctions—was lost in the power of one Spirit common to all, who united them all as redeemed ones in one only Body. The apostle in this verse (13) speaks of the baptism of the Holy Ghost; but the word suggests to him the Supper, the second ordinance of the Lord, and he speaks of drinking into one spirit, alluding, I doubt not, to the Lord's Supper. He does not speak of the Holy Ghost: one spirit was the state of the believers, the word being used in contrast with one Body, associated in one heart and mind by the Spirit —participating in Christ.

The baptism of the Holy Spirit forming Christians into one Body

It is not faith which is union, nor even life, though both are the portion of those united, but the Holy Ghost. The baptism of the Holy Ghost, then, is that which forms Christians into one only Body, and they are all made partakers of, are animated individually by, one and the same Spirit. Thus there are many members but one only Body, and a Body composed of these members, which are dependent the one on the other, and have need of each other. And even those gifts which were the most shining were comparatively of the least value, even as a man clothes and ornaments the least honorable parts of his body, and leaves the more beautiful parts uncovered.

Members of the one Body: their common interest

Another point which the apostle marks, is the common interest that exists among them in that they are members of the one and the same Body. If one suffers, all suffer, since there is but one Body animated by one Spirit. If one is honored, all rejoice. This also depends on the one self-same Spirit who unites and animates them. Moreover this Body is the Body of Christ. "Ye are," says the apostle, "the Body of Christ, and members in particular."

The Christians in one place representing the whole assembly, because inseparably united to the other members of the one Body

Observe, also, here that, although that assembly at Corinth was only a part of the Body of Christ, the apostle speaks of the whole Body; for the assembly there was, according to the principle of its gathering, the Body of Christ as assembled at Corinth. It is true that at the beginning he speaks of all those who call on the name of the Lord Jesus; but in fact he addresses the Corinthian assembly. And the general expression shows that, in the walk of the assembly, and in its general interests, a local assembly cannot be separated from the whole Body of Christians on earth; and the language employed here shows that, as to their position before God, the Christians of one town were considered as representing the whole assembly, as far as regarded that locality; not as independent of the rest, but, on the contrary, as inseparably united to the others, living and acting, with respect to that locality as members of the Body of Christ, and looked upon as such in it, because every Christian formed a part of that Body, and they formed a part of it likewise. From the verses that follow we see that the apostle, while looking upon the Christians there as the Body of Christ, the members of which they were, has in his mind the whole assembly as the assembly of God. In the New

Testament there is no other membership than that of Christ, except that they are members of each other, as forming the entire Body, but never members of *a* church; the idea is different. The word speaks of the members of a body, like that of man as a figure, never of the members of an assembly in the modern sense of the word. We are members of Christ, and consequently of the Body of Christ; so were the Corinthians, as far as that Body was manifested at Corinth.

The Body of Christ, the assembly, looked upon as on the earth

Moreover the Body of Christ, the assembly, is looked at here as a whole upon the earth. God has set in the assembly apostles, prophets, &c.; miracles, healings, tongues. It is very plain that this is on the earth, as were the Corinthians, and that it is the assembly as a whole. Healings and tongues were not in heaven, and the apostles were not those of an individual assembly. In a word it was the Holy Ghost, come down from heaven, who had formed the unity of the Body on earth, and who acted in it by the especial gifts which distinguished the members.

The gifts distinguished from sign-gifts: their character, purpose and promise of continuance

The apostle then points out these gifts, not to give a formal and complete list of them, but to mark the order and importance of those he mentions. Tongues, of which the Corinthians were so proud, are the last gifts named in the list. Some gifts, then, were more excellent than others; they were to be estimated according to the measure in which they served for the edification of the assembly. Those which served this end were to be desired.

It is interesting to remark here the difference of this

chapter and Ephesians 4. Here it is simply power, and men are told in certain cases to be silent, when the power was there; it was the Holy Ghost working as power. In Ephesians 4 it is Christ's care as Head of the Body. No gifts which are signs of power to others are mentioned; only what founds the assembly, edifies the saints, and builds the assembly up; and then there is promise of continuance till we all come. For Christ cannot cease to care for His Body; but sign-gifts may disappear, and they have. Apostles and prophets were the foundation, and in that sense they were, when the foundation was laid, no longer in exercise.

Chapter 13

Something more excellent than gifts—love, as conformity to the nature of God, acting and feeling according to His likeness

NEVERTHELESS there was something more excellent than all gifts. They were the manifestations of the power of God and of the mysteries of His wisdom; love, that of His nature itself.

They might speak with all tongues; they might have prophecy, the knowledge of mysteries, the faith which can remove mountains; they might give all their possessions to feed the poor, and their bodies to be tortured: if they had not love, it was nothing. Love was conformity to the nature of God, the living expression of what He was, the manifestation of having been made partakers of His nature: it was the acting and feeling according to His likeness. This love is developed in reference to others; but others are not the motive, although they are the object. It has its source within; its strength is independent of the objects with which it is occupied.

Thus it can act where circumstances might produce irritation or jealousy in the human heart. It acts according to its own nature in the circumstances; and by judging them according to that nature, they do not act upon the man who is full of love, except so far as they supply occasion for its activity and direct its form. Love is its own motive. In us participation in the divine nature is its only source. Communion with God Himself alone sustains it through all the difficulties it has to surmount in its path. This love is the opposite of selfishness and of self-seeking, and shuts it out, seeking the good of others, even (as to its principle) as God has sought us in grace. (See Eph. 4: 32; 5: 1, 2.) What a power to avoid evil in oneself, to forget all in order to do good!

The qualities of divine love: the time and place of its exercise

It is worthy of note that the qualities of divine love are almost entirely of a passive character.

The first eight qualities pointed out by the Spirit are the expression of this renunciation of self. The three that follow, mark that joy in good which sets the heart free also from that readiness to suppose evil, which is so natural to human nature, on account of its own depth of evil, and that which it also experiences in the world. The last four show its positive energy, which—the source of every kind thought—by the powerful spring of its divine nature, presumes good when it does not see it, and bears with evil when it sees it, covering it by long-suffering and patience; not bringing it to light, but burying it in its own depth—a depth which is unfathomable, because love never changes. One finds nothing but love where it is real; for circumstances are but an occasion for it to act and show itself. Love is always itself, and it is love which is exercised and displayed. It is that which fills the mind: everything else is but a means of awakening the soul that dwells in love to its exercise. This is the divine character. No doubt the time of judgment will come; but our relationships with God are in grace. Love is His nature. It is now the time of its exercise. We represent Him on earth in testimony.

The unchangeable and everlasting character of divine love

In that which is said of love in this chapter we find the reproduction of the divine nature, except that what is said is but the negative of the selfishness of the flesh in us. Now the divine nature changes not and never ceases; love therefore abides ever. Communications from God; the means by which they are made; knowledge, as attained here below, according to which we apprehend the truth in part only, although the whole truth is revealed to us (for we apprehend it in detail, so that we have never the whole at once, the character of our knowledge being to lay hold of different truths singly); all that is characterized by being in part—passes away. Love will not pass away. A child learns; he rejoices too in things that amuse him; when he becomes a man, he requires things in accordance with his intelligence as a man. It was thus with tongues and the edification of the assembly. The time however was coming when they should know even as they were known, not by communications of truths to a capacity that apprehended the truth in its different parts, but they should understand it as a whole in its unity.

Now love subsists already; there are faith and hope also. Not only shall these pass away, but even now, here below, that which is of the nature of God is more excellent than that which is connected with the capacity of human nature, even though enlightened by God, and having for its object the revealed glory of God.

Chapter 14

The edification of the assembly: prophecy and speaking with tongues

BELIEVERS therefore were to follow after and seek for love, while desiring gifts, especially that they might prophesy, because thus they would edify the assembly, and that was the thing to aim at; it was that which love desired and sought, it was that which intelligence required, the two marks of a *man* in Christ, of one to whom Christ is all.

Two verses in this chapter 14 demand a little attention —the 3rd and the 6th. Verse 3 is the effect, or rather the quality, of that which a prophet says, and not a definition. He edifies, he encourages, he comforts, by speaking. Nevertheless these words show the character of what he said. Prophecy is in no wise simply the revelation of future events, although prophets as such have revealed them. A prophet is one who is so in communication with God as to be able to communicate His mind. A teacher instructs according to that which is already written, and so explains its import. But, in communicating the mind of God to souls under grace, the prophet encouraged and edified them. With regard to verse 6, it is plain that coming with tongues (by the use of which the Corinthians, like children, loved to shine in the assembly) he that so spoke edified no one, for he was not understood. Perhaps he did not understand himself, but was the unintelligent instrument of the Spirit, whilst having the powerful impression of the fact that God spoke by his means, so that in the Spirit he felt that he was in communication with God, although his understanding was unfruitful. In any case no one could speak for the edification of the assembly unless he communicated the mind of God.

Revelation and knowledge: prophecy and doctrine

Of such communication the apostle distinguishes two kinds—revelation and knowledge. The latter supposes a revelation already given, of which some one availed himself by the Holy Ghost for the good of the flock. He then points out the gifts which were respectively the means of edifying in these two ways. It is not that the two latter terms (ver. 6) are the equivalents of the two former; but the two things here spoken of as edifying the church were accomplished by means of these two gifts. There might be "prophecy" without its being absolutely a new revelation, although there was more in it than knowledge. It might contain an application of the thoughts of God, an address on the part of God to the soul, to the conscience, which would be more than knowledge, but which would not be a new revelation. God acts therein without revealing a new truth or a new fact. "Knowledge," or "doctrine," teaches truths or explains the Word, a thing very useful to the assembly; but in it there is not the direct action of the Spirit in application, and thus not the direct manifestation of the presence of God to men in their own conscience and heart. When any one teaches, he who is spiritual profits by it; when one prophesies, even he who is not spiritual may feel it, he is reached and judged; and it is the same thing with the Christian's conscience. Revelation, or knowledge, is a perfect division and embraces everything. Prophecy, and doctrine, are in intimate connection with the two; but prophecy embraces other ideas, so that this division does not exactly answer to the first two terms.

The necessity of making oneself understood in speaking with tongues: gifts only to be used as instruments for good

The apostle insists largely on the necessity for making oneself understood, whether one speaks, or sings, or prays.

He desires—and the remark is of all importance in judging men's pretensions to the Spirit—that the understanding be in exercise. He does not deny that they might speak with tongues without the understanding being at all in it—a thing of evident power and utility when persons were present who understood no other language, or whose natural language it was. But, in general, it was an inferior thing when the Spirit did not act upon, and therefore by means of, the understanding in him who spoke. Communion between souls in a common subject, through the unity of the Spirt, did not exist when he who spoke did not understand what he said. The individual speaking did not himself enjoy, as from God, what he communicated to others. If others did not understand it either, it was child's play to utter words without meaning to the hearers. But the apostle desired to understand himself that which he said, although he spoke in many tongues; so that it was not jealousy on his part. He spoke more foreign tongues, by the gift of the Holy Ghost, than they all. But his soul loved the things of God—loved to receive truth intelligently from Him—loved to hold intelligent intercourse with others; and he would rather say five words with his understanding than ten thousand without it in an unknown tongue.

What a marvellous power, what a manifestation of the presence of God—a thing worthy of the deepest attention —and, at the same time, what superiority to all carnal vanity, to the lustre reflected upon the individual by means of gifts—what moral power of the Spirit of God, where love saw nothing in these manifestations of power in gift but instruments to be used for the good of the assembly and of souls! It was the practical force of that love, to the exercise of which, as being superior to gifts, he exhorted the faithful. It was the love and the wisdom of God directing the exercise of His power for the good of those whom He loved. What a position for a man! What simplicity is imparted by the grace of God to one who forgets self in humility and love, and what power in that humility! The apostle confirms his argument by the effect that would be produced on strangers who might come into the assembly, or on unenlightened Christians, if they heard languages spoken which no one understood: they would think them mad. Prophecy, reaching their conscience, would make them feel that God was there— was present in the assembly of God.

The exercise of gifts regulated

Gifts were abundant in Corinth. Having regulated that which concerned moral questions, the apostle in the second place regulates the exercise of those gifts. Every one came with some manifestation of the power of the Holy Ghost, of which they evidently thought more than of conformity to Christ. Nevertheless the apostle acknowledges in it the power of the Spirit of God, and gives rules for its exercise. Two or three might speak with tongues, provided there was an interpreter, so that the assembly might be edified. And this was to be done one at a time, for it appears they even spoke several at once. In the same way as to the prophets: two or three might speak, the others would judge if it really came from God. For, if it were given to them of God, all might prophesy; but only one at a time, that all might learn—a dependence always good for the most gifted prophets—and that all might be comforted. The spirits of the prophets (that is to say, the impulse of the power in the exercise of gifts) were subject to the guidance of the moral intelligence which the Spirit bestowed on the prophets. They were, on God's part, masters of themselves in the use of these gifts, in the exercise of this marvellous power which wrought in them. It was not a divine fury, as the pagans said of their diabolical inspiration, which carried them away; for God could not be the author of confusion in the assembly, but of peace. In a word we see that this power was committed to man in his moral responsibility; an important principle, which is invariable in the ways of God. God saved man by grace, when he had failed in his responsibility; but all that He has committed to man, whatever may be the divine energy of the gift, man holds as responsible to use it for the glory of God, and consequently for the good of others and especially for the assembly.

Directions as to women's silence in the assembly or in public

Women were to be silent in the assembly: it was not permitted to them to speak. They were to remain in obedience and not to direct others. The law moreover held the same language. It would be a shame to hear them speak in public. If they had questions to ask, they might inquire of their husbands at home.

The proof of being filled by the Spirit — the acknowledgment that what the apostle wrote came from God

With all their gifts, the Word did not come out from the Corinthians, nor had it come unto them only; they ought to submit to the universal order of the Spirit in the assembly. If they pretended to be led by the Spirit, let them acknowledge (and this would prove it) that the things which the apostle wrote to them were the commandments of the Lord: a very important assertion; a responsible and serious position of this wonderful servant of God.

What a mixture of tenderness, of patience, and of authority! The apostle desires that the faithful should come to the truth and to order, conducted by their own affections; not fearing, if necessary for their good, to avail himself of an authority without appeal, as speaking directly from God—an authority which God would justify if the apostle was forced unwillingly to use it. If any were

ignorant that he wrote by the Spirit with the authority of
God, it was ignorance indeed; let such be given up to their
ignorance. Spiritual and simple men would be delivered
from such pretensions. Those who were really filled with
the Spirit would acknowledge that what the apostle wrote
came immediately from God, and was the expression of
His wisdom, of that which became Him: for often there
may be the recognition of divine or even human wisdom
when it is found, where there was not the ability to find
it, nor, if it were perceived in part, the power to set it
forth with authority. Meanwhile the man of pretension,
reduced to this place, would find the place profitable, and
that which he needed.

The apostle's assertion as to the inspiration
of the Epistles

We shall also observe here the importance of this assertion of the apostle's with regard to the inspiration of the
epistles. That which he taught for the details even of the
order of the assembly, was so really given of God, came
so entirely from God, that they were the commandments
of the Lord. For doctrine we have, at the end of the
Epistle to the Romans, the same declaration that it was
by means of prophetic writings that the gospel was dis-
seminated among the nations.

Encouragement of the exercise of gifts in due order

The apostle resumes his instructions by saying, that
they should desire to prophesy, not forbid to speak with
tongues, and that all should be done with order and
propriety.

Chapter 15

The denial of the resurrection of the dead

BUT other evils had found means to introduce themselves into the midst of the shining gifts which were
exercised in the bosom of the flock at Corinth. The resur-

rection of the dead was denied. Satan is wily in his dealings. Apparently it was only the body that was in question; nevertheless the whole gospel was at stake, for if the
dead rose not, then Christ was not risen. And if Christ
was not risen, the sins of the faithful were not put away,
and the gospel was not true. The apostle therefore reserved this question for the end of his epistle, and he
enters into it thoroughly.

Salvation dependent on the fact of the resurrection: complete and positive testimony as to it.

First, he reminds them of that which he had preached
among them as the gospel, that Christ died for our sins
according to the Scriptures, and was raised again according to the Scriptures. This then was the means of their
salvation, if they continued in it, unless they had believed
in vain. Here at least was a very solid foundation for his
argument: their salvation (unless all that they had believed was but a profitless fable) depended on the fact of
the resurrection, and was bound up with it. But if the
dead rose not, Christ was not risen, for He had died. The
apostle begins therefore by establishing this fact through
the most complete and positive testimonies, including his
own testimony, since he had himself seen the Lord. Five
hundred persons had seen Him at once, the greater part
of whom were still alive to bear witness of it.

Christ is risen: if not, the preaching and faith of Christians are vain

Observe, in passing, that the apostle can speak of nothing without a moral effect being produced in his heart,
because he thinks of it with God. Thus, verses 8-10, he
calls to mind the state of things with regard to himself
and to the other apostles, and that which grace had done;
and then, his heart unburdened, he returns to his subject.
The testimony of every divine witness was the same. Every-

thing declared that Christ was risen; everything depended on the fact that He was so. This was his starting-point. If, said he, that which was preached among you is that Christ was raised from the dead, how happens it that some among you say there is no resurrection of the dead? If there is none, Christ is not risen; if He is not risen, the preaching of His witnesses is vain, the faith of Christians vain. Nor that only; but these witnesses are false witnesses, for they had declared, with respect to God, that He had raised up Christ from the dead. But God had not raised Him up if the dead do not rise. And in that case their faith was vain: they were yet in their sins; and those who had already fallen asleep in Christ had perished. Now, if it be in this life only that the believer has hope in Christ, he is of all men the most miserable; he does but suffer as to this world. But it is not so, for Christ is risen.

Christ risen from among all the other dead

Here, however, it is not only a general doctrine that the dead are raised. Christ, in rising, came up *from among* the dead. It is the favor and the power of God come in,[17] to bring back from among the dead the One who had in His grace gone down into death to accomplish and to display the deliverance of man in Christ from the power of Satan and of death; and to put a public seal on the work of redemption, to exhibit openly in man the victory over all the power of the enemy. Thus Christ arose from among all the other dead (for death could not hold Him), and established the glorious principle of this divine and

---

[17] Christ could say, "Destroy this temple, and in three days I will raise it up," for He who dwells in the temple is God. It is also said that He was raised up by the Spirit, and at the same time by the glory of the Father. But here He is viewed as Man who has undergone death; and God intervenes, that He may not remain in it, because here the object is, not to show forth the glory of the Lord's Person, but to prove our resurrection, since He, a dead Man, has been raised. By man came death; by Man, resurrection. While demonstrating that He was the Lord from heaven, the apostle always speaks here of the Man Christ.

complete deliverance, and He became the first-fruits of them that slept, who having His life, await the exercise of His power, which will awaken them by virtue of the Spirit that dwells in them.

The peculiar character of resurrection and the peculiar place of Christ: Christ and His people inseparably identified

This evidently gives a very peculiar character to the resurrection. It is not only that the dead rise, but that God, by His power, brings back certain persons from among the dead, on account of the favor which He has for them, and in connection with the life and the Spirit which are in them. Christ has a quite peculiar place. Life was in Him, and He is our life. He gained this victory by which we profit. He is of right the first-fruits. It was due to His glory. Had He not gained the victory, we should always have remained in prison. He had power Himself to resume life, but the great principle is the same; it is not only a resurrection of the dead, but those who are alive according to God arise as the objects of His favor, and by the exercise of that power which wills to have them for Himself and with Himself—Christ, the first-fruits; those who are Christ's, at His coming. We are associated with Christ in resurrection. We come out like Him, not only from death, but from the dead. We mark, too, here how Christ and His people are inseparably identified. If they do not rise, He is not risen. He was as really dead as we can be, has taken in grace our place under death, was a Man as we are men (save sin) so truly that, if you deny this result for us, you deny the fact as to Him; and the object and foundation of faith itself fails. This identification of Christ with men, so as to be able to draw a conclusion from us to Him, is full of power and blessing. If the dead do not rise, He is not risen; He was as truly dead as we can be.

Victory over death and him who had the power of it by One who became Man

It needed to be by man. No doubt the power of God can call men back from the tomb. He will do so, acting in the Person of His Son, to whom all judgment is given. But that will not be a victory gained in human nature over death which held men captive. This it is which Christ has done. He was willing to be given up to death for us, in order (as Man) to gain the victory for us over death and over him who had the power of death. By man came death; by Man, resurrection. Glorious victory! Complete triumph! We come out of the state where sin and its consequences fully reached us. Evil cannot enter the place into which we are brought out. We have crossed the frontiers for ever. Sin, the power of the enemy, remains outside this new creation, which is the fruit of the power of God after evil had come in, and which the responsibility of man shall not mar. It is God who maintains it in connection with Himself: it depends on Him.

Adam and Christ as heads of two families characterized by death and life

There are two great principles established here: by man, death; by Man, the resurrection of the dead; Adam and Christ as heads of two families. In Adam all die; in Christ all shall be made alive. But here there is an all-important development in connection with the position of Christ in the counsels of God. One side of this truth is the dependence of the family, so to call it, upon its head. Adam brought death into the midst of his descendants—those who are in relation with himself. This is the principle which characterizes the history of the first Adam. Christ, in whom is life, brings life into the midst of those who are His—communicates it to them. This principle characterizes the second Adam, and those who are His in Him. But it is life in the power of resurrection, without which it could not have been communicated to them. The grain of wheat would have been perfect in itself, but would have remained alone. But He died for their sins, and now He imparts life to them, all their sins being forgiven them.

God's order in the resurrection: its three steps: the resurrection of judgment—of those who are not Christ's

Now, in the resurrection, there is an order according to the wisdom of God for the accomplishment of His counsels—Christ, the first-fruits; those who are Christ's, at His coming again. Thus those who are in Christ are quickened according to the power of the life which is in Christ; it is the resurrection of life. But this is not the whole extent of resurrection as acquired by Christ, in gaining the victory over death according to the Spirit of holiness. The Father has given Him power over *all* flesh, that He should give eternal life to as many as the Father had given Him. The latter are those of whom this chapter treats essentially, because its subject is resurrection among Christians; and the apostle, the Spirit Himself, loves to speak on the subject of the power of eternal life in Christ. Yet he cannot entirely omit the other part of the truth. The resurrection of the dead, he tells us, is come by man. But he is not here speaking of the communication of life in Christ. In connection with this last and nearer part of his subject, he does not touch upon the resurrection of the wicked; but after the coming of Christ he introduces the end, when He shall have given up the kingdom to the Father. With the kingdom is introduced the power of Christ exercised over all things—a different thought entirely from the communication of life to His own.

There are three steps therefore in these events: first, the resurrection of Christ; then, the resurrection of those who are His, at His coming; afterwards, the end, when

He shall have given up the kingdom to the Father. The first and the second are the accomplishment in resurrection of the power of life in Christ and in His people. When He comes, He takes the kingdom; He takes His great power and acts as King. From His coming then to the end is the development of His power, in order to subdue all things to Himself; during which all power and all authority shall be abolished. For He must reign till all His enemies are under His feet; the last subdued will be death. Here then, as the effect of His power only, and not in connection with the communication of life, we find the resurrection of those who are not His; for the destruction of death is their resurrection. They are passed over in silence: only that death, such as we see it, has no longer dominion over them. Christ has the right and the power, in virtue of His resurrection and of His having glorified the Father, to destroy the dominion of death over them, and to raise them up again. This will be the resurrection of judgment. Its effect is declared elsewhere.

The Son Himself subject as Man that God may be all in all

When He has put all His enemies under His feet, and has given back the kingdom to His Father (for it is never taken from Him, nor given to another, as happens with human kingdoms), then the Son Himself is subject to Him who has put all things under Him, in order that God may be all in all. The reader should observe, that it is the counsels of God with regard to the government of all things which is here spoken of, and not His nature; and moreover it is the Son, as Man, of whom these things are said. This is not an arbitrary explanation: the passage is from Psalm 8, the subject of which is the exaltation of Man to the position of head of all things, God putting all things under His feet. Nothing, says the apostle, is excepted (Heb. 2:8) save, as he adds here, that He is

necessarily excepted who put all things under Him. When
the Man Christ, the Son of God, has in fact accomplished this subjugation, He gives back to God the universal power which had been committed to Him, and the
mediatorial *kingdom,* which He held as man, ceases. He
is again subject, as He was on earth. He does not cease
to be one with the Father, even as He was so while living
in humiliation on the earth, although saying at the same
time, "Before Abraham was, I am." But the mediatorial
government of man has disappeared—is absorbed in the
supremacy of God, to which there is no longer any opposition. Christ will take His eternal place, a Man, the
Head of the whole redeemed family, being at the same
time God blessed for ever, one with the Father. In Psalm
2 we see the Son of God, as born on earth, King in Zion,
rejected when He presented Himself on earth; in Psalm
8 the result of His rejection, exalted as Son of Man at the
head of all that the hand of God has made. Then we
find Him here laying down this conferred authority, and
resuming the normal position of humanity, namely, that
of subjection to Him who has put all things under Him;
but through it all, never changing His divine nature, nor
—save so far as exchanging humiliation for glory—His
human nature either. But God is now all in all, and the
special government of man in the Person of Jesus—a government with which the assembly is associated (see Eph.
1: 20-23, which is a quotation from the same psalm)—is
merged in the immutable supremacy of God, the final and
normal relationship of God with His creature. We shall
find the Lamb omitted in that which is said in Revelation
21: 1-8, speaking of this same period.

Resurrection by the Man Christ Jesus: a revelation to Paul of all the ways of God with regard to resurrection

Thus we find in this passage resurrection by Man—
death having entered by man; the relationship of the

saints with Jesus, the source and the power of life, the consequence being His resurrection, and theirs at His coming; power over all things committed to Christ, the risen Man; afterwards the kingdom given back to God the Father, the tabernacle of God with men, and the Man Christ, the Second Adam, eternally a Man subject to the Supreme—this last a truth of infinite value to us (the resurrection of the wicked, though supposed in the resurrection brought in by Christ, not being the direct subject of the character). The reader must now remark that this passage is a *revelation*, in which the Spirit of God, having fixed the apostle's thoughts upon Jesus and the resurrection, suddenly interrupts the line of his argument, announcing—with that impulse which the thought of Christ always gave to the mind and heart of the apostle—all the ways of God in Christ with regard to the resurrection, to the connection of those that are His with Him in that resurrection, and the government and dominion which belong to Him as risen, as well as the eternal nature of His relationship, as Man, to God. Having communicated these thoughts of God, which were revealed to him, he resumes the thread of his argument in verse 29. This part ends with verse 34, and after which he treats the question, which they had brought forward as a difficulty—in what manner should the dead be raised?

Baptized for the dead

By taking the verses 20-28 (which contain so important a revelation in a passage that is complete in itself) as a parenthesis, the verses 29-34 become much more intelligible, and some expressions, which have greatly harassed interpreters, have a tolerably determined sense. The apostle had said, in verse 16, "If the dead rise not," and then, that if such were the case, those who had fallen asleep in Jesus had perished, and that the living were of all men most miserable. At verse 29 he returns to these points, and speaks of those who are baptized for the dead, in connection with the assertion, that if there were no resurrection those who had fallen asleep in Christ had perished; "If," he says, repeating more forcibly the expression in verse 16, "the dead rise not at all;" and then shows how entirely he is himself in the second case he had spoken of, "of all men most miserable," and almost in the case of perishing also, being every moment in danger, striving as with wild beasts, dying daily. Baptized, then, for the dead is to become a Christian with the view fixed on those who have fallen asleep in Christ, and particularly as being slain for Him, taking one's portion with the dead, yea, with the dead Christ; it is the very meaning of baptism (Rom. 6). How senseless if they do not rise! As in 1 Thessalonians 4, the subject, while speaking of all Christians, is looked at in the same way. The word translated *"for"* is frequently used in these epistles for "in view of," "with reference to."

Resurrection proving that death does not touch the soul though dissolving its intimate union with the body

We have seen that verses 20-28 form a parenthesis. Verse 29 then is connected with verse 18. Verses 30-32 relate to verse 19. The historical explanation of these last verses is found in the second epistle. (See chap. 1: 8, 9; 4: 8-12.) I do not think that verse 32 should be taken literally. The word translated, "I have fought with beasts," is usually employed in a figurative sense, to be in conflict with fierce and implacable enemies. In consequence of the violence of the Ephesians he had nearly lost his life, and even despaired of saving it; but God had delivered him. But to what purpose all these sufferings, if the dead rise not? And observe here, that although the resurrection proves that death does not touch the soul (compare Luke 20: 38), yet the apostle does not think of immortality,[18] apart from resurrection. God has to do so, with man, and man is composed of body and of soul. He gives account in the judgment of the things done in the body. It is when raised from the dead that he will do so. The intimate union between the two, quite distinct as they are, forms the spring of life, the seat of responsibility, the means of God's government with regard to His creatures, and the sphere in which His dealings are displayed. Death dissolves this union; and although the soul survives, and is happy or miserable, the existence of the complete man is suspended, the judgment of God is not applied, the believer is not yet clothed with glory. Thus to deny the resurrection, was to deny the true relationship of God with man, and to make death the end of man, destroying man as God contemplates him, and making him perish like a beast. Compare the Lord's argument in that passage in Luke of which I have already quoted one verse.

The desire with which the denial of the resurrection is linked: the reason for it

Alas, the denial of the resurrection was linked with the desire to unbridle the senses. Satan introduced it into the heart of Christians through their communication with persons with whom the Spirit of Christ would have had no communion.

They needed to have their conscience exercised, to be awakened, in order that righteousness might have its place there. It is the lack of that which is commonly the true source of heresies. They failed in the knowledge *of God*. It was to the shame of these Christians. God grant us to take heed to it! It is the great matter even in questions of doctrine.

[18] But, remark, mortality in the New Testament is never applied to anything, but the body, and that exclusively and emphatically, "this mortal" and the like. The separate existence of the soul, as not dying with the body, is taught plainly enough in Scripture, and not merely for the Christian (as to whom it is evident, for we are with Christ) but for all, as in Luke 20: 38; 12: 4, 5, and the end of chapter 16.

The physical mode of the resurrection: the glorious abode of the soul — a body suited to the creature that possessed it

But further, the inquisitive spirit of man would fain be satisfied with respect to the physical mode of the resurrection. The apostle did not gratify it, while rebuking the stupid folly of those who had occasion every day to see analogous things in the creation that surrounded them. Fruit of the power of God, the raised body would be, according to the good pleasure of Him who gave it anew for the glorious abode of the soul, a body of honor, which, having passed through death, would assume that glorious condition which God had prepared for it—a body suited to the creature that possessed it, but according to the supreme will of Him who clothed the creature with it. There were different kinds of bodies; and as wheat was not the bare grain that had been sown, although a plant of its nature and not another, so should it be with the raised man. Different also were the glories of heavenly and earthly bodies: star differed from star in glory. I do not think that this passage refers to degrees of glory in heaven, but to the fact that God distributes glory as He pleases. Heavenly glory and earthly glory are however plainly put in contrast, for there will be an earthly glory.

The character of the resurrection

And observe here, that it is not merely the fact of the resurrection which is set forth in this passage, but also its character. For the saints it will be a resurrection to heavenly glory. Their portion will be bodies incorruptible, glorious, vessels of power, spiritual. This body, sown as the grain of wheat for corruption, shall put on glory and incorruptibility.[19] It is only the saints that are here spoken

[19] It is a striking collateral proof of the completeness of our redemption, and the impossibility of our coming into judgment, that we are raised in glory. We are glorified before we arrive before the judgment-seat. Christ will have come and changed our vile body and fashioned it like His glorious body.

of—"They also that are heavenly," and in connection with
Christ, the Second Adam. The apostle had said that the
first body was "natural." Its life was that of the living
soul; as to the body it partook of that kind of life which
the other animals possessed—whatever might be its superiority as to its relationship with God, in that God Himself
had breathed into his nostrils the spirit of life, so that
man was thus in a special way in relationship with God
(of His race, as the apostle said at Athens). "Adam, the
son of God," said the Holy Ghost in Luke—made in the
image of God. His conduct should have answered to it,
and God had revealed Himself to him in order to place
him morally in the position that was suitable to this
breath of life which he had received. He had become—
free as he was from death by the power of God who sustained him, or mortal by the sentence of Him who had
formed him—a living soul. There was not the quickening
power in himself. The first Adam was simply a man—
"the first man Adam."

The Last Adam giving life to whom He would

The Word of God does not express itself thus with regard to Christ, when speaking of Him in this passage as
the Last Adam. He could not be the Last Adam without
being a Man; but it does not say, "The last Man was a
quickening Spirit," but "the Last Adam;" and when it
speaks of Him as the Second Man, adds that He was
"from heaven." Christ had not only life as a living soul,
He had the power of life, which could impart life to
others. Although He was a Man on earth, He had life
in Himself; accordingly He quickened whom He would.
Nevertheless it is as the Last Adam, the Second Man,
the Christ, that the Word here speaks of Him. It is not
only that God quickens whom He will, but the Last Adam,
Christ, the Head, spiritually, of the new race, has this
power in Himself: and therefore it is said—for it is al-

ways Jesus on earth who is in question—"He hath given
to the Son to have life *in Himself*." Of us it is said, "God
hath given to us eternal life, and this life is *in His Son:*
he who hath the Son hath life, and he that hath not the
Son of God hath not life." Howbeit that which is of the
Spirit is not that which was first, but that which is natural, that is, that which has the natural life of the soul.
That which is spiritual, which has its life from the power
of the Spirit, comes after. The first man is of the earth—
has his origin, such as he is (God having breathed into
his nostrils a spirit or breath of life), from the earth.
Therefore he is of the dust, even as God said, "Dust thou
art, and unto dust shalt thou return." The Last Adam,
though He was as truly Man as the first, is from heaven.

United to the Head of a spiritual race and bearing His image

As belonging to the first Adam, we inherit his condition,
we are as he is: as participating in the life of the Second,
we have part in the glory which He possesses as Man,
we are as He is, we exist according to His mode of being,
His life being ours. Now the consequence here is that, as
we have borne the image of the earthy, we shall also bear
the image of the heavenly. Observe here, that the first
Adam and the Last or Second Man, respectively, are
looked at as in that condition into which they entered
when their respective trials under responsibility had ended;
and those who are connected with the one and the other
inherit the condition and the consequences of the work of
the one and the other, as thus tested. It is the fallen
Adam who is the father of a race born after his image—
a fallen and guilty race, sinful and mortal. He had failed,
and committed sin, and lost his position before God, was
far from Him, when he became the father of the human
race. If the corn of wheat falling into the ground does not
die, it bears no fruit; it it die, it bears much fruit. Christ

had glorified God, made expiation for sin, and was raised in righteousness; had overcome death and destroyed the power of Satan, before He became as a quickening Spirit, the Head of a spiritual race,[20] to whom—united to Himself—He communicates all the privileges that belong to the position before God which He has acquired, according to the power of that life by which He quickens them.* It is a risen and glorified Christ whose image we shall bear, as we now bear the image of a fallen Adam.

A positive revelation as to the enjoyment of incorruptibility by all the saints: immortality of the mortal body

Flesh and blood, not merely sin, cannot enter the kingdom of heaven. Corruption (for such we are) cannot inherit that which is incorruptible. This leads the apostle to a positive revelation of that which will take place with regard to the enjoyment of incorruptibility by all the saints. Death is conquered. It is not necessary that death should come upon all, still less that all should undergo actual corruption; but it is not possible for flesh and blood to inherit the kingdom of glory. But we shall not all sleep; there are some who will be changed without dying. The dead shall be raised incorruptible, and we (for redemption being accomplished and Christ ready to judge the quick and the dead, the apostle always looked at it as a thing immediately before his eyes, ready to take place any moment) shall be changed (a change equivalent to resurrection); for that which is corruptible, if not already in dust and corruption, shall put on incorruptibility; that which is mortal, immortality. We see that this relates to the body; it is in his body that man is mortal, even when he has eternal life, and shall live by Christ and with

---

[20] It is not that as Son of God He could not quicken at all times, as indeed He did. But in order to our partaking with Him, all this was needed and accomplished, and here He is looked at as Himself risen from the dead, the heavenly Man. Thus also it is founded in divine righteousness.

Christ. The power of God will form the saints whether living or dead for the inheritance of glory.

Death entirely conquered for the Christian: the dead are raised and the living changed at the coming of Christ

Take especial notice of what has just been said. Death is entirely conquered—annulled in its power—for the Christian. He possesses a life (Christ risen), which sets him above death, not perhaps physically, but morally. It has lost all its power over his soul, as the fruit of sin and judgment. It is so entirely conquered, that there are some who will not die at all. All Christians have Christ for their life. If He is absent and if He does not return—as will be the case as long as He sits on His Father's throne, and our life is hid with Him in God—we undergo death physically according to the sentence of God; that is to say, the soul is separated from the mortal body. When He shall return and exercise His power, having risen up from the Father's throne to take His people to Himself before He exercises judgment, death has no power at all over them: they do not pass through it. That the others are raised from the dead is a proof of power altogether divine, and more glorious even than that which created man from the dust. That the living are changed proves a perfection of accomplished redemption, and a power of life in Christ which had left no trace, no remains, of the judgment of God as to them, nor of the power of the enemy, nor of the thraldom of man to the consequences of his sin. In place of all that, is an exercise of divine power, which manifests itself in the absolute, complete, and eternal deliverance of the poor guilty creature who before was under it —a deliverance that has its perfect manifestation in the glory of Christ, for He had subjected Himself in grace to the condition of man under death for sin; so that to faith it is always certain, and accomplished in His Person. But the resurrection of the dead and the change of the living will be its actual accomplishment for all who are His at His coming. What a glorious deliverance is that which is wrought by the resurrection of Christ, who—sin entirely blotted out, righteousness divinely glorified and made good, Satan's power destroyed—transports us by virtue of an eternal redemption, and by the power of a life which has abolished death, into an entirely new sphere, where evil cannot come, nor any of its consequences, and where the favor of God in glory shines upon us perfectly and for ever! It is that which Christ has won for us, according to the eternal love of God our Father, who gave Him to us to be our Saviour.

The instantaneous accomplishment of this change at an unexpected moment, by the power of God

At an unexpected moment we shall enter into this scene, ordained by the Father, prepared by Jesus. The power of God will accomplish this change in an instant: the dead shall rise; we shall be changed. The last trumpet is but a military allusion, as it appears to me, when the whole troop wait for the last signal to set out all together.

Death's character completely changed by what its Victor has done: fear gives place to thanks

In the quotation from Isaiah 25: 8 we have a remarkable application of Scripture. Here it is only the fact that death is thus swallowed up in victory, for which the passage is quoted; but the comparison with Isaiah shows us that it will be, not at the end of the world, but at a period when, by the establishment of the kingdom of God in Zion, the veil, under which the heathen have dwelt in ignorance and darkness, shall be taken off their face. The whole earth shall be enlightened, I do not say at the moment, but at the period. But this certainty of the destruction of death procures us a present confidence, although death still exists. Death has lost its sting, the grave its victory. All is changed by the grace which, at the end, will bring in this triumph. But meantime, by revealing to us the favor of God who bestows it, and the accomplishment of the redemption which is its basis, it has completely changed the character of death. Death, to the believer who must pass through it, is only leaving that which is mortal; it no longer bears the terror of God's judgment, nor that of the power of Satan. Christ has gone into it and borne it and taken it away totally and for ever. Nor that only,—He has taken its source away. It was sin which sharpened and envenomed that sting. It was the law which, presenting to the conscience exact righteousness, and the judgment of God which required the accomplishment of that law, and pronounced a curse on those who failed in it,—it was the law which gave sin its force to the conscience, and made death doubly formidable. But Christ was made sin, and bore the curse of the law, being made a curse for His own who were under the law; and thus, while glorifying God perfectly with regard to sin, and to the law in its most absolute requirements, He has completely delivered us from the one and the other, and, at the same time, from the power of death, out of which He came victorious. All that death can do to us, is to take us out of the scene in which it exercises its power, to bring us into that in which it has none. God, the Author of these counsels of grace, in whom is the power that accomplishes them, has given us this deliverance by Jesus Christ our Lord. Instead of fearing death, we render thanks to Him who has given us the victory by Jesus. The great result is to be with Jesus and like Jesus, and to see Him as He is. Meanwhile we labor in the scene where death exercises its power—where Satan uses it, if God allows him, to stop us in our way. We labor although there are difficulties, with entire confidence, knowing what will be the infallible result. The path may be beset by the enemy; the end will be the fruit of the counsels and the power of our God, exercised on our behalf according to that which we have seen in Jesus, who is the

Head and the manifestation of the glory which His own shall enjoy.

Christ's power over all things: His association of His own with Himself

To sum up what has been said, we see the two things in Christ: first, power over all things, death included; He raises up even the wicked: and secondly, the association of His own with Himself. With reference therefore to the latter, the apostle directs our eyes to the resurrection of Christ Himself. He not only raises up others, but He has been raised up Himself from the dead. He is the first-fruits of them that *sleep*. But before His resurrection He died for our sins. All that separated us from God is entirely put away—death, the wrath of God, the power of Satan, sin, disappear, as far as we are concerned, in virtue of the work of Christ; and He is made to us that righteousness which is our title to heavenly glory. Nothing remains of that which appertained to His former human estate, except the everlasting favor of God who brought Him there. Thus it is a resurrection from among the dead by the power of God in virtue of that favor, because He was the delight of God, and in His exaltation His righteousness is accomplished.

The foundation of resurrection

For us it is a resurrection founded on redemption, and which we enjoy even now in the power of a life which brings the effect and the strength of both into our hearts, enlightened by the Holy Ghost who is given to us. At the coming of Christ the accomplishment will take place in fact for our bodies.

The Corinthians exhorted and encouraged as to practice

With regard to practice, the assembly at Corinth was in a very poor condition; and being asleep as to righteousness, the enemy sought to lead them astray as to faith also. Nevertheless, as a body, they kept the foundation; and as to external spiritual power, it shone very brightly.

Chapter 16

Paul's plans: the collection for the poor saints at Jerusalem: the open door and many adversaries his motive for remaining at Ephesus

THE apostle, in his letter, had treated of the disorder that reigned among these believers, and his spirit was to a certain degree relieved by fulfilling this duty towards them; for, after all, they were Christians and an assembly of God. In the last chapter he speaks to them in the sense of this, although he could not make up his mind to go to Corinth, for he had intended to visit them in going to Macedonia, and a second time in returning thence. He does not say here why he did not go thither on his way to Macedonia, and he speaks with uncertainty as to his sojourn at Corinth when he should arrive there on his return from Macedonia; if the Lord permitted, he would tarry awhile with them. The Second Epistle will explain all this. In their existing state his heart would not allow him to visit them. But he treats them tenderly, nevertheless, as still beloved Christians, giving them directions suited to the circumstances of the moment. They were to make a collection for the poor saints at Jerusalem, as had been arranged with the apostles when Paul left Jerusalem as the recognized apostle of the Gentiles. This was not to be done in haste when he came, but by laying up every week in proportion to their prosperity. He would send persons chosen by the Corinthians, or take them with him if he went himself to Jerusalem. He thought of remaining till Pentecost at Ephesus, where a great door was opened to him and there were many adversaries. If these two things go together, it is a motive for remaining; the open door is an inducement on the part of God, the activity of adversaries makes it necessary with regard to the enemy. A closed door is a different thing from opposition. People do not hearken if the door is shut; God does not act to draw attention. If God is acting, the assiduity of the enemy is but a reason for not abandoning the work. It appears (chap. 15: 32) that Paul had already suffered much at Ephesus, but he still continued his work there. He could not pour out his heart on the subject to the Corinthians, seeing the state they were in. He does it in the Second Epistle, when the first had produced the effect he desired. There was a tumult afterwards at Ephesus, stirred up by the craftsmen, in consequence of which Paul left the city (Acts 19). Verses 21, 22, of this chapter in Acts show us the period at which he wrote this letter. The danger to his life had preceded it, but he remained at Ephesus after that. The tumult closed the door and sent him away.

Apollos as sharing Paul's feeling and one with him

In Acts 19: 22 we see that he had sent Timothy into Macedonia. In our epistle he supposes that he might go on as far as Corinth. If he came, the Corinthians were to receive him as they would have received Paul. He had begged Apollos to go to them; he had already been made a blessing to them; and Paul thought he might be so again. He did not fear that Apollos would displace him in the heart of the Corinthians. But Apollos shared the apostle's feeling; he was not inclined to recognize, or by his presence to have the appearance of upholding, that which prevented Paul going thither; and the more so because there were some in the assembly at Corinth who wished to use his name as the standard of a party. Free in his movements, he would act according to the judgment which the Lord would enable him to form.

Paul's ardent desire for their blessing: his joyful recognition of the active charity of three brethren

After speaking of Apollos, the apostle's mind turns again to his children in the faith, dear to him, whatever their faults might be. Verses 13, 14, are the effusion of a heart which forgot these faults in the ardent desire of a charity that only thought of their blessing according to the Spirit. Three Corinthians had brought him supplies; it does not appear to have been on the part of the assembly, nor that it was any testimony of its love which had refreshed the apostle's heart. He would have the Corinthians to rejoice at it. He does not doubt that they loved him enough to be refreshed because it was so. Their charity had not thought of it beforehand; but he expresses his conviction that they took pleasure in the thought of his heart being refreshed. It is touching to see here, that the apostle's charity suggests that which grace would produce on the heart of the Corinthians, communicating that which they probably would not otherwise have known of—the active charity of three brethren of the assembly; and, in love uniting them to his joy, if they had not been united to that which occasioned it. The flame of charity communicates itself by rising above coldness, and reaching the depths of divine life in the heart; and, once communicated, the soul, before unkindled, glows now with the same fire.

Four channels of ministry

We find in this chapter four channels, so to speak, of ministry. First, the apostle, sent direct from the Lord and by the Holy Ghost. Secondly, persons associated with the apostle in his work, and acting at his desire, and (in the case of Timothy) one pointed out by prophecy. Thirdly, an entirely independent laborer, partly instructed by others (see Acts 17: 26), but acting where he saw fit,

according to the Lord and to the gift he had received.
Fourthly, one who gives himself to the service of the
saints, as well as others who helped the apostle and
labored. Paul exhorts the faithful to submit themselves
to such, and to all those who helped in the work and
labored. He would also have them acknowledge those
who refreshed his heart by their service of devotedness.
Thus we find the simple and important principle according
to which all the best affections of the heart are developed,
namely, the acknowledgment of every one according to the
manifestation of grace and of the power of the Holy Ghost
in him. The Christian man submits to those who addict
themselves to the service of the saints; he acknowledges
those who manifest grace in a special way. They are not
persons officially nominated and consecrated who are
spoken of here. It is the conscience and the spiritual
affection of Christians which acknowledges them according to their work—a principle valid at all times, which
does not permit this respect to be demanded, but which
requires it to be paid.

Elders who serve and are acknowledged without official appointment: all the members of the assembly recognized as real Christians

We may remark, here, that this epistle, although entering into all the details of the interior conduct of an
assembly, does not speak of elders or of any formally
established officers at all. It is certain, that in general
there were such; but God has provided in the Word for
the walk of an assembly at all times, and, as we see,
principles which oblige us to acknowledge those who
serve in it through personal devotedness without being
officially appointed. General unfaithfulness, or the absence
of such established officers, will not prevent those who
obey the Word from following it in all that is needful for
Christian order. We see moreover that, whatever might

be the disorder, the apostle recognizes the members of
the assembly as being all real Christians; he desires them
to acknowledge one another by the kiss of love, the
universal expression of brotherly affection.   This is so
entirely the case that he pronounces a solemn anathema
on every one who loved not the Lord Jesus.   There
might be such, but he would in no way recognize them.
If there were any, let them be anathema.   Is this an
allowed mixture?   He will not believe it, and he embraces
them all in the bonds of Christian love (ver. 24).

Even when God's discipline is exercised or that of man is required, the guilty are looked upon as Christians, but unreality of love for the Lord calls for the most terrible anathema

The last point is important.   The state of the assembly at Corinth might give room for some uncertainty as
to the Christianity of certain members or persons in
connection with them, although not dwelling at Corinth.
He admonishes them; but in fact, in cases of the most
grievous sin where the discipline of God was exercised
or that of man was required, the guilty are looked upon
as Christians.   (See chap. 10 for the warning; chap.
11: 32 for the Lord's discipline; for that of man, chap.
5: 5 in this epistle; for the principle, 2 Cor. 2: 8.)   Besides, he denounces with an anathema those who do not
love the Lord Jesus.   Discipline is exercised towards the
wicked man who is called a brother.   He who calls himself a Christian, yet does not really love the Lord—for
there may be such—is the subject of the most terrible
anathema.

Christ the sole spring of the apostle's love

It is sweet to see that, after faithfully (although with
anguish of heart) correcting every abuse, the spirit of the
apostle returns by grace into the enjoyments of charity

in his relationship with the Corinthians. The terrible
verse 22 was not felt to be inconsistent with the love that
dictated the other verses. It was the same spirit, for
Christ was the sole spring of his charity.

The importance of the closing salutation written with the apostle's own hand

We may notice (ver. 21) that the apostle, as other
passages testify, employed some one to write for him. The
Epistle to the Galatians is an exception. He verified his
epistles to the assemblies by writing the salutation at the
end with his own hand, marking the importance he
attached to the exactitude of the verbal contents, and
confirming the principle of an exact inspiration. His
heart flows out (ver. 24), and he comforts himself in
being able to acknowledge them all in love.

2 CORINTHIANS

Chapter I

The circumstances occasioning the writing of the Epistle

THE apostle writes the Second Epistle to the Corinthians under the influence of the consolations of Christ—consolations experienced when the troubles which came upon him in Asia were at their height; and renewed at the moment when he wrote his letter, by the good news which Titus had brought him from Corinth—consolations which (now that he is happy about them) he imparts to the Corinthians; who, by grace, had been their source in the last instance.

The first letter had awakened their conscience, and had re-established the fear of God in their heart and integrity in their walk. The sorrowing heart of the apostle was revived by hearing this good news. The state of the Corinthians had cast him down and a little removed from his heart the feelings produced by the consolations with which Jesus filled it during his trials at Ephesus. How various and complicated are the exercises of him who serves Christ and cares for souls! The spiritual restoration of the Corinthians, by dissipating Paul's anguish, had renewed the joy of these consolations, which the tidings of their misconduct had interrupted. He afterwards returns to this subject of his sufferings at Ephesus; and develops, in a remarkable way, the power of the life by which he lived in Christ.

He addresses all the saints of that country, as well as those in the city of Corinth, which was its capital; and, being led by the Holy Ghost to write according to the real sentiments which that Spirit produced in him, he at once places himself in the midst of the consolations which flowed into his heart, in order to acknowledge in them the God who poured them into his tried and exercised spirit.

The Spirit's work in a human heart

Nothing more touching than the work of the Spirit in the apostle's heart. The mixture of gratitude and worship towards God, of joy in the consolations of Christ, and of affection for those on whose account he now rejoiced, has a beauty entirely inimitable by the mind of man. Its simplicity and its truth do but enhance the excellence and exalted character of this divine work in a human heart. "Blessed be God, even the Father of our Lord Jesus Christ, the Father of mercies, and the God of all comfort, who comforteth us in all our tribulation, that we may be able to comfort them which are in any trouble, by the comfort wherewith we ourselves are comforted of God. For as the sufferings of Christ abound in us, so our consolation also aboundeth by Christ. And whether we be afflicted, it is for your consolation and salvation, which is effectual in the enduring of the same sufferings which we also suffer; or whether we be comforted it is for your consolation and salvation." Blessing God for the consolations which he had received, content to suffer, because his participation in suffering encouraged the faith of the Corinthians who suffered, by showing them the path ordained of God for the most excellent, he pours into their hearts the consolation of his own, as soon as comfort comes to him from God. His first thought (and it is always so with one who realizes his dependence on God, and who abides in His presence—see Genesis 24) is to bless God, and to acknowledge Him as the source of all consolation. The Christ, whom he has found both in the sufferings and in the consolation, turns his heart immediately to the beloved members of His Body.

Man's perversity and God's patience: grace concludes that evil will be corrected

Mark at once the perversity of man's heart and the patience of God. In the midst of sufferings for the sake of Christ, they could take part in the sin that dishonored His name—a sin unknown among the Gentiles. In spite of this sin God would not deprive them of the testimony, which those sufferings gave them, of the truth of their Christianity—sufferings which assured the apostle that the Corinthians would enjoy the consolations of Christ, which accompanied sufferings for His sake. It is beautiful to see how grace lays hold of the good, in order to conclude that the evil will surely be corrected, instead of discrediting the good because of the evil. Paul was near Christ—the source of strength.

The power of life in Christ

He continues by presenting, experimentally, the doctrine of the power of life in Christ,[1] which had its development and its strength in death to all that is temporal, to all that links us with the old creation, to mortal life itself. He then touches upon almost every subject that had occupied him in the first epistle, but with an unburdened heart, although with a firmness that desired their good, and the glory of God, let it cost him what sorrow it might.

The effect of the Spirit's work when the conscience is touched

Observe here the admirable connection between the personal circumstances of God's laborers, and the work

---

[1] The beginning of this Epistle presents the experimental power of that which is doctrinally taught in Romans 5: 12 to chap. 8, and is extremely instructive in this respect. It is not so much Colossians and Ephesians; the practical fruit of the doctrine there is the display of God's own character. However we have in a measure what is taught in Colossians carried out.

to which they are called, and even the circumstances of that work. The first epistle had produced that salutary effect on the Corinthians to which the apostle, under the guidance of the Holy Spirit, had destined it. Their conscience had been awakened, and they had become zealous against the evil in proportion to the depth of their fall. This is always the effect of the work of the Spirit, when the conscience of the Christian who has fallen is really touched. The apostle's heart can open with joy to their complete and sincere obedience. Meanwhile he had himself passed through terrible trials, so that he had despaired of life; and he had been able through grace to realize the power of that life in Christ which gained the victory over death, and could pour abundantly into the hearts of the Corinthians the consolations of that life, which were to raise them up again. There is a God who conducts all things in the service of His saints—the sorrow through which they pass, as all the rest.

Thanksgiving for God's comfort in suffering, a token of His favor, to be shared with others

Observe, also, that he does not need to begin by reminding the Corinthians, as he had done in the first epistle, of their calling and their privileges as sanctified in Christ. He breaks out in thanksgiving to the God of all consolation. Holiness is brought forward when it is practically wanting among the saints. If they are walking *in* holiness, they enjoy God, and they speak of Him. The way in which the various parts of the work of God are linked together, in and by means of the apostle, is seen in the expressions that flow from his grateful heart. God comforts him *in* his sufferings; and the consolation is such that it is suited to comfort others, in whatsoever affliction it may be; for it is God Himself who is the consolation, by pouring into the heart His love and His communion, as it is enjoyed in Christ.

If afflicted, it was for the comfort of others by the sight of similar afflictions in those who were honored of God, and the consciousness of unison in the same blessed cause, and relationship with God (the heart being touched and brought back to these affections by this means). If comforted, it was to comfort others with the consolations that he himself enjoyed in affliction. And the afflictions of the Corinthians were a testimony to him that, however great their moral weakness had been, they had part in those consolations which he enjoyed himself, and which he knew to be so deep, so real, which he knew to be of God, and a token of His favor. Precious bonds of grace! And how true it is in our little measure, that the sufferings of those who labor re-animate on the one hand love towards them, and on the other re-assure the laborer as to the sincerity of the objects of his Christian affection, by presenting them anew to him in the love of Christ. The affliction of the apostle had helped him in writing to the Corinthians with the grief that was suitable to their condition; but what faith was that which occupied itself with such energy and such entire forgetfulness of self about the sad state of others, amid such circumstances as then surrounded the apostle! His strength was in Christ.

Paul explains the motives of his movements to demonstrate his love for the Corinthians

His heart expands toward the Corinthians. We see that his affections flow freely—a thing of great value. He reckons on the interest they will take in the account of his sufferings; he is sure that they will rejoice in what God has given him, even as he rejoices in them as the fruit of his labors, and that they will acknowledge what he is; and he is content to be a debtor to their prayers with regard to the gifts displayed in himself, so that his success in the gospel was to them as a personal interest of their own. He could truly demand their prayers, for his course had been run in unmingled sincerity, and especially among them. This leads him to explain to them the motives of his movements, of which he had not spoken to them before, referring these movements to his own plans and motives, subject to the Lord. He is always master (under Christ) of his movements; but he can now speak freely of that which had decided him, which the Corinthians were not before in a state to know. He wishes to satisfy them, to explain things to them, so as to demonstrate his perfect love for them; and, at the same time, to maintain his entire liberty in Christ, and not make himself responsible to them for what he did. He was their servant in affliction, but free to be so, because he was amenable only to Christ, although he satisfied their conscience (because he served Christ) if their conscience was upright.

His own conscience however was clear; and he only wrote to them that which they knew and acknowledged, and, as he trusted, would acknowledge to the end; so that they should rejoice in him, as he in them.

The reason Paul had not visited them: their laxity and the groundwork of Christianity

But had there been any lightness in his decisions, since, as he now informed them, he had intended to visit them on his way to Macedonia (where he was at the moment of writing this letter), and then a second time on his return from that country? In no wise; they were not intentions lightly formed, according to the flesh, and then abandoned. It was his affection, it was to spare them. He could not bear the idea of going with a rod to those whom he loved. Observe in what manner, although showing his affection and tenderness, he maintains his authority; and they needed the exercise of this authority. And while reminding them of his authority, he displays all his tenderness. They were not Cretans, perhaps, whom it was necessary to rebuke sharply; but there was laxity of morals which required delicacy and care lest they should become restive, but also authority and a bridle, lest, in giving them liberty, they should fall into all sorts of bad ways. But he turns immediately to the certainty which was in Christ, the basis of all his own. He would not press too much upon the chord he had touched at the beginning. He lets his authority be known as that which might have been exercised, and he does not employ it. The groundwork of Christianity was needed, in order to put their souls into a condition to judge themselves healthily. They were quite disposed, through the intrigues of false teachers and their habit of schools of philosophy, to separate from the apostle, and, in spirit, from Christ. He brings them back to the foundation, to the sure doctrine that was common to all those that had labored among them at the beginning. He would give Satan no occasion to detach them from him. (See chap. 2: 11.)

The great principles of Christian joy and assurance established: simple certainty in Christ

He establishes therefore the great principles of Christian joy and assurance. I do not speak of the blood, the only source of peace of conscience before God as a judge, but of the manner in which we are placed by the power of God in His presence, in the position and state into which that power introduces us according to the counsels of His grace. Simple certainty was in Christ, according to that which had been said. It was not first Yea, and then Nay: the yea remained always yea—a principle of immense importance, but for the establishment of which there was needed the power and the firmness and even perfection, and the wisdom, of God; for to assure and make stedfast that which was not wise and perfect would certainly not have been worthy of Him.

It will be seen that the question was, whether Paul had lightly changed his purpose. He says that he had not; but he leaves the thought of that which concerned him personally to speak of that which pre-occupied . his thoughts—of Christ; and to him, in fact, to live was Christ. But there was a difficulty to solve, when the immutability of God's promises was the question. It is that we are not in a state to profit by that which was immutable on account of our weakness and inconstancy. He solves this difficulty by setting forth the mighty operations of God in grace.

The immutability of God's promises: their fulfilment in Christ alone

There are two points therefore:—the establishment of all the promises in Christ, and the enjoyment, by us, of the effect of these promises. The thing is, as we have seen, not merely to say, to promise, something; but not to change one's intentions, not to depart from what was said but to keep one's word. Now there had been promises. God had made promises, whether to Abraham unconditionally, or to Israel at Sinai under the condition of obedience. But in Christ there was, not promises, but the Amen to God's promises, the verity and realization of them. Whatever promises there had been on God's part, the Yea was in Him, and the Amen in Him. God has established—deposited, so to speak—the fulfilment of all His promises in the Person of Christ. Life, glory, righteousness, pardon, the gift of the Spirit, all is in Him; it is in Him that all is true—Yea and Amen. We cannot have the effect of any promise whatsoever out of Him. But this is not all: we, believers, are the objects of these counsels of God. They are to the glory of God by us.

But, in the first place, the glory of God is that of Him who ever glorifies Himself in His ways of sovereign grace towards us; for it is in these ways that He unfolds and displays what He is. The Yea and Amen therefore of the promises of God, the accomplishment and the realization of the promises of God for His glory by us, are in Christ.

The enjoyment of the promises: in Christ

But how can we participate in it, if all is Christ and in Christ? It is here that the Holy Ghost presents the second part of the ways of grace. *We* are in Christ, and we are in Him not according to the instability of the will of man, and the weakness that characterizes him in his transitory and changeable works. He who has firmly established us in Christ is God Himself. The accomplishment of all the promises is in Him. Under the law, and under conditions the fulfilment of which depended on the stability of man, the effect of the promise was never attained; the thing promised eluded the pursuit of man, because man needed to be in a state capable of attaining it by righteousness, and he was not in that state; the accomplishment of the promise therefore was always suspended; it would have its effect *if*—but the "if" was not accomplished, and the Yea and Amen did not come. But all that God has promised *is* in Christ. The second part is the "by us," and how far we enjoy it. We are firmly established by God in Christ, in whom all the promises subsist, so that we securely possess in Him all that is promised us. But we do not enjoy it as that which subsists in our own hands.

Anointed, sealed, and given the earnest of the Spirit for the enjoyment of what is in Christ

But, further, God Himself has anointed us. We have by Jesus received the Holy Ghost. God has taken care that we should understand by the Spirit that which is freely given us in Christ. But the Spirit is given to us, according to the counsels of God, for other things than

understanding merely His gifts in Christ. He who has
received Him is sealed. God has marked him with His
seal, even as He marked Christ with His seal when He
anointed Him after His baptism by John. Moreover the
Spirit becomes the earnest, in our own hearts, of that
which we shall fully possess hereafter in Christ. We
understand the things that are given us in the glory; we
are marked by the seal of God to enjoy them; we have
the earnest of them in our hearts—our affections are
engaged by them. Established in Christ, we have the
Holy Ghost, who seals us when we believe, to bring us
into the enjoyment, even while here below, of that which
is in Christ.

Chapter 2

The guilty sinner and the effect of discipline: Satan's aim

HAVING again spoken of the care which manifested
his affection for them, he expresses his conviction
that that which had pained him had pained them also;
and this was demonstrated by the way in which they
had treated the transgressor. He exhorts them to receive
again and comfort the poor guilty one, who was in
danger of being entirely overwhelmed by the discipline
that had been exercised towards him by the mass of the
Christians; adding, that if the Christians forgave him his
fault, he forgave it likewise. He would not that Satan
should get any advantage through this case to bring in
dissension between himself and the Corinthians; for Paul
well knew what the enemy aimed at, the object with which
he made use of this affair.

Led by God in His way: the perfume of the gospel

This gives him occasion to show how much he had them always in his heart. Coming to Troas for the gospel, and a wide door being opened to him, nevertheless he could not remain there, because he had not found Titus; and he left Troas and continued his journey into Macedonia. It will be remembered that, instead of passing by the western shores of the Archipelago, in order to visit Macedonia, taking Corinth on his way, and then returning by the same route, the apostle had sent Titus with his first letter, and had gone by way of Asia Minor, or the eastern coast of the sea, which led him to Troas, where Titus was to meet him. But not finding him at Troas, and being uneasy with regard to the Corinthians, he could not be satisfied with there being a work to be done at Troas, but journeyed on to meet Titus and repaired to Macedonia. There he found him, as we shall see presently. But this thought of having left Troas affected him, for in fact it is a serious thing, and painful to the heart, to miss an opportunity of preaching Christ, and the more so when people are disposed to receive Him, or at least to hear of Him. To have left Troas was indeed a proof of his affection for the Corinthians; and the apostle recalls the circumstance as a strong demonstration of that affection. He comforts himself for having missed this work of evangelization by the thought that after all God led him as in triumph (not "caused him to triumph"). The gospel which he carried with him, the testimony of Christ, was like the perfume caused by burning aromatic drugs in triumphal processions—a token of death to some of the captives, of life to others. And this perfume of the gospel was pure in his hands. The apostle was not like some who adulterated the wine they furnished; he labored in Christian integrity before God.

Chapter 3

The apostle's letters of commendation of his ministry

THESE words give rise to an exposition of the gospel in contrast with the law, which the false teachers mixed up with the gospel. He gives this exposition with the most touching appeal to the heart of the Corinthians, who had been converted through his means. Did he begin speaking of his ministry to commend himself anew, or did he need, as others, letters of commendation to them or from them? *They* were his letters of commendation, the striking proof of the power of his ministry, a proof which he carried always in his heart, ready to bring it forward on every occasion. He can say this now, being happy in their obedience. And why did they serve as a letter in his favor? Because in their faith they were the living expression of his doctrine. They were Christ's letter of commendation, which, by means of his ministry, had been written on the fleshy tables of the heart by the power of the Holy Ghost, as the law had been graven on tables of stone by God Himself.

The ministry of the new covenant of life and that of death and condemnation

This was Paul's confidence with regard to his ministry; his competency came from God for the ministry of the new covenant, not of the letter (not even the letter of this covenant, any more than the letter of anything else) but of the Spirit, the true force of the purpose of God, as the Spirit gave it. For the letter kills, as a rule imposed on man; the Spirit quickens, as the power of God in grace— the purpose of God communicated to the heart of man

by the power of God, who imparted it to him that he
might enjoy it. Now the subject of this ministry brought
out the difference between it and the ministry of the law
yet more strongly. The law, graven on stones, had been
introduced with glory, although it was a thing that was
to pass away as a means of relation between God and
men. It was a ministry of death, for they were only to
live by keeping it. Nor could it be otherwise ordered
than on this principle. A law was to be kept; but man
being already a sinner by nature and by will, having
desires which the law forbade, that law could only be
death to him—it was a ministry of death. It was a ministry of condemnation because the authority of God came
in to give to the law the sanction of condemnation against
every soul that should break it. It was a ministry of
death and of condemnation because man was a sinner.

Grace mingled with the law aggravates guilt: the glory of the ordinances

And observe, here, that to mingle grace with the law
changes nothing in its effect, except to aggravate the
penalty that results from it by aggravating the guilt of
him who violated the law, inasmuch as he violated it in
spite of the goodness and the grace. For it was still the
law, and man was called to satisfy the responsibility under
which the law placed him. "The soul that sinneth," said
Jehovah to Moses, "will I blot out of my book." The
figure used by the apostle shows that he is speaking of
the second descent of Moses from Mount Sinai, when he
had heard the name of Jehovah proclaimed, merciful and
gracious. The face of Moses did not shine the first time
that he came down: he broke the tables before he went
into the camp. The second time God made all His goodness pass before him, and the face of Moses reflected the
glory which he had seen, partial as it may have been.
But Israel could not bear this reflection; for how can it

be borne, when it must judge the secrets of the heart after all? For, though grace had been shown in sparing on Moses' intercession, the exigency of the law was still maintained, and every one was to suffer the consequences of his own disobedience. Thus the character of the law prevented Israel from understanding even the glory which was in the ordinances, as a figure of that which was better and permanent; and the whole system ordained by the hand of Moses was veiled to their eyes, and the people fell under the letter, even in that part of the law which was a testimony of things to be spoken afterwards. It was according to the wisdom of God that it should be so; for in this way all the effect of the law, as brought to bear on the heart and conscience of man, has been fully developed.

Making a law of Christ Himself, an obligation to love Him

There are many Christians who make a law of Christ Himself, and in thinking of His love as a fresh motive to oblige them to love Him, think of it only as an obligation, a very great increase to the measure of the obligation which lies upon them, an obligation which they feel bound to satisfy. That is to say, they are still under the law, and consequently under condemnation.

The apostle's ministry revealing righteousness, not as requiring it

But the ministry which the apostle fulfilled was not this; it was the ministry of righteousness and of the Spirit, not as requiring righteousness in order to stand before God, but as revealing it. Christ was this righteousness, made such on God's part for us; and we are made the righteousness of God in Him. The gospel proclaimed righteousness on God's part, instead of requiring it from man according to the law. Now the Holy Ghost could be the seal of that righteousness. He could come down upon the Man Christ, because He was perfectly approved of God. He was righteous—the righteous One. He came down upon us, because we are made the righteousness of God in Christ. Thus it was the ministry of the Spirit; His power wrought in it. He was bestowed when that which it announced was received by faith; and with the Spirit they also received understanding of the mind and purposes of God, as they were revealed in the Person of a glorified Christ, in whom the righteousness of God was revealed and subsisted eternally before Him.

Christ's glory, hidden in the letter, revealed by the Holy Spirit

Thus the apostle unites, in the self-same thought, the mind of God in the Word according to the Spirit, the glory of Christ who had been hidden in it under the letter, and the Holy Ghost Himself, who gave its force, revealed that glory, and, by dwelling and working in the believer, enables him to enjoy it. Thus, where the Spirit was, there was liberty; they were no longer under the yoke of the law, of the fear of death, and of condemnation. They were in Christ before God, in peace before Him, according to perfect love and that favor which is better than life, even as it shone upon Christ, without a veil, according to the grace which reigns by righteousness. When it is said, "Now the Lord is that spirit," allusion is made to verse 6: 7-16 is a parenthesis. Christ glorified is the true thought of the Spirit which God had previously hidden under figures. And here is the practical result: they beheld the Lord with open (that is, with unveiled) face; they were able to do it. The glory of the face of Moses judged the thoughts and intents of the hearts, causing terror by threatening the disobedient and the sinner with death and condemnation. Who could stand in the presence of God? But the glory of the face of

Jesus, a Man on high, is the proof that all the sins of those who behold it are blotted out; for He who is there bore them all before He ascended, and He needed to put them all away in order to enter into that glory. We contemplate that glory by the Spirit, who has been given us in virtue of Christ's having ascended into it. He did not say, "I will go up; peradventure I shall make atonement." He made the atonement and went up. Therefore we gaze upon it with joy, we love to behold it: each ray that we see is the proof that in the eyes of God our sins are no more. Christ has been made sin for us; He is in the glory. Now, in thus beholding the glory with affection, with intelligence, taking delight in it, we are changed into the same image from glory to glory, even as by the power of the Holy Ghost, who enables us to realize and to enjoy these things; and in this is Christian progress. Thus the assembly too becomes the epistle of Christ.

The veil taken away in Christ, but on the hearts of Jews till Israel turns to the Lord

The allusion made at the same time to the Jews at the end of the parenthesis, where the apostle makes a comparison between the two systems, is most touching. The veil, he says, is taken away in Christ. Nothing is now veiled. The glorious substance is accomplished. The veil is on the *heart of the Jews*, when they read the Old Testament. Now every time that Moses entered into the tabernacle to speak to God, or to hear Him, he took off his veil. Thus, says the apostle, when Israel shall turn to the Lord, the veil shall be taken away.

The glorious things of which the gospel treats

There is but one more remark to be made. "The things that remain" are the subject the gospel treats of, not the ministry which announces it—the glory of the Person of

Jesus Christ, the substance of that which the Jewish ordinances represented only in figure.

Chapter 4

Christ victorious over death makes us victorious over its fear and over suffering

THE apostle returns to the subject of his ministry in connection with his sufferings, showing that this doctrine of a Christ victorious over death, truly received into the heart, makes us victorious over all fear of death, and over all the sufferings that are linked with the earthen vessel in which this treasure is carried.

Paul proclaiming the glorious Person of Christ to the world making men responsible for submission to this glorious Christ

Having received this ministry of righteousness and of the Spirit, the foundation of which was Christ glorified beheld with open face, he not only used great boldness of speech, but his zeal was not abated, nor his faith enfeebled by difficulties. Moreover, with the courage which through grace was imparted to him by this doctrine, he held back nothing, weakened nothing of this glory; he did not corrupt the doctrine; he manifested it in all the purity and brightness in which he had received it. It was the Word of God; such as he had received it, so they received it from him, the unaltered Word of God; the apostle thus approving himself, commending himself to every man's conscience in the sight of God. All could not say this. The glory of the Lord Jesus was set forth by Paul's preaching in all the clearness and brightness of its revelation to himself. If, therefore, the good news which he proclaimed was hidden, it was not as in the case of

Moses; not only was the glory of the Lord fully revealed
with open face in Christ, it was also manifested without
a veil in the pure preaching of the apostle. This is the
link established between the glory accomplished in the
Person of Christ, as the result of the work of redemption,
and the ministry which, by the power of the Holy Ghost
acting in the instrument chosen of the Lord, proclaimed
this glory to the world, and made men responsible for the
reception of the truth—responsible for submission to this
glorious Christ, who announced Himself in grace from
heaven, as having established righteousness for the sinner,
and as inviting him to come freely and enjoy the love and
the blessing of God.

The only means of coming to God: the light of the glory of Christ shining in the heart or blindness

Now there was no other means of coming to God. To
set up any other would be to put aside and declare imperfect and insufficient that which Christ had done, and that
which Christ was, and to produce something better than
He. But this was not possible: for that which he announced was the manifestation of the glory of God in the
Person of the Son, in connection with the revelation of
perfect love, and of the making good perfect and divine
righteousness; so that the pure light was the happy abode
of those who by this means entered into it. There could
not be anything more, unless there was something more
than God in the fulness of His grace and of His perfection. If then this revelation was hidden, it was in the
case of those who were lost, whose minds were blinded
by the god of this world, lest the light of the good news
of the *glory* of Christ, who is the image of God, should
shine into their hearts.

This is translated "glorious gospel." But we have seen
that the fact of Christ's being in glory, the glory of God
being seen in His face, was the special subject of the

preceding chapter. To that the apostle here alludes as characterizing the gospel which he preached. It was the proof of the sin Christ had borne being utterly put away, of victory over death, of the introduction of man into the presence of God in glory according to God's eternal counsels of love. It was withal the full display of the divine glory in man according to grace, which the Holy Ghost takes to show to us in order to form us after the same likeness. It was the glorious ministration of righteousness, and of the Spirit, which opened the free way for man to God, even into the holiest in entire liberty.

The shining forth of the gospel of the glory of Christ the work of God's power in the heart: the treasure in earthen vessels

When Christ was thus proclaimed, there was either the joyful acceptance of the good news, submission of heart to the gospel, or else the blinding of Satan. For Paul did not preach himself (which others did not fail to do) but Jesus Christ the Lord, and himself their servant for Jesus' sake. Because in fact (and this is another important principle) the shining forth of this gospel of the glory of Christ is the work of God's power—of the same God who, by His Word alone, caused the light instantaneously to shine out of the midst of darkness. He had shone into the apostle's heart to give forth the light of the knowledge of His own glory in the face of Jesus Christ. The gospel shone forth by a divine operation similar to that which had, in the beginning, caused the light to shine out of darkness by a single word. The heart of the apostle was the vessel, the lamp, in which this light had been kindled to shine in the midst of the world before the eyes of men. It was the revelation of the glory which shone in the Person of Christ by the power of the Spirit of God in the heart of the apostle, in order that this glory should shine out in the gospel before the world.

It was the power of God which wrought in it, in the same manner as when light was caused by the word "Let there be light!" "and there was light." But the treasure of this revelation of the glory was deposited in earthen vessels, in order that power which wrought in it should be of God alone, and not that of the instruments. In all, the weakness of the instrument showed itself in the trying circumstances which God, for this very purpose (among others), made the testimony pass through. Nevertheless the power of God was manifested in it so much the more evidently, from the vessel's showing its weakness in the difficulties that beset its path. The testimony was rendered, the work was done, the result was produced, even when man broke down and found himself without resource in presence of the opposition raised up against truth.

The earthen vessel and God: death realized: the life of Jesus manifested

Afflicted by the tribulation, this was the vessel's part; not straitened, for God was with the vessel. Without means of escape, that was the vessel; yet not without resource, for God was with it. Persecuted, that was the vessel; not forsaken, for God was with it. Cast down, that was the vessel; but not destroyed, for God was with it. Always bearing about in his body the dying[2] of the Lord Jesus (made like Him, in that the man as such was reduced to nothing), in order that the life of Jesus, which death could not touch, which has triumphed over death, should be manifested in his body, mortal as it was. The more the natural man was annihilated, the more was it evident that a power was there which was not of man. This was the principle, but it was morally realized in the heart by faith. As the Lord's servant, Paul realized in his heart the death of all that was human life, in order that the power might be purely of God through Jesus

---

[2] Or rather, "putting to death."

risen. But besides this, God made him realize these things by the circumstances through which he had to pass; for, as living in this world, he was always delivered unto death for Jesus' sake, in order that the life of Jesus might be manifested in his mortal flesh. Thus death wrought in the apostle; what was merely of man, of nature and natural life, disappeared, in order that life in Christ, developing itself in him on the part of God and by His power, should work in the Corinthians by his means. What a ministry! A thorough trial of the human heart, a glorious calling, for a man to be thus assimilated to Christ, to be the vessel of the power of His pure life, and by means of an entire self-renunciation, even that of life itself, to be morally like unto Jesus. What a position by grace! What a conformity to Christ! And yet in a way in which it passed through man's heart to reach man's heart (which indeed is of the essence of Christianity itself), not surely by man's strength, but God's made good in man's weakness.

Bearing testimony for Christ and suffering with Him

Therefore it was that the apostle could use the language of the Spirit of Christ in the Psalms, "I believed, and therefore have I spoken." That is to say, "At whatever cost, in spite of everything, of all the danger, all the opposition, I have spoken for God, I have borne my testimony. I have had confidence enough in God to bear testimony to Him and to His truth, whatever the consequences might be, even if I had died in doing it." That is, the apostle said, "I have acted as Christ Himself did, because I know that He who raised up Jesus would do the same for me, and would present me, together with you, before His face in that same glory in which Christ is now in heaven, and for my testimony to which, I have suffered death like Him." We must clearly distinguish here between Christ's sufferings for righteousness and for His work of love, and

His sufferings for sin. The former it is our privilege to share with Him; in the latter He is alone.

Light affliction for a moment and an eternal weight of glory

The apostle said, "Will present me with you," for, he adds, according to the heart and mind of Christ towards His own, "All things are for your sakes, that the abundant grace might, through the thanksgiving of many, redound to the glory of God." And therefore it was that he did not allow himself to be discouraged; but on the contrary, if the outward man perished, the inward man was renewed day by day. For the light affliction, which was but for a moment (for such he esteemed it in view of the glory—it was but the temporary affliction of this poor dying body), worked out for him an eternal weight of glory which was beyond all the most exalted expression of human thought or language. And this renewing took place; and he was not disheartened come what might, in that he looked not at the things that are seen, which are temporal, but at the things that are not seen, which are eternal. Thus the power of the divine life, with all its consequences, was developed in his soul by faith. He knew the result of everything on God's part.

Chapter 5

The Christian's body: the certainty of a building of God eternal in the heavens as a real and practical hope while groaning in this tabernacle

IT was not only that there were things invisible and glorious. Christians had their part in them. We know, the apostle says in their name, that if this earthly house (passing away as it is) were destroyed—and it had very nearly been the case with himself—we have a building of God, a house not made with hands, eternal in the heavens. Precious certainty! He *knew* it. Christians know it as a part of their faith. *We* know[3]—a certainty which caused this glory, which he knew to be his, to be a real and practical hope in the heart by the power of the Holy Ghost— a reality present by faith. He saw this glory as that which belonged to him, with which he was to be invested. And therefore also he groaned in his tabernacle, not (as so many do) because the desires of his flesh could not be fulfilled; and because satisfaction of heart cannot be found for man, even when those desires are fulfilled; nor because he was uncertain whether he was accepted, and the glory his or not; but because the body was a hindrance, tending to depress the divine life, to deprive him of the full enjoyment of that glory which the new life saw and desired, and which Paul saw and admired as his own. It was a burden, this earthly human nature, it was no distress to him that he could not satisfy its desires; his distress was to find himself still in this mortal nature, because he saw something better.

The apostle's desire to be "clothed upon": mortality disappearing before the power of life in Jesus

Not however that he desired to be unclothed, for he saw in Christ glorified a power of life capable of swallowing up and annihilating every trace of mortality; for the fact that Christ was on high in the glory was the result of this power, and at the same time the manifestation of the heavenly portion that belonged to them that were His. Therefore the apostle desired, not to be unclothed but clothed upon, and that that which was mortal in him should be absorbed by life that the mortality that characterized his earthly human nature should disappear be-

---

[3] This "we know" is in fact a technical expression for the portion of Christians, known to them as such. "We know that the law is spiritual," "We know that the Son of God is come," and so on.

fore the power of life which he saw in Jesus, and which
was his life. That power was such that there was no need
to die. And this was not a hope which had no other foundation than the desire awakened by a view of the glory
might produce: God had formed Christians for this very
thing. He who was a Christian was formed for this, and
not for anything else. It was God Himself who had
formed him for *this*—this glory, in which Christ, the
last Adam, was at the right hand of God. Precious assurance! Happy confidence in the grace and the mighty
work of God! Ineffable joy to be able to attribute all to
God Himself, to be thus certified of His love, to glorify
Him as the God of love—our Benefactor, to know that
it was His work, and that we rest upon a finished work
—the work of God. It is not here resting upon a work
done for us; but the blessed consciousness that God has
wrought *us* for this: we are His workmanship.

The glory before us: the earnest of the Spirit given: the transforming power of Christ at His coming

Nevertheless something else was necessary to our enjoying this, since we are not yet glorified in fact; and God
has given it—the earnest of the Spirit.

Thus, we have the glory before us, we are wrought for
it by God Himself, and we have the earnest of the Spirit
till we are there, and know that Christ has so entirely
overcome death that, if the time were come, we should
be transformed into glory without dying at all. Mortality
would be swallowed up of life. This is our portion through
grace in the last Adam, through the power of life in
which Christ was raised.

The present effect of the possession of life in Christ as to death and judgment: in the light

But next the apostle will treat of the effect as to the

natural portion of the first fallen man, death and judgment; for the testimony here is very complete.

What then is the effect of the possession of life in
Christ as applied to death and judgment, the two natural
objects of men's fears, the fruit of sin? If our bodies are
not yet transformed; and if that which is mortal is not
yet swallowed up, we are equally full of confidence, because, being formed for glory, and Christ (who has manifested the victorious power that opened the path of
heaven to Him) being our life, if we should leave this
tabernacle and be absent from the body before we are
clothed upon with the glory, this life remains untouched;
it has already in Jesus triumphed over all these effects of
the power of death. We should be present with the Lord;
for we walk by faith, not by the sight of these excellent
things. Therefore we prefer to be absent from the body,
and to be present with the Lord. For this reason we seek
to be well-pleasing to Him, whether we are found absent
from this body, or present in this body, when Christ shall
come to take us to Himself and make us share His glory.

And this leads on to the second point—judgment. For
we must all be manifested before the tribunal of Christ,
in order that each may receive according to that which
he shall have done in the body, be it good or evil. A
happy and precious thought, after all, solemn as it may
be; for, if we have really understood grace, if we are
standing in grace, if we know what God is, all love for
us, all light for us, we shall like to be in the full light.
It is a blessed deliverance to be in it. It is a burden, an
encumbrance, to have anything concealed, and although
we have had much sin in us that no one knows (perhaps even some that we have committed, and which it
would be no profit for any one to know), it is a comfort
—if we know the perfect love of God—that all should be
in perfect light since He is there. This is the case by
faith and for faith, wherever there is solid peace: we are
before God as He is, and as we are—all sin in ourselves

alas, except so far as He has wrought in us by quickening us; and He is all love in this light in which we are placed; for God is light, and He reveals Himself. Without the knowledge of grace, we fear the light: it cannot be otherwise. But knowing grace, knowing that sin has been put away as regards the glory of God, and that the offence is no longer before His eyes, we like to be in the light, it is joy to us, it is that which the heart needs, without which it cannot be satisfied, when there is the life of the new man. Its nature is to love the light, to love purity in all that perfection which does not admit the evil of darkness, which shuts out all that is not itself. Now to be thus in the light, and to be manifested, is the same thing, for the light makes everything manifest.

We are in the light by faith when the conscience is in the presence of God. We shall be according to the perfection of that light when we appear before the tribunal of Christ. I have said that it is a solemn thing—and so it is, for everything is judged according to that light; but it is that which the heart loves, because—thanks to our God!—we *are* light in Christ.

Looking back, after the tribunal of Christ

But there is more than this. When the Christian is thus manifested, he is already glorified, and, perfectly like Christ, has then no remains of the evil nature in which he sinned. And he now can look back at all the way God has led him in grace, helped, lifted up, kept from falling, not withdrawn His eyes from the righteous. He knows as he is known. What a tale of grace and mercy! If I look back now, my sins do not rest on my conscience; though I have horror of them, they are put away behind God's back. I am the righteousness of God in Christ, but what a sense of love and patience, and goodness and grace! How much more perfect then, when all is before me! Surely there is great gain as to light and love, in giving an account of ourselves to God; and not a trace remains of the evil in us. We are like Christ. If a person fears to have all out thus before God, I do not believe he is free in soul as to righteousness—being the righteousness of God in Christ, not fully in the light. And we have not to be judged for anything: Christ has put it all away.

Retribution: loss or gain, and the cause seen in the light

But there is another idea in the passage—retribution. The apostle does not speak of judgment on persons, because the saints are included, and Christ has stood in their place for all that regards the judgment of their persons: "There is no condemnation for those who are in Christ." They do not come into judgment. But they shall be manifested before His tribunal, and receive that which they have done in the body. The good deserves nothing: they received that by which they have wrought what is good— grace produced it in them; nevertheless they shall receive its reward. What they have done is counted as their own act. If, by neglecting grace and the witness of the Spirit in them, the fruits which He would have produced have been turned aside, they will bear the consequences. It is not that, in this case, God will have forsaken them; it is not that the Holy Ghost will not act in them with regard to the condition they are in; but it will be in their conscience that He acts, judging the flesh which has prevented the man's bearing the natural fruit of His presence and operation in the new man. So that the Holy Ghost will have done all that is necessary with respect to their state of heart; and the perfect counsel of God with regard to the person will have been accomplished, His patience manifested, His wisdom, His ways in governing, the care which He deigns to take of each one individually in His most condescending love. Each one will have his place, as it was prepared for him of the Father. But the natural fruit of the presence and operation of the Holy Ghost in a soul which has (or, according to the advantages it has enjoyed, ought to have had) a certain measure of light, will not have been produced. It will be seen what it was that prevented. It will judge, according to the judgment of God, all that was good and evil in itself, with a solemn reverence for that which God is, and a fervent adoration on account of what He has been for us. The perfect light will be appreciated; the *ways* of God known and understood in all their perfection, by the application of the perfect light to the whole course of our life and of His dealings with us, in which we shall thoroughly recognize that love—perfect, sovereign above all things—has reigned, with ineffable grace.

God's majesty maintained: the perfection and tenderness of His dealings known and understood

Thus the majesty of God will have been maintained by His judgment, at the same time that the perfection and tenderness of His dealings will be the eternal recollection of our souls. Light without cloud or darkness will be understood in its own perfection. To understand it is to be in it and to enjoy it. And light is God Himself. How wonderful to be thus *manifested!* What love is that which in its perfect wisdom, in its marvellous ways overruling all evil, could bring such beings as we are to enjoy this unclouded light—beings knowing good and evil (the natural prerogative of those only of whom God can say "one of Us"), under the yoke of the evil which they knew, and driven out by a bad conscience from the presence of God to whom that knowledge belonged, having testimony enough in their conscience as to the judgment of God, to make them avoid Him and be miserable, but nothing to draw them to Him who alone could find a remedy! What love and holy wisdom which could bring such to the source of good, of pure happiness, in whom the power of good repels absolutely the evil which it judges!

The personal responsibility of the unrighteous

With regard to the unrighteous, at the judgment-day they will have to answer personally for their sins, under a responsibility which rests entirely on themselves.

God's grace and government leading the believer to please the Lord

However great the happiness of being in the perfect light (and this happiness is complete and divine in its character), it is on the side of conscience that the subject is here presented. God maintains His majesty by the judgment which He executes, as it is written, "The Lord is known by the judgment that He executeth:" there, in His government of the world; here, final, eternal, and personal judgment. And, for my part, I believe that it is very profitable for the soul to have the judgment of God present to our minds, and the sense of the unchangeable majesty of God maintained in the conscience by this means. If we were not under grace, it would be—it ought to be—insupportable; but the maintenance of this sentiment does not contradict grace. It is indeed only under grace that it can be maintained in its truth; for who otherwise could bear the thought, for an instant, of receiving that which he had done in the body? None but he who is completely blinded.

But the authority, the holy authority of God, which asserts itself in judgment, forms a part of our relationship with Him; the maintenance of this sentiment, associated with the full enjoyment of grace, a part of our holy spiritual affections. It is the fear of the Lord. It is in this sense, that "Happy is he who feareth always." If this weakens the conviction that the love of God rests fully, eternally, upon us, then we get off the only possible ground of any relation whatever with God, unless perdition could be so called. But, in the sweet and peaceful atmosphere of grace, conscience maintains its rights and its authority against the subtle encroachments of the flesh, through the sense of God's judgment, in virtue of a holiness which cannot be separated from the character of God without denying that there is a God: for if there is a God, He is holy. This sentiment engages the heart of the accepted believer, to endeavor to please the Lord in every way; and, in the sense of how solemn a thing it is for a sinner to appear before God, the love that necessarily accompanies it in a believer's heart urges him to persuade men with a view to their salvation, while maintaining his own conscience in the light. And he who is now walking in the light, whose conscience reflects that light, will not fear it in the day when it shall appear in its glory. We must be manifested; but, walking in the light in the sense of the fear of God, realizing His judgment of evil, we are already manifested to God: nothing hinders the sweet and assured flow of His love. Accordingly the walk of such a one justifies itself in the end to the consciences of others; one is manifested as walking in the light.

Walking in the light and seeking those in danger of judgment, constrained by Christ's love

These are therefore the two great practical principles of the ministry: to walk in the light, in the sense of God's solemn judgment for every one; and, the conscience being thus pure in the light, the sense of the judgment (which in this case cannot trouble the soul for itself, or obscure its view of the love of God) impels the heart to seek in love those who are in danger of this judgment. This connects itself with the doctrine of Christ, the Saviour, through His death upon the cross; and the love of Christ

constrains us, because we see that, if one died for all, it is
that all were dead. This was the universal condition of
souls. The apostle seeks them in order that they may live
unto God by Christ. But this goes farther. First, as regards fallen man's lot, death is gain. The saint, if absent
from the body, is present with the Lord. As to judgment,
he owns the solemnity of it, but it does not make him
tremble. He is in Christ—will be like Christ; and Christ,
before whom he is to appear, has put away all the sins
he had to be judged for. The effect is the sanctifying one
of bringing him fully manifested into the presence of God
now. But it stimulates his love as to others, nor is it only
by fear of judgment to come for them; Christ's love constrains him—love manifested in death. But this proves
more than the acts of sin which bring judgment: Christ
died because all were dead. The Spirit of God goes to the
source and spring of their whole condition, their state, not
merely the fruits of an evil nature—all were dead. We
find the same important instruction in John 5: 24, "He
that heareth My word, and believeth Him that sent Me,
hath everlasting life, and shall not come into judgment
[that which applies to sins], but is passed from death
unto life;" he has come out of the whole state and condition, as an already lost one, into another and different one
in Christ. This is a very important aspect of the truth.
And the distinction, largely developed in Romans, is found
in many passages.

The sight of sin and failures before and since con-
version awakening humility and adoration of
God's grace

The work of manifestation before God in the light is
already true, in so far as we have realized the light. Cannot I, being now in peace, look back at what I was before
conversion, and at all my failures since my conversion,
humbled but adoring the grace of God in all He has done

for me, but without a thought of fear, or imputation of
sin? Does not this awaken a very deep sense of all that
God is in holy grace and love, in unbounded patience towards me, both keeping and helping and restoring? Such
will be the case perfectly when we are manifested, when
we shall know as we are known.

All judged by the soul as God judges it, communion is enjoyed

That this point may be still more clear, for it is an
important one, let me add some further observations here.
What we find in this passage is the perfect manifestation
of all that a person is and has been before a throne characterized by judgment, without judgment as to the person
in question being guilty. No doubt when the wicked receives the things done in the body, he is condemned. But
it is not said "judged" here, because all then must be
condemned. But this manifestation is exactly what brings
all morally before the heart, when it is capable of judging
evil for itself: were it under judgment, it could not. Freed
from all fear, and in the perfect light and with the comfort of perfect love (for where we have the conscience of
sin, and of its not being imputed, we have the sense,
though in a humbling way, of perfect love), and at the
same time the sense of authority and divine government
fully made good in the soul, all is judged by the soul itself
as God judges it, and communion with Himself entered
into. This is exceedingly precious.

The believer already glorified before his appearance before Christ's judgment-seat

We have to remember that, at our appearing before
the judgment-seat of Christ, we are *already glorified*.
Christ has come Himself in perfect love to fetch us; and
has changed our vile body according to the resemblance

of His glorious body. We are glorified and like Christ before the judgment takes place. And mark the effect on Paul. Does the thought of being manifested awaken anxiety or dread? Not the least. He realizes all the solemnity of such a process. He knows the terror of the Lord; he has it before his eyes; and what is the consequence? He sets about to persuade others who are in need of it.

God's righteousness and perfect love for the believer in Christ: manifested now to God

There are, so to speak, two parts in God's nature and character: His righteousness, which judges everything; and His perfect love. These are one for us in Christ, ours in Christ. If indeed we realize what God is, both will have their place: but the believer in Christ *is* the righteousness which God, from His very nature, must have before Him on His throne, if we are to be with Him and enjoy Him. But the Christ, in the judgment-seat, before whom we are, is our righteousness. He judges by the righteousness which He is; but we are that righteousness, the righteousness of God in Him. Hence this point can raise no question in the soul, will make us adore such grace, but can raise no question, only enhance the sense we have of grace ourselves, make us understand it, as suited to man as he is, and feel the solemn and awful consequences of not having part in it, since there is such a judgment. Hence that other and indeed essential part of the divine nature, love, will work in us towards others; and, knowing the terror of the Lord, we shall persuade men. Thus Paul (it is conscience in view of that most solemn moment) possessed the righteousness which he saw in the Judge, for that which judged was His righteousness; but then he consequently seeks others earnestly, according to the work which had thus brought him near to God, to which he then turns (vers. 13, 14). But this view of judgment and our complete manifestation in that day, has a present effect on the saint according to its own nature. He realizes it by faith. He *is* manifested. He does not fear being manifested. It will unfold all God's past ways towards him when he is in glory; but he is manifested now to God, his conscience exercised in the light. It has thus a present sanctifying power.

Three apparently contradictory principles united to give complete character to the Christian ministry

Observe here the assemblage of powerful motives, of pre-eminently important principles; contradictory in appearance, but which, to a soul which walks in light, instead of clashing and destroying each other, unite to give its complete and thoroughly furnished character to the Christian minister and ministry.

First of all, the glory, in such a power of life, that he who realizes it does not desire death, because he sees in the power of life in Christ that which can absorb whatever in him is mortal, and he sees it with the certainty of enjoying it—such a consciousness of possessing this life (God having formed him for it, and given him the earnest of the Spirit), that death if it arrive to him is but a happy absence from the body in order to be present with the Lord.

Now the thought of ascending to Christ gives the desire of being acceptable to Him, and presents Him (the second motive or principle that gives a form to this ministry) as the Judge who will render to every one that which he has done. The solemn thought of how much this judgment is to be feared takes possession of the apostle's heart. What a difference between this thought and the "building of God," for which he was waiting with certainty! Nevertheless this thought does not alarm him; but, in the solemn sense of the reality of that judgment, it impels him to persuade others.

But here a third principle comes in, the love of Christ with reference to the condition of those whom Paul sought to persuade. Since this love of Christ's shows itself in His death, there is in it the witness that all were already dead and lost.

Thus we have here set before us glory, with the personal certainty of enjoying it, and death become the means of being present with the Lord; the tribunal of Christ, and the necessity of being manifested before it; and the love of Christ in His death, all being already dead. How are such diverse principles as these to be reconciled and arranged in the heart? It is that the apostle *was* manifested to God. Hence the thought of being manifested before the tribunal produced, along with the present sanctification, no other effect on him than that of solemnity, for he was not to come into judgment; but it became an urgent motive for preaching to others, according to the love which Christ had manifested in His death. The idea of the tribunal did not in the least weaken his certainty of glory.[4] His soul, in the full light of God, reflected what was in that light, namely, the glory of Christ ascended on high as man. And the love of this same Jesus was strengthened in its active operation in him by the sense of the tribunal which awaits all men.

A pure conscience

What a marvellous combination of motives we find in this passage, to form a ministry characterized by the development of all that in which God reveals Himself, and by which He acts on the heart and conscience of man! And it is in a pure conscience that these things can have their force together. If the conscience were not pure, the tribunal would obscure the glory, at least as belonging to oneself, and weaken the sense of His love. At any rate

[4] The truth is, the judgment-seat is what most brings out our assurance before God; for as He is, so are we in this world; and it is when Christ shall appear we shall be *like Him*.

one would be occupied with self in connection with these things, and ought to be so. But when pure before God, it only sees a tribunal which excites no sense of personal uneasiness, and therefore has all its true moral effect, as an additional motive for seriousness in our walk, and a solemn energy in the appeal which the known love of Jesus impels it to address to man.

The result of Christ's death and resurrection: new creatures with a new nature in a new creation: reconciliation proclaimed

As to how far our own relations with God enter into the service which we have to render to others, the apostle adds another thing that characterized his walk, and that was the result of the death and resurrection of Christ. He lived in an entirely new sphere, in a new creation, which had left behind, as in another world, all that belonged to a natural existence in the flesh here below. The proof that Christ had died for all proved that all were dead; and that He died for all in order that those who live should live no longer to themselves but to Him who died for them and rose again. They are in connection with this new order of things in which Christ exists as risen. Death is on everything else. Everything is shut up under death. If I live, I live in a new order of things, in a new creation, of which Christ is the type and the head. Christ, so far as in connection with this world below, is dead. He might have been known as the Messiah, living on the earth, and in connection with promises made to men living on the earth in the flesh. The apostle no longer knew Him thus. In fact Christ, as bearing that character, was dead; and now, being risen, He has taken a new and a heavenly character.

Therefore if any one is in Christ, he belongs to this new creation, he is of the new creation. He belongs no more at all to the former; the old things have passed away; all things are become new. The system is not the fruit of human nature and of sin, like all that surrounds us here below, according to the flesh. Already, looked at as a system existing morally before God, in this new creation, all things are *of* God. All that is found in it is of God, of Him who *has* reconciled us to Himself by Jesus Christ. We live in an order of things, a world, a new creation, entirely of God. We are there in peace, because God, who is its centre and its source, has reconciled us to Himself. We enjoy it, because we are new creatures in Christ; and everything in this new world is of Him, and corresponds with that new nature. He had also committed to the apostle a ministry of reconciliation, according to the order of things into which he had been himself introduced. Being reconciled, and knowing it by the revelation of God who had accomplished it for him, he proclaimed a reconciliation, the effect of which he was enjoying.

God was in Christ: the apostle as an ambassador for the absent Christ: Christ made sin by God to make us His righteousness

All this flowed from an immense and all-powerful truth. God was in Christ. But then, in order that others might have a part with him, and the apostle be the minister of this, it was also necessary that Christ should be made sin for us. One of these truths presents the character in which God has drawn nigh to us; the other, the efficacy of that which has been wrought for the believer.

Here is the first of these truths, in connection with the apostle's ministry, which form the subject of these chapters. God was in Christ (that is to say, when Christ was on earth). The day of judgment had not been waited for. God had come down in love into the world alienated from Him. Such was Christ. Three things were connected with and characterized this great and essential truth: reconciling the world, not imputing transgression, and putting the word of reconciliation into the apostle. As the result of this third consequence of the incarnation, the apostle assumes the character of ambassador for Christ; as though God exhorted by his means, he besought men, in the name of Christ, to be reconciled to God. But such an embassy supposed the absence of Christ; His ambassador acted in His stead. It was in fact based upon another truth of immeasurable importance, namely, that God had made Him who knew no sin to be sin for us, in order that we should be made the righteousness of God in Him. This was the true way to reconcile us, and that entirely, to God, according to the perfection of God fully revealed. For He had set His love upon us where we were, giving His Son, who was without spot or motion or principle of sin; and making Him (for He offered Himself to accomplish the will of God) sin for us, in order to make us in Him, who in that condition had perfectly glorified Him— the expression of His divine righteousness, before the heavenly principalities through all eternity; to make us His delight, as regards righteousness; "That we should be the righteousness of God in Him." Man has no righteousness for God; God has made the saints, in Jesus, His righteousness. It is in us that this divine righteousness is seen fully verified—of course in Christ first, in setting Him at His right hand, and in us as in Him. Marvellous truth, which, if its results in us cause thanksgiving and praise to resound when looking at Jesus, silences the heart, and bows it down in adoration, astonished at the sight of His wonderful acts in grace![5]

---

[5] It should be observed that, in verse 20, the word "you" ought to be omitted. It was the way in which the apostle fulfilled his ministry to the world.

Chapter 6

Paul approving himself as God's witness: God's power in a vessel of weakness

PAUL had said that God exhorted by his means. In chapter 6 the affection of the apostle carries on by the Spirit this divine work, beseeching the Corinthians that it might not be in vain in their case that this grace had been brought to them. For it was the acceptable time, the day of salvation.[6] The apostle had spoken of the great principles of his ministry, and of its origin. He reminds the Corinthians of the way in which he had exercised it in the varied circumstances through which he had been led. The cardinal point of his service is that he was the minister of God, that he represented Him in his service. This rendered two things needful: first, that he should be in all things without reproach; and then that he should maintain this character of God's minister, and the exercise of his ministry, through all the opposition, and in all the circumstances through which the enmity of man's heart, and the cunning even of Satan, could make him pass. Everywhere and in all things he avoided, by his conduct, all real occasion of being reproached, in order that no one should have room to blame the ministry. He approved himself in all things as a minister of God, worthily representing Him in whose name he spoke to men; and that with a patience, and in the midst of persecution and contradiction of sinners, which showed an inward energy, a sense of obligation to God, and a dependence on Him, which the realization of His presence and of our duty to Him can alone maintain. It was a quality which reigned through all the circumstances of which the apostle speaks, and had dominion over them.

[6] The passage is a quotation from Isaiah 49: 8, which speaks of the blessing that should be brought to the Gentiles when Christ was rejected by the Jews, but through Christ's work and by the resurrection.

Thus he showed himself to be the minister of God in everything which could test him; in pureness, in kindness, in love; as a vessel of power; whether disgraced or applauded; unknown to the world, and known and eminent; outwardly trodden under foot of man and chastened, inwardly victorious and joyful, enriching others, and in possession of all things. Here ends his description of the sources, the character, the victory over circumstances, of a ministry which displayed the power of God in a vessel of weakness, whose best portion was death.

The Corinthians exhorted to maintain their God-given place of new creatures

The restoration of the Corinthians to a moral state befitting the gospel, associated with the circumstances through which he had just been passing, had allowed him to open his heart to them. Pre-occupied till now with his subject of the glorious Christ, who, having accomplished redemption, sent him as the messenger of the grace to which that redemption had given free course, and having spoken with a free heart of all that was comprised in his ministry, he returns with affection to his beloved Corinthians, showing that it was with them that he had all this openness, this enlargement of heart. "My mouth is open unto you, O Corinthians," he says, "my heart is enlarged; ye are not straitened in me, but in your own affections." As a recompense for the affections that overflowed from his heart towards them, he only asks for the enlargement of their own hearts.

He spoke as to his children. But he avails himself of this tender relationship to exhort the Corinthians to maintain the place in which God had set them: "Be not in the same yoke with unbelievers." Having a hold upon their affections, and rejoicing deeply before God in the grace which had restored them to right sentiments, his heart is free to give way, as though beside himself, to the

joy that belonged to him in Christ glorified: and, with a
sober mind after all when his dear children in the faith
were in question,[7] he seeks to detach them from all that
recognized the flesh, or implied that a relationship which
recognized it were possible for a Christian—from everything that denied the position of a man who has his life
and his interests in the new creation, of which Christ is
the Head in glory. An angel can serve God in this world:
little would it concern him in what way, provided that way
was God's; but to associate himself with its interests, as
forming a part of it, to ally himself with those who are
governed by the motives that influence the men of this
world, so that a common conduct would show that the
one and the other acted according to the principles that
form its character, would be, to those heavenly beings,
to lose their position and their character. The Christian,
whose portion is the glory of Christ—who has his world,
his life, his true associations, there where Christ has entered in—should not either; nor can he, as a Christian,
put himself under the same yoke with those who can have
only worldly motives, to draw the chariot of life in a path
common to both.

Separation: coming out from among the worldly to enter into the relationship of sons and daughters to God as a Father and be so owned of Him

What communion is there between Christ and Belial;
between light and darkness; faith and unbelief; the temple of God and idols? Christians are the temple of the
living God who dwells and walks among them. He is a
God to them; they are a people to Him. Therefore must
they come out from all fellowship with the worldly, and

[7] What a blessed state is that of a man, who, when he is taken out of
himself and a state of calm reflection, is entirely absorbed with, or turned
towards, God, and, when he does think soberly and calculates, is occupied
in love in seeking the good of his brethren, the members of Christ: who
is either rapt up into the contemplation *of* God and communion with
Him, or filled *with* Him, so as to think only of others in love!

be separate from them. As Christians, they must stand apart, for they are the temple of God. God dwells among them and walks there, and He is their God. They are therefore to come out from the world and be separate, and God will own them, and will be to them in the relationship of a Father with sons and daughters who are dear to Him.

This, observe, is the special relationship which God assumes with us. The two preceding revelations of God with men are named here, and He takes a third. To Abraham He revealed Himself as Almighty; to Israel as Jehovah or Lord. Here the Lord Almighty declares that He will be a Father to His own, to His sons and daughters. We come out from among the worldly, for it is just that (not physically out of the world, but while in it), in order to enter into the relationship of sons and daughters to the Almighty God: otherwise we cannot practically realize this relationship. God will not have worldlings in relation with Himself as sons and daughters; they have not entered into this position with regard to Him. Nor will He recognize those who remain identified with the world, as having this position; for the world has rejected His Son, and the friendship of the world is enmity against God: and he who is the friend of the world is the enemy of God. It is not being His child in a practical sense. God says therefore, "Come out from among them, and be separate, and ye shall be to Me for sons and daughters." Remember that it is not a question of coming out of the world—it is while we are in it—but of coming out from among the world, to *enter into the relationship* of sons and daughters, in order to be to Him for sons and daughters, to be owned of Him in this relationship.[8]

---

[8] The reader may remark that the passage sets two things before us: that God is present in the assembly of those who are separated from the world, and walks among them, as He did in the case of Israel in the wilderness when they had come out of Egypt; and that the individuals who compose the assembly enter into the relationship of sons and daughters.

Chapter 7

The legitimate consequences of God's promises: holiness of walk and purity of thought

BUT it is not only that from which we are separated to be in this position of sons and daughters that engages the apostle's attention, but the legitimate consequences of such promises. Sons and daughters of the Lord God Almighty, holiness becomes us. It is not only that we are to be separate from the world; but, in relationship with God, to cleanse ourselves from all filthiness of the flesh and spirit: holiness in the outward walk, and that which is quite as important with regard to our relationship to God, purity of thought. For, although man does not see the thoughts, the flow of the Spirit is stopped in the heart. There is not enlargement of heart in communion with God. It is much if His presence is felt, His relationship to us realized; grace is known, but God scarcely at all, in the way in which He makes Himself gradually known in communion.

The heart of Christ's minister revealed

The apostle returns to his own relationships with the Corinthians—relations formed by the word of his ministry. And now, having laid open what this ministry really was, he seeks to prevent the bonds being broken, which had been formed by this ministry between the Corinthians and himself through the power of the Holy Ghost.

"Receive us: we have wronged no one"—he is anxious not to wound the feelings of these restored ones, who found themselves again in their old affection for the apostle, and thus in their true relation with God. "I do not say this to condemn you," he adds; "for I have said before that ye are in my heart to die and live with you.

My boldness is great towards you, great is my glorying of
you. I am filled with comfort, I am exceeding joyful in
all my tribulation." He is not now unfolding the principles of the ministry, but the heart of a minister, all that
he had felt with regard to the state of the Corinthians.
When he had arrived in Macedonia (whither, it will be
remembered, he had gone without visiting Corinth), after
he had left Troas, because he did not find Titus there, who
was to bring him the answer to his first letter to the Corinthians—when he was come into Macedonia, his flesh had
no rest there either; he was troubled on every side: without were fightings, within were fears. There however God,
who comforts those who are cast down, comforted him
by the arrival of Titus, for whom he had waited with so
much anxiety; and not only by his coming, but by the
good news he brought from Corinth. His joy went beyond
all his sorrow, for his heart was to live and die with them.
He saw the moral fruits of the operation of the Spirit,
their desire, their tears, their zeal with regard to the
apostle; and his heart turns again to them in order to
bind up, by the expression of his affection, all the wounds
(needful as they were) which his first letter might have
made in their hearts.

Nothing more touching than the conflict in his heart
between the necessity he had felt, on account of their
previous state, to write to them with severity, and in some
sort with a cold authority, and the affections which, now
that the effect had been produced, dictated almost an
apology for the grief he might have caused them. If, he
says, I made you sorry by the letter, I do not repent:
even though he might have repented and had done so for
a moment. For he saw that the letter had grieved them,
were it but for a season. But now he rejoiced, not that
they had been made sorry, but that they had sorrowed
unto repentance. What solicitude! What a heart for the
good of the saints! If they had a fervent mind towards
him, assuredly he had given them the occasion and the

motive. No rest till he had tidings: nothing, not open doors, nor distress, could remove his anxiety. He regrets perhaps having written the letter, fearing that he had alienated the hearts of the Corinthians; and now, still pained at the thought of having grieved them, he rejoices, not at having grieved them, but because their godly sorrow had wrought repentance.

Paul's two letters: the difference between Paul the individual and Paul the inspired writer

He writes a letter according to the energy of the Holy Ghost. Left to the affections of his heart, we see him, in this respect, below the level of the energy of inspiration which had dictated that letter which the spiritual were to acknowledge as the commandments of the Lord; his heart trembles at the thought of its consequences, when he receives no tidings. It is very interesting to see the difference between the individuality of the apostle and inspiration. In the first letter we remarked the distinction which he makes between that which he said as the result of his experience, and the commandments of the Lord communicated through him. Here we find the difference in the experience itself. He forgets the character of his epistle for a moment, and, given up to his affections, he fears to have lost the Corinthians by the effort he had made to reclaim them. The form of the expression he uses shows that it was but for a moment that this sentiment took possession of his heart. But the fact that he had it plainly shows the difference between Paul the individual and Paul the inspired writer.

Paul's greatness of heart in speaking of his strong affection

Now he is satisfied. The expression of this deep interest which he feels for them is a part of his ministry, and valuable instruction for us, to show the way in which the heart enters into the exercise of this ministry, the flexibility of this mighty energy of love, in order to win and bend hearts by the opportune expression of that which is passing in our own: an expression which will assuredly take place when the occasion makes it right and natural, if the heart is filled with affection; for a strong affection likes to make itself known to its object, if possible, according to the truth of that affection. There is a grief of heart which consumes it, but a heart that feels godly sorrow is on the way to repentance.[9]

The fruits of godly sorrow

The apostle then sets forth the fruits of this godly sorrow, the zeal against sin it had produced, the heart's holy rejection of all association with sin. Now also that they had morally separated themselves, he separates those who were not guilty from those who were so. He will no longer confound them together. They had confounded themselves together morally by walking at ease with those who were in sin. By putting away the sin they were now outside the evil: and the apostle shows that it was with a view to their good, because he was devoted to them, that he had written to testify the loving occupation of his thoughts about them, and to put to the test their love for him before God. Sad as their walk had been, he had assured Titus, when encouraging him to go to Corinth, that he would certainly find hearts there that would respond to this appeal of apostolic affection. He had not been disappointed, and as he had declared the truth among them, that which he had said of them to Titus was found true

[9] Greatness of heart does not readily talk about feelings, because it thinks of others, not of itself. But it is not afraid, when occasion arises, to do so; because it thinks of others, and has a depth of purpose in its affections, which is behind all this movement of them. And Christianity gives greatness of heart. And besides, from its nature, it is confiding, and this wins, and gives unsought, influence this greatness of heart does not seek, for it is unselfish. His true relationship for their good the apostle did maintain.

also, and the affections of Titus himself were strongly awakened when he saw it.

Chapters 8, 9

Exhortation to help Israel's poor: the money collection: honesty before men as well as before God

IN the next chapter the apostle (being on his way to Judea) exhorts the Corinthians to prepare relief for the poor of Israel; sending Titus that all might be ready as of a willing mind—a disposition of which he had spoken on his journey as existing among these Christians, so that others had been stirred up to give likewise. And now, while reckoning upon their goodwill, and knowing that they had begun a year before, he would run no risk of finding that facts gave the lie to what he had said of them. Not that he would burden the Corinthians and ease those of Judea, but that the rich should provide for the need of the poor brethren, in order that none should be in want. Every one, if his will were in it, should be accepted of God according to his ability. He loved a cheerful giver. Only they should reap according as they sowed. Titus, happy at the result of his first visit, and attached to the Corinthians, was ready to go again and gather this fruit also for their own blessing. With him went the messengers of the other churches, charged with the collection made among them for the same purpose—a brother known to all the churches, and another of approved diligence, stimulated by Paul's confidence in the Corinthians. The apostle would not take charge of the money without having companions whose charge it should also be, avoiding all possibility of reproach in affairs of this kind, taking care that everything should be honest before men as well as before God. Nevertheless he did not speak by commandment in all this, but on account of the zeal of other churches, and to prove the sincerity of their love.

It will be remembered that it was this collection which occasioned all that happened to Paul at Jerusalem—that which put an' end to his ministry, stopped him on his way into Spain, and perhaps other places; and which, on the other hand, gave occasion to write the Epistles to the Ephesians, Philippians, Colossians, Philemon, and, it may be, to the Hebrews. How little we know the bearing of the circumstances we enter upon, happy that we are led by Him who knows the end from the beginning, and who makes all things work for good to those who love Him!

The happy and manifold effects of practical charity

In closing those exhortations to give according to their ability, he commends them to the rich goodness of God, who was able to make them abound in all things, so that they should be in circumstances to multiply their good works, enriched to all bountifulness, so as to produce in others (by means of the apostle's services in this respect) thanksgiving unto God. For, he adds, the happy effect of your practical charity, exercised in the name of Christ, would not only supply the want of the saints (through his administration of the collection made at Corinth) but abound also in thanksgiving to God; for, those who received it blessed God that their benefactors had been brought to confess the name of Christ, and to act with this practical liberality to them and to all. And this thought stirred them up to pray with fervent desire for those who provided in this way for their need, because of the grace of God manifested in them. Thus the bonds of eternal charity were strengthened on both sides, and glory redounded to God. Thanks be to God, says the apostle, for His unspeakable gift; for whatsoever may be the fruits of grace, we have the proof and the power in that which God has given. Here ends the matter of the epistle properly so called.

Chapter 10

Paul's connections with the Corinthians: the truth and authority of his apostleship: the principle on which he acted

THE apostle returns to the subject which pre-occupied him—his connections with the Corinthians, and the truth of his apostleship, which was questioned by those who seduced them, throwing contempt on his person. He was weak, they said, when present, and his speech contemptible, though bold when absent (his letters being boastful, but his bodily presence contemptible). "I beseech you," says the apostle, "by the meekness and gentleness of Christ [showing thus the true character of his own meekness and humility when among them], not to compel me to be bold among you, as I think of being with regard to some who pretend that I walk after the flesh." The strength of the war that he waged against evil was founded on spiritual weapons, with which he brought down all that exalted itself against the knowledge of God. This is the principle on which he acted, to seek to bring to obedience all who hearkened to God, and then severity to all disobedience, when once obedience should be fully established, and those who would hearken were restored to order. Precious principle!—the power and the guidance of the Spirit acting in full, and with all patience, to restore to order, and to a walk worthy of God; carrying the remonstrances of grace to the utmost, until all those who hearken to them and willingly obey God were restored; and then to assert divine authority in judgment and discipline, with the weight which was added to the apostolic action by the conscience and common action of all those who had been brought back to obedience.

Observe, that the apostle refers to his personal authority

as an apostle; but that he uses it in patience (for he possessed it for the purpose of edification and not for destruction) in order to bring back to obedience and uprightness all those who would hearken; and thus, preserving Christian unity in holiness, he clothes the apostolic authority with the power of the universal conscience of the assembly, guided by the Spirit, so far as there was a conscience at work.

He then declares that such as he is in his letters, such shall they find him when he is present; and he contrasts the conduct of those who took advantage of his labors, beguiling a people who had already become Christians, in order to stir them up against him, with his own conduct in going where Christ had not yet been known, seeking to bring souls to the knowledge of a Saviour of whom they were ignorant. Also he hoped that, when he visited the Corinthians, his ministry would be enlarged among them by their increase of faith, in order that he might go on beyond them to evangelize regions that still lay in darkness. But he who gloried, let him glory in the Lord.

Chapter 11

False teachers and the absolute devotedness manifested in the apostle's life: the living Source

IN chapter 11, jealous with regard to his beloved Corinthians with a godly jealousy, he carries yet further his arguments relating to false teachers. He asks the faithful in Corinth to bear with him a little, while he acts like a fool in speaking of himself. He had espoused them as a chaste virgin to Christ, and he feared lest any should corrupt their minds, leading them away from the simplicity that is in Him. If the Corinthians had received another Christ from the teachers lately come among them, or another Spirit, or another gospel, they might well bear with what these teachers did. But certainly the apostle had not been a whit behind in his instructions, even if they compared him with the most renowned of the apostles. Had he wronged them by receiving nothing at their hands (as these new teachers boasted of doing), and in taking money from other assemblies, and never being a burden to them? —a subject for boasting, of which no one should deprive him in the regions of Achaia. Had he refused to take anything from them because he loved them not? God knew —No; it was to deprive the false teachers of a means of commending themselves to them by laboring gratuitously among them, while the apostle received money. He would deprive them of this boast, for they were false apostles. As Satan transformed himself into an angel of light, so his instruments made themselves ministers of righteousness. But again let them bear with him while he spoke as a fool in speaking of himself. If these ministers of Satan accredited themselves as Jews, as of the ancient religion of God, consecrated by its antiquity and its traditions, he could do as much, a Hebrew of the Hebrews, and possessing all the titles to glory of which they boasted. And if it was a question of Christian service—to speak as a fool—certainly the comparison would not fail to show where the devotedness had been. Here in fact God has allowed this invasion of the apostle's work by these wretched judaizing men (calling themselves Christians) to be the means of acquainting us with something of the indefatigable labors of the apostle, carried on in a thousand circumstances of which we have no account. In the Acts God has given us the history of the establishment of the assembly in the great principles on which it was founded, and the phases through which it passed on coming out of Judaism. The apostle will have his own reward in the kingdom of glory, not by speaking of it among men. Nevertheless it is profitable for our faith to have some knowledge of Christian devotedness, as it was manifested in the life of the apostle. The folly of the Corinthians has been the means of furnishing us with a little glimpse of it.

Troubles and dangers without, incessant anxieties within, a courage that quailed before no peril, a love for poor sinners and for the assembly that nothing chilled—these few lines sketch the picture of a life of such absolute devotedness that it touches the coldest heart; it makes us feel all our selfishness, and bend the knee before Him who was the living source of the blessed apostle's devotedness, before Him whose glory inspired it.

Chapter 12

Glorying in infirmities: glorying in the sovereign power of God in a wonderful revelation

NEVERTHELESS, though forced to speak of himself, the apostle would glory only in his infirmities. But he is, as it were, outside his natural work. His past life unfolds before his eyes. The Corinthians obliged him to think of things which he had left behind. After having ended his account, and declared that he would glory in his infirmities alone, there was one circumstance that recurred to him. Nothing can be more natural, more simple, than all these communications. Must he glory? It is but unprofitable. He would come to that of which a man —as in the flesh—could not glory. It was the sovereign power of God in which the man had no part. It was a man in Christ of whom he spoke—such a one had been caught up to the third heaven, to paradise; in the body, or out of the body, he knew not. The body had no part in it. Of such a one he would glory.

That which exalted him on the earth he would put aside. That which took him up to heaven—that which gave him a portion there—that which he was "in Christ" —was his glory, the joy of his heart, the portion in which he readily would glory. Happy being, whose portion in

Christ was such that, in thinking of it, he is content to forget all that could exalt him as man! As he says elsewhere as to his hope, "That I may win Christ." The man, the body, had no share in a power, to taste of which he had to be caught up into heaven; but of such a one he would glory. There, where God and His glory are everything, separated from his body as to any consciousness of being in it, he heard things which men in the body were not capable of entering into, and which it was not fitting that a mortal man should declare, which the mode of being of a man in the body could not admit. These things had made the deepest impression on the apostle; they strengthened him for the ministry; but he could not introduce them into the manner of understanding and communicating which belongs to man's condition here below.

Caught up to the third heaven: its lessons

But many practical lessons are connected with this marvellous favor shown to the apostle. I say, "marvellous;" for in truth one feels what a ministry his must have been, whose strength, and whose way of seeing and judging, were drawn from such a position. What an extraordinary mission was that of this apostle! But he had it in an earthen vessel. Nothing amends the flesh. Once come back into the consciousness of his human existence on earth, the apostle's flesh would have taken advantage of the favor he had enjoyed to exalt him in his own eyes, to say, "None have been in the third heaven but thou, Paul." To be near God in the glory, as out of the body, does not puff up. All is Christ, and Christ is all: self is forgotten. To *have been* there is another thing. The presence of God makes us feel our nothingness. The flesh can avail itself of our having been in it, when we are no longer there. Alas, what is man? But God is watchful; in His grace He provided for the danger of His poor servant. To have taken him up to a fourth heaven—so to speak—would only have increased the danger. There is no way of amending the flesh; the presence of God silences it. It will boast of it as soon as it is no longer there. To walk safely, it must be held in check, such as it is. We have to reckon it dead; but it often requires to be bridled, that the heart be not drawn away from God by its means, and that it may neither impede our walk nor spoil our testimony. Paul received a thorn in the flesh, lest he should be puffed up on account of the abundant revelations which he had received. We know, by the Epistle to the Galatians, that it was something which tended to make him contemptible in his preaching: a very intelligible counterpoise to these remarkable revelations.

Paul's thorn in the flesh: Satan as God's servant

God left this task to Satan, as He used him for the humiliation of Job. Whatever graces may be bestowed on us, we must go through the ordinary exercises of personal faith, in which the heart only walks safely when the flesh is bridled, and so practically nullified, that we are not conscious of it as active in us when we wish to be wholly given to God, and to think of Him and with Him according to our measure.

The way of prevention: the lesson of humility to escape humiliation

Three times (like the Lord with reference to the cup He was to drink) the apostle asks Him that the thorn be taken away; but the divine life is fashioned in the putting off of self, and—imperfect as we are—this putting off as to practice that which, as to truth, if we look at our standing in Christ, we have put off, is wrought by our being made conscious of the humiliating unsuitableness

of this flesh, which we like to gratify, to the presence of
God and the service to which we are called. Happy
for us when it is by way of prevention, and not by the
humiliation of a fall, as was the case with Peter! The
difference is plain. There it was self-confidence mingled
with self-will in spite of the Lord's warnings. Here,
though still the flesh, the occasion was the revelations
which had been made to Paul. If we learn the tendency
of the flesh in the presence of God, we come out of it
humble, and we escape humiliation. But in general (and
we may say in some respects with all) we have to experience the revelations that lift us up to God, whatever their
measure may be, and we have to experience what the
vessel is in which it is contained, by the pain it gives us
through the sense of what it is—I do not say through
falls.

Man is nothing and Christ everything, in practical experience here

God, in His government, knows how to unite suffering
for Christ, and the discipline in the flesh, in the same
circumstance; and this explains Hebrews 12: 1-11. The
apostle preached: if he was despised in his preaching it
was truly for the Lord that he suffered; nevertheless the
same thing disciplined the flesh, and prevented the apostle
priding himself on the revelations he enjoyed, and the
consequent power with which he unfolded the truth. In
the presence of God, in the third heaven, he truly felt
that man was nothing, and Christ everything. He must
acquire the practical experience of the same thing below.
The flesh must be annulled, where it is not a nullity, by
the experimental sense of the evil which is in it, and
must thus become consciously a nullity in the personal
experience of that which it is. For what was the flesh
of Paul—which only hindered him morally in his work,
by drawing him away from God—except a troublesome

companion in his work? The suppression of the flesh
felt and judged was a most profitable exercise of the
heart.

Self lost sight of in the enjoyment of unutterable heavenly things

Observe here the blessed position of the apostle, as
caught up into the third heaven. He could glory in such
a one, because self was entirely lost in the things with
which he was in relation. He did not merely glory in
the things, neither does he say "in myself." Self was
completely lost sight of in the enjoyment of things that
were unutterable by the man when he returned into the
consciousness of self. He would glory in such a one; but
in himself, looked at in flesh, he would not glory, save in
his infirmities. On the other hand, is it not humiliating
to think that he who had enjoyed such exaltation should
have to go through the painful experience of what the
flesh is, wicked, despicable, and selfish?

The difference between Christ and any man

Observe also the difference between Christ and any
man whatsoever. Christ could be on the mount in glory
with Moses, and be owned as His Son by the Father
Himself; and He can be on the plain in the presence of
Satan and of the multitude; but, although the scenes
are different, He is alike perfect in each. We find
admirable affections in the apostles, and especially in
Paul; we find works, as Jesus said, greater than His
own; we find exercises of heart, and astonishing heights
by grace; in a word we see a marvellous power developed
by the Holy Ghost in this extraordinary servant of the
Lord; but we do not find the evenness that was in Christ.
He was the Son of Man who was in heaven. Such as
Paul are chords on which God strikes and on which He
produces a wondrous music; but Christ is all the music
itself.

Needed humiliation used by Christ to display His power: dependence learned

Finally, observe that the humiliation needed to reduce the rebellious flesh to its nothingness is used by Christ to display His power in it. Thus humbled, we learn our dependence. All that is of us, all that constitutes self, is a hindrance; the infirmity is that in which it is put down, laid low, in which weakness is realized. The power of Christ is perfected in it. It is a general principle; humanly speaking, the cross was weakness. Death is the opposite of the strength of man. Nevertheless it is in it that the strength of Christ revealed itself. In it He accomplished His glorious work of salvation.

Infirmity here is utter weakness: Christ's strength made perfect and manifested in man's infirmity

It is not sin in the flesh that is the subject here when infirmity is spoken of, but what is contrary to the strength of man. Christ never leant on human strength for a moment; He lived by the Father, who had sent Him. The power of the Holy Ghost alone was displayed in Him. Paul needed to have the flesh reduced to weakness, in order that there might not be in it the motion of sin which was natural to it. When the flesh was reduced to its true nothingness as far as good is concerned, and in a manifest way, then Christ could display His strength in it. That strength had its true character. Remark it well: that is always its character—strength made perfect in infirmity. The blessed apostle could glory in a man in Christ above, enjoying all this beatitude, these marvellous things which shut out self, so much were they above all we are. While enjoying them, he was not conscious of the existence of his body. When he was again conscious of it, that which he had heard could not be translated into those communications which had the body for their instrument, and human ears as the means of intelligence.

He gloried in that man in Christ above. Here below he only gloried in Christ Himself, and in that infirmity which gave occasion for the power of Christ to rest on him, and which was the demonstration that this power was that of Christ, that Christ made him the vessel of its manifestation. But this nevertheless was realized by painful experiences. The first was the man in Christ, the second the power of Christ resting on the man. For the first the man as to flesh is nothing; as to the second it is judged and put down—turned to weakness, that we may learn, and Christ's power may be manifested. There is an impulse, an ineffable source of ministry on high. Strength comes in on, the humiliation of man as he is in this world, when the man is reduced to nothingness—his true value in divine things—and Christ unfolds in him that strength which could not associate itself with the strength of man, nor depend on it in any way whatsoever. If the instrument was weak, as they alleged, the power which had wrought must have been—not its power, but that of Christ.

The practical strength and source of Paul's ministry

Thus, as at the beginning of the epistle we had the true characteristics of the ministry in connection with the objects that gave it that character, so we have here its practical strength, and the source of that strength, in connection with the vessel in which the testimony was deposited, the way in which this ministry was exercised by bringing a mortal man into connection with the ineffable sources from which it flowed, and with the living, present, active energy of Christ, so that the man should be capable of it, and yet that he should not accomplish it in his own carnal strength—a thing moreover impossible in itself.[10]

[10] This chapter is altogether a striking one. We have Christians in the highest and lowest condition; in the third heaven, and in actual low sin. In the first, a man in Christ (true in position, if not in vision, of us all),

The apostle giving the most striking proofs of his ministry and showing the love that "beareth all things"

Thus the apostle gloried in his sufferings and his infirmities. He had been obliged to speak as a fool; they who ought themselves to have proclaimed the excellence of his ministry had forced him to do it. It was among them all the most striking proofs of an apostolic ministry had been given. If in anything they had been behind other churches with regard to proofs of his apostleship, it was in their not having contributed anything to his maintenance. He was coming again. This proof would still be wanting. He would spend himself for them, as a kind father; even although the more he loved, the less he should be loved. Would they say that he had kept up appearances by taking nothing himself, but that he knew how to indemnify himself by using Titus in order to receive from them? It was no such thing. They well knew that Titus had walked among them in the same spirit as the apostle. Sad work, when one who is above these wretched motives and ways of judging and estimating things, and full of these divine and glorious motives of Christ, is obliged to come down to those which occupy the selfish hearts of the people with whom he has to do—hearts that are on a level with the motives which animate and govern the world that surrounds them! But love must bear all things and must think for others, if one cannot think with them, nor they with oneself.

the apostle glories, and we are right to glory—that is a man in Christ. As to what he is in himself he has to be brought to utter nothingness. But neither the glorying in the man in Christ, nor his being made nothing of in flesh, is power: the latter is the path to it; but then, being nothing, Christ's power is with him, rests on him, and here he has power in service, the man in Christ his own place—Christ in, or His power on, the man, his strength to serve. So that we have the highest apprehension of the Spirit, the lowest failure in flesh, and the way of power in making nothing of the latter, Christ's power being thereon with us, practical power while in the body. But there will be the sense of weakness, the want of proportion between what we are as to the earthen vessel, and what is ministered and enjoyed. It is not merely what is evil but the earthen vessel in which the treasure is.

Paul's fear of what he might find and have to do

Is it then that the apostle took the Corinthians for judges of his conduct? He spoke before God in Christ; and only feared lest, when he came, he should find many of those who professed the name of Christ like the world of iniquity that surrounded them; and that he should be humbled amongst them, and have to bewail many who had already sinned and had not repented of their misdeeds.

Chapter 13

Paul's delayed visit: his justice

FOR the third time he was coming. Everything should be proved by the testimony of two or three witnesses; and this time he would not spare. The apostle says, "This is the third time I am coming;" yet he adds, "as if I were present the second time, and being absent now." This is, because he had been there once, was to have gone there on his way to Macedonia, was coming a second time, but did not on account of the state the Corinthians were in; but this third time he was coming, and he had told them beforehand; and he said beforehand, as if he had gone the second time, although now absent, that if he came again he would not spare.

The Corinthians' dilemma: if Paul's apostleship were questioned, their own Christianity was overturned

He then puts an end to the question about his ministry by presenting an idea which ought to confound them utterly. If Christ had not spoken by him, Christ did not dwell in them. If Christ was in them, He must have spoken by the apostle, for he had been the means of their conversion. "Since," he says, "ye seek a proof that Christ speaketh in me, examine yourselves, whether ye be in the faith. Do ye not know yourselves, that Christ dwelleth in you, unless ye be reprobates?" and that they did not at all think. This was quite upsetting them, and turning their foolish and stupid opposition, their unbecoming contempt of the apostle, to their own confusion. What folly to allow themselves to be led away by a thought which, no doubt, exalted them in their own eyes; but which, by calling in question the apostleship of Paul, necessarily overturned, at the same time, their own Christianity!

The apostle's self-effacing desire for their blessing and perfection lest he should have to exercise his God-given authority

From "which to you-ward is not weak" to the end of verse 4 is a parenthesis, referring to the character of his ministry, according to the principles brought forward in the previous chapter: weakness, and that which tended to contempt, on the side of man; power on God's part: even as Christ was crucified in weakness and was raised again by divine power. If the apostle himself was weak, it was in Christ; and he lived in Him, by the power of God, towards the Corinthians. Whatever might be the case with them, he trusted they should know that he was not reprobate; and he only prayed to God that they should do no evil, not in order that he should not be reprobate (that is, worthless in his ministry, for here he is speaking of ministry), but that they might do good even if he were reprobate. For he could do nothing against the truth, but for the truth. He was not master of the Corinthians for his own interests, but was content to be weak that they might be strong; for what he desired was their perfection. But he wrote, being absent, as he had said, in order that when present he might not be obliged to act with severity, according to the authority which the

Lord had given him for edification, and not for destruction.

The touching and loving conclusion

He had written what his heart, filled and guided by the Holy Ghost, impelled him to say; he had poured it all out; and now, wearied, so to speak, with the effort, he closes the epistle with a few brief sentences:—"Rejoice, be perfect, be of good comfort, be of one mind, live in peace." Happen what might, it was this which he desired for them; and that the God of love and of peace should be with them. He rests in this wish, exhorting them to salute one another with affection, as all the saints, including himself, saluted them; praying that the grace of the Lord Jesus Christ, and the love of God, and the communion of the Holy Ghost, might be with them all.

GALATIANS

The subject of the Epistle: justification by grace: the impossibility of uniting the law and the gospel

THE Epistle to the Galatians sets before us the great source of the afflictions and conflicts of the apostle in the regions where he had preached the glad tidings; that which was at the same time the principal means employed by the enemy to corrupt the gospel. God, it is true, in His love, has suited the gospel to the wants of man. The enemy brings down that which still bears its name to the level of the haughty will of man and the corruption of the natural heart, turning Christianity into a religion that suits that heart, in place of one that is the expression of the heart of God—an all-holy God—and the revelation of that which He has done in His love to bring us into communion with His holiness. We see, at the same time, the connection between the judaizing doctrine—which is the denial of full redemption, and looking for good in flesh and man's will, power in man to work out righteousness in himself for God—in those who hindered the apostle's work, and the attacks that were constantly aimed against his ministry; because that ministry appealed directly to the power of the Holy Ghost and to the immediate authority of a glorified Christ, and set man as ruined, and Judaism which dealt with man, wholly aside. In withstanding the efforts of the judaizers, the apostle necessarily establishes the elementary principles of justification by grace. Traces both of this combat with the spirit of Judaism, by which Satan endeavored to destroy true Christianity, and of the maintenance by the apostle of this liberty, and of the authority of his ministry, are found in a multitude of passages in Corinthians, in Philippians, and Colossians, in Timothy, and historically in the Acts. In Galatians the two subjects are treated in a direct and formal way. But the gospel is consequently reduced to its most simple elements, grace to its most simple expression. But, with regard to the error, the question is but the more decisively settled; the irreconcilable difference between the two principles, Judaism and the gospel, is the more strongly marked.

God allowed this invasion of His assembly in the earliest days of its existence, in order that we might have the answer of divine inspiration to these very principles, when they should be developed in an established system which would claim submission from the children of God as being the Church that He had established and the only ministry that He acknowledged. The immediate source of true ministry, according to the gospel that Paul preached to the Gentiles, the impossibility of uniting the law and that gospel—of binding up together subjection to its ordinances and distinction of days—with the holy and heavenly liberty into which we are brought by a risen Christ, the impossibility, I repeat, of uniting the religion of the flesh with that of the Spirit, are plainly set forth in this epistle.

Chapters 1, 2

A different gospel, not the gospel of Christ

THE apostle begins, at the very outset, with the independence, as to all other men, of the ministry which he exercised, pointing out its true source, from which he received it without the intervention of any intermediate instrument whatsoever: adding, in order to show that the Galatians were forsaking the common faith of the saints, "all the brethren which are with me." Also, in opening the subject of his epistle, the apostle declares at once, that the doctrine introduced by the judaizers among the Galatians was a different gospel (but which was not really another), not the gospel of Christ.

The origin and authority of Paul's commission

He begins then by declaring that he is not an apostle either of men or by man. He does not come on the part of men as though sent by them, and it is not by means of any man that he had received his commission, but by Jesus Christ and God the Father who raised Him from the dead. It was by Jesus Christ, on the way to Damascus; and by the Father, it appears to me, when the Holy Ghost said, "Separate to me Barnabas and Paul." But he speaks thus, in order to carry up the origin of his ministry to the primary source of all real good, and of all legitimate authority.[1]

Deliverance from this present evil age

He wishes, as usual, to the assembly, grace and peace from God in His character of Father, and from Jesus in His character of Lord. But he adds here to the name of Jesus, that which belongs to that character of the gospel which the Galatians had lost sight of, namely, that Christ had given Himself for our sins that He might deliver us from this present evil age. The natural man, in his sins, belongs to this age. The Galatians desired to return to it under the pretext of a righteousness according to the law. Christ had given Himself for our sins in order to take us out of it: for the world is judged. Looked at as in the flesh, we are of it. Now the righteousness of the law has to do with men in the flesh. It is man as in the flesh who is to fulfil it, and the flesh has its sphere in this world;

---

[1] Not "of men" what calls itself the clergy would freely admit, but not "by man" they cannot. It strikes at the root of their existence as such. They boast its descent from man, but (it is remarkable enough) none from St. Paul, the true minister of the assembly, and, where most insisted on, from Peter, the apostle of the circumcision. Peter was not the apostle to the Gentiles at all, and, as far as we know, never went to them.

the righteousness which man would accomplish in the
flesh is directed according to the elements of this world.
Legal righteousness, man in the flesh, and the world, go
together. Whereas Christ has viewed us as sinners, having
no righteousness, and has given Himself for our sins and
to deliver us from this condemned world, in which men
seek to establish righteousness by putting themselves on
the ground of the flesh which can never accomplish it.
This deliverance is also according to the will of our God
and Father. He will have a heavenly people, redeemed
according to that love which has given us a place on high
with Himself, and a life in which the Holy Ghost works,
to make us enjoy it and cause us to walk in the liberty
and in the holiness which He gives us in this new creation, of which Jesus Himself, risen and glorified, is the
head and the glory.

The true gospel perverted: any addition can only alter and corrupt it

The apostle opens his subject without preamble: he was
full of it, and the state of the Galatians who were giving
up the gospel in its foundations forced it out from an
oppressed, and I may say, an indignant heart. How was
it possible that the Galatians had so quickly forsaken him,
who had called them according to the power of the grace
of Christ, for a different gospel? It was by this call of
God that they had part in the glorious liberty, and in the
salvation that has its realization in heaven. It was by the
redemption that Christ had accomplished and the grace
that belongs to us in Him, that they enjoyed heavenly and
Christian happiness. And now they were turning to an
entirely different testimony; a testimony which was not
another gospel, another true glad tidings. It did but
trouble their minds by perverting the true gospel. "But,"
says the apostle, reiterating his words on the subject, "if
an angel from heaven, or he [Paul himself], preached

anything besides the gospel that he had already preached to them, let him be accursed." Observe here, that he will allow nothing in addition to that which he had preached.

They did not formally deny Christ; they wished to add circumcision. But the gospel which the apostle had preached was the complete and whole gospel. Nothing could be added to it without altering it, without saying that it was not the perfect gospel, without really adding something that was of another nature, that is to say, corrupting it. For the entirely heavenly revelation of God was what Paul had taught them. In his teaching he had completed the circle of the doctrine of God. To add anything to it was to deny its perfection; and to alter its character, to corrupt it. The apostle is not speaking of a doctrine openly opposed to it, but of that which is outside the gospel which he had preached. Thus, he says, there cannot be *another* gospel; it is a different gospel, but there are no glad tidings except that which he had preached. It is but a corruption of the true, a corruption by which they troubled souls. Thus, in love to souls, he could anathematize those who turned them away from the perfect truth that he had preached. It was the gospel of God Himself. Everything else was of Satan. If Paul himself brought it, let him be anathema. The pure and entire gospel was already proclaimed, and it asserted its claims in the name of God against all that pretended to associate itself with it. Did Paul seek to satisfy the minds of men in his gospel, or to please men? In no wise; he would not thus be the servant of Christ.

Paul's gospel not according to nor received from man

He then speaks historically of his ministry, and of the question whether man had anything to do with it. His gospel was not according to man, for he had not received it from any man; he had not been taught it. That which

he possessed was his by the immediate revelation made
to him by Jesus Christ. And when God, who, from his
mother's womb, set him apart, and had called him by His
grace, was pleased to reveal His Son in him, the revelation had at once all its own power as such. He did not
consult any one. He did not put himself into communication with the other apostles, but at once acted independently of them, as being directly taught of God. It was not
till three years after that he went to make acquaintance
with Peter, and also saw James. The churches of Judea
did not know him by sight; only they glorified God for
the grace he had received. Moreover he was only fifteen
days in Jerusalem. He then went into Syria and Cilicia.
Fourteen years afterwards he went up to Jerusalem (we
have the account in Acts 15) with Barnabas, and took
Titus with him. But Titus, Gentile as he was, had not
been circumcised; an evident proof of the liberty in which
the apostle publicly stood. It was a bold step on his
part to take Titus with him, and thus decide the question
between himself and judaizing Christians. He went up
because of false brethren, who sought to spy out the
liberty into which Paul (enjoying it in the Spirit) introduced believers; and he went up by virtue of a revelation.

God's over-ruling guidance: the proofs of Paul's special and independent ministry

We may observe here, how the communications of God
may be inwardly the guides of our conduct, although we
yield to motives presented by others. In Acts 15 we find
the outward history; here, that which governed the apostle's heart. God (in order that the thing might be decided
at Jerusalem, to shut every mouth and to maintain unity)
did not allow the apostle to have the upper hand at Antioch, or to arrange on the spot the walk of the assembly
formed in that place. Neither did He allow him to iso-
late himself in his own convictions, but made him go up

to Jerusalem and communicate to the chief apostles that
which he taught, so that there should be community of
testimony on this important point; and that they also
should acknowledge Paul as taught of God independently
of them, and at the same time recognize his ministry as
sent of God, and that he was acting on the part of God
as much as themselves. For, although God would have
him communicate to them that which he had taught
others, he received nothing from them. The effect of his
communication was, that they owned the grace which
God had granted him and the ministry he had received for
the Gentiles, and they gave to him and to Barnabas the
right hands of fellowship.

Had he gone up earlier, whatever his knowledge might
have been, the proofs of his special and independent ministry would not have existed. But he had labored fruit-
fully for many years without receiving any mission from
the other apostles, and they had to recognize his apostleship as the immediate gift of God, as well as the truths
which God had imparted to him: the proofs were there;
and God had owned this apostleship, as He had given it.
The twelve had nothing to do but to acknowledge it, if
they acknowledged God as the source of all these excellent
gifts. Paul was an apostle from God without their intervention. They could acknowledge his ministry, and in it
the God who had given them that which they themselves
exercised.

Paul's firmness, ardor and clear-sightedness

Moreover Paul had always acted independently in the
fulfilment of his mission. When Peter came to Antioch,
he withstood him to the face, because he was to be blamed.
He was not, as to Paul, as a superior before whom his
subordinates must maintain a respectful silence. Although
God had wrought mightily in Peter, yet his companion in
apostleship (faithful to Him who had called him) could

not allow the gospel to be falsified which had been committed to his own care by the Lord Himself. Ardent as he was, poor Peter always cared too much about the opinion of others. Now the opinion that prevails in the world is always that which influences the heart of man; and this opinion is always one which gives a certain glory to man after the flesh. Paul, taught from above and full of the power of the Spirit, who by revealing heavenly glory had made him feel that all which exalted the flesh obscured that glory and falsified the gospel that declared it—Paul, who lived and moved morally in the new creation, of which a glorified Christ is the centre; and as firm as he was ardent, because he realized the things that are not seen; as clear-sighted as firm, because he lived in the realization of spiritual and heavenly things in Christ—Paul, for whom to win Christ thus glorified was everything, clearly sees the carnal walk of the apostle of the circumcision. He is not deterred by man; he is occupied with Christ who was his all, and with the truth. He does not spare one who overturned this truth, be his position in the assembly what it might.

Peter's dissimulation: its cause and effects

It was dissimulation in Peter. While alone, where the influence of heavenly truth prevailed, he ate with the Gentiles, surrounding himself with the reputation of walking in the same liberty as others. But when certain persons came from James, from Jerusalem, where he himself habitually lived, the centre where religious flesh and its customs still had (under the patient goodness of God) so much power, he no longer dared to use a liberty which was condemned by those Christians who were still Jewish in their sentiments; he withdrew himself. What a poor thing is man! And we are weak in proportion to our importance before men; when we are nothing, we can do all things, as far as human opinion is concerned. We exercise, at the same time, an unfavorable influence over others in the degree in which they influence us—in which we yield to the influence which the desire of maintaining our reputation among them exercises over our hearts: and all the esteem in which we are held, even justly, becomes a means of evil.[2] Peter, who fears those that came from Jerusalem, draws away all the Jews and even Barnabas with him in his dissimulation.

Paul's faithful and open rebuke

Paul, energetic and faithful, through grace, alone remains upright: and he rebukes Peter before them all. Why compel Gentiles to live as Jews in order to enjoy full Christian communion, when he, being a Jew, had felt himself free to live as the Gentiles? Themselves Jews by nature, and not poor sinners of the Gentiles, they had given up the law as a means of securing the favor of God, and had taken refuge in Christ. But if they sought to rebuild the edifice of legal obligations, in order to acquire righteousness, why had they overturned it? Thus acting, they made themselves transgressors in having overturned it. And more than that; since it was in order to come to Christ—in exchange for the efficacy which they had formerly supposed to exist in the law as a means of justification—that they had ceased to seek righteousness by the law, Christ was a minister of sin. His doctrine had made them transgressors! For in rebuilding the edifice of the law, they made it evident that they ought not to have overthrown it; and it was Christ who made them do so.

The purpose of ordinances: their use and mis-use

What a result from the weakness which, in order to please men, had returned to those things that were grati-

[2] It is practically important to remark that worldliness or any allowance of what is not of God, by a godly man, gives the weight of his godliness to the evil he allows.

fying to the flesh! How little did Peter think of this! How little do many Christians suspect it! To rest upon ordinances is to rest upon the flesh; there are none in heaven. When Christ; who is there, is everything, it cannot be done. Christ has indeed established ordinances to distinguish His people from the world, by that which signified on the one hand that they were not of it but dead with Him to it, and, on the other hand, to gather them on the ground of that which alone can unite them all— on the ground of the cross and of accomplished redemption, in the unity of His body. But if, instead of using them with thanksgiving according to His will, we rest upon them, we have forsaken the fulness, the sufficiency, of Christ, to build upon the flesh, which can thus occupy itself with these ordinances, and find in them its fatal sustenance and a veil to hide the perfect Saviour, of whose death, as in connection with this world and with man living in the flesh, these ordinances so plainly speak to us. To rest upon Christian ordinances is exactly to deny the precious and solemn truth which they present to us, that there is no longer righteousness after the flesh, since Christ is dead and risen.

Condemned to death under the law: dead with Christ and dead to the law

This the apostle deeply felt; this he had been called to set before the eyes and consciences of men by the power of the Holy Ghost. How many afflictions, how many conflicts, his task cost him! The flesh of man likes to have some credit; it cannot bear to be treated as vile and incapable of good, to be excluded and condemned to annihilation, not by efforts to annul itself, which would restore it all its importance, but by a work that leaves it in its true nothingness, and that has pronounced the absolute judgment of death upon it, so that, convicted of being nothing but sin, it has only to be silent. If it acts, it is only to do evil. Its place is to be dead, and not better. We have both right and power to hold it as such, because Christ has died, and we live in His risen life. He has Himself become our life. Alive in Him, I treat the flesh as dead; I am not a debtor to it. God *has* condemned sin in the flesh, in that His Son came in the likeness of sinful flesh and for sin. It is this great principle of our being dead with Christ which the apostle sets forth at the end of the chapter (only first recognizing the force of the law to bring death into the conscience). He had discovered that to be under a law was to find himself condemned to death. He had undergone in spirit the whole force of this principle; his soul had realized death in all its power. He was dead; but, if so, he was dead to the law. The power of a law does not reach beyond life; and, its victim once dead, it has no more power over him. Now Paul had acknowledged this truth; and, attributing to the principle of law its whole force, he confessed himself to be dead by law—dead then to law. But how? Was it by undergoing the eternal consequences of its violation; for if the law killed, it condemned too? (See 2 Cor. 3.) By no means. It is quite another thing here. He did not deny the authority of the law, he acknowledged its force in his soul, but in death, in order that he might live to God.

Law reaching Saul the sinner in the Person of Christ who died: life since Christ lived in him: the disappearance of the law's dominion

But where could he find this life, since the law only slew him? This he explains. It was not himself in his own responsibility, exposed as he was to the final consequences of the violation of the law—who could find life in it? Christ had been crucified—He who could suffer the curse of the law of God, and death, and yet live in the mighty and holy life which nothing could take away; which made it impossible for death to hold Him, although in grace He tasted it. But the apostle (whom this same grace had reached) owning it according to the truth as a poor sinner in subjection to death, and blessing the God who granted him the grace of life and of free acceptance in Christ, had been associated with Christ in God's counsels in His death (now realized by faith, and become true practically by Christ, who had died and risen again, being his life). He was crucified with Him, so that the condemnation of it was gone for Paul. It is Christ whom death under the law had reached. The law had reached Saul the sinner, in the Person of Him who had given Himself for him, in fact, and now Saul himself in conscience, and brought death there—but the death of the old man (see Rom. 7: 9, 10)—and it had now no more right over him; for the life to which the dominion of the law was attached had come to its end upon the cross.[3] Nevertheless he lived: yet not he, but Christ, in that life in which Christ rose from among the dead—Christ lived in him. Thus the dominion of the law over him disappeared (while ascribing to the law all its force), because that dominion was connected with the life in regard to which he reckoned himself to be dead in Christ, who had really undergone death for this purpose. And Paul lived in that mighty and holy life, in the perfection and energy of which Christ was risen from among the dead, after having borne the curse of the law. He lived to God, and held the corrupt life of his flesh as dead. His life drew all its character, all its mode of being, from the source whence it flowed.

Christ the Source and Object of our life: individual, intimate faith in the Son of God

But the creature must have an object to live for, and so it was as to Paul's soul, it was by the faith of Jesus

---

[3] Christ had also borne his sins; but this is not the subject here spoken of; it is the dominion of the law over him while living on earth.

Christ. By faith in Jesus Christ Paul lived indeed. The Christ who was the source of his life, who was his life, was its object also. It is this which always characterizes the life of Christ in us; He Himself is its object—He alone. The fact, that it is by dying for us in love that He —who was capable of it, the Son of God—has given us thus freed from sin this life as our own, being ever before the mind, in our eyes He is clothed with the love He has thus shown us. We live by faith of the Son of God, who has loved us, and given Himself for us. And here it is personal life, the individual faith that attaches us to Christ, and makes Him precious to us as the object of the soul's intimate faith. Thus the grace of God is not frustrated: for, if righteousness were established on the principle of law, Christ died in vain, since it would be by keeping the law ourselves that we should, in our own persons, acquire righteousness.

Chapter 3

Saved by works or by grace through faith?
Believing God's testimony

WHAT a loss, dreadful and irreparable, to lose such a Christ, as we, under grace, have known Him; such a righteousness; such a love; the Son of God our portion, our life; the Son of God devoted for us, and to us! It is. indeed this which awakens the strong feelings of the apostle: "Oh foolish Galatians," he continues, "who hath bewitched you?" Christ had been portrayed as crucified before their eyes. Thus their folly appeared still more surprising, in thinking of what they had received, of what in fact they were enjoying under the gospel, and of their sufferings for the sake of that gospel. Had they received the Spirit through works done on the principle of law, or through a testimony received by faith? Having begun by the power of the Spirit, would they carry the thing on to perfection by the wretched flesh? They had suffered for the gospel, for the pure gospel, unadulterated with Judaism and the law: was it then all in vain? Again, he who ministered to them the Spirit, and worked miracles among them, was it through works on the principle of law, or in connection with a testimony received by faith? Even as Abraham believed God, and it was accounted to him for righteousness. It was the principle established by God in the case of the father of the faithful. Therefore they who placed themselves by grace on the principle of faith, —they were the "children of Abraham." And the Scripture, foreseeing that God would justify the Gentiles through faith, preached this gospel beforehand to Abraham, saying, "In thee shall all nations be blessed."

Abraham's standing before God and the blessing of believing Gentiles

The epistle is necessarily elementary, for the Galatians were forsaking the foundation, and the apostle insists on that. The great principles of the epistle are, connected with the known presence of the Spirit, promise according to grace in contrast with and before law, Christ the accomplishment of the promise, the law coming in by the bye meanwhile. The Gentiles were thus heirs in Christ, true and sole heir of promise, and the Jews acquiring the position of sons.

The law's true character: its curse borne that blessing might reach Jew and Gentile: the Holy Spirit the subject of God's promises

We have then the principle on which Abraham stood before God, and the declaration that it was in him the Gentiles should be blessed. Thus they who are on the principle of faith are blessed with Abraham the believer; while the law pronounced an express curse on those who did not keep it in every point. This use of Deuteronomy 27 has been considered elsewhere. I would call to mind only that (the twelve tribes having been divided into two companies of six each, the one to announce the blessing and the other the curse) the curses alone are recited, the blessings entirely omitted—a striking circumstance, used by the apostle to show the true character of the law. At the same time the Scripture plainly set forth that it was not the works of the law that justified; for it said, "The just shall live on the principle of faith." Now the law was not on the principle of faith, but he who *has done* these things shall live by them. But was not this authority of the law to be maintained, as being that of God? Assuredly. But Christ had borne its curse (having redeemed and thus delivered those who—subject before to the sentence of the law—had now believed in Him), in order that the blessing of Abraham might reach the Gentiles through Him, so that all believers, both Jew and Gentile, should receive the Spirit who had been promised.

Christ had exhausted for the believer—who before was subject to the law and guilty of having broken it—all the curse that it pronounced on the guilty: and the law which distinguished Israel had lost its power over the Jew who believed in Jesus, through the very act that bore the most striking testimony to its authority. The barrier therefore no longer existed, and the former promise of blessing could flow freely (according to the terms in which it was made to Abraham) upon the Gentiles through the channel of Christ, who had put away the curse that the law brought upon the Jews; and both Jew and Gentile, believing in Him, could receive the Holy Ghost, the subject of God's promises, in the time of blessing.

The unconditional promises confirmed to Christ and given long before the law: the reason the law was given

Having thus touched on this point, the apostle now

treats, not the effect of the law upon the conscience, but the mutual relationship that existed between the law and the promise. Now the promise had been given first, and not only given, but it had been confirmed; and, had it been but a human covenant solemnly confirmed, it could neither be added to nor annulled. But God had engaged Himself to Abraham by promise 430 years before the law, having deposited, so to say, the blessing of the Gentiles in his person. (Gen. 12.) This promise was confirmed to his seed[4] (Isaac: Gen. 22), and to only one; he does not say to the seeds, but "to the Seed," and it is Christ who is this Seed. A Jew would not deny this last point. Now the law, coming so long after, could not annul the promise that was made before and solemnly confirmed by God, so as to render it of no effect. For if the inheritance were on the principle of law, it was no more on that of promise: but God gave it to Abraham by promise. "Wherefore then the law?" since the unchangeable promise was already given, and the inheritance must come to the object of that promise, the law having no power to change it in any way. It is because there is another question between the

---

[4] We must read, "It is to Abraham that the promise was made, and to his seed:" not, "to Abraham and to his seed." The promises relating to the temporal blessings of Israel were made to Abraham and to his seed, with the addition that this seed should be as the stars in multitude. But here Paul is not speaking of the promises made to the Jews, but of the blessing granted to the Gentiles. And the promise of blessing for the Gentiles was made to Abraham alone, without mentioning his seed (Gen. 12), and, as the apostle says here, it was confirmed to his seed—without naming Abraham (chap. 22)—in the alone person of Isaac, the type of the Lord Jesus offered up in sacrifice and raised from the dead, as Isaac was in a figure. Thus the promise was confirmed, not *in* Christ, but *to* Christ the true seed of Abraham. It is on this fact, that the promises were confirmed to Christ, that the whole argument of the apostle depends. The importance of the typical fact, that it is after the figurative sacrifice and resurrection of Isaac that the promise was confirmed to the latter, is evident. Doubtless that which realized this figure secured thus the promise to David; but at the same time the middle wall of partition was broken down, the blessing can flow to the Gentiles—and, let us add, to the Jews also—by virtue of the expiation made by Christ; the believer, made the righteousness of God in Him, can be sealed with the Holy Ghost who had been promised. When once the import of Genesis 12 and 22 has been apprehended, in that which relates to the promises of blessing made to the Gentiles, one sees most clearly the foundation on which the apostle's argument rests.

soul and God, or, if you will, between God and man, namely, that of righteousness. Grace, which chooses to bestow blessing, and which promises it beforehand, is not the only source of blessing for us. The question of righteousness must be settled with God, the question of sin and of the guilt of man.

The question of man's sin, guilt and unrighteousness

Now the promise which was unconditional and made to Christ, did not raise the question of righteousness. It was necessary that it should be raised, and in the first place by requiring righteousness from man, who was responsible to produce it and walk in it before God. Man ought to have been righteous before God. But sin had already come in, and it was in reality to make sin manifest that the law was brought in. Sin was indeed present, the will of man was in rebellion against God; but the law drew out the strength of that evil will, and it manifested its thorough contempt of God by overleaping the barrier which the prohibition of God raised between it and its desires.

Man's moral condition manifested: God's majesty and glory at Sinai

The law was added that there might be transgressions, not (as we have seen already, when meditating on the Romans, where this same subject is treated) that there might be sin, but that there might be transgressions, through which the consciences of men might be reached, and the sentence of death and condemnation made to be sensibly felt in their light and careless hearts. The law was therefore introduced between the promise and its fulfilment, in order that the real moral condition of man should be made manifest. Now the circumstances under which it was given rendered it very obvious that the law was in no wise the means of the fulfilment of the promise, but that on the contrary it placed man upon an altogether different ground, which made him know himself, and at the same time made him understand the impossibility of his standing before God on the ground of his own responsibility. God had made an unconditional promise to the seed of Abraham. He will infallibly perform it, for He is God. But in the communication of the law there is nothing immediate and direct from God simply. It is ordained by the hand of angels. It is not God who, in speaking, engages Himself simply by His own Word to the person in whose favor the promise is to be fulfilled. The angels of glory, who had no part in the promises (for it was angels who shone in the glory of Sinai; see Psalm 68) invested, by the will of God, the proclamation of the law with the splendor of their dignity. But the God of the angels and of Israel stood apart, hidden in His sanctuary of clouds and fire and thick darkness. He was encompassed with glory; He made Himself terrible in His magnificence; but He did not display Himself. He had given the promise in Person; a mediator brought the law. And the existence of a mediator necessarily supposes two parties. But God was one (and it was the foundation of the whole Jewish religion). There was therefore another on whom the stedfastness of the covenant made at Sinai depended. And in fact Moses went up and down, and carried the words of Jehovah to Israel, and the answer of Israel who engaged themselves to perform that which Jehovah imposed on them as a condition of the enjoyment of the effect of His promise.

The conditions of blessing under the law: man's utter failure: the reason why the Scripture shuts up all under sin

"If ye will indeed obey My voice," said Jehovah. "All that Jehovah hath spoken we will do," replied Israel intermediately through Moses. What were the consequences? The apostle, with touching tenderness, as it appears to me, does not answer this question—does not deduce the necessary consequences of his argument. His object was to show the difference between the promise and the law, without needlessly wounding the heart of a people whom he loved. On the contrary, he endeavors at once to prevent any offence that might arise from what he had said (further developing at the same time his thesis). Was the law against the promises of God? By no means. If a law had been given that was to impart life, then righteousness (for that is our subject in this passage) should have been by the law. Man, possessing divine life, would have been righteous in the righteousness that he had accomplished. The law promised the blessing of God on the terms of man's obedience: if it could have given life at the same time, this obedience would have taken place, righteousness would have been accomplished on the ground of law; they to whom the promise had been made would have enjoyed its fulfilment by virtue of their own righteousness. But it was the contrary which happened, for after all man, whether Jew or Gentile, is a sinner by nature; without law, he is the slave of his unbridled passions; under law, he shows their strength by breaking the law. The Scripture has shut up all under sin, in order that this promise, by faith in Jesus Christ, should be accomplished in favor of those who believe.

The law as a child's tutor to the Jews until faith came

Now before faith came (that is, Christian faith, as the principle of relationship with God, before the existence of the positive objects of faith in the Person, the work, and the glory of Christ as Man, had become the means of establishing the faith of the gospel), the Jews were kept under the law, shut up with a view to the enjoyment of this privilege which was to come. Thus the law had been to the Jews as a child's conductor up to Christ, in order that they might be justified on the principle of faith. Meanwhile they were not without restraint; they were kept apart from the nations not less guilty than they, but kept separate for a justification, the necessity of which was made more evident by the law which they did not fulfil, but which demanded righteousness from man (thus showing that God required this righteousness). But when once faith had come, those until then subject to the law were no longer under the tutelage of this law, which only bound them until faith was come. For this faith, placing man immediately in the presence of God, and making the believer a son of the Father of glory, left no more place for the guidance of the tutor employed during the nonage of one who was now set free and in direct relationship with the Father.

Set free, in direct relationship with the Father as sons: in Christ and heirs of the promise

The believer then is a son in immediate connection with his Father, with God (God Himself being manifested). He is a son, because all who have been baptized to have part in the privileges that are in Christ have put on Christ. They are not before God as Jews or Gentiles, bond or free, male or female; they are before God according to their position in Christ, all one thing in Him, Christ being for all the common and only measure of their relationship with God. But this Christ was, as we have seen, the one Seed of Abraham: and if the Gentiles were in Christ, they entered consequently into this privileged position; they were, in Christ, the seed of Abraham, and heirs according to the promise made to that seed.

Chapter 4

The relative positions of the Jew before Christ's coming and of the believing Jew or Gentile after His manifestation

THE relative position therefore of the Jew (even though he were godly) before the coming of Christ, and of the believing Jew or Gentile when Christ had been revealed, is clearly set forth; and in the commencement of chapter 4 the apostle sums up that which he had said. He compares the believer before the coming of Christ to a child under age, who has no direct relation with his father as to his thoughts, but who receives his father's orders, without his accounting for them to him, as a servant would receive them. He is under tutors and governors until the time appointed of the father. Thus the Jews, although they were heirs of the promises, were not in connection with the Father and His counsels in Jesus, but were in tutelage to principles that appertained to the system of the present world, which is but a corrupt and fallen creation. Their walk was ordained of God in this system, but did not go beyond it. We speak of the system by which they were guided, whatever divine light they might receive from time to time to reveal heaven to them, to encourage them in hope, while making the system under the rule of which they were placed yet darker. Under the law then, heirs as they were, they were still in bondage. But when the time was fulfilled and ripe for it, God sent forth His Son—an act flowing from His sovereign goodness for the accomplishment of His eternal counsels, and for the manifestation of all His character. It was God who did it. It was He who acted. The law required man to act, and it manifested man to be just the contrary of that which he ought to have been according to the law. But the Son of God comes from God. *He requires noth-*

ing. He is manifested in the world in relation with men under the double aspect of a Man born of woman and a Man under law.

Christ manifested in the world as born of a woman: a Man under law: His redemption and its efficacy: sons and heirs

If sin and death came in by the woman, Christ came into this world by the woman also. If through law man is under condemnation, Christ puts Himself under law also. Under this double aspect He takes the place in which man was found; He takes it in grace without sin, but with the responsibility that belonged to it—a responsibility which He alone has met. But still the object of His mission went much farther than the manifestation in His Person of Man without sin, in the midst of evil, and having the knowledge of good and evil. He came to redeem those that were under the law, in order that believers (be they who they may) should receive the adoption. Now that the Gentile believers had been admitted to share the adoption was proved by the sending of the Spirit who made them cry, "Abba, Father." For it is because they are sons, that God sent the Spirit of His Son into their heart as well as into that of the Jews without distinction. The Gentile, a stranger to the house, and the Jew, who under age differed in nothing from a servant, had each taken the position of a son in direct relation with the Father—a relation of which the Holy Ghost was the power and the witness—in consequence of the redemption wrought in their behalf by the Son (the Jew under the law needing it as much as the Gentile in his sins). But its efficacy was such that the believer was not a bondman but a son, and if a son, an heir also of God by Christ. Previously the Gentiles had been in bondage, not indeed to the law, but to that which, in its nature, was not God. They knew not God, and were the slaves of everything

that boasted of the name of God, in order to blind the
heart of man alienated from Him who is the true God and
from His knowledge.

Desiring to go back again into bondage

But what were these Gentiles, become Christians, now
doing? They desired to be again in bondage to these
wretched elements, worldly and carnal, to which they
had formerly been in subjection; these things of which
the carnal man could form his religion, without one moral
or spiritual thought, and which placed the glory due to
God, in outward observances which an unbeliever and a
heathen ignorant of God could call his religion and glory
in it.

The true value of the figures of the realities in Christ: leaving the substance of the shadows

As figures, which God used to bear testimony beforehand to the realities that are in Christ, they had their
true value. God knew how to reconcile the employment
of these figures, which are profitable to faith, with a religious system that tested man in the flesh, and that
served to answer the question, whether, with every kind
of help, man was able to stand before God and to serve
Him. But to go back to these ordinances made for man
in the flesh, now that God had shown man's incapability
of becoming righteous before Him—now that the substance of these shadows was come, was to go back to the
position of men in the flesh, and to take that standing
without any command of God that sanctioned it. It was
to go back to the ground of idolatry, that is to say, to a
carnal religion, arranged by man without any authority
from God, and which in no way brought man into connection with Him. For things done in the flesh had not
certainly that effect. "Ye observe days and months and
seasons and years." This the heathen did in their human

religion. Judaism was a human religion ordained of God, but, by going back to it when the ordinance of God was no longer in force, they did but go back to the paganism out of which they had been called to have part with Christ in heavenly things.

Ritualism after the cross: the apostle's love and concern for those to whom he had brought the gospel

Nothing can be more striking than this statement of what ritualism is after the cross. It is simply heathenism, going back to man's religion, when God is fully revealed: "I fear concerning you," said the apostle, "that I have labored in vain." But they reproached the apostle with not being a faithful Jew according to the law, with freeing himself from its authority. "Be ye then," says he, "as I am; for I am as ye are" (namely, free from the law). Ye have done me no wrong in saying so. Would to God ye were as much so! He then reminds them of his thorn in the flesh. It was some circumstance adapted to make him contemptible in his ministry. Nevertheless they had received him as an angel of God, as Jesus Christ. What was become of that blessedness? Had he become their enemy because he had told them the truth? Zeal was good; but if it had a right thing for its object, they should have persevered in their zeal, and not merely have maintained it while he was with them. These new teachers were very zealous to have the Galatians for their partisans, and to exclude them from the apostle, that they might be attached to themselves. He labored again, as though travailing in birth, in order that Christ should be formed as if anew in their hearts—a touching testimony of the strength of his Christian love. This love was divine in its character; it was not weakened by the disappointment of ingratitude, because its source was outside the attraction of its objects. Moses said, "Have I conceived all this people, that I should carry them in my bosom?" Paul is ready to travail in birth with them a second time.

The two systems, law and grace: Hagar and Sarah, bondage and liberty, Jerusalem above and Jerusalem on earth

He does not know what to say. He would like to be present with them, that he might, on seeing them, adapt his words to their condition, for they had really forsaken Christian ground. Would they then, since they desired to be under the law, hear the law? In it they might see the two systems, in the type of Hagar and Sarah: that of law, gendering to bondage; and that of grace, to liberty; not that only, but the positive exclusion of the child of bondage from the inheritance. The two could not be united; the one shut out the other. The bond-child was born according to the flesh, the free-child according to promise. For the law and the covenant of Sinai were in connection with man in the flesh. The principle of man's relationship with God, according to the law (if such relations had been possible), was that of a relationship formed between man in the flesh and the righteous God. As to man, the law and the ordinances were only bondage. They aimed at bridling the will without its being changed. It is all-important to understand, that man under the law is man in the flesh. When born again, dead and risen again, he is no longer under law, which has only dominion over man in that he is alive here below. Read "Jerusalem which is above is our mother"—not "the mother of us all." It is in contrast with Jerusalem on earth, which in its principle answered to Sinai. And observe that the apostle is not here speaking of the violation of the law, but of its principle. The law itself puts man in a state of bondage. It is imposed on man in the flesh, who is opposed to it. By the very fact that he has self-will, the law and that will are in conflict. Self-will is not obedience.

The children of Jerusalem now: the children of promise

Verse 27 presents some difficulty to many minds, because it is generally confounded with Hagar and Sarah. But it is a separate consideration, suggested by the idea of Jerusalem above. The verse is a quotation from Isaiah 54, which celebrates the joy and glory of the earthly Jerusalem at the beginning of the millennium. The apostle quotes it to show that Jerusalem had more children during the time of her desolation than when she had a husband. In the millennium Jehovah, the Lord, will be her husband. He had been so before. At present she is desolate, she bears not. Nevertheless there are more children than previously when she was married. Such were the marvellous ways of God. All Christians are reckoned, when earth takes its course again, as the children of Jerusalem with no husband and desolate, so that the Galatians were not to own it as if God did still. Sarah was not without a husband. Here is a different order of thought. Without a husband and desolate (so that, properly speaking, she has none) Jerusalem has more children now than in the best days of her career, when Jehovah was a husband to her. For, as regards the promise, the gospel came forth from her. The assembly is not of promise. It was a counsel hid in God, of which the promises had never spoken. Its position is a yet higher one; but in this place the apostle's instruction does not rise to that height. But we are also the children of promise, and not of the flesh. Israel after the flesh had no other pretension than to be the children of Abraham after the flesh; we are so only by promise. Now the word of God cast out the child of the bondwoman, born after the flesh, that he might not be heir with the child of promise. As to us, we are the children of promise.

Chapter 5

The liberty of Christ and the yoke of the law

IT is in this liberty, the liberty of Christ, alluding to the free woman and Jerusalem above, that they were to stand fast, and not put themselves again under the yoke of the law. If they took that ground they made themselves responsible to keep it personally and wholly, and Christ was of no effect to them. They could not rest upon the work of Christ for righteousness, and then hold themselves responsible to fulfil righteousness themselves according to the law. The two things contradict each other. Hence too it would be no longer grace on which they stood. They forsook grace, in order to satisfy the requirements of the law. This is not the Christian's position.

The Christian's position

Here is the Christian's position. He does not seek for righteousness before God as a man who does not possess it; he is the righteousness of God in Christ, and Christ Himself is the measure of that righteousness. The Holy Ghost dwells in him. Faith rests in this righteousness, even as God rests in it, and this faith is sustained by the Holy Ghost, who turns the heart that is established in that righteousness towards the glory that is its recompense—a recompense which Christ enjoys already, so that we know what that righteousness deserves. Christ is in the glory due to righteousness, to the work which He accomplished. We know this righteousness in virtue of that which He has wrought, because God has owned His work and set Him at His right hand on high. The glory in which He is is His just reward, and the proof of that righteousness. The Spirit reveals the glory, and seals to us that righteousness on which faith builds. It is thus that the apostle expresses it: "We, through the Spirit, wait for the hope [the hoped-for glory] of righteousness by faith." To us it is faith, for we have not yet the thing hoped for—the glory due to that righteousness which is ours. Christ possesses it, so that we know what we hope for. It is by the Spirit that we know it, and that we have the assurance of the righteousness which gives us the title to possess it. It is not righteousness we wait for, but, by the Spirit in faith, the hope that belongs to it. It is by faith; for in Christ neither circumcision nor uncircumcision avails anything, but faith working by love. There must be a moral reality.

The apostle's distress at the Galatian error: the glory of Christ at stake: his confidence in Christ's grace for His own regained

The apostle's heart is oppressed at the thought of what they were rejecting, and the mischief this doctrine was doing. It overflows. In the midst of his argument he interrupts himself. "Ye did run well: who has hindered you from obeying the truth?" To be so easily persuaded of this judaizing doctrine, which was but a fatal error, was not the work of Him who had called them. It was not thus that through grace they had become Christians. A little leaven corrupted the whole.

Nevertheless the apostle regains his confidence by looking higher. By resting on the grace which is in Christ towards His own, he can re-assure himself with regard to the Galatians. He stood in doubt when he thought of them; he had confidence when he thought of Christ, that they would surely not be otherwise minded. Thus delivered from the evil by grace, as in the moral case of the Christians, he was ready to punish all disobedience, when all that knew how to obey had been brought fully back to obedience; so here also, every heart that was susceptible of the influence of the truth would be brought back to the power of the truth of Christ; and those who, active in evil, troubled them by false doctrine, those whose will was engaged in propagating error, should bear their burden. It is very beautiful to see the apostle's uneasiness, when he thinks of men—the fruit moreover of his love for them —and the confidence which he regains as soon as he lifts up his heart to the Lord. But his abrupt style, his broken and unconnected words, show how deeply his heart was engaged. The error that separated the soul from Christ was to him more terrible than the sad fruits of practical separation. We do not find the same marks of agitation in the Epistle to the Corinthians; here the foundation of everything was in question. In the case of the Galatians the glory of Christ the Saviour was at stake, the only thing that could bring a soul into connection with God; and on the other hand it was a systematic work of Satan to overthrow the gospel of Christ as needed for the salvation of men.

The spirit of Judaism as Satan's great instrument in opposing the gospel

Here, interrupting himself, he adds, "And I, if I preach circumcision, why am I persecuted?" It will in fact be seen that the Jews were habitually the instigators of the persecution which the apostle suffered from the Gentiles. The spirit of Judaism, as has been the case in all ages, the religious spirit of the natural man, has been Satan's great instrument in his opposition to the gospel. If Christ would put His sanction on the flesh, the world would come to terms and be as religious as you please, and would value itself upon its devotion. But in that case it would not be the true Christ. Christ came, a witness that the natural man is lost, wicked, and without hope, dead in his trespasses and sins; that redemption is necessary, and a new man. He came in grace, but it was because man was incapable of being restored; and consequently all must be pure grace, and emanate from God. If Christ would have to do with the old man, all would be well; but, I repeat, He would no longer be Christ. The world then, the old man, does not endure Him. But there is a conscience, there is a felt need of religion, there is the prestige of an ancient religion held from one's fathers; true perhaps in its original foundations, although perverted. Thus the prince of the world will use carnal religion to excite the flesh, the ready enemy, when once awakened, of the spiritual religion which pronounces sentence upon it.

Adding something to Christ or a needed and accomplished redemption

It is only to add something to Christ. But what? If it is not Christ and the new man, it is the old man, it is sinful man; and, instead of a needed and *accomplished* redemption, and an entirely new life from above, you have a testimony that agreement between the two is possible; that grace is not necessary, except at most as a little help; that man is not already lost and dead in his trespasses and sins, that the flesh is not essentially and absolutely evil. Thus the name of Christ is made subservient to the flesh, which willingly adorns itself with the credit of His name, in order to destroy the gospel from its very foundations. Only preach circumcision, accept the religion of the flesh, and all difficulty will cease; the world will accept your gospel, but it will not be the gospel of Christ. The cross in itself (that is, the total ruin of man—man proved to be the enemy of God), and perfect finished redemption by grace, will always be a stumbling-block to one who desires to maintain some credit for the flesh. "Would to God," says the apostle—for he sees the whole gospel falling into ruin before this device, and souls destroyed— "would to God that they who trouble you were cut off!"

What have we seen since then? Where is the holy indignation of the apostle?

The practical consequences of the religion of the flesh contrasted with God's perfect grace and a worthy walk

He then touches on the point of the practical consequences of this doctrine, and explains how the doctrine of perfect grace was connected, without the law, with a walk worthy of the people of God. Ye have then been called, he says, unto liberty: only use not your liberty for an occasion to the flesh—which the flesh would readily do. God gave the law to convince of sin; the flesh would use it to work out righteousness. He acts in grace, that we may be above sin and outside its dominion: the flesh would use grace as an occasion to sin without restraint. The Christian, truly free from the yoke of sin, as well as from its condemnation (for Christ risen is his life as well as his righteousness, and the Spirit is the power and guide of his walk towards glory, and according to Christ), instead of serving his lusts, seeks to serve others, as free to do it in love. Thus the law itself is fulfilled, without our being under its yoke; for the whole practical law is summed up in this word: "Thou shalt love thy neighbor as thyself."

Walking in the Spirit who is the Christian's strength: the works of the flesh and the fruit of the Spirit

If, yielding to the flesh, and attacking those who were not circumcized, they devoured one another, they were to take heed that they were not consumed one of another. But the apostle would give something more positive. "This I say then," he continues, after the interruption of his subject, "Walk in the Spirit, and ye shall not fulfil the lust of the flesh." It is not by putting oneself under the law that one has power against sin. It is the Spirit (given in virtue of the ascension of Christ, our righteousness, to the right hand of God) who is the Christian's strength. Now the two powers, the flesh and the Spirit, are antagonistic. The flesh strives to hinder us when we would walk according to the Spirit, and the Spirit resists the working of the flesh to prevent it from accomplishing its will.[5] But if we are led of the Spirit, we are not under the law. Holiness, true holiness, is accomplished without the law, even as righteousness is not founded on it. Nor is there any difficulty in judging between what is of the flesh and what is of the Spirit; the apostle enumerates the sad fruits of the former, adding the sure testimony that they which do such things shall not inherit the Kingdom of God. The fruits of the Spirit are equally evident in their character, and assuredly against such things there was no law. If we walk according to the Spirit, the law will find nothing to condemn in us. And they that are Christ's have crucified the flesh and its lusts. This is what they are, inasmuch as they are Christians; it is that which distinguishes them. If these Galatians really lived, it was in the Spirit: let them then walk in the Spirit.

Chapter 6

The strength and rule for holiness: the law of Christ

HERE is the answer to those who then sought, and now seek, to bring in law for sanctification and as a guide: the strength and the rule for holiness are in the Spirit. The law does not give the Spirit. Moreover (for it is evident that these pretensions of observing the law had given liberty to the pride of the flesh) the Christian was not to be desirous of vain-glory, provoking one another, envying one another. If any one, through careless-

---

[5] It is not, "So that ye cannot," but "In order that ye might not."

ness, committed some fault, the Christian's part was to
restore this member of Christ, dear to Christ and to the
Christian, according to the love of Christ, in a spirit of
meekness, remembering that he himself might fall. If
they wished for a law, here was one: to bear each other's
burdens, and so fulfil the law of Christ (that is, the rule
of all His own life here below). It is not by boasting,
when one is nothing, that true glory was acquired. It is
but deceiving oneself, says the apostle, in language which,
by its simplicity, pours unspeakable contempt on those
who did so. These legalists boasted much of themselves,
imposed burdens on others; and investing themselves with
their Judaic glory—that which was a burden to others,
and one which they did not help them to bear, was vain-
glory to themselves they gloried in their Judaism, and
in making others subject to it. But what was their work?
Had they labored really for the Lord? In no wise. Let
them prove their own work; then they would have reason
to glory in what they had done themselves, if there was
any Christian work of which they had been the instruments. It certainly would not be in what they were doing
then, for it was another who had done the work of Christ
in Galatia. And after all, every one should bear his own
burden.

Practical words: effects and cause: sowing and reaping

The apostle adds a few practical words. He who was
taught should, in temporal things, succor those who taught
him. Furthermore, although grace was perfect and redemption complete, so that the believer received the Holy
Ghost as a seal thereof, God had attached infallible consequences to a man's walk, be it after the flesh or after
the Spirit. The effects followed the cause; and they could
not mock God by making a profession of grace or Christianity, if they did not walk according to its spirit, as led,

in a word, by the Holy Ghost, who is its practical power. Of the flesh they would reap corruption; of the Spirit, life everlasting. But, as Christians, they must have patience in order to reap, and not grow weary of well-doing: the harvest was sure. Let believers, then, do good to all, especially to those of the house of God.

The apostle's letters carefully invested with apostolic authority: the reason this one was written with his own hand

Paul had written this letter with his own hand—an unusual thing for him. He generally employed others (as Tertius for the Epistle to the Romans), dictating to them that which he wished to say, adding the benediction with his own hand, as certifying the correctness of that which was written (1 Cor. 16; 2 Thess. 3: 17): a remarkable proof of the importance that the apostle attached to his writings, and that he did not send them forth as ordinary letters from man to man, but as being furnished with an authority that required the use of such precautions. They were carefully invested with the apostolic authority. In this case, full of sorrow, and feeling that the foundations had been overthrown, he wrote the whole with his own hand. Accordingly, in saying this, he returns immediately to the subject which had caused him to do so.

The reproach of the cross: its sentence of death on nature and its wisdom and glory

Those who desired to make a fair show after the flesh constrained the Gentiles to be circumcized, in order to avoid the persecution that attached to the doctrine of the cross—to free salvation by Christ. The circumcized were Jews, of a religion known and received even in this world; but to become the disciples of a crucified Man, a Man who had been hung as a malefactor, and to confess Him as the only Saviour—how could the world be expected to receive it? But the reproach of the cross was the life of Christianity; the world was judged, it was dead in its sin; the prince of the world was judged, he had only the empire of death, he was (with his followers) the impotent enemy of God. In the presence of such a judgment, Judaism was honorable wisdom in the eyes of the world. Satan would make himself a partisan of the doctrine of one only God; and those who believed in it join themselves to their former adversaries, the worshippers of devils, in order to withstand this new enemy who cast reproach on the whole of fallen humanity, denouncing them as rebels against God, and as devoid of the life which was manifested in Jesus only. The cross was the sentence of death upon nature; and the Jew in the flesh was offended at it, even more than the Gentile, because he lost the glory with which he had been invested before others on account of his knowledge of the only true God.

A fleshly religion accepted by self or God's grace doing all and condemning the flesh as incapable

The carnal heart did not like to suffer, and to lose the good opinion of the world, in which a certain measure of light was accepted or tolerated by people of sense (and by sincere persons when there was no greater light to be had), provided they did not set up pretensions that condemned everybody, and judged everything which the flesh desired and relied on for its importance. A compromise which more or less accepts the flesh—which does not judge it as dead and lost, which, in however small a degree, will acknowledge that the world and the flesh are its basis—the world will accept. It cannot hope to strive against the truth that judges the whole conscience, and it will accept a religion that tolerates its spirit and adapts itself to the flesh, which it desires to spare even when painful sacrifices must be made; provided only that the flesh itself be not entirely set aside. Man will make himself a fakeer—sacrifice his life—provided that it is self that does it, and that God shall not have done the whole in grace, condemning the flesh as incapable of well doing, having nothing good in itself.

What the world is: the cross telling what man was, and what God and His holiness and love were; glorying in that cross

The circumcized did not observe the law—that would have been too wearisome, but they desired to glory in proselytes to their religion. In the world the apostle has seen nothing but vanity and sin and death; the spirit of the world, of the carnal man, was morally degraded, corrupt, and guilty, boasting in self, because ignorant of God. Elsewhere he had seen grace, love, purity, obedience, devotedness to the Father's glory and to the happiness of poor sinners. The cross declared the two things: it told what man was; it told what God was, and what holiness and love were. But it was the utmost degradation in the eyes of the world, and put down all its pride. It was another who had accomplished it at the cost of His own life, bearing all possible sufferings; so that the apostle could give free course to all the affections of his heart without boasting himself of anything; on the contrary, forgetting himself. It is not self that we glory in when we look at the cross of Christ: one is stript of self. It was He who hung upon that cross who was great in Paul's eyes. The world which had crucified Him was thus seen by the apostle in *its* true character; the Christ who had suffered on the cross in *His* likewise. In that cross would the apostle glory, happy, by this means, to be dead to the world, and to have the world ended, crucified, put to shame, as it deserved to be, for his heart. Faith in the crucified Son of God overcomes the world.

New creatures, the Israel of God

To the believer the world has its true character; for, in fact, in Christ Jesus neither circumcision nor uncircumcision has any value (all that has passed away with a dead Christ), but a new creature, according to which we estimate everything as God estimates it. It is to such, the true children of God, that the apostle wishes peace. It was not Israel circumcized after the flesh that was the Israel of God. If there were any of that people who were circumcized in heart, who gloried in the cross according to the sentiments of the new creature, those were the Israel *of God*. Moreover every true Christian was of them according to the spirit of his walk.

The apostle's Master shown by Satan's marks—the beautiful initials of Jesus

Finally, let no one trouble him with regard to his ministry. He bore the stigmata of the Lord. It is known that marks were printed on a slave with a hot iron to indicate the person to whom he belonged. The wounds which the apostle had received fully showed who was his Master. Let his right then to call himself the servant of Christ be no more questioned. Touching appeal from one whose heart was wounded at finding his service to the Master whom he had loved called in question! Moreover Satan, who imprinted those marks, ought indeed to recognize them—those beautiful initials of Jesus.

The duty of love: the heart turned to the dishonored Christ

The apostle desires that grace be with them (according to the divine love that animated him) as souls dear to Christ, whatever their state might be. But there is no outpouring of heart in greetings affectionately addressed to Christians. It was a duty—a duty of love—which he fulfilled; but for the rest, what bonds of affection could he have with persons who sought their glory in the flesh, and who accepted that which dishonored Jesus and which weakened and even annulled the glory of His cross? Without any wish of his, the current of affection was checked. The heart turned to the dishonored Christ, although loving those that were His in Him. This is the real feeling contained in the last verses of this epistle.

The whole Epistle a judgment of all return to Judaism as identical with heathen idolatry

In Galatians we have indeed Christ living in us, in contrast with the flesh or *I* still living in flesh. But, as systematic truth, we have neither the believer in Christ nor Christ in the believer. We have the Christian's practical state at the end of chapter 2. Otherwise the whole epistle is a judgment of all return to Judaism, as identical with heathen idolatry. The law and man in the flesh were correlative; law came in between the promise and Christ, the Seed; was a most useful testing of man, but when really known putting him to death, and condemning him. Now this was fully met in grace in the cross, the end in death of man in flesh, of sin, in Christ made sin. All return to law was giving up both promise and the work of grace in Christ, and going back again to flesh proved to be sin and lost, as if there could be relationship with God in it, denying grace, and denying even the true effect of law, and denying man's estate proved in the cross. It was heathenism. And days and years, etc., took man up as alive in flesh, was not the end of the old man in the cross in grace. We have Christ as our life thereupon, or death would leave us of course hopeless. But we have not the Christian condition, we in Christ and Christ in us. It is the discussion of the work that brings us there, and where man is, and of vital importance in this respect. Man in the flesh is wholly gone from all relationship with God, and none can be formed: there must be a new creation.

EPHESIANS

The rich and blessed scope of the Ephesian Epistle

THE Epistle to the Ephesians gives us the richest exposition of the blessings of the saints individually, and of the assembly, setting forth at the same time the counsels of God with regard to the glory of Christ. Christ Himself is viewed as the One who is to hold all things united in one under His hand, as Head of the assembly. We see the assembly placed in the most intimate relationship with Him, as those who compose it are with the Father Himself, and in the heavenly position dispensed to her by the sovereign grace of God. Now these ways of grace to her reveal God Himself, and in two distinct characters; as well in connection with Christ as with Christians. He is the God and Father of our Lord Jesus Christ. He is the God of Christ, when Christ is looked at as Man; the Father of Christ, when Christ is looked at as the Son of His love. In the first character the nature of God is revealed; in the second, we see the intimate relationship which we enjoy to Him who bears this character of Father, and that according to the excellence of Christ's own relationship to Him. It is this relationship to the Father, as well as that in which we stand to Christ as His Body and His Bride, that is the source of blessing to the saints and to the assembly of God, of which grace has made us members as a whole.

Chapter I

The blessings of the assembly and of the saints individually

THE form even of the epistle shows how much the apostle's mind was filled with the sense of the blessing

that belongs to the assembly. After having wished grace
and peace to the saints and the faithful[1] at Ephesus from
God, the Father of true Christians, and from Jesus Christ
their Lord, he begins at once to speak of the blessings in
which all the members of Christ participate. His heart
was full of the immensity of grace; and nothing in the
state of the Ephesian Christians required any particular
remarks adapted to that state. It is nearness of heart to
God that produces simplicity, and that enables us in
simplicity to enjoy the blessings of God as God Himself
bestows them, as they flow from His heart, in all their
own excellence—to enjoy them in connection with Him
who imparts them, and not merely in a mode adapted to
the state of those to whom they are imparted; or through
a communication that only reveals a part of these blessings, because the soul would not be able to receive more.
Yes, when near to God, we are in simplicity, and the
whole extent of His grace and of our blessings unfolds
itself as it is found in Him.

Moral nearness to God and conduct suited to it: the believer not forsaken because of faults, but grace is adapted to our wants and need

It is important to remark two things here in passing:
first, that moral nearness to God, and communion with
Him, is the only means of any true enlargement in the
knowledge of His ways and of the blessings which He
imparts to His children, because it is the only position in
which we can perceive them, or be morally capable of so
doing; and, also, that all conduct which is not suitable to

---

[1] The word translated "faithful" might be rendered "believers." It is
used as a term of superscription both here and in the Epistle to the
Colossians. We must remember that the apostle was now in prison, and
that Christianity had been established for some years, and was exposed
to all kinds of attack. To say that one was a believer as at the beginning,
was to say that he was faithful. The word then does not merely express
that they believed, nor that each individual walked faithfully, but that
the apostle addressed himself to those who by grace faithfully maintained
the faith they had received.

this nearness to God, all levity of thought, which His presence does not admit of, makes us lose these communications from Him and renders us incapable of receiving them. (Compare John 14: 21-23.) Secondly, it is not that the Lord forsakes us on account of these faults or this carelessness; He intercedes for us, and we experience His grace, but it is no longer communion or intelligent progress in the riches of the revelation of Himself, of the fulness which is in Christ. It is grace adapted to our wants, an answer to our misery. Jesus stretches out His hand to us according to the need that we feel—need produced in our hearts by the operation of the Holy Ghost. This is infinitely precious grace, a sweet experience of His faithfulness and love: we learn by this means to discern good and evil by judging self; but the grace had to be adapted to our wants, and to receive a character according to those wants, as an answer made to them: we have had to think of ourselves.

Restoring grace is not communion: the positive Source of everlasting joy

In a case like this the Holy Ghost occupies us with ourselves (in grace, no doubt), and when we have lost communion with God, we cannot neglect this turning back upon ourselves without deceiving and hardening ourselves. Alas, the dealings of many souls with Christ hardly go beyond this character. It is with all too often the case. In a word, when this happens, the thought of sin having been admitted into the heart, our dealings with the Lord to be true must be on the ground of this sad admission of sin (in thought, at least). It is grace alone which allows us again to have to do with God. The fact that He restores us enhances His grace in our eyes; but this is not communion. When we walk with God, when we walk after the Spirit without grieving Him, He maintains us in communion, in the enjoyment of God, the positive source of joy—of an everlasting joy. This is a position in which He can occupy us—as being ourselves interested in all that interests Him—with all the development of His counsels, His glory, and His goodness, in the Person of Jesus the Christ, Jesus the Son of His love; and the heart is enlarged in the measure of the objects that occupy it. This is our normal condition. This, in the main, was the case with the Ephesians.

Paul's special gift: the secret of the assembly's blessing: in Christ and in His relationship with God, in the heavenly places

We have already remarked, that Paul was specially gifted of God to communicate His counsels and His ways in Christ; as John was gifted to reveal His character and life as it was manifested in Jesus. The result of this particular gift in our apostle is naturally found in the epistle we are considering. Nevertheless we, as being ourselves in Christ, find in it a remarkable development of our relationships with God, of the intimacy of those relationships, and of the effect of that intimacy. Christ is the foundation on which our blessings are built. It is as being in Him that we enjoy them. We thus become the actual and present object of the favor of God the Father, even as Christ Himself is its object. The Father has given us to Him; Christ has died for us, has redeemed, washed, and quickened us, and presents us, according to the efficacy of His work, and according to the acceptance of His Person, before God His Father. The secret of all the assembly's blessing is, that it is blessed *with* Jesus Himself; and thus—like Him, viewed as a man—is accepted before God; for the assembly is His Body, and enjoys in Him and by Him all that His Father has bestowed on Him. Individually the Christian is loved as Christ on earth was loved; he will hereafter share in the glory of Christ before the eyes of the world, as a proof that he was so loved, in connection with the name of Father, which God maintains in regard to this. (See John 17: 23-26.) Hence in general we have in this epistle the believer in Christ, not Christ in the believer, though that of course be true. It leads up to the privileges of the believer and of the assembly, more than to the fulness of Christ Himself, and we find more the contrast of this new position with what we were as of the world than development of the life of Christ: this is more largely found in Colossians, which looks more at Christ in us. But this epistle, setting us in Christ's relationship with God and the Father and sitting in heavenly places, gives the highest character of our testimony here.

Christ's two relationships with God, His Father

Now Christ stands in two relationships with God, His Father. He is a perfect Man before His God; He is a Son with His Father. We are to share both these relationships. This He announced to His disciples ere He went back to heaven: it is unfolded in all its extent by the words He spoke, "I go to My Father and your Father, to My God and your God." This precious—this inappreciable truth is the foundation of the apostle's teaching in this place. He considered God in this double aspect, as the God of our Lord Jesus Christ, and as the Father of our Lord Jesus Christ; and our blessings are in connection with these two titles.

God's ways, thoughts and counsels first considered here

But before attempting to set forth in detail the apostle's thought, let us remark that he begins here entirely with God, His thoughts and His counsels, not with what man is. We may lay hold of the truth, so to speak, by one or the other of two ends—by that of the sinner's condition in connection with man's responsibility, or by that of the thoughts and eternal counsels of God in view of His own glory. The latter is that side of the truth on which the Spirit here makes us look. Even redemption, all glorious as it is in itself, is consigned to the second place, as the means by which we enjoy the effect of God's counsels.

It was necessary that the ways of God should be considered on this side, that is, His own thoughts, not merely the means of bringing man into the enjoyment of the fruit of them. It is the Epistle to the Ephesians which thus presents them to us; as that to the Romans, after saying it is God's goodness, begins with man's end, demonstrating the evil and presenting grace as meeting and delivering from it.

Summary of Chapter I

The God and Father of our Lord Jesus Christ has blessed us with all spiritual blessings in the heavenly places in Christ, having chosen us in Him. Chapter 1 unfolds (vers. 4-7) these blessings, and the means of sharing them; verses 8-10, the settled purpose of God for the glory of Christ, in whom we possess them. Next, verses 11-14 set before us the inheritance, and the Holy Ghost given as a seal to our persons, and as the earnest of our inheritance. Then follows a prayer, in which the apostle asks that his dear children in the faith—let us say that we —may know our privileges and the power that has brought us into them, the same as that by which Christ was raised from the dead and set at the right hand of God to possess them; as the Head of the assembly, which is His Body, which, with Him, shall be established over all things that were created by its Head as God and that He inherits as Man, filling all things with His divine and redeeming glory. In a word, we have first the calling of God, what the saints are before Him in Christ; then, having stated the full purpose of God as to Christ, God's inheritance in the saints; then the prayer that we may know these two things, and the power by which we are brought into them, and the enjoyment of them.

"All spiritual blessings": their character, extent, origin and measure

But we must examine these things more closely. We have seen the establishment of the two relationships between man and God—relationships in which Christ Himself stands. He ascended to His God and our God, to His Father and our Father. We share all the blessings that flow from these two relationships. He has blessed us with all spiritual blessings: not one is lacking. And they are of the highest order; they are not temporal, as was the case with the Jews. It is in the most exalted capacity of the renewed man that we enjoy these blessings: and they are adapted to that capacity, they are spiritual. They are also in the highest sphere: it is not in Canaan or Emmanuel's land. These blessings are granted us in the heavenly places; they are granted us in the most excellent way—one which leaves room for no comparison—it is *in Christ*. The God and Father of our Lord Jesus Christ has blessed us with *all spiritual* blessings in *heavenly places* in *Christ*. But this flows from the heart of God Himself, from a thought outside the circumstances in which He finds us in time. Before the world was, this was our place in His heart. He purposed to give us a place in Christ. He chose us *in Him*.

What blessing, what a source of joy, what grace, to be thus the objects of God's favor, according to His sovereign love! If we would measure it, it is by Christ we must attempt to do so; or, at least, it is thus that we must feel what this love is. Take especial notice here of the way in which the Holy Ghost keeps it continually before our eyes, that all is in Christ—in the heavenly places *in Christ*—He had chosen us *in Him*—unto the adoption *by Jesus Christ*—made acceptable *in the Beloved*. This is one of the fundamental principles of the Spirit's instruction in this place. The other is that the blessing has its origin in God Himself. He is its source and author. His own heart, if we may so express it, His own mind, are its origin and its measure. Therefore it is in Christ alone that we can have any measure of that which cannot be measured. For He is, completely and adequately, the delight of God. The heart of God finds in Him a sufficient object on which to pour itself out entirely, towards which His infinite love can all be exercised.

The blessing then is of God; but moreover it is *with* Himself and *before* Him, to gratify Himself, to satisfy His love. It is He who has chosen us, He who has predestined us, He who has blessed us; but it is that we should be before Him, and adopted as sons unto Himself. Such is grace in these great foundations. This consequently is what grace was pleased to do for us.

Chosen in Christ, in the counsels of God, before the world existed: man's responsibility from Adam's creation up to the cross

But there is another thing we have to note here. We are chosen in Him before the foundation of the world. Now this expression is not simply that of the sovereignty of God. If God chose some out of men now, it would be as sovereign as if before the world; but this shows that we belong in the counsels of God to a system set up by Him in Christ before the world existed, which is not of the world when it does exist, and exists after the fashion of this world has passed away. This is a very important aspect of the Christian system. Responsibility came in (for man of course) with the creation of Adam in this world. Our place was given us in Christ before the world existed. The development of all the characters of this responsibility went on up to the cross and there closed; innocent, a sinner without law, under law, and, when every way guilty, grace—God Himself comes into the world of sinners in goodness and finds hatred for His love. The world stood judged and men lost, and this the individual now learns as to himself. But then redemption was accomplished, and the full purpose and counsel of God in the new creation in Christ risen, the Last Adam, was brought out, "the mystery hidden from ages and generations," while the first man's responsibility was being tested. Compare 2 Timothy: 9-11; Titus 1: 2, where this truth is very distinctly brought out.

Responsibility and grace reconciled only in Christ

This responsibility and grace cannot be reconciled really but in Christ. The two principles were in the two trees of the garden; then promise to Abraham unconditionally, that we might understand blessing was free grace; then the law again brought both forward, but put life consequent on responsibility. Christ came, is life, took on Himself for all who believe in Him the consequence of responsibility, and became, as the divine Son and withal as risen Head, the source of life, our sin being put away; and here, as risen with Him, we not only have received life, but are in a new position quickened out of death with Him, and have a portion according to the counsels which established all in Him before the world existed, and are established according to righteousness and redemption, as a new creation, of which the Second Man is the head. The following chapter will explain our being brought into this place.

Our blessings connected with the two characters in which God has revealed Himself

We have said that God reveals Himself in two characters, even in His relationship to Christ; He is God, and He is Father. And our blessings are connected with this (that is, with His perfect nature as God, and with the intimacy of a positive relationship with Him as Father). The apostle does not yet touch on the inheritance, nor on the counsels of God, with regard to the glory of which Christ is to be the centre as a whole; but he speaks of our relationship with God, of that which we are with God and before Him, and not of our inheritance—of that which He has made us to be, and not of that which He has given us. In verses 4-6 our own portion in Christ before God is developed. Verse 4 depends on the name of God; verse 5, on that of Father.

God's character depicted in what is ascribed to the saints: like God in His nature and capable of enjoying it in Christ

The character of God Himself is depicted in that which is ascribed to the saints (ver. 4). God could find His moral delight only in Himself and in that which morally resembles Him. Indeed this is a universal principle. An honest man can find no satisfaction in a man who does not resemble him in this respect. With still greater reason God could not endure that which is in opposition to His holiness, since, in the activity of His nature, He must surround Himself with that which He loves and delights in. But, before all, Christ is this in Himself. He is personally the image of the invincible God. Love, holiness, blameless perfection in all His ways, are united in Him. And God has chosen us in Him. In verse 4 we find our position in this respect. First, we are before Him: He brings us into His presence. The love of God must do this in order to satisfy itself. The love which is in us also must be found in this position to have its perfect object. It is there only that perfect happiness can be found. But this being so, it is needful that we should be like God. He could not bring us into His presence in order to take delight in us, and yet admit us there such as He could not find pleasure in. He has therefore chosen us in Christ, that we should be holy, without blame before Him in love. He Himself is holy in His character, unblamable in all His ways, love in His nature. It is a position of perfect happiness—in the presence of God, like God; and that, in Christ, the object and the measure of divine affection. So God takes delight in us; and we, possessing a nature like His own as to its moral qualities, are capable of enjoying this nature fully and without hindrance, and of enjoying it in its perfection in Him. It is also His own choice, His own affection, which has placed us there, and which has placed us there in Him, who, being His eternal delight, is worthy of it; so that the heart finds its rest in this position, for there is agreement in our nature with that of God, and we were also chosen to it, which shows the personal affection that God has for us. There is also a perfect and supreme object with which we are occupied.

The unalterable joy of God's nature

Remark here that, in the relationship of which we here speak, the blessing is in connection with the nature of God; therefore it is not said that we are predestined to *this* according to the good pleasure of His will. *We* are chosen in Christ to be blessed in His presence; it is His infinite grace; but the joy of His nature could not (nor could ours in Him) be other than it is, because such is His nature. Happiness could not be found elsewhere or with another.

Predestined to particular privileges as sons

But in verse 5 we come to particular privileges, and we are *predestined to those* privileges. "He has predestined us unto the adoption, according to the good pleasure of His will." This verse sets before us, not the nature of God, but the intimacy, as we have said, of a positive relationship. Hence it is according to the good pleasure of His will. He may have angels before Him as servants; it was His will to have sons.

The form and character of the believer's relationship to God dependent on His sovereign will

Perhaps it might be said that, if admitted to take delight in the nature of God, one could hardly not be in an intimate relationship; but the form, the character of this relationship depends certainly on the sovereign will of God. Moreover, since we possess these things in Christ, the reflection of this divine nature and the relationship of son go together, for the two are united in us. Still we must remember that our participation in these things depends on the sovereign will of God our Father; even as the means of sharing them, and the manner in which we share them, is that we are in Christ. God our Father, in His sovereign goodness, according to His counsels of love, chooses to have us near Himself. This purpose, which links us to Christ in grace, is strongly expressed in this verse, as well as that which precedes it. It is not only our position which it characterizes, but the Father introduces Himself in a peculiar way with regard to this relationship. The Holy Ghost is not satisfied with saying "He has predestined us unto the adoption," but He adds "unto Himself." One might say this is implied in the word "adoption." But the Spirit would particularize this thought to our hearts, that the Father chooses to have us in an intimate relationship with Himself as sons. We are sons to *Himself* by Jesus Christ, according to the good pleasure of His will. If Christ is the image of the invisible God, we bear that image, being chosen in Him. If Christ is a Son, we enter into that relationship.

The glory of God's grace: in the Beloved

These then are our relationships, so precious, so marvellous, with God our Father in Christ. These are the counsels of God. We find nothing yet of the previous condition of those who were to be called into this blessing. It is a heavenly people, a heavenly family, according to the purposes and counsels of God, the fruit of His eternal thoughts, and of His nature of love—that which is here called the "glory of His grace." We cannot glorify God by adding anything to Him. He glorifies Himself when He reveals Himself. All this is therefore to the praise of the glory of His grace, according to which He has acted towards us in grace in Christ; according to which Christ is the measure of this grace, its form towards us, He in whom we share it. All the fulness of this grace reveals itself in His ways towards us—the original thoughts, so to speak, of God, which have no other source than Himself, and in and by the accomplishment of which He glorifies Himself. And observe here, that the Spirit does not say "the Christ," at the end of verse 6. When He speaks of Him, He would put emphasis on the thoughts of God. He has acted towards us in grace *in the Beloved*—in Him who is peculiarly the object of His affections. He brings this characteristic of Christ out into relief when He speaks of the grace bestowed upon us in Him. Was there an especial object of the love, of the affection of God? He has blessed us *in* that object.

Who are chosen to be blessed, and where

And where is it that He found us when He would bring us into this glorious position? What is it that He chooses to bless in this way? Poor sinners, dead in their trespasses and sins, the slaves of Satan and of the flesh.

Redemption: God's eternal counsels revealing Himself as glorious in grace

If it is in Christ that we see our position according to the counsels of God, it is in Him also that we find the redemption that set us in it. We have redemption through His blood, the remission of our sins. Those whom He would bless were poor and miserable through sin. He has acted towards them according to the riches of His grace.

We have already observed, that the Spirit brings out in this passage the eternal counsels of God with regard to the saints in Christ, before He enters on the subject of the state from which He drew them, when He found them in their condition of sinners here below. Now the whole mind of God respecting them is revealed in His counsels, in which He glorifies Himself. Therefore it is said, that that which He saw good to do with the saints was according to the *glory* of His grace. He makes Himself known in it. That which He has done for poor sinners is according to the *riches* of His grace. In His counsels He has revealed Himself; He is glorious in grace. In His work He thinks of our misery, of our wants, according to the riches of His grace; we share in them, as being their object in our poverty in our need. He is rich in grace. Thus our position is ordered and established according to the counsels of God, and by the efficacy of His work in Christ—our position, that is, in reference to Him. If we are to think here, where God's thoughts and counsels are revealed, if remission and redemption come of this, we are to think not according to our need as its measure, but according to the riches of God's grace.

The purposed glory of Christ: our inheritance in Him

But there is more: God having placed us in this intimacy, reveals to us His thoughts respecting the glory of Christ Himself. This same grace has made us the depositaries of the settled purpose of His counsels, with regard to the universal glory of Christ, for the administration of the fulness of times. This is an immense favor granted us. We are interested in the glory of Christ as well as blessed in Him. Our nearness to God and our perfectness before Him enable us to be interested in the counsels of God as to the purposed glory of His Son. And this leads to the inheritance. (Compare John 14: 28.) Thus Abraham, though on lower ground, was the friend of God. God our Father has given us to enjoy all blessings in heavenly places ourselves; but He would unite all things in heaven and on the earth under Christ as Head, and our relationship with all that is put under Him, as well as our relationship with God His Father, depends on our position in Him: it is in Him that we have our inheritance.

The position in virtue of which the inheritance falls to us: the praise of His glory and the praise of the glory of His grace

The good pleasure of God was to unite all that is created under the hand of Christ. This is His purpose for the administration of the times in which the result of all His ways shall be manifested.[2] In Christ we inherit our part, heirs of God, as it is said elsewhere, joint-heirs of Christ. Here however the Spirit sets before us the position, in virtue of which the inheritance has fallen to us, rather than the inheritance itself. He ascribes it also to the sovereign will of God, as He did before with regard to the special relationship of sons unto God. Remark also here, that in the inheritance we shall be to the praise of *His glory;* as in our relationship to Him we are to the praise of the glory of *His grace.* Manifested in possession of the inheritance, we shall be the display of His glory made visible and seen in us; but our relationships with Him are the fruit, for our own souls, with Him and before Him, of the infinite grace that has placed us in these relationships and made us capable of them.

[2] It will be a grand spectacle, as the result of the ways of God, to see all things united in perfect peace and union under the authority of Man, of the Second Adam, the Son of God; ourselves associated with Him in the same glory with Himself, His companions in the heavenly glory, as the objects of the eternal counsels of God. I do not enlarge here upon this scene, because the chapter we are considering directs our attention to the communications of the counsels of God respecting it, and not to the scene itself. The eternal state, in which God is all in all, is again another thing. The administration of the fulness of times is the result of the ways of God in government; the eternal state, that of the perfection of His nature. We, even in the government, are brought in according to His nature as sons. Wonderful privilege!

The glory bestowed on Christ as Man: Jewish believers in Christ before He returns, and the Jewish remnant in the last days

Such then, with regard to the glory bestowed on Him as Man, are the counsels of God our Father with respect to Christ. He shall gather together in one all things in Him as their Head. And as it is in Him that we have our true position as to our relationship with God the Father, so also is it with regard to the inheritance bestowed upon us. We are united to Christ in connection with that which is above us; we are so likewise with regard to that which is below. The apostle is speaking here first of Jewish Christians, who have believed in Christ before He is manifested; this is the force of "we who have first trusted in Christ." If I may venture to use a new word, "who have pre-trusted in Christ"—trusted in Him before He appears. The remnant of the Jews in the last days will believe (like Thomas) when they shall see Him. Blessed is he who shall have believed without seeing. The apostle speaks of those among the Jews who had already believed in Him.

Sealed with the Holy Spirit of promise

In verse 13 he extends the same blessing to the Gentiles, which gives occasion for another precious truth with regard to us—a thing that is true of every believer, but that had special force with regard to those from among the Gentiles. God had put His seal on them by the gift of the Holy Ghost. They were not, according to the flesh, heirs of the promises; but, when they believed, God sealed them with the Holy Spirit of promise, who is the earnest of the inheritance both of the one and the other, Jews and Gentiles, until the possession acquired by Christ should be delivered to Him, until He should in fact take possession of it by His power—a power which will allow no adversary to subsist. Remark here, that the subject is not being born again, but a seal put on believers, a demonstration and earnest of their future full participation in the heritage that belongs to Christ—an inheritance to which He has a right through redemption, whereby He has purchased all things to Himself, but which He will only appropriate by His power when He shall have gathered together all the co-heirs to enjoy it with Him.

The Holy Spirit as the earnest of the inheritance not yet possessed

The Holy Ghost is not the earnest of love. The love of God *is* shed abroad in our hearts by the Holy Ghost who is given unto us. God loves us as He will love us in heaven. Of the inheritance the Holy Ghost is but an earnest. We do not yet possess anything of the inheritance. Then we shall be to the praise of His glory. The glory of His grace is already revealed.

Thus we have here the grace which ordered the position of the children of God—the counsels of God respecting the glory of Christ as Head over all—the part which we have in Him as Heir—and the gift of the Holy Ghost to believers, as the earnest and seal (until they are put in possession with Christ) of the inheritance that He has won.

The apostle's prayer based on God's power in Christ's resurrection: its two parts

From verse 15 to the end, we have the apostle's prayer for the saints, flowing from this revelation—a prayer founded on the way in which the children of God have been brought into their blessings in Christ, and leading thus to the whole truth respecting the union of Christ and the assembly, and the place which Christ takes in the universe that He created as Son, and which He reassumes as Man; and on the power displayed in placing us, as well as Christ Himself, at the height of this position which

God has given us in His counsels. This prayer is founded on the title of "God of our Lord Jesus Christ;" that of chapter 3 on the title of "Father of our Lord Jesus Christ." There it is more communion than counsels. God is called the Father of glory here, as being its Source and Author. But not only is it said, "The God of our Lord Jesus Christ," but we shall see also that Christ is viewed as Man. God has wrought in Christ (ver. 20), He has raised Him from among the dead—has made Him sit at His right hand. In a word, all that happened to Christ is considered as the effect of the power of God who has accomplished it. Christ could say, "Destroy this temple, and I will raise it up again in three days," for He *was* God; but here He is viewed as Man; it is God who raises Him up again.

There are two parts in this prayer: first, that they may understand what the calling and the inheritance of God are; and secondly, what the power is that puts them in possession of that which this calling confers upon them—the same power which sets Christ at the right hand of God, having raised Him from among the dead.

The understanding of two things given us: our calling of God and the inheritance

First, the understanding of the things given us. We find, it appears to me, the two things which, in the previous part of the chapter, we have seen to be the saint's portion—the hope of the calling of God, and the glory of His inheritance in the saints. The first is connected with verses 3-5, that is, our calling; the second, with verse 11, that is, the inheritance. In the former we have found grace (that is, God acting towards us because He is love); in the latter, the glory—man manifested as enjoying in His Person and inheritance the fruits of the power and the counsels of God. God calls us to be before Him, holy and unblamable in love, and at the same time to be His

sons. The glory of His inheritance is ours. Take notice
that the apostle does not say "*our* calling," although we
are the called. He characterizes this calling by connecting it with Him who calls in order that we may understand it according to its excellence, according to its true
character. The calling is according to God Himself. All
the blessedness and character of this calling are according
to the fulness of His grace—arc worthy of Himself. It is
this which we hope for. It is also *His* inheritance, as the
land of Canaan was His, as He had said in the law, and
which nevertheless He inherited in Israel. Even so the
inheritance of the whole universe, when it shall be filled
with glory, belongs to Him. but He inherits it in the saints.
It is the riches of the glory of His inheritance in the saints.
He will fill all things with His glory, and it is in the saints
that He will inherit them. These are the two parts of the
first thing to which the eyes of the saints were to be
opened. By the calling of God we are called to enjoy the
blessedness of His presence, near to Himself, to enjoy that
which is above us. The inheritance of God applies to that
which is below us, to created things, which are all made
subject to Christ, with whom and in whom we enjoy the
light of the presence of God near to Him. The apostle's
desire is, that the Ephesians may understand these two
things.

**Paul's prayer that we may know God's power al-
ready manifested: the rightful and glorious
place given to Christ as Man: the Head of the
Body: union with Christ the saints' marvellous
portion**

The second thing that the apostle asks for them is, that
they may know the power already manifested, which had
already wrought to give them part in this blessed and
glorious position. For, even as they were introduced by
the sovereign grace of God into the position of Christ

before God His Father; so also the work which has been wrought in Christ, and the display of the power of God, which took place in raising Him from the grave to the right hand of God the Father above every name that is named, are the expression and the model of the action of the same power which works in us who believe, which has raised us from our state of death in sin to have part in the glory of this same Christ. This power is the basis of the assembly's position in her union with Him and of the development of the mystery according to the purposes of God. In person Christ raised up from among the dead is set at the right hand of God, far above all power and authority, and above every name that is named among the hierarchies by which God administers the government of the world that now is, or among those of the world to come. And this superiority exists, not only with regard to His divinity, the glory of which changes not, but with regard to the place given Him as Man; for we speak here—as we have seen—of the *God* of our Lord Jesus Christ. It is He who has raised Him from the dead, and who has given Him glory and a place above all; a place of which no doubt He was personally worthy, but which He receives, and ought to receive, as Man from the hand of God, who has established Him as Head over all things, uniting the assembly to Him as His Body, and raising up the members from their death in sins by the same power as that which raised up and exalted the Head—quickening them together with Christ, and seating them in the heavenly places in Him, by the same power that exalted Him. Thus the assembly, His Body, is His fulness. It is indeed He who fills all in all, but the Body forms the complement of the Head. It is He, because He is God as well as Man, who fills all things—and that, inasmuch as He is Man, according to the power of redemption, and of the glory which He has acquired; so that the universe which He fills with His glory enjoys it according to the stability of that redemption from the power and effect of which nothing can withdraw it.[3] It is He, I repeat, who fills the universe with His glory; but the Head is not isolated, left, so to speak, incomplete as such, without its Body. It is the Body that completes it in that glory, as a natural body completes the head; but not to be the head or to direct, but to be the Body of the head, and that the head should be the head *of its Body*. Christ is the Head of the Body over all things. He fills all in all, and the assembly is His fulness. This is the mystery in all its parts. Accordingly we may observe that it is when Christ (having accomplished redemption) was exalted to the right hand of God, that He takes the place in which He can be the Head of the Body.

Marvellous portion of the saints, in virtue of their redemption, and of the divine power that wrought in the resurrection of Christ, when He had died under our trespasses and sins, and set Him at the right hand of God: a portion which, save His personal session at the right hand of the Father, is ours also through our union with Him!

Chapter 2

God's power bringing dead souls into enjoyment of heavenly privileges

IN chapter 2[4] the operation of the power of God on earth, for the purpose of bringing souls into the enjoy-

[3] Compare chapter 4: 9, 10: and this introduction of redemption, and the place Christ has taken as Redeemer, as filling all in all, is full of interest.

[4] It is this power which, raising the saints from the death of sin, and uniting them to Him the Head, forms their relationship to Him as His Body. The first part of the chapter gave our individual relationship to the Father, in that Christ is the firstborn among many brethren. Here we come to corporate relationship to Christ, the last and risen Man. Up to the second part of the prayer we have the counsels of God. From the latter part we have the operations of power to accomplish them. And it is here our union with Christ first comes in, which, though God's counsels as to it are revealed, yet spiritually is wrought now, as seen in chapter 2.

ment of their heavenly privileges, and thus of forming the assembly here below, is presented, rather than the unfolding of the privileges themselves, and consequently that of the counsels of God. It is not even these counsels; it is the grace and the power which work for their fulfilment, by leading souls to the result which this power will produce according to those counsels. Christ is first seen, not as God come down here and presented to sinners, but as dead, that is, where we were by sin, but raised from it by power. He for sin had died; God had raised Him from the dead, and set Him at His own right hand. We were dead in our trespasses and sins: He has quickened us together with Him. But as it is the earth that is in question, and the operation of power and grace on the earth, the Spirit naturally speaks of the condition of those in whom this grace works, in fact of the condition of all. At the same time, in the earthly forms of religion, in the system that existed on earth, there were those who were nigh and those who were far off. Now we have seen that in the full blessing of which the apostle speaks the nature of God Himself is concerned; in view of which, and to glorify which, all His counsels were settled. Therefore outward forms, although some of them had been established provisionally on the earth by God's own authority, could now have no value. They had served for the manifestation of the ways of God as shadows of things to come, and had been connected with the display of God's authority on earth among men, maintaining some knowledge of God—important things in their place; but these figures could do nothing as to bringing souls into relationship with God, in order to enjoy the eternal manifestation of His nature, in hearts made capable of it by grace, through their participation in that nature and reflecting it. For this, these figures were utterly worthless; they were not the manifestation of these eternal principles. But the two classes of man, Jews and Gentiles, were there; and the apostle speaks of them both. Grace takes up persons from both to form one Body, one new man, by a *new creation* in Christ.

Man's distance from God under the power of darkness

In the first two verses of this chapter he speaks of those who were brought out from among the nations that knew not God—Gentiles, as they are usually called. In verse 3 he speaks of the Jews—"We all also," he says. He does not enter here into the dreadful details contained in Romans 3,[5] because his object is not to convince the individual, in order to show him the means of justification, but to set forth the counsels of God in grace. Here then he speaks of the distance from God in which man is found under the power of darkness. With regard to the nations, he speaks of the universal condition of the world. The whole course of the world, the entire system, was according to the prince of the power of the air; the world itself was under the government of him who worked in the hearts of the children of disobedience, who in self-will evaded the government of God, although they could not evade His judgment.

Jews and Gentiles all children of wrath by nature

If the Jews had external privileges; if they were not in a direct way under the government of the prince of this world (as was the case with the nations that were plunged in idolatry, and sunk in all the degradation of that system in which man wallowed, in the licentiousness into which demons delighted to plunge him in derision of his

[5] Take especial notice here that, in the Ephesians, the Spirit does not describe the life of the old man in sin. God and His own work are everything. Man is viewed as dead in his sins; that which is produced is therefore entirely of God, a new creation on His part. A man who lives in sin must die, must judge himself, must repent, by grace be cleansed; that is, he is dealt with as a living man. Here man is without any movement of spiritual life: God does everything; He quickens and raises up. It is a new creation.

wisdom); if the Jews were not, like the Gentiles, under the government of demons, nevertheless in their nature they were led by the same desires as those by which demons influenced the poor heathen. The Jews led the same life as to the desires of the flesh; they were children of wrath, even as others, for that is the condition of *men;* they are in their nature the children of wrath. In their outward privileges the Israelites were the people of God; by nature they were men as others. And remark here these words, "by nature." The Spirit is not speaking here of a judgment pronounced on the part of God, nor of sins committed, nor of Israel having failed in their relationship to God through falling into idolatry and rebellion, nor even of their having rejected the Messiah and so deprived themselves of all resources—all of which Israel had done. Neither does He speak of a positive judgment from God pronounced on the manifestation of sin. They were, even as all men, in their nature the children of wrath. This wrath was the natural consequence of the state in which they were.[6]

God's mercy, love and power to those dead in trespasses and sins: passed out of death into life as a new creation, all distinctions ended

Man as he was, Jew or Gentile, and wrath, naturally went together, even as there is a natural link between good and righteousness. Now God, though in judgment taking cognizance of all that is contrary to His will and glory, in His own nature is above all that. To those who are worthy of wrath He can be rich in mercy, for He is so in Himself. The apostle therefore presents Him here as acting according to His own nature towards the objects of His grace. We were dead, says the apostle—dead

[6] Faith, when taught by the Word, always goes back to this: judgment refers to deeds done in the body. But we were dead in sins—no living movement of the heart towards God. We do not (John 5) come into judgment, but are passed from death unto life.

in our trespasses and sins. God comes, in His love, to
deliver us by His power—"God, who is rich in mercy,
according to *His* great love wherewith He loved us."
There was no good working in us: we were dead in our
trespasses and sins. The movement came from Him,
praised be His name! He has quickened us; nor only that
—He has quickened us together with Christ. He had not
said in a direct way, that Christ had been quickened,
although it may be said, where the power of the Spirit
in Himself is spoken of. He was however raised from
the dead; and, when we are in question, we are told that
all the energy by which He came forth from death is
employed also for our quickening; and not only that;
even in being quickened we are associated with Him. He
comes forth from death—we come forth *with* Him. God
has imparted this life to us. It is His pure grace, and a
grace that has saved us, that found us dead in sins, and
brought us out of death even as Christ came out of it,
and by the same power, and brought us out with Him
by the power of life in resurrection—with Christ,[7] to set
us in the light and in the favor of God, as a new creation,
even as Christ Himself is there. Jews and Gentiles are
found together in the same new position in Christ. Resurrection has put an end to all those distinctions; they have
no place in a risen Christ. God has quickened the one
and the other with Christ.

[7] Here it is a wholly new creation, and the new estate is looked at
simply in itself. We were dead towards God in our old one. Man is not
looked at here as alive in sins and responsible, but as entirely dead in
them, and created again: hence in this part of the epistle we have no
forgiveness, no justification. The man is not looked at as a living responsible man. In Colossians we are risen with Christ, but "having forgiven you all trespasses" which Christ had borne in coming down into
death. Here, too, we have not the old man, and death brought in to it,
though both walk and the old man are recognized as facts, though not in
connection with resurrection. In Colossians we have; even when "dead
in your sins" is spoken of, it is added, "and the uncircumcision of your
flesh," for it is dead towards God. The Epistle to the Romans looks at
responsible man in the world; hence you have fully justification, death
to sin, and no resurrection with Christ. The man is a living man here,
though justified, and alive in Christ.

In Christ in a new condition: all the gift of God's grace and not of works

Now, Christ having done this, Jews and Gentiles, without the differences which death had abolished, are found together in the risen and ascended Christ, sitting together in Him in a new condition common to both—a condition described by that of Christ Himself.[8] Poor sinners from among the Gentiles, and from among the disobedient and gainsaying Jews, are brought into the position where Christ is by the power which raised Him from the dead and set Him at God's right hand,[9] to show forth in the ages to come the immense riches of the grace which had accomplished it. A Mary Magdalene, a crucified thief, companions in glory with the Son of God, all we who believe, will bear witness to it. It is by grace we are saved. Now we are not yet in the glory: it is by faith. Would any one say that at least the faith is of man? No;[10] it is not of ourselves in this respect either; all is the gift of God; not of works, in order that no one may boast. For we are His workmanship.

[8] It is not merely life communicated (that we had in Romans), but a totally new place and standing which we have taken, life having the character of resurrection out of a state of death in sins. And here we are not viewed as quickened by Christ, but quickened *with Him*. He is the raised and glorified Man.

[9] In Colossians the saints are only seen risen with Christ, with a hope laid up for them in heaven, and are called to set their affections on things above, when Christ and their life with Him are hid. Moreover their resurrection with Christ is only an administrative one for this world in baptism, in connection with faith in the power which raised Christ. We have no union of Jews and Gentiles in Him as risen and in heavenly places. Indeed in Colossians, Gentiles only are before the mind of the apostle.

[10] I am quite aware of what critics have to say here as to gender; but it is equally true as to grace, and to say, "By grace . . . . . and that not of yourselves," is simply nonsense; but by faith might be supposed to be of ourselves, though grace cannot. Therefore the Spirit of God adds, "And that [not it] not of yourselves: it is the gift of God." That is, the believing is God's gift, not of ourselves. And this is confirmed by what follows, "not of works." But the object of the apostle is to show that the whole thing was of grace and of God—God's workmanship—a new creation. So far, grace and faith and all go together.

Created anew for good works in accordance with the new creation

In how powerful a way the Spirit puts God Himself forward, as the Source and Operator of the whole, and the sole one! It is a creation, but, as His work, of a result which is in accordance with His own character. Now it is in us that this is done. He takes up poor sinners to display His glory in them. If it is the operation of God, assuredly it will be for good works: He has created us in Christ for them. And observe here that if God has created us for good works, these must in their nature be characterized by Him who has wrought in us, creating us according to His own thoughts. It is not man who seeks to draw nigh to God, or to satisfy Him by doing works that are pleasing to Him according to the law—the measure of that which man ought to be; it is God who takes us up in our sins, when there is not one moral movement in our hearts ("None that understandeth, none that seeketh after God"), and creates us anew for works in accordance with this new creation. It is an entirely new position that we are placed in, according to this new creation of God—a new character that we are invested with according to the pre-determination of God. The works are pre-determined also according to the character which we put on by this new creation. All is absolutely according to the mind of God Himself. It is not duty according to the old creation.[11] All is the fruit of God's own thoughts in the new creation. The law disappears with regard to us even as to its works, together with the nature to which it applied. Man obedient to the law was man as he ought to be according to the first Adam; the man in Christ must walk according to the heavenly life of the Second Adam, and walk worthy of Him as the Head of a new creation, being raised up with Him, and

[11] Not that God does not recognize the relationships He had originally formed—He does fully when we are in them; but the measure of the new creation is another thing.

being the fruit of the new creation—worthy of Him who
has formed him for this very thing (2 Cor. 5: 5).

Jew and Gentile one new man: enmity destroyed and peace made and proclaimed

The Gentiles therefore enjoying this ineffable privilege
—although the apostle does not recognize Judaism as a
true circumcision—were to remember from whence they
had been taken; without God and without hope as they
were in the world, strangers to all the promises. But however far off they had been, now in Christ they were
brought nigh by His blood. He had broken down the
middle wall, having annulled the law of commandments
by which the Jew, who was distinguished by these ordinances, was separated from the Gentiles. These ordinances
had their sphere of action in the flesh. But Christ (as
living in connection with all that), being dead, has abolished the enmity to form in Himself of the two—Jew and
Gentile—one new man; the Gentiles brought nigh by the
blood of Christ, and the middle wall of partition broken
down, to reconcile both to God in one Body; having by
the cross not only made peace, but destroyed—by grace
that was common to both, and to which one could make
no more claim than the other, since it was for sin—the
enmity that existed, till then, between the privileged Jew
and the idolatrous Gentile far from God, abolishing in
His flesh the enmity, the law of commandments contained
in ordinances.

Access to God as our Father and part of His family: the true house of God viewed both as a progressive work and as His house on earth at the moment

Having made peace, He proclaimed it with this object
to the one and the other, whether far off or nigh. For by

Christ we all—whether Jews or Gentiles—have access by one Spirit to the Father. It is not the Jehovah of the Jews (whose name was not called upon the Gentiles); it is the Father of Christians, of the redeemed by Jesus Christ, who are adopted to form part of the family of God. Thus, albeit a Gentile, one is no longer a stranger or foreigner; one is of the Christian and heavenly citizenship, of the true house of God Himself. Such is grace. As to this world, being thus incorporated in Christ, this is our position. All, Jew or Gentile, thus gathered together in one Body, constitute the assembly on earth. The apostles and prophets (of the New Testament) form the foundation of the building, Christ Himself being the chief corner stone. In Him the whole building rises to be a temple, the Gentiles having their place, and forming with the others the dwelling-place on earth of God, who is present by His Spirit. First, he looks at the progressive work which was being built on the foundation of the apostles and prophets, the whole assembly according to the mind of God; and, secondly, he looks at the union which existed between the Ephesians and other believing Gentiles and the Jews, as forming God's house on the earth at that moment. God dwells in it by the Holy Ghost.[12]

[12] It is exceedingly important in these days to see the difference between this progressive building, never complete till all believers who are to form Christ's Body are gathered in, and the present temple of God on earth. In the former Christ is the Builder. He carries it on without fail, and the gates of hell cannot prevail against it. This is not yet complete nor viewed as a whole till built. Hence in the Epistles we never find a builder in this case: in Peter, "Unto whom coming as to a living stone, ye also as living stones are built up;" so here, in Ephesians, it grows to a holy temple in the Lord. But, besides this, the present manifested professing body is looked at as a whole on earth; and man is looked at as building. "Ye are God's building" (1 Cor. 3). "I, as a wise masterbuilder, have laid the foundation: let every man take heed how he buildeth thereon." Man's responsibility comes in, and the work is the subject of judgment. It is the attributing to this the privileges of the Body, and of that which Christ builds, that has produced popery and all that is akin to it. The corrupt thing which is to come under judgment is falsely clothed with the security of Christ's work. Here in Ephesians 2 we find not only the progressive and surely constructed work, but the present building together as a fact in the blessing of it, without reference to human responsibility in building.

The subjects of Chapters 1 and 2

Chapter 1 had set before us the counsels and purposes of God; beginning with the relationship of the sons and the Father, and, when the operation of God is spoken of, the assembly as the Body of Christ united to Him who is Head over all things. Chapter 2, treating of the work which calls out the assembly, which creates it here below by grace, sets before us this assembly on the one hand, growing up to a holy temple, and then as the present habitation of God here below by the Spirit.[13]

[13] Chapter 2 speaks indeed of the Body (ver. 16); but the introduction of the house is a new element and requires some development. Although the work which is accomplished in the creation of the members who are to compose the Body is all of God, it is accomplished on earth. The counsels of God have in view, first individuals, to place them near Himself, such as He would have them; then, having exalted Christ above every name now or hereafter, gives Him to be Head of the Body, formed of individuals united to Christ in heaven over all things. They will be perfect according to their Head. But the work on earth, if it gathers together the new-born, gathers them together on the earth. Now that which answers here below to the presence of Christ in heaven is the presence of the Holy Ghost on earth. The individual believer is indeed the temple of God, but in this chapter it is the whole body of Christians formed on earth that is spoken of; they become the house, the dwelling-place, of God on the earth. Wonderful and solemn truth. Immense privilege and source of blessing; but equally great responsibility.

It will be observed that, in speaking of the Body of Christ, we speak of the fruit of God's eternal purpose and own operation; and, although the Spirit may apply this name to the assembly of God on earth, as accounted to be composed of real members of Christ, nevertheless the Body of Christ, as formed by the quickening power of God according to His eternal purpose, is composed of persons united to the Head as real members. The house of God, as now set up on earth, is the fruit of a work of God, here entrusted to men, not the proper object of His counsels (though the city in Revelation in a measure answers to it). In so far as it is the work of God, it is evident that this house is composed of those who are truly called of God, and so God set it up, and as it is spoken of here. (Compare Acts 2: 47.) But we must not confound the practical result of this work, accomplished in the hands of men, and under their responsibility (1 Cor. 3), with the object of the counsels of God. A true member of Christ can no one be without being really united to the Head, neither a *true* stone in the house; but the house can be the dwelling-place of God, although that which is not a true stone may enter into its construction. But it is impossible that one not born of God should be a member of the Body of Christ. See the preceding note.

Chapter 3

The connection of Chapter 3 with what precedes it

THE whole of chapter 3 is a parenthesis unfolding the mystery; and presenting at the same time, in the prayer that concludes it, the second character of God set before us at the beginning of the epistle, namely, that of Father of our Lord Jesus Christ; and this is the way in which it is here introduced. Chapter 1 gives the counsels of God as they are in themselves, adding His raising Christ and setting Him above all on high at the end. Chapter 2, His work in quickening others with Him and forming the whole assembly of those who are risen in Christ, taken by grace from among Jews and Gentiles; these are God's thoughts and work. Chapter 3 is Paul's administration of it; it speaks especially of the bringing in of the Gentiles on the same footing as the Jews. This was the entirely new part of the ways of God.

Paul's particular ministry: a special revelation of the mystery, once necessarily hidden, made known by the Spirit

Paul was a prisoner for having preached the gospel to the Gentiles—a circumstance that brought out his particular ministry very clearly. This ministry in the main is presented as in Colossians 1. Only in the latter epistle the whole subject is treated more briefly, and the essential principle and character of the mystery according to its place in the counsels of God is less explained, is viewed only on a special side of it, suited to the purpose of the epistle, that is, Christ and the Gentiles. Here the apostle assures us that he had received it by a special revelation, as he had already taught them in words which; though few, were suited to give a clear understanding of his knowledge of the mystery of Christ—a mystery never made known in the past ages, but now revealed by the Spirit to the apostles and prophets. Here it will be observed that the prophets are most evidently those of the New Testament, since the communications made to them are put in contrast with the degree of light granted in the previous ages. Now the mystery had been hidden in all former times; and in fact it needed so to be; for to havè put the Gentiles on the same footing as the Jews would have been to demolish Judaism, such as God had Himself established it. In it He had carefully raised a middle wall of partition. The duty of the Jew was to respect this separation; he sinned, if he did not strictly observe it. The mystery set it aside. The Old Testament prophets, and Moses himself, had indeed shown that the Gentiles should one day rejoice with the people: but the people remained a separate people. That they should be co-heirs, and of the same body, all distinction being lost, had indeed been entirely hid in God (part of His eternal purpose before the world was), but formed no part of the history of the world, nor of the ways of God respecting it, nor of the revealed promises of God.

The place of the redeemed, now and in the future, in the mind of God

It is a marvellous purpose of God which, uniting redeemed ones to Christ in heaven as a body to its head, gave them a place in heaven. For, although we are journeying on the earth, and although we are the habitation of God by the Spirit on the earth, yet in the mind of God our place is in heaven.

The Gentile and Israel in the age to come: no earthly distinction in the assembly, as one in Christ and having a place in heaven

In the age to come the Gentiles will be blessed; but Israel will be a special and separate people.

In the assembly all earthly distinction is lost: we are all one in Christ, as risen with Him.

A Christ whose riches are unsearchable proclaimed to the Gentiles: the two parts of Paul's ministry

Thus the gospel of the apostle was addressed to the Gentiles, to announce this good news to them according to the gift of God, which had been granted to Paul by the operation of His power, to proclaim to them not merely a Messiah according to the promises made to the fathers, a Jewish Christ, but a Christ whose riches were unsearchable. No one could trace to the end, and in all its development in Him, the accomplishment of the counsels, and the revelation of the nature of God. They are the incomprehensible riches of a Christ in whom God reveals Himself, and in whom all God's thoughts are accomplished and displayed. These purposes of God with regard to a Christ, the Head of His Body, the assembly, Head over all things in heaven and earth, Christ, God manifest in the flesh, were now made known and being accomplished, so far as gathering the joint-heirs in one Body went. Saul, the inveterate enemy of Jesus proclaimed as Messiah, even if by the Holy Ghost from heaven—the worst therefore of all men—becomes by grace Paul, the instrument and witness of that grace to announce these incomprehensible riches to the Gentiles. This was his apostolic function with regard to the Gentiles. There was another—to enlighten all with regard to this mystery, which, from the beginning of the world, had been hidden in God. This answers to the two parts of the apostle's ministry pointed out in Colossians 1: 23-25: as verse 27 in that chapter corresponds with verse 17 here. God, who created all things, had this thought, this purpose before creation, in order that, when He should subject all creation to His Son become a man and glorified, that Son should have companions in His glory, who should be like Himself, members of His body spiritual, living of His life.

The administration of the mystery, the secret of God's counsels revealed by the establishment of the assembly on earth

He made known to the Gentiles the unsearchable riches of Christ, which gave them a portion in the counsels of God in grace. He enlightened all with regard not precisely to the mystery, but to the administration[14] of the mystery; that is to say, not only the counsel of God, but the accomplishment in time of that counsel by bringing the assembly together under Christ its Head. He who had created all things, as the sphere of the development of His glory, had kept this secret in His own possession, in order that the administration of the mystery, now revealed by the establishment of the assembly on earth, should be in its time the means of making known to the most exalted of created beings the manifold and various wisdom of God. They had seen creation arise and expand before their eyes; they had seen the government of God, His providence, His judgment; His intervention in loving-kindness on the earth in Christ. Here was a kind of wisdom altogether new; a thing outside the world, hitherto shut up in the mind of God, hid in Himself so that there was no promise or prophecy of it, but the special object of His eternal purpose; connected in a peculiar way with the One who is the centre and the fulness of the mystery of godliness; which had its own place in union with Him; which, although it was manifested on earth and set with Christ at the head of creation, formed properly no part of it. It was a new part of it. It was a new creation, a distinct manifestation of the wisdom of God; a part of His thoughts which until then had been reserved in the

---

[14] This appears to me to be the true word, and not "the fellowship."

secret of His counsels; the actual administration of which,
on the earth in time by the apostle's work, made known
the wisdom of God according to His settled purpose, according to His eternal purpose in Christ Jesus. "In
whom," the apostle adds, "we draw nigh with all boldness by faith in Him:" and it is according to this relationship that we do so.

The Gentile believers encouraged

Therefore these Gentile believers were not to be discouraged on account of the imprisonment of him who
had proclaimed to them this mystery; for it was the
proof and the fruit of the glorious position which God
had granted them, and of which the Jews were jealous.

Christ as the Centre of all God's ways: every family ranging itself under the name of His Father

This revelation of the ways of God does not, as the
first chapter, present Christ to us as Man raised up by
God from the dead, in order that we should be raised up
also to have part with Him, and that the administration
of the counsels of God should thus be accomplished. It
presents Him as the centre of all the ways of God, the
Son of the Father, the Heir of all things as the Creator
Son, and the centre of the counsels of God. It is to the
Father of our Lord Jesus Christ that the apostle now
addresses himself; as in chapter 1 it was to the God of
our Lord Jesus Christ. Every family (not "the whole
family") ranges itself under this name of Father of our
Lord Jesus Christ. Under the name of Jehovah there
were only the Jews. "You only have I known of all the
families of the earth," had Jehovah said to the Jews in
Amos, "therefore will I punish you for your iniquities;"
but under the name of Father of Jesus Christ all families
—the assembly, angels, Jews, Gentiles, all—range themselves. All the ways of God in that which He had ar-

ranged for His glory were co-ordained under this name, and were in relation with it: and that which the apostle asked for the saints to whom he addressed himself was, that they should be enabled to apprehend the whole import of those counsels, and the love of Christ which formed the assured centre for their hearts.

Strengthened by the Spirit: Christ dwelling in and filling the heart

For this purpose he desires that they should be strengthened with all might by the Spirit of the Father of our Lord Jesus Christ, and that the Christ, who is the centre of all these things in the counsels of God the Father, should dwell also in their hearts, and thus be the intelligent centre of affection to all their knowledge—a centre which found no circle to limit the view that lost itself in infinitude which God alone filled—length, breadth, height, depth.[15] But this centre gave them at the same time a sure place, a support immovable and well known, in a love which was as infinite as the unknown extent of the glory of God in its display around Himself. "That Christ," says the apostle, "may dwell in your hearts." Thus He, who fills all things with His glory, fills the heart Himself, with a love more powerful than all the glory of which He is the centre. He is to us the strength which enables us in peace and love to contemplate all that He has done, the wisdom of His ways, and the universal glory of which He is the centre.

Christ filling our hearts: ourselves the centre of His affections: the fulness of God

I repeat it—He who fills all things fills above all our

[15] Christ is the centre of all the display of divine glory, but He thus dwells in our hearts so as to set them, so to speak, in this centre, and make them look out thence on all the glory displayed. Here we might lose ourselves; but he brings them back to the well-known love of Christ, yet not as anything narrower, for He is God, and it passes knowledge, so that we are filled up to all the fulness of God.

hearts. God strengthens us according to the riches of that glory which He displays before our wondering eyes as rightly belonging to Christ. He does it, in that Christ dwells in us, with tenderest affection, and He is the strength of our heart. It is as rooted and grounded in love; and thus embracing as the first circle of our affections and thoughts, those who are so to Christ—all the saints the objects of His love: it is as being filled with Him, and ourselves as the centre of all *His* affections, and thinking His thoughts, that we throw ourselves into the whole extent of God's glory; for it is the glory of Him whom we love. And what is its limit? It has none; it is the fulness of God. We find it in this revelation of Himself. In Christ He reveals Himself in all His glory. He is God over all things blessed for ever.

The realization of Paul's desire for us

But dwelling in love we dwell in God and God in us: and that in connection with the display of His glory, as He develops it in all that He has formed around Himself, to exhibit Himself in it, in order that Christ, and Christ in the assembly, His Body, should be the centre of it, and the whole the manifestation of Himself in His entire glory. We are filled unto all the fulness of God: and it is in the assembly that He dwells for this purpose. He works in us by His Spirit with this object. Therefore Paul's desire and prayer is that glory may be unto God in the assembly throughout all ages by Jesus Christ: Amen. And note, it is here realization of what is spoken of that is desired. It is not, as chapter 1, objective, that they may know what is certainly true, but that it may be true for them, they being strengthened with might by His Spirit. It is very beautiful to see how, after launching us into the infinitude of God's glory, he brings us back to a known centre in Christ—to know the love of Christ, but not to narrow us. It is more properly divine, though familiar to us, than the glory. It passes knowledge.

Divine love working in us

Observe too here, that the apostle does not now ask
that God should act by a power, as it is often expressed,
which works for us, but by a power that works in us.[16]
He is able to do above all that we can ask or think according to His power that works in us. What a portion for
us! What a place is this which is given us in Christ! But
he returns thus to the thesis proposed at the end of chapter 2, God dwelling in the assembly by the Spirit, and
Christians, whether Jews or Gentiles, united in one. He
desires that the Ephesian Christians (and all of us)
should walk worthy of this vocation. Their vocation was
to be *one*, the Body of Christ; but this Body in fact manifested on earth in its true unity by the presence of the
Holy Ghost. We have seen (chap. 1) the Christian
brought into the presence of God Himself; but the fact
that these Christians formed the Body of Christ, and that
they were the dwelling-place of God here below, the house
of God on the earth—in a word, their whole position—
is comprised in the expression, "their vocation." Chapter
1, note, gives the saints before God; the prayer of chapter
3, Christ in them.

Chapters 4, 5

The individual state Paul desired to be realized among the Ephesians

NOW the apostle was in prison for the testimony which
he had borne to this truth, for having maintained
and preached the privileges that God had granted to the
Gentiles, and in particular that of forming by faith, to-

[16] This fully distinguishes the prayer of chapter 1 and this. There the
calling and inheritance were in the sure purpose of God, and his prayer
is that they may know them, and the power that brought them there.
Here it is what is in us, and he prays that it may exist, and that as
present power in the Church.

gether with the believing Jews, one Body united to Christ. In his exhortation he makes use of this fact as a touching motive. Now the first thing that he looked for on the part of his beloved children in the faith, as befitting this unity and as a means of maintaining it in practice, was the spirit of humility and meekness, forbearance with one another in love. This is the individual state which he desired to be realized among the Ephesians. It is the true fruit of nearness to God, and of the possession of privileges; if they are enjoyed in His presence.

The result of Christ's work: the Christian's "vocation": its development and application

At the end of chapter 2 the apostle had unfolded the result of the work of Christ in uniting the Jew and the Gentile, in making peace, and in thus forming the dwelling-place of God on the earth (Jew and Gentile having access to God by one Spirit through the mediation of Christ, both being reconciled to God in one body). To have access to God; to be the dwelling-place of God through His presence by the Holy Ghost; to be one body reconciled to God—such is the vocation of Christians. Chapter 3 had developed this in its whole extent. The apostle applies it in chapter 4.

The triple exhortation: the unity of the Spirit maintained in the bond of peace

The faithful were to seek—in the dispositions mentioned above—to maintain this unity of the Spirit by the bond of peace. There are three things in this exhortation: first, to walk worthy of their calling; second, the spirit in which they were to do so; third, diligence in maintaining the unity of the Spirit by the bond of peace. It is important to observe, that this unity of the Spirit is not similarity of sentiment, but the oneness of the members of the Body of Christ established by the Holy Ghost, maintained practically by a walk according to the Spirit of grace. It is evident that the diligence required for the maintenance of the unity of the Spirit relates to the earth and to the manifestation of his unity on the earth.

The three spheres of unity

The apostle now founds his exhortation on the different points of view under which this unity may be considered —in connection with the Holy Ghost, with the Lord, and with God.

There is one Body and one Spirit; not merely an effect produced in the heart of individuals, in order that they might mutually understand each other, but one Body. The hope was one, of which this Spirit was the source and the power. This is the essential, real, and abiding unity.

There is also one Lord. With Him was connected "one faith" and "one baptism." This is the public profession and recognition of Christ as Lord. Compare the address in 1 Corinthians.

Finally, there is one God and Father of all, who is above all, and through all, and in us all.

What mighty bonds of unity! The Spirit of God, the Lordship of Christ, the universal ubiquity of God, even the Father, all tend to bring into unity those connected with each as a divine centre. All the religious relationships of the soul, all the points by which we are in contact with God, agree to form all believers into one in this world, in such a manner that no man can be a Christian without being one with all those who are so. We cannot exercise faith, nor enjoy hope, nor express Christian life in any form whatever, without having the same faith and the same hope as the rest, without giving expression to that which exists in the rest. Only we are called on to maintain it practically.

The enlarged extent of each circle of unity: essential and real unity and outward profession, with the Father's universal claims and rights

We may remark, that the three spheres of unity presented in these three verses have not the same extent. The circle of unity enlarges each time. With the Spirit we find linked the unity of the Body, the essential and real unity produced by the power of the Spirit uniting to Christ all His members: with the Lord, that of faith and of baptism. Here each individual has the same faith, the same baptism: it is the outward profession, true and real perhaps, but a profession, in reference to Him who has rights over those that call themselves by His name. With regard to the third character of unity, it relates to claims that extend to all things, although to the believer it is a closer bond, because He who has a right over all things dwells in believers.[17]

Realization and manifestation of the unity of the one Body

Observe here, that it is not only a unity of sentiment, of desire, and of heart. That unity is pressed upon them;

[17] To recapitulate, there is, first, one Body and one Spirit, one hope of our calling; second, one Lord, with whom are connected one faith and one baptism; third, one God and Father of all, who is above all things, everywhere, and in all Christians. Moreover, while insisting upon these three great relationships in which all Christians are placed, as being in their nature the foundations of unity, and the motives of its maintenance, these relationships extend successively in breadth. The direct relationship applies properly to the same persons; but the character of Him who is the basis of the relationship enlarges the idea connected with it. With regard to the Spirit, His presence unites the Body—is the bond between all the members of the Body: none but the members of the Body —and they, as such—are seen here. The Lord has wider claims. In this relationship it is not the members of the Body that are spoken of; there is one faith and one baptism, one profession in the world: there could not be two. But although the persons who are in this outward relationship may stand also in the other relationships and be members of the Body, yet the relationship here is one of individual *profession*. It is not a thing which cannot exist at all except in reality (one is a member of Christ's Body, or one is not). God is the Father of these same members, as being His children, but He who maintains this relationship is necessarily and always above all things—personally above all things, but divinely everywhere.

but it is in order to maintain the realization, and the manifestation here below, of a unity that belongs to the existence and to the eternal position of the assembly in Christ. There is one Spirit, but there is one Body. The union of hearts in the bond of peace, which the apostle desires, is for the public maintenance of this unity; not that there might be patience with one another when that has disappeared, Christians contenting themselves with its absence. One does not accept that which is contrary to the Word, although in certain cases those who are in it ought to be borne with. The consideration of the community of position and of privilege, enjoyed by all the children of God in the relationships of which we have now been speaking, served to unite them with each other in the sweet enjoyment of this most precious position, leading them also, each one, to rejoice in love at the part which every other member of the Body had in this happiness.

Christ the Head over all things: the necessity of redemption if men were to be united to Christ: Satan overcome and led captive

But, on the other hand, the fact that Christ was exalted to be in heaven the Head over all things brought in a difference which appertained to this supremacy of Christ —a supremacy exercised with divine sovereignty and wisdow. "Unto every one of us is given grace [gift] according to the measure of the gift of Christ" (that is to say, as Christ sees fit to bestow). With regard to our position of joy and blessing in Christ, we are one. With regard to our service, we have each an individual place according to His divine wisdom, and according to His sovereign rights in the work. The foundation of this title, whatever may be the divine power that is exercised in it, is this: man was under the power of Satan—miserable condition, the fruit of his sin, a condition to which his self-

will had reduced him, but in which (according to the
judgment of God who had pronounced on him the sentence of death) he was a slave in body and mind to the
enemy who had the power of death—with reservation of
the sovereign rights and sovereign grace of God. (See
chap. 2:2.) Now Christ has made Himself Man, and
began by going as Man, led by the Spirit, to meet Satan.
He overcame him. As to His personal power, He was
able to drive him out everywhere, and to deliver man.
But man would not have God with him; nor was it possible for men, in their sinful condition, to be united to
Christ without redemption. The Lord however, carrying
on His perfect work of love, suffered death, and overcame
Satan in that his last stronghold, which God's righteous
judgment maintained in force against sinful man—a judgment which Christ therefore underwent, accomplishing a
redemption that was complete, final, and eternal in its
value; so that neither Satan, the prince of death and
accuser of the children of God on earth, nor even the
judgment of God, had anything more to say to the redeemed. The kingdom of Satan was taken from him; the
just judgment of God was undergone and completely
satisfied. All judgment is committed to the Son, and
power over all men, because He is the Son of Man. These
two results are not yet manifested, although the Lord possesses all power in heaven and in earth. The thing here
spoken of is another result which is accomplished meanwhile. The victory is complete. He has led the adversary
captive. In ascending to heaven He has placed victorious
Man above all things, and has led captive all the power
that previously had dominion over man.

The Lord's power over Satan exhibited in His Body, the assembly

Now before manifesting in person the power He had
gained as Man by binding Satan, before displaying it in

the blessing of man on earth, He exhibits it in the assembly, His Body, by imparting, as He had promised, to men delivered from the enemy's dominion gifts which are the proof of that power.

The contents and connection of Chapters 1, 2, 3 and 4

Chapter 1 had laid open to us the thoughts of God; chapter 2 the fulfilment, in power, of His thoughts with regard to the redeemed—Jews or Gentiles, all dead in their sins—to form them into the assembly. Chapter 3 is the especial development of the mystery in that which concerned the Gentiles in Paul's administration of it on earth. Here (chap. 4) the assembly is presented in its unity as a Body, and in the varied functions of its members; that is to say, the positive effect of those counsels in the assembly here below. But this is founded on the exaltation of Christ, who, the conqueror of the enemy, has ascended to heaven as man.

Gifts for men from the Head of the Body, the ascended Man

Thus exalted, He has received gifts in Man, that is, in His human character. (Compare Acts 2: 33.) It is thus "in Man," that it is expressed in Psalm 68, from whence the quotation is taken. Here, having received these gifts as the Head of the Body, Christ is the channel of their communication to others. They are gifts for men.

Three things here characterize Him—a Man ascended on high—a Man who has led captive him who held man in captivity—a Man who has received for men, delivered from that enemy, the gifts of God, which bear witness to this exaltation of man in Christ, and serve as a means for the deliverance of others. For this chapter does not speak of the more direct signs of the Spirit's power, such as tongues, miracles—such as are usually termed miraculous gifts. But what the Lord as Head confers on individuals, they are the gifts, as His servants for forming the saints to be with Him, and for the edification of the body—the fruit of His care over them. Hence, as already remarked, their continuance (till we all, one after another, grow up to the Head) is stated as to power, by the Spirit; in 1 Corinthians 12 it is not.

The Lord's complete and glorious work: Satan's captives made Christ's servants, the vessels of His power

But let us pause here for a moment, to contemplate the import of that which we have been considering.

What a complete and glorious work is that which the Lord has accomplished for us, and of which the communication of these gifts is the precious testimony! When we were the slaves of Satan and consequently of death, as well as the slaves of sin, we have seen that He was pleased to undergo for the glory of God that which hung over us. He went down into death of which Satan had the power. And so complete was the victory of Man in Him, so entire our deliverance, that (exalted Himself as Man to the right hand of God's throne—He who had been under death) He has rescued us from the enemy's yoke, and uses the privilege which His position and His glory give Him to make those who were captives before, the vessels of His power for the deliverance of others also. He gives us the right, as under His jurisdiction, of acting in His holy war, moved by the same principles of love as Himself. Such is our deliverance that we are the instruments of His power against the enemy—His fellow-laborers in love through His power. Hence the connection between practical godliness, the complete subjugation of the flesh, and the capacity to serve Christ as instruments in the hand of the Holy Ghost, and the vessels of His power.

The significance of the Lord's ascension in connection with His Person and work

Now the Lord's ascension has immense significancy in connection with His Person and work. He ascended indeed as Man, but He first descended as Man even into the darkness of the grave and of death; and from thence— victorious over the power of the enemy who had the power of death, and having blotted out the sins of His redeemed ones, and accomplished the glory of God in obedience—He takes His place as Man above the heavens in order that He may fill all things; not only as being God, but according to the glory and the power of a position in which He was placed by the accomplishment of the work of redemption—a work which led Him into the depths of the power of the enemy, and placed Him on the throne of God—a position that He holds, not only by the title of Creator, which was already His, but by that of Redeemer, which shelters from evil all that is found within the sphere of the mighty efficacy of His work—a sphere filled with blessing, with grace, and with Himself. Glorious truth, which belongs at the same time to the union of the divine and human natures in the Person of Christ, and to the work of redemption accomplished by suffering on the cross!

The Lord's descent and ascent

Love brought Him down from the throne of God, and, being found as a Man,[18] through the same grace, into the darkness of death. Having died, bearing our sins, He has gone up again to that throne as Man, filling all things. He went below the creature into death, and is gone above it.

[18] The descent into the lower parts of the earth is viewed as from His place as Man on earth; not His coming down from heaven to be a Man. It is Christ who descended.

The object of Christ's work: His Body, His Bride: gifts communicated to gather together the members of His Body

But while filling all things by virtue of His glorious Person, and in connection with the work which He accomplished, He is also in immediate relation with that which in the counsels of God is closely united to Him who thus fills all things, with that which has been especially the object of His work of redemption. It is His Body, His assembly, united to Him by the bond of the Holy Ghost to complete this mystical Man, to be the Bride of this Second Man, who fills all in all—a Body which, as manifested here below, is set in the midst of a creation that is not yet delivered, and in the presence of enemies that are in the heavenly places, until Christ shall exercise, on the part of God His Father, the power that has been committed to Him as Man. When Christ shall thus exercise His power, He will take vengeance on those who have defiled His creation by seducing man, who had been its head down here, and the image of Him who was to be its Head everywhere. He will also deliver creation from its subjection to evil. Meanwhile, personally exalted as the glorious Man, and seated at God's right hand until God shall make His enemies His footstool, He communicates the gifts necessary for the gathering together of those who are to be the companions of His glory, who are the members of His Body, and who shall be manifested with Him when His glory shines forth in the midst of this world of darkness.

The work of the Spirit in the assembly: its spiritual power

The apostle shows us here an assembly already delivered, and exercising the power of the Spirit; which on the one side delivers souls, and on the other builds them up in Christ, that they may grow up to the measure of their

Head in spite of all the power of Satan which still subsists.

But an important truth is connected with this fact. This spiritual power is not exercised in a manner simply divine. It is Christ ascended (He however who had previously descended into the lower parts of the earth) who, as Man, has received these gifts of power. It is thus that Psalm 68 speaks as well as Acts 2: 33. The latter passage speaks also of the gifts bestowed on His members. In our chapter it is only in the latter way that they are mentioned. He has given gifts unto men.

The purpose and character of the gifts of the Head of the Body

I would also remark, that these gifts are not here presented as gifts bestowed by the Holy Ghost come down to earth, and distributing to every one according to His will: nor are those gifts spoken of which are tokens of spiritual power suited to act as signs upon those that are outside: but they are ministrations for gathering together and for edification established by Christ as Head of the Body by means of gifts with which He endows persons at His choice. Ascended on high, and having taken His place as Man at the right hand of God, and filling all things, whatever may be the extent of His glory, Christ has first for His object to fulfil the ways of God in love in gathering souls, and in particular towards the saints and the assembly; to establish the manifestation of the divine nature, and to communicate to the assembly the riches of that grace which the ways of God display, and of which the divine nature is the source. It is in the assembly that the nature of God, the counsels of grace, and the efficacious work of Christ are concentrated in their object; and these gifts are the means of ministering, in the communication of these, in blessing to man.

Apostles, prophets, evangelists, pastors, and teachers:

apostles and prophets laying, or rather being laid, as the foundations of the heavenly building, and acting as coming directly from the Lord in an extraordinary manner; the two other classes (the last being subdivided into two gifts, connected in their nature) belonging to ordinary ministry in all ages. It is important to remark also, that the apostle sees nothing existing before the exaltation of Christ save man the child of wrath, the power of Satan, the power which raised us up (dead in sins as we were) with Christ, and the efficacy of the cross, which had reconciled us to God, and abolished the distinction between Jew and Gentile in the assembly, to unite them in one Body before God—the cross in which Christ drank the cup and bore the curse, so that wrath has passed away for the believer, and in which a God of love, a Saviour God, is fully manifested.

The New Testament apostles and prophets exclusive of the twelve apostles

So the existence of the apostles dates here only from the gifts that followed the exaltation of Jesus. The twelve as sent out by Jesus on earth have no place in the instruction of this epistle, which treats of the Body of Christ, of the unity and the members of this Body; and the Body could not exist before the Head existed and had taken His place as such. Thus also we have seen that, when the apostle speaks of the apostles and prophets, the latter are to him those exclusively of the New Testament, and those who have been made such by Christ after His ascension. It is the new heavenly Man who, being the exalted Head in heaven, forms His Body on the earth. He does it for heaven, putting the individuals who compose it spiritually and intelligently in connection with the Head by the power of the Holy Ghost acting in this Body on the earth (the gifts, of which the apostle here speaks, being the channels by which His graces are communicated according to the bonds which the Holy Ghost forms with the Head).

The effect of the gifts as channels to the Body

The proper and immediate effect is the perfecting of individuals according to the grace that dwells in the Head. The shape which this divine action takes, further, is the work of the ministry, and the formation of the Body of Christ, until all the members are grown up into the measure of the stature of Christ their Head. Christ has been revealed in all His fulness: it is according to this revelation that the members of the Body are to be formed in the likeness of Christ, known as filling all things, and as the Head of His Body, the revelation of the perfect love to God, of the excellency of man before Him according to His counsels, of man the vessel of all His grace, all His power, and all His gifts. Thus the assembly, and each one of the members of Christ, should be filled with the thoughts and the riches of a well-known Christ, instead of being tossed to and fro by all sorts of doctrines brought forward by the enemy to deceive souls.

Love and truth: Christ the perfect expression of them

The Christian was to grow up according to all that was revealed in Christ, and to be ever increasing in likeness to his Head; using love and truth for his own soul —the two things of which Christ is the perfect expression. Truth displays the real relation of all things with each other in connection with the centre of all things, which is God revealed now in Christ. Love is that which God is in the midst of all this. Now Christ, as the light, put everything precisely in its place—man, Satan, sin, righteousness, holiness, all things, and that in every detail, and in connection with God. And Christ was love, the expression of the love of God in the midst of all this. And this is our pattern; and our pattern as having overcome, and, as having ascended into heaven, our Head, to which we are united as the members of His Body.

The members of the Body channels of Christ's grace to each member that all may be nourished and grow

There flows from this Head, by means of its members, the grace needed to accomplish the work of assimilation to Himself. His Body, compacted together, increases by the working of His grace in each member, and edifies itself in love.[19] This is the position of the assembly according to God, until all the members of the Body attain to the stature of Christ. The manifestation, alas, of this unity is marred; but the grace, and the operation of the grace of its Head to nourish and cause its members to grow, is never impaired, any more than the love in the Lord's heart from which this grace springs. We do not glorify Him, we have not the joy of being ministers of joy to each other as we might be; but the Head does not cease to work for the good of His Body. The wolf indeed comes and scatters the sheep, but he cannot pluck them out of the Shepherd's hands. His faithfulness is glorified in our unfaithfulness without excusing it.

The union of Christ and the assembly in its double character

With this precious object of the ministration of grace (namely, for the growth of each member individually unto the measure of the stature of the Head Himself), with the ministration of each member in its place to the edifying itself in love, ends this development of the counsels of God in the union of Christ and the assembly, in its double

[19] Verse 11 gives special and permanent gifts; verse 16, what every joint supplies in its place. Both have their place in the forming and growth of the Body.

character of the Body of Christ in heaven, and the habitation of the Holy Ghost on earth—truths which cannot be separated, but each of which has its distinctive importance, and which reconcile the certain immutable operations of grace in the Head with the failures of the assembly responsible on the earth.

Exhortations to a suited walk: putting off the old man, putting on Christ

Exhortations to a walk befitting such a position follow, in order that the glory of God in us and by us, and His grace towards us, may be identified in our full blessing. We will notice the great principles of these exhortations.

The first is the contrast[20] between the ignorance of a heart that is blind, and a stranger to the life of God, and consequently walking in the vanity of its own understanding, that is, according to the desires of a heart given up to the impulses of the flesh without God—the contrast, I say, between this state, and that of having learnt Christ, as the truth is in Jesus (which is the expression of the life of God in man, God Himself manifested in the flesh), the having put off this old man, which is corrupt itself according to its deceitful lusts, and put on this new Man, Christ. It is not an amelioration of the old man; it is a putting it off, and a putting on of Christ.

Even here the apostle does not lose sight of the oneness of the Body; we are to speak the truth, because we are members one of another. "Truth," the expression of simplicity and integrity of heart, is in connection with "the truth as it is in Jesus," whose life is transparent as the light, as falsehood is in connection with deceitful lusts.

---

[20] I have already noticed, that contrast of the new state and the old characterizes the Ephesians more than Colossians, where we find more development of life.

New creation: Adam's fall and its result

Moreover, the old man is without God, alienated from the life of God. The new man is created, it is a new creation, and a creation[21] after the model of that which is the character of God, righteousness and holiness of truth. The first Adam was not in that manner created after the image of God. By the fall the knowledge of good and evil entered into man. He can no longer be innocent. When innocent, he was ignorant of evil in itself. Now, fallen, he is a stranger to the life of God in his ignorance: but the knowledge of good and evil which he has acquired, the moral distinction between good and evil in itself, is a divine principle. "The man," said God, "is become as one of Us, to know good and evil." But in order to possess this knowledge, and subsist in what is good before God, there must be divine energy, divine life.

God as the Centre of all true relationship and moral obligation

Everything has its true nature, its true character, in the eyes of God. That is the truth. It is not that He is the truth. The truth is the right and perfect expression of that which a thing is (and, in an absolute way, of that which all things are), and of the relations in which it stands to other things, or in which all things stand towards each other. Thus God could not be the truth. He is not the expression of some other thing. Everything relates to Him. He is the centre of all true relationship, and of all moral obligation. Neither is God the measure of all things, for He is above all things; and nothing else can be so above them, or He would not be so.[22] It is God become Man; it is Christ, who is the truth, and the measure of

[21] In Colossians we have "renewed in knowledge after the image of Him that created us."

[22] There is a sense in which God is, morally, the measure of other beings—a consideration that brings out the immense privilege of the

all things. But all things have their true character in the eyes of God: and He judges righteously of all, whether morally or in power. He acts according to that judgment. He is just. He also knows evil perfectly, being Himself goodness, that it may be perfectly an abomination to Him, that He may repel it by His own nature. He is holy. Now the new man, created after the divine nature, is so in righteousness and holiness of truth. What a privilege! What a blessing! It is, as another apostle has said, to be "partakers of the divine nature." Adam had nothing of this.

Adam's responsibility for obedience, not for knowledge

Adam was perfect as an innocent man. The breath of life in his nostrils was breathed into him by God, and he was responsible for obedience to God in a thing wherein neither good nor evil was to be known, but simply a commandment. The trial was that of obedience only, not the knowledge of good or evil in itself. At present, in Christ, the portion of the believer is a participation in the divine nature itself, in a being who knows good and evil, and who vitally participates in the sovereign good, morally in the nature of God Himself, although always thereby dependent on Him. It is our evil nature which is not so, or at least which refuses to be dependent on Him.

Partakers of the divine nature and indwelt by the Holy Spirit to be imitators of God

Now there is a prince of this world, a stranger to God; and, besides participation in the divine nature, there is

child of God. It is the effect of grace, in that, being born of Him and partaking of His nature, the child of God is called to be the imitator of God, to be perfect as His Father is perfect. He who loves is born of God, and knows God, for God is love. He makes us partakers of His holiness, consequently we are called to be imitators of God, as His dear children. This shows the immense privileges of grace. It is the love of God in the midst of evil, and which, superior to all evil, walks in holiness, and rejoices also together, in a divine way, in the unity of the same joys and the same sentiments. Therefore Christ says (John 17), "as We are," and "in Us."

the Spirit Himself who has been given to us. These solemn truths enter also as principles into these exhortations. "Give no place to the devil," on the one hand—give him no room to come in and act on the flesh; and, on the other hand, "Grieve not the Holy Spirit" who dwells in you. The redemption of the creature has not yet taken place, but ye have been sealed unto that day: respect and cherish this mighty and holy Guest who graciously dwells in you. Let all bitterness and malice therefore cease, even in word, and let meekness and kindness reign in you according to the pattern you have in the ways of God in Christ towards you. Be imitators of God—beautiful and magnificent privilege!—but which flows naturally from the truth that we are made partakers of His nature, and that His Spirit dwells in us.

The Christian pattern of life founded on new creation: subjectively, putting off the old and putting on the new

These are the two great subjective principles of the Christian—the having put off the old man and put on the new, and the Holy Ghost's dwelling in him. Nor can anything be more blessed than the pattern of life here given to the Christian, founded on our being a new creation. It is perfect subjectively and objectively. First, subjectively, the truth in Jesus is the having put off the old man and put on the new, which has God for its pattern. It is created *after God* in the perfection of His moral character. But this is not all. The Holy Spirit of God by which we are sealed to the day of redemption dwells in us: we are not to grieve Him. These are the two elements of our state, the new man created after God, and the presence of the Holy Spirit of God; and He is emphatically here called the Spirit of God, as in connection with God's character.

Objectively, God the pattern as love and light

And next objectively: created after God, and God dwelling in us, God is the pattern of our walk, and thus in respect of the two words which alone give God's essence —love and light, We are to walk in love, as Christ loved us and gave Himself for us a sacrifice to God. *"For us"* was divine love; *"to God"* is perfection of object and motive. Law takes up the love of self as the measure of love to others. Christ gives up self wholly and for us, but to God. Our worthlessness enhances the love; but, on the other hand, an affection and a motive have their worth from the object (and with Christ that was God Himself), self wholly given up. For, so to speak, we may love up and love down. When we look upward in our affections, the nobler the object the nobler the affection; when it is downwards, the more unworthy the object, the more pure and absolute the love. Christ was perfect in both, and absolutely so. He gave *Himself* for us, and to God. Afterwards we are light in the Lord. We cannot say we are love, for love is sovereign goodness in God; we walk in it, like Christ. But we *are* light in the Lord. This is the second essential name of God, and as partaker of the divine nature we are light in the Lord. Here again Christ is the pattern. "Christ shall give thee light." We are called on, then, as His dear children to imitate God.

Life perfectly and fully presented to us in Christ

This life, in which we participate and of which we live as partakers of the divine nature, has been objectively presented to us in Christ in all its perfection and in all its fulness; in man, and in man now brought to perfection on high, according to the counsels of God respecting Him. It is Christ, this eternal life, who was with the Father and has been manifested unto us—He who, having then first descended, has ascended now into heaven to carry humanity thither, and display it in the glory—the glory of

God—according to His eternal counsels. We have seen this life here in its earthly development: God manifest in the flesh; Man, perfectly heavenly, and obedient in all things to His Father, moved, in His conduct to others, by the motives that characterize God Himself in grace. Hereafter He will be manifested in judgment; and already, here below, He has gone through all the experiences of a man, understanding thus how grace adapts itself to our wants, and displaying it now, according to that knowledge, even as hereafter He will exercise judgment with a knowledge of man, not only divine, but which, having gone through this world in holiness, will leave the hearts of men without excuse and without escape.

The image of God

But it is the image of God in Him, of which we are now speaking. It is in Him that the nature which we have to imitate is presented to us, and presented in man as it ought to be developed in us here below, in the circumstances through which we are passing. We see in Him the manifestation of God, and that in contrast with the old man. There we see "the truth as it is in Jesus," save that in us it involves the putting off of the old man and putting on the new, answering to Christ's death and resurrection. (Compare particularly as to His death, 1 Peter 3: 18; 4: 1.) Thus, in order to attract and to lead on our hearts, to give us the model on which they are to be formed, the aim to which they should tend, God has given us an object in which He manifests Himself, and which is the object of all His own delight.

God's object in the new man and that of the new man himself

The reproduction of God in man is the object that God proposed to Himself in the new man; and that the new man proposes to himself, as he is himself the reproduction of the nature and the character of God. There are two principles for the Christian path, according to the light in which he views himself. Running his race as man towards the object of his heavenly calling, in which he follows after Christ ascended on high: he is running the heavenward race; the excellency of Christ to be won there, his motive—that is not the Ephesian aspect. In the Ephesians he is sitting in heavenly places in Christ, and he has to come out as from heaven, as Christ really did, and manifest God's character upon earth, of which, as we have seen, Christ is the pattern. We are called, as in the position of dear children, to show our Father's ways.

We are not created anew according to that which the first Adam was, but according to that which God is: Christ is its manifestation. And He is the Second Man, the Last Adam.[23]

Characteristic features of the new man: the picture of the life of Christ

In detail we shall find these characteristic features: truthfulness, the absence of all anger that has the nature of hatred (lying and hatred are the two characteristics of the enemy); practical righteousness connected with labor according to the will of God (man's true position); and the absence of corruption. It is man under the rule of God since the fall, delivered from the effect of the deceitful lusts. But it is more than this. A divine principle brings in the desire of doing good to others, to their body and their soul. I need not say how truly we find here the picture of the life of Christ, as in the preceding remarks it was the putting off of the spirit of the enemy and of the old man. The spirit of peace and love (and

[23] It is useful to note here the difference of Romans (12: 1, 2) and this epistle. The Romans, we have seen, contemplates a living man on earth; hence he is to give his body up as a living sacrifice—alive in Christ, he is to yield his members up wholly to God. Here the saints are seen as sitting in heavenly places already, and they are to come out in testimony of God's character before men, walking as Christ did in love, and light.

that, in spite of evil in others and the wrongs they may do us) completes the picture, adding that which will be easily understood after what has been said, that, in "forgiving one another," we are to be imitators of God, and to walk in love as Christ has loved us, and has given Himself for us. Beautiful picture, precious privilege! May God grant us so to look at Jesus as to have His image stamped upon us, and in some sort to walk like Him.

God's grace and love acting in man go up again to God in devotedness

Moreover, let us remark here, and it is an important feature in this picture of the fruits of grace and of the new man, that when the grace and love, which come down from God, act in man, they always go up again to God in devotedness. Walk, he says, in love, even as Christ loved us and gave Himself up for us, an offering and a sacrifice to God for a sweet-smelling savor. We see it in Christ. He is this love which comes down in grace, but this grace, acting in man, makes Him devote Himself to God, although it is on behalf of others. So it is in us; it is the touchstone of the Christian heart's activity.

Plain speaking as to sin and the neglect of ordinary morality: the most profound truths connected with daily practice

The apostle then speaks plainly as to sin, in order that no one may deceive himself; nor be occupied with deep truths, using them intellectually, to the neglect of ordinary morality—one of the signs of heresy, properly so called. He has connected the profoundest doctrines in his teaching with daily practice. If Christ be glorified, the Head of the assembly, He is the model of the New Man, the Last Adam; the assembly being one with Him on high, and the habitation of God on earth by the Spirit, with whom every Christian is sealed. Every Christian, if indeed he has learned the truth as it is in Jesus, has learned that it consists in having put off the old man, and having put on the new man, created after God in righteousness and holiness (of which Christ is the model, according to the counsels of God in glory); and he is to grow up unto the measure of the stature of Christ, who is the Head, and not grieve the Holy Spirit wherewith he is sealed. The fullest revelation of grace does not weaken the immutable truth that God had a character proper to Himself; it unfolds that character to us by means of the most precious revelations of the gospel, and of the closest relationships with God, which were formed by these revelations: but this character could not alter, nor could the kingdom of God allow of, any characters contrary to it. The wrath of God therefore against evil, and against those who commit it, is plainly set forth.

The fruit of the light and the unfruitful works of darkness

Now we were that which is contrary to His character, we were darkness; not only in the dark, but darkness in our nature, the opposite of God who is light. No one ray of that which He is was found in our will, our desires, our understanding. We were morally destitute of it. There was the corruptness of the first Adam, but no share in any feature of the divine character. We are now partakers of the divine nature, we have the same desires, we know what it is that He loves, and we love what He loves, we enjoy that which He enjoys, we are light (poor and weak indeed, yet such by nature) in the Lord—looked at as in Christ. They are the fruits of light[24] that are developed in the Christian; he is to avoid all association with the unfruitful works of darkness.

[24] We should read "fruit of the light," not "fruit of the Spirit."

Called to awake from sleep: Christ Himself the light of the soul: the Spirit the Source of joy and thanksgiving

But, in speaking of motives, the apostle returns to the great subjects that pre-occupied him, and he returns to them, not only that we should put on the character set forth by that of which he speaks, but that we should realize all its extent, that we should experience all its force. He had told us that the truth in Christ was the having put on the new man, in contrast with the old man, and that we are not to grieve the Holy Spirit. Now he exhorts those that sleep to awake, and Christ should be their light. Light makes all things manifest; but he who sleeps, although not dead, does not profit by it. For hearing, seeing, and all mental reception and communication, he is in the state of a dead man. Alas, how apt this sleep is to overtake us! But in awaking, it was not that they should see the light dimly, but Christ Himself should be the light of the soul; they should have all the full revelation of that which is well-pleasing to God, that which He loves; they should have divine wisdom in Christ; they should be able to profit by opportunities, should find them, being thus enlightened, in the difficulties of a world governed by the enemy, and should act according to spiritual understanding in every case that presented itself. Further, if they were not to lose their senses through means of excitement used in the world, they were to be filled with the Spirit, that is, that He should take such possession of our affections, our thoughts, our understanding, that He should be their only source according to His proper and mighty energy to the exclusion of all else. Thus, full of joy, we should praise, we should sing for joy; and we should give thanks for all that might happen, because a God of love is the true source of all. We should be full of joy in the spiritual realization of the objects of faith, and the heart continuing to be filled with the Spirit and sustained by this grace, the experience of the hand of God in everything here below will give rise only to thanksgiving. It comes from His hand whom we trust and whose love we know. But giving thanks in all things is a test of the state of the soul; because the consciousness that all things are from God's hand, full trust in His love, and deadness as to any will of our own, must exist in order to give thanks in everything—a single eye which delights in His will.

The fruit of grace in our relationships and duties

In entering into the details of relationships and particular duties, the apostle cannot give up the subject that is so dear to him. The command which he addresses to wives, that they are to submit themselves to their husbands, immediately suggests the relationship between Christ and the assembly, not now as a subject for knowledge, but to unfold His affection and tender care. We have seen that the apostle, having established the great principles displayed in the revelation of our relationship with God—our vocation—then deduces their practical consequences with regard to the life and conduct of Christians: they were to walk as having put on the new man, to have Christ for their light, not to grieve the Spirit, to be filled with the Spirit. Now all this, while the fruit of grace, was either knowledge or practical responsibility.

Christ's grace: three steps in the work of His love to the assembly

But here the subject is viewed in another aspect. It is the grace that acts in Christ Himself, His affections, His guardian care, His devotedness to the assembly. Nothing can be more precious, more tender, more intimate. He loved the assembly—that is the source of all. And there are three steps in the work of this love. He gave Himself for it, He washes it, He presents it all glorious to Himself. This is not precisely the sovereign election of the individual by God; but the affection that displays itself in the relationship which Christ maintains with the assembly.[25] See also the extent of the gift, and how marvellous the ground of confidence that it contains. He gives *Himself;* it is not only His life, true as that is, but Himself.[26] All that Christ was has been given, and given by Himself; it is the entire devotedness and giving of Himself. And now all that is in Him—His grace, His righteousness, His acceptancy with the Father, the excellent glory of His Person, His wisdom, the energy of divine love that can give itself—all is consecrated to the welfare of the assembly. There are no qualities, no excellencies in Christ, which are not ours in their exercise consequent on the gift of Himself. He has already given them, and consecrated them to the blessing of the assembly which He has given Himself to have. Not only are they given, but *He* has given them; His love has accomplished it.

Christ's love to the assembly—unutterable, inexhaustible and unchangeable

We know well that it is on the cross that this giving of Himself was accomplished, it is there that the consecration of Himself to the good of the assembly was complete. But here that glorious work is not exactly viewed on the side of its atoning and redeeming efficacy, but on

[25] It is well to notice here this character of love—love in an established relationship. The Word of God is more exact than is generally thought in its expressions; because the expression has its origin in the thing itself. It is not said that *Christ* loved the *world*—He has no relationship with the world as it is. It is said that "God so loved the world," this is what He is towards it in His own goodness. It is not said that *God* loved the *assembly.* The proper relationship of the assembly as such is with Christ, her heavenly Bridegroom. The *Father* loves us, we are His dear children. God, in this character, loves us. Thus *Jehovah* loves *Israel.* On the other hand, all the tenderness and faithfulness that belong to the relationship in which Christ stands are our portion in Him, as well as all that the name of Father means on its side also.

[26] It is specially the devotedness of His love; He gives and gives Himself.

that of the devotedness and love to the assembly which
Christ manifested in it. Now we can always reckon upon
this love which was perfectly displayed in it. It is not
altered. Jesus—blessed and praised be His name for it!
—is for me according to the energy of His love in all that
He is, in all circumstances and for ever, and in the
activity of that love according to which He gave Himself.
He loved the assembly and gave Himself for it. This is
the source of all our blessings, as members of the assembly.

But this love of Christ is inexhaustible and unchangeable. It effects the blessing of its cherished object, by
preparing it for a happiness of which His heart is alike
the measure and the source,[27] to happiness of perfect
purity, the excellence of which He knows in heaven—
purity suited to the presence of God, and to her who
should be in that presence for ever, the Bride of the Lamb
—purity which renders it capable of enjoying perfect love
and glory; even as that love tends to purify the soul by
making itself known to it, and attracting it, divesting it
of self, and filling it with God as the centre of blessing
and joy.

The Church made Christ's own to sanctify it:
the means He uses

It is important to remark that Christ does not here
sanctify the assembly to make it His own, but makes it
His own to sanctify it. It is first His, then He suits it to
Himself. Christ, who loves the Church as being His own,
and who has already made it His own by giving Himself
for it, and who chooses to have it such as His heart desires, occupies Himself with it, when He has won it, to
render it such. He gave Himself for it, that He might

[27] When I say (here and above) that the love of Christ is its source, it
is not as if the love of the Father and the counsels of God had not their
place in it. I speak of the blessing applied and carried out in the relationship presented in this passage; and this relationship exists with
Christ. Nevertheless it is the same divine love.

sanctify it by the washing of water by the Word. Here we find the moral effect produced by the care of Christ, the object which He proposes to Himself in His work accomplished in time, and the means He uses to attain it. He appropriates the assembly morally, sets it morally apart for Himself, when He has made it His; for He can only desire holy things—holy according to the knowledge He has of purity—by virtue of His eternal and natural abode in heaven. He then puts the assembly in connection with heaven, from whence He is, and into which He will introduce it. He gave Himself in order to sanctify it. For this purpose He uses the Word, which is the divine expression of the mind of God, of heavenly order and holiness, of truth itself (that is to say, of the true relation of all things with God; and that according to His love in Christ), and which consequently judges all that deviates from it as to purity or love.

The assembly as the Bride of Christ

He forms the assembly for His Bride, a helpmeet for Him, in which all is according to the glory and the love of God, by the revelation (through the word, which comes from thence) of these things as they exist in heaven. Now Christ Himself is the full expression of these things, the image of the invisible God. Thus, in communicating them to the assembly, He prepares it for Himself. When speaking therefore in this sense of His own testimony, He says, "We speak that we do know, and testify that we have seen."

The Word: its cleansing effect

But it is this which the Word is, as we have received it from Jesus; and more especially as speaking from heaven, with the character of the new commandment, the darkness passing away, and the true light now shining; and consequently, the thing being true, not only in Him but in us. (The ministry of chapter 1 is occupied with this, forming the hearts of the saints on earth in fellowship with the Head from which the grace and the light descended.) In this manner then Christ sanctifies the assembly for which He gave Himself. He has formed it for heavenly things by the communication of heavenly things, of which He is Himself the fulness and the glory. But this Word finds the assembly mixed up with things that are contrary to this heavenly purity and love. Alas, its affections—as to the old man at least—mixed up with these earthly things, which are contrary to the will of God and to His nature. Thus in sanctifying the assembly He must needs cleanse it. This is therefore the work of the love of Christ during the present time, but for the eternal and essential happiness of the assembly.

The use of the Word in grace and love by Christ Himself

He sanctifies the assembly, but He does it by the Word, communicating heavenly things—all that belongs to the nature, to the majesty, and to the glory of God—in love, but at the same time applying them to judge everything in her present affections, which is at variance with that which He communicates. Precious work of love, which not only loves us but labors to make us fit to enjoy that love; fit to be with Christ Himself in the Father's house!

How deeply is He interested in us! He not only accomplished the glorious work of our redemption by giving Himself for us, but He acts continually with perfect love and patience to make us such as He would have us to be in His own presence—fit for the heavenly places and heavenly things.

What a character this shows to belong also to the Word, and what grace in His use of it! It is the communication of divine things according to their own perfection, and now as God Himself is in the light. It is the revelation of God Himself, as we know Him in a glorified Christ, in a perfect love to form us also according to that perfection for the enjoyment of Him; and yet it is addressed to us, yea is suited in its very nature to us down here (compare John 1:4) to impart these things to us by bringing in light amid the darkness, thus necessarily judging all that is in the darkness, but in order to purify us in love.

The order in which Christ's work for His Church is presented: the source of all: its result and proof

Observe, also, the order in which this work of Christ is presented to us, beginning with love. He loved the assembly; this, as we have already said, is the source of all. *All* that follows is the result of that love and cannot gainsay it. The perfect proof of it is then stated: He gave Himself for the assembly. He could not give more. It was to the glory of the Father, no doubt, but it was for the assembly. Had he reserved anything, the love in giving Himself would not have been perfect, not absolute; it would not have been a devotedness that left nothing for the awakened heart to desire. It would not have been Christ, for He could not but be perfect. We know love and perfection in knowing Him. But He has won the heart of the assembly by giving Himself for it. He has won her thus. She is His according to that love. Yea; it is there that we have learnt what love is. Hereby know we love in that He gave Himself for us. All was for the glory of the Father: without that it would not have been perfection; and the revelation of the heavenly things would not have taken place, for that depended on the Father's being perfectly glorified. In this the things to be revealed were manifested and verified, so to speak, in spite of evil; but all is entirely for us.

If we have learnt to know love, we have learnt to know Jesus, such as He is for us; and He is wholly for us.

The result of perfect love

Thus the entire work of cleansing and of sanctification is the result of perfect love. It is not the means of obtaining the love, or of being its object. It is indeed the means of enabling us to enjoy it; but it is the love itself which, in its exercise, works this sanctification. Christ wins the assembly *first*. He then in His perfect love makes it such as He would have it to be—a truth that is precious to us in every way, and first, in order to free the soul from all servile fear, to give sanctification its true character of grace and its true extent here. It is joy of heart to know that Christ Himself will make us all He desires us to be.

Three effects of Christ's love for His Church

We have considered two effects of the love of Christ for the assembly. The first was the gift of Himself, which in a certain sense comprises the whole; it is love perfect in itself. He gave Himself. The second is the moral formation of the object of His love, that it may be with Him; according, we may add, to the perfections of God Himself, for that indeed is what the Word is—the expression of the nature, the ways, and the thoughts of God.

Presented to Himself glorious, without spot or wrinkle: Eve presented to Adam by God

There is yet a third effect of this love of Christ's which completes it. He presents it to Himself a glorious assembly without spot or wrinkle. If He gave Himself for the assembly, it was in order to have it with Him; but if He would have it with Him, He must render it fit to be in His glorious presence; and He has sanctified it by cleansing it according to the revelation of God Himself, and the heavenly things of which He is in Himself the centre in glory. The Holy Ghost has taken the things of Christ, and has revealed them to the assembly; and all that the

Father has is Christ's. Thus perfected according to the perfection of heaven, He presents it to Himself a glorious assembly. Morally the work was done; the elements of heavenly glory had been communicated to her who was to stand in that glory, had entered into her moral being, and thus formed her to participate in it. The power of the Lord is needed to make her participate in it in fact, to make her glorious, to destroy every trace of her earthly abode, save the excellent fruit that results from it. He presents her glorious to Himself—this is the result of all. He took her for Himself, He presents her to Himself, the fruit and the proof of His perfect love; and for her it is the perfect enjoyment of that same love. But there is yet more. That sentence discloses to us all the import of this admirable display of grace. The Spirit carries us back to the case of Adam and Eve, in which God, having formed Eve, presents her to Adam all complete according to His own divine thoughts and at the same time suited to be the delight of Adam, as a helpmeet adapted to his nature and condition. Now Christ is God. He has formed the assembly, but with this additional right over her heart that He has given Himself for her; but He is also the Last Adam in glory; and He presents her glorified to Himself, such as He had formed her for Himself. What a sphere for the development of spiritual affections is this revelation! What infinite grace is that which has given place for such an exercise of these affections!

The connection between the cleansing and the glory

We cannot fail to notice the connection between the cleansing and the glory, that is, that the cleansing is according to the glory and by it; and that the glory is the completeness of, and completely answers to, the cleansing. For the cleansing is by the Word, which reveals the whole glory and mind of God. Presented in glory she has neither spot nor wrinkle; she is holy and unblamable.

This is a most important truth, and recurs elsewhere. Compare 2 Corinthians 3: 18, and Philippians 3: 11 to the end. So in 1 Thessalonians 3: 13. What is complete in glory there, is wrought into the soul now by the Spirit operating with the Word.

This then is the purpose, the mind of the Lord, with regard to the assembly, and this the sanctifying work which prepares her for Himself and for heaven. But these are not all the effects of His love. He watches tenderly over her during all the time of her sojourn here below.

Human love and care called forth by wants and weaknesses, the figure of Christ's affections

The apostle, who did not lose sight of the thesis which gave rise to this digression that is so instructive to us, says that the husband ought to love his wife as his own body —that it was loving himself. He was naturally led to this by the allusion to Genesis; but he immediately returns to the subject that occupies him. No one, he says, ever hated his own flesh; he nourishes and cherishes it, *even as the Lord the assembly*. This is the precious aspect, during time, of Christ's love, which the apostle here presents. Not only has Christ a heavenly aim, but His love performs the work which, so to speak, is natural to it. He tenderly cares for the assembly here below; He nourishes it, He cherishes it. The wants, the weaknesses, the difficulties, the anxieties of the assembly are only opportunities to Christ for the exercise of His love. The assembly needs to be nourished, as do our bodies; and He nourishes her. She is the object of His tender affections; He cherishes her. If the end is heaven, the assembly is not left desolate here. She learns His love where her heart needs it. She will enjoy it fully when need has passed away for ever. Moreover it is precious to know that Christ cares for the assembly, as a man cares for his own flesh. For we are members of His own Body. We are of His flesh, and of His bones. Eve is here alluded to. We are, as it were, a part of Himself, having our existence and our being from Him, as Eve from Adam. He can say, "I am Jesus whom thou persecutest." Our position is, on the one hand, to be members of His Body; on the other hand, we have our existence as Christians from Him. Therefore it is that a man is to leave his natural relations, in order to be united to his wife. It is a great mystery. Now it was just this that Christ did as Man, in a certain sense, divinely. Nevertheless every one ought thus to love his own wife, and the wife to reverence her husband.

Chapter 6

Relationships of life: the children of Christians

THERE remain yet certain relationships in life, with which the doctrine of the Spirit of God is connected: those of children and parents, of fathers and children, and of servants and masters. It is interesting to see the children of believers introduced as objects of the Holy Spirit's care, and even slaves (for servants were such), raised by Christianity to a position which the circumstances of their social degradation could not affect.

All the children of Christians are viewed as subjects of the exhortations in the Lord, which belong to those who are within, who are no longer in this world, of which Satan is the prince. Sweet and precious comfort to the parent, that he may look upon them as having a right to this position, and a part in those tender cares which the Holy Ghost lavishes on all who are in the house of God! The apostle marks the importance which God attached, under the law, to this duty. It is the first command with which He linked a promise. Verse 3 is only the quotation of that which he alludes to in verse 2.

Exhortation to Christian fathers

The exhortation to fathers is also remarkable—that they should not provoke their children; that their *hearts* should be turned towards them; that they should not repel them, nor destroy that influence which is the strongest guard against the evil of the world. God forms the heart of children around this happy centre: the father should watch over this. But there is more. The Christian father (for it is always those within to whom he speaks) ought to recognize the position in which, as we have seen, the children are placed, and to bring them up under the yoke of Christ in the discipline and admonition of the Lord. Christian position is to be the measure and the form of the influences which the father exercises, and of the education which he gives his children. He treats them as brought up for the Lord, and as the Lord would bring them up.

Submission and obedience the healing principle of humanity, the starting-point of the Christian's life

It will be remarked, that in the two relationships we are considering, as well as in that of wives with their husbands, it is on the side from which submission is due that the exhortations begin. This is the genius of Christianity in our evil world, in which man's will is the source of all the evil, expressing his departure from God to whom all submission is due. The principle of submission and of obedience is the healing principle of humanity: only God must be brought into it, in order that the will of man be not the guide after all. But the principle that governs the heart of man in good, is always and everywhere obedience. I may have to say that God must be obeyed rather than man; but to depart from obedience is to enter into sin. A man may have, as a father, to command and direct; but he does it ill if he do it not in obedience to

God and to His Word. This was the essence of the life of Christ: "I come to do Thy will, O My God." Accordingly the apostle begins his exhortations with regard to relationships by giving the general precept: "Submit yourselves one to another." This renders order easy, even when the order of institutions and of authority may fail. Submission, moral obedience, can never in principle be wanting to the true Christian. It is the starting-point of his whole life. He is sanctified unto the obedience of Christ (1 Pet. 1: 2).

The slave in the happy service of Christ to be rewarded by this Lord: the master reminded he has the same Master in heaven

In the case which has led to these remarks, it is striking to see how this principle elevates the slave in his condition: he obeys by an inward divine principle, as though it were Christ Himself whom he obeyed. However wicked his master may be, he obeys as if he obeyed Christ Himself. Three times the apostle repeats this principle of obedience to Christ or the service of Christ, adding "doing the will of God from the heart." What a difference this made in the poor slave's condition! Moreover, whether bond or free, each should receive his reward from the Lord. The master himself had the same Master in heaven, with whom there is no respect of persons. Still it is to masters that he says this, not to the slave; for Christianity is delicate in its propriety, and never falsifies its principles. The master was also to treat the slave with perfect equity—even as he expected it from the slave—and was not to threaten.

The fragrance of the perfection of divine doctrine in every duty and relationship

It is beautiful to see the way in which divine doctrine enters into the details of life, and throws the fragrance of

its perfection into every duty and every relationship;
how it acknowledges existing things, as far as they can
be owned and directed by its principles, but exalts and
enhances the value of everything according to the perfection of those principles; by touching not the relationships
but the man's heart who walks in them; taking the moral
side, and that of submission, in love and in the exercise of
authority which the divine doctrine can regulate, bringing in the grace which governs the use of the authority of
God.

Conflict: the Christian's enemies

But it is not only that there is a line of conduct to follow, a model to imitate, a Spirit with whom one may be
filled; it is not only relationships between oneself and
God, and those in which we stand here below; this is not
all that must occupy the Christian. He has enemies to
fight. The people of Israel under Joshua in the land of
Canaan were indeed in the promised land, but they were
in conflict there with enemies who were in it before them,
although not according to the rights by which Israel possessed the land through the gift of God. God had set it
apart for Israel (see Deut. 32: 8); Ham had taken possession of it.

Spiritual blessings and spiritual wickednesses in the heavenlies

Now, with regard to us, it is not with flesh and blood
that we have to fight, as was the case with Israel. Our
blessings are spiritual in the heavenly places. We are
sitting in Christ in the heavenlies. We are a testimony to
principalities and powers in the heavenlies; we have to
wrestle with spiritual wickednesses in the heavenlies.
Israel had passed through the wilderness—had crossed
the Jordan; the manna had ceased; they ate the corn of
the land. They were settled in the land of Canaan as

though it were all their own without striking a blow. They ate the produce of this good land in the plains of Jericho. So it is with regard to the Christian. Although we are in the wilderness, we are also in the heavenly places in Christ. We have crossed the Jordan, we have died and are risen again with Him. We are sitting in the heavenly places in Him, that we may enjoy the things of heaven as the fruit of our own country. But conflict is before us, if we desire to enjoy them practically. The promise is of every blessing, of all the promised land, but wheresoever we shall set our foot on it. (Joshua 1.) For this we need the Lord's strength, and of this the apostle now speaks. "Be strong," he says, "in the Lord." The enemy is subtle. We have to withstand his stratagems even more than his power. Neither the strength nor even the wisdom of man can do anything here. We must be armed with the panoply, that is the whole armor of God.

God Himself as strength: the whole armour of God supplied

But observe first, that the Spirit turns our thoughts upon God Himself before speaking of that which has to be overcome. "Be strong in the Lord." It is not, first of all, a refuge from the face of the enemy; we are in it for ourselves before we use it against the wiles of the enemy. It is in the intimacy of the counsels and the grace of God that man fortifies himself for the warfare from which he cannot escape, if he would enjoy his Christian privileges. And he must have the *whole* armour. To be wanting in one piece exposes us to Satan on that side. The armour must be that of God—divine in its nature. Human armour will not ward off the attacks of Satan; confidence in that armour will engage us in the battle only to make us fall in combat with a spirit who is more mighty and more crafty than we are.

The Christian's enemies characterized: their will and energy independent of God

These enemies are thus characterized; they are principalities and powers—beings possessing an energy of evil which has its source in a will that has mastery over those who do not know how to resist it; they have also strength to carry it out. Their energy they have from God, the will that uses it comes from themselves; they have forsaken God; the spring of their actions is in their own will. In this respect it is a source of action independent of God, and the energy and the qualities which they have from God are the instruments of that will—a will which has no bridle except from outside itself. They are *principalities and powers*. There are good ones; but in them the will is only to do that which God wills, and to employ in His service the strength they have received from Him.

Evil principalities ruling in the darkness: their power in the world: their religious and delusive ascendency in the heavens: the sphere of their power in man

These rebellious principalities and powers rule over the darkness of this world. Light is the atmosphere in which God dwells, which He diffuses all around Himself. Wicked spirits deceive and reign in darkness. Now this world, not having the light of God, is entirely in darkness, and demons reign in it; for God is not there—except in supreme power after all, turning everything to His glory, and, in the end to the good of His children.

But if these principalities rule in the darkness of this world, they do not possess merely an outward force; they are in the heavenlies, and are occupied with spiritual wickedness there. They exercise a spiritual influence, as having the place of gods. There is then, first, their intrinsic character, their mode of being, and the state in which they are found: second, their power in the world as governing it; and third, their religious and delusive ascendency, as lodging in the heavens. They have also, as a sphere for the exercise of their power, the lusts of man, and even the terrors of his conscience.

Where, when and why the armour of God is needed

To resist enemies like these we need the armour of God. The manifestations of this power, when God permits it, constitute the evil days. All this present period of Christ's absence is, in a certain sense, the evil day. Christ has been rejected by the world, of which, while in it, He was the light, and is hidden in God. This power, which the enemy displayed when he led the world to reject Christ, he still exercises over it: we oppose it by the action and the power of the Holy Ghost, who is here during the Lord's absence. But there are moments when this power is allowed to show itself in a more especial manner, when the enemy uses the world against the saints, darkening the light which shines in it from God, troubling and leading astray the minds of professors and even of believers—days, in a word, in which his power makes itself felt. We have to wrestle with this power, to resist it all, to stand against everything in the confession of Christ, of the light; we have to do all that the confession of His name requires in spite of all and at whatever cost, and to be found standing when the storm and the evil day are past.

Thus we have not only to enjoy God and the counsels of God and their effect in peace; but, since these very counsels introduce us into heavenly places and make us the light of God on earth, have also to encounter the spiritual wickednesses which are in the heavenly places, and which seek to make us falsify our high position, to mislead us, and to darken the light of Christ in us on the earth. We have to escape the snares of heavenly spiritual wickedness for ourselves, and to maintain the testimony here below incorrupt and pure.[28]

The order of the armour and its practical use

Now by the power of the Holy Ghost, who has been given to us for this purpose, we shall find that the armour of God relates first to that which, by setting the flesh aside, and by maintaining the existence of a good conscience, takes all hold from the enemy; then, to the preservation of complete objective trust in God; and next, to the active energy which stands with confidence in the presence of the enemy, and using the weapons of the Holy Ghost against him. The defensive armour, our own state, comes first. The whole ends with the expression of the entire and continual dependence on God in which the Christian warrior stands.

We will examine this armour of God, that we may know it. It is all practical—founded on that which has been accomplished, but in itself practical. For it is not a question here of appearing before the bar of God, but of resisting the enemy, and of maintaining our ground against him.

The loins girt about with truth: the heart having truth for its rule

Before God our righteousness is perfect, it is Christ Himself, and we are the righteousness of God in Him: but we do not need armour there, we are *sitting* in the heavenly places: all is peace, all is perfect. But here we need armour, real practical armour, and first of all to have the loins girt about with truth. The loins are the place of strength when duly girt, but represent the intimate affec-

---

[28] Still what we have to overcome are the wiles of the devil. His power over us is broken. He may rouse the world in persecution and be a roaring lion; but as regards personal temptation, if we resist the devil he flees from us; he knows he has met Christ, and Christ has overcome. But his wiles are ever there.

tions and movements of the heart. If we allow our hearts to wander where they will, instead of abiding in communion with God, Satan has easy hold upon us. This piece of armour is then the application of the truth to the most intimate movements, the first movements of the heart. We gird up the loins. This is done, not when Satan is present; it is a work with God, which is done by applying the truth to our souls in His presence, judging everything in us by this means, and putting a bridle on the heart that it may only move under His eye. This is true liberty and true joy, because the new man enjoys God in uninterrupted communion; but here the Spirit speaks of it with respect to the safeguard which it will be to us against the attacks of the enemy. At the same time it is not merely the repression of evil thoughts—that is its consequence: it is the action of the truth, of the power of God, acting by the revelation of everything as it is—of all that He Himself teaches, bringing the conscience into His presence, keeping it thus in His thoughts; all that God has said in His Word, and the unseen realities having their true force and their application to the heart that stirs in us, so that its movements should have their character from God's own Word and not from its own desires, everything going on in the presence of God.[29]

The Lord's perfect application of the Word to Himself

Satan has no hold on a heart thus kept in the truth, as revealed by God: there is nothing in its desires that answers to the suggestions of Satan. Take Jesus as an example. His safeguard was not in judging all that Satan said. In the wilderness at the beginning of His public service, except in the last temptation, it was in the perfect application of the Word for Himself, for that which concerned His own conduct, to the circumstances around Him.

[29] It is a common figure of Scripture for a mind and heart kept in godly order as in God's presence by the Word of God.

The truth governed His heart, so that it only moved according to that truth in the circumstance that presented itself. "Man shall not live by bread alone, but by every word that proceedeth out of the mouth of God." No word has come forth—He does nothing. There was no motive for acting. It would have been to act of His own accord, of His own will. That truth kept His heart in connection with God in the circumstance that met Him. When the circumstance arose, His heart was already in intercourse with God, so that it had no other impulse than that which the Word of truth suggested. His conduct was purely negative, but it flowed from the light which truth threw upon the circumstance, because His heart was under the absolute government of the truth. The suggestion of Satan would have brought Him out of this position. That was enough. He will have nothing to do with it. He does not yet drive away Satan: it was only a matter of conduct, not of flagrant opposition to the glory of God. In the latter case He drives him away; in the former He acts according to God without concerning Himself with anything farther. Satan's device *totally* failed of its effect. It simply produced nothing. It is absolutely powerless against the truth, because it is not the truth; and the heart has truth for its rule. Wiles are not the truth: this is quite enough to prevent our being caught by them, that is, if the heart be thus governed.

The breastplate of righteousness: a good conscience: the feet shod with peace in the path of peace

In the second place there is the breastplate of righteousness—a conscience that has nothing to reproach itself with. The natural man knows how a bad conscience robs him of strength before men. There is only to be added here the way in which Satan uses it to entrap man in his snares. By maintaining the truth we have Satan for our enemy. If we yield ourselves up to error, he will leave us in that respect at peace, except in using our faults and crimes to enslave us more, to bind us hand and foot in that which is false. How would a man who has the truth, who has perhaps even escaped error, if his conduct were bad, bear to have it exposed to the eyes of all? He is silent before the enemy. His own conscience even will make him silent, if he is upright, without thinking of consequences, unless a confession be necessary. Besides this the strength of God and spiritual understanding will fail him: where could he have gained them in a wrong walk? We go forward boldly when we have a good conscience. But it is when we are walking with God, for the love of God, for the love of righteousness itself, that we have this breastplate on, and thus we are fearless when called to go forward and face the enemy. We gain a good conscience before God by the blood of the Lamb. By walking with God we maintain it before men and for communion with God, in order to have strength and spiritual understanding, and to have them increasingly. This is the practical strength of good conduct, of a conscience without rebuke. "I exercise myself" always to this, said the apostle. What integrity in such a walk, what truthfulness of heart when no eye sees us! We are peremptory with ourselves, with our own hearts, and with regard to our conduct; we can therefore be peaceful in our ways. God also is there. So walk, says the apostle, and the God of peace shall be with you. If the fruits of righteousness are sown in peace, the path of peace is found in righteousness. If I have a bad conscience, I am vexed with myself, I grow angry with others. When the heart is at peace with God and has nothing to reproach itself with, when the will is held in check, peace reigns in the soul. We walk on the earth, but the heart is above it in intercourse with better things; we walk in a peaceful spirit with others, and nothing troubles our relations with God. He is the God of peace. Peace, the peace of Jesus, fills the heart. The feet are shod with it; we walk in the spirit of peace.

The shield of faith: full and entire trust in God's love and faithfulness as well as His power

But, together with all this, a piece of defensive armour is needed over all the rest, that we may be able to stand in spite of all the wiles of the enemy—an armour, however, which is practically maintained in its soundness by the use of the preceding ones, so that, if the latter is essential, the others have the first place in practice. This is the shield, faith; that is to say, full and entire trust in God, the consciousness of grace and of His favor maintained in the heart. Here faith is not simply the reception of God's testimony (although it is founded on that testimony), but the present assurance of the heart with regard to that which God is for us, founded, as we have just said, on the testimony which He has given of Himself—trust in His love and in His faithfulness, as well as in His power. "If our hearts condemn us not, then have we confidence towards God." The work of the Spirit in us is to inspire this confidence. When it exists, all the attacks of the enemy, who seeks to make us believe that the goodness of God is not so sure—all his efforts to destroy or to weaken in our hearts this confidence in God and to hide Him from us, prove fruitless. His arrows fall to the ground without reaching us. We stand fast in the consciousness that God is for us: our communion is not interrupted. The fiery darts of the enemy are not the desires of the flesh, but spiritual attacks.

The helmet of salvation: the knowledge of God

Thus we can hold up our heads: moral courage, the energy which goes forward, is maintained. Not that we have anything to boast of in ourselves, but the salvation and the deliverance of God are fresh in our minds. God has been *for* us; He is for us: who shall be against us? He was for us when we had no strength; it was salvation, when we could do nothing. This is our confidence—God

Himself—not looking at ourselves. We have the helmet
of salvation on our heads. The former parts of the armor
give us freedom to enjoy the two latter.

The one offensive weapon—the sword of the Spirit, the Word of God

Thus furnished with that which protects us in our walk,
and in the practical confidence in God, and the knowledge
of God that flows from it, we are in a state to use offensive
weapons. We have but one against the enemy, but it is
one that he cannot resist if we know how to handle it:
witness the Lord's conflict in the wilderness with Satan.
It is the Word of God. There Jesus always answered with
the Word by the power of the Spirit. It sets man in his
true position according to God as obedient man in the
circumstances around him. Satan can do nothing there:
we have but to maintain that position. If Satan openly
tempts us to disobedience, there is no wile in that. Not
being able to do anything else, Satan acted thus with the
Lord, and manifested himself as he is. The Lord drove
him away by the Word. Satan has no power when he is
manifested as Satan. We have to resist the wiles of the
devil. Our business is to act according to the Word, come
what may; the result will show that the wisdom of God
was in it. But observe here, this sword is the sword of
the Spirit. It is not the intelligence or the capacity of
man, although it is man who uses the Word. His sword
is highly tempered, but he can neither draw it nor strike
with it if the Holy Ghost is not acting in him. The
weapons are spiritual; they are used by the power of the
Spirit. God must speak, however weak the instrument
may be.

Complete dependence on God expressed in prayer

The sword is also used actively in the spiritual warfare,
in which it judges all that is opposed to us. In this sense

it is both defensive and offensive. But, behind all this armour, there is a state, a disposition, a means of strength, which quickens and gives all the rest its power: this is a complete dependence on God, united to trust in Him, which expresses itself in prayer. "Praying always;" this dependence must be constant. When it is real, and I feel that I can do nothing without God, and that He wills my good in all things, it expresses itself. It seeks the strength which it has not: it seeks it from Him in whom it trusts. It is the motion of the Spirit in our hearts in their intercourse with God, so that our battles are fought in the communion of His strength and His favor, and in the consciousness that we can do nothing, and that He is all. "At all times;" "With supplication." This prayer is the expression of the man's need, of the heart's desire, in the strength that the Spirit gives him, as well as in confidence in God. Also since it is the Spirit's act, it embraces all saints, not one of whom can be forgotten by Jesus (and the Spirit in us answers the affections of Christ, and reproduces them). We must be watchful and diligent in order to use this weapon; avoiding all that would turn us away from God, availing ourselves of every opportunity, and finding, by the grace of the Spirit, in everything that arises, an occasion (by means of this diligence) for prayer and not for distraction.[30]

Paul's heartfelt request: his confidence in the Ephesians' affection for him

The apostle asks from his heart for this intercession on their part, in the sense of his own need and of that which he desired to be for Christ.

The mission of Tychicus expressed Paul's assurance of the interest which the love of the Ephesians made them take in having tidings of him, and that which he himself

[30] Prayer is founded on the immense privilege of having common interests with God both as to ourselves and as to all that are His, yea, even as to Christ's glory. Wondrous thought! Unspeakable grace!

felt in ascertaining their welfare and spiritual state in Christ. It is a touching expression of his confidence in their affection—an affection which his own devoted heart led him to expect in others.

The standpoint of the Epistle as written to the believers in the heavenly places in Christ: the position and privileges of the children and of the assembly as united to Christ

He presents the Ephesians as enjoying the highest privileges in Christ, and as being able to appreciate them. He blames them in nothing. The armour of God—by which to repel the assaults of the enemy, and to grow up in peace unto the Head in all things, the preservative armour of God—was naturally the last thing that he had to set before them. It is to be noticed that he does not speak to them in this epistle of the Lord's coming. He supposes believers in the heavenly places in Christ; and not as on earth going through the world, waiting till He should come to take them to Himself, and restore happiness to the world. That which is waited for in this epistle is the gathering together of all things under Christ, their true Head, according to the counsels of God. The blessings are in the heavens, the testimony is in the heavens, the Church is sitting in the heavens, the warfare is in the heavens.

The apostle repeats his desire for them of peace, love, and faith; and concludes his epistle with the usual salutation by his own hand.

This epistle sets forth the position and the privileges of the children, and of the assembly in its union with Christ.

PHILIPPIANS

Philippians as the Epistle of proper Christian experience

IN the Epistle to the Philippians we find much more of Christian experience, and the development of the exercise of the heart, than in the generality of the epistles. It is in fact proper Christian experience. Doctrine and practice are found in them all, but, with the exception of the Second to Timothy which is of another nature, there is none that contains like this, the expression of the Christian's experience in this toilsome life, and the resources which are open to him in passing through it, and the motives which ought to govern him. We may even say that this epistle gives us the experience of Christian life in its highest and most perfect expression—say, rather, its normal condition under the power of the Spirit of God. God has condescended to furnish us with this beautiful picture of it, as well as with the truths that enlighten us, and the rules that direct our walk.

The occasion for the Epistle: Paul in prison: his need and the Philippians' love

The occasion for it was quite natural. Paul was in prison, and the Philippians (who were very dear to him, and who, at the commencement of his labors, had testified their affection for him by similar gifts) had just sent assistance to the apostle by the hand of Epaphroditus at a moment when, as it appears, he had been for some time in need. A prison, need, the consciousness that the assembly of God was deprived of his watchful care, this expression on the part of the Philippians of the love that thought of him in his necessities, although at a distance—what could be more adapted to open the apostle's heart, and lead to his expressing the confidence in God that animated him, as well as what he felt with regard to the assembly, unsupported now by his apostolic care, and having to trust God Himself without any intermediate help? And it was most natural that he should pour out his feelings into the bosom of these beloved Philippians, who had just given him this proof of their affection. The apostle therefore speaks more than once of the Philippians' fellowship with the gospel: that is to say, they took part in the labors, the trials, the necessities which the preaching of the gospel occasioned to those who devoted themselves to it. Their hearts united them to it—like those of whom the Lord speaks who received a prophet in the name of a prophet.

Chapter I

The inner life, the common affections of Christians towards each other, experienced by Paul

THIS brought the apostle into a peculiarly intimate connection with this assembly; and he and Timotheus, who had accompanied him in his labors in Macedonia, his true son in the faith and in the work, address themselves to the saints and to those who bore office in this particular assembly. This is not an epistle which soars to the height of God's counsels, like that to the Ephesians, or which regulates the godly order which becomes Christians everywhere, like the two to the Corinthians; nor is it one which lays the foundation for the relationship of a soul with God, like that to the Romans. Neither was it destined to guard Christians against the errors that were creeping in among them, like some of the others which were written by our apostle. It takes the ground of the precious inner life, of the common affection of Christians towards each other, but of that affection as experienced in the heart of Paul, animated and directed by the Holy Ghost. Hence also we find the ordinary relationships which existed within an assembly: there are bishops and deacons, and it was the more important to remember them, since the immediate care of the apostle was no longer possible. The absence of this immediate care forms the basis of the apostle's instructions here, and gives its peculiar importance to the epistle.

The evidences of God's work in the Philippians: the true and living Source of all blessing, remaining and unchangeable

The affection of the Philippians, which expressed itself by sending help to the apostle, reminded him of the spirit they had always shown; they had cordially associated themselves with the labors and trials of the gospel. And this thought leads the apostle higher, to that which governs the current of thought (most precious to us) in the epistle. Who had wrought in the Philippians this spirit of love and of devotedness to the interests of the gospel? Truly it was the God of the glad tidings and of love; and this was a security that He who had begun the good work would fulfil it unto the day of Christ. Sweet thought!—now that we have no longer the apostle, that we have no longer bishops and deacons, as the Philippians had in those days. God cannot be taken from us; the true and living source of all blessing remains to us, unchangeable, and above the infirmities, and even the faults, which deprive Christians of all intermediate resources. The apostle had seen God acting in the Philippians. The fruits bore witness of the source. Hence he counted on the perpetuity of the blessing they were to enjoy.[1] But there must be faith in order to draw these conclusions. Christian love is clear-sighted and full of trust with regard to its objects, because God Himself, and the energy of His grace, are in that love.

[1] Read in verse 7 as in the margin, "Because ye have me in your heart."

The fruits of God's essential grace in the walk of the Philippians leading the apostle to the Source of confidence

To return to the principle—it is the same thing with the assembly of God. It may indeed lose much, as to outward means, and as to those manifestations of the presence of God which are connected with man's responsibility; but the essential grace of God cannot be lost. Faith can always count upon it. It was the *fruits* of grace which gave the apostle this confidence, as in Hebrews 6: 9, 10; 1 Thessalonians 1: 3, 4. He counted indeed, in 1 Corinthians 1: 8, and in Galatians, on the faithfulness of Christ in spite of many painful things. The faithfulness of the Lord encouraged him with regard to Christians, whose condition in other respects was the cause of great anxiety. But here—surely a much happier case—the walk itself of the Christian led him to the source of confidence about them. He remembered with affection and tenderness the way in which they had always acted towards him, and he turned it into a desire for them that the God who had wrought it would produce for their own blessing the perfect and abundant fruits of that love.

Paul's earnest desire for them of every excellence and likeness to Christ

He opens his own heart also to them. They took part, by the same grace acting in them, in the work of God's grace in him, and that with an affection that identified itself with him and his work; and his heart turned to them with an abundant return of affection and desire. God, who created these feelings, and to whom he presented all that passed in his heart, this same God who acted in the Philippians, was a witness between them (now that Paul could give no other by his labor among them) of his earnest desire for them all. He felt their love, but he desired moreover that this love should be not only cordial and active, but that it should be guided also by wisdom and understanding from God, by a godly discernment of good and evil, wrought by the power of His Spirit; so that, while acting in love, they should also walk according to that wisdom, and should understand that which, in this world of darkness, was truly according to divine light and perfection, so that they should be without reproach until the day of Christ. How different from the cold avoidance of positive sin with which many Christians content themselves! The earnest desire of every excellence and likeness to Christ which divine light can show them is that which marks the life of Christ in us.

The Christian's normal condition in his daily walk

Now the fruits produced were already a sign that God was with them; and He would fulfil the work unto the end. But the apostle desired that they should walk throughout the whole of the way according to the light that God had given, so that when they came to the end there should be nothing with which they could be reproached: but that, on the contrary, set free from all that might weaken or lead them astray, they should abound in the fruits of righteousness, which are by Jesus Christ to the glory and praise of God. A fine practical picture of the Christian's normal condition in his daily walk towards the end; for, in the Philippians, we are always on the way towards our heavenly rest in which redemption has set us.

Such is the introduction to this epistle. After this expression of the wishes of his heart for them, reckoning on their affection, he speaks of his bonds, which they had remembered; but he does so in connection with Christ and the gospel, which he had most of all at heart. But, before I go beyond the introduction into the matter of the epistle, I would notice the thoughts which lie at the foundation of the sentiments expressed in it.

Pilgrimage in the wilderness: salvation as a result at the end of the journey

There are three great elements which stamp their character on it.

First, it speaks of the Christian's pilgrimage in the wilderness: salvation is viewed as a result to be obtained at the end of the journey. Redemption accomplished by Christ is indeed established as the foundation of this pilgrimage (as was the case with Israel at their entrance into the wilderness), but the being presented risen and in glory before God, when victorious over every difficulty, is the subject in this epistle, and is that which is here called salvation.

The assembly by itself maintaining the conflict and having to overcome

In the second place, the position is characterized by the apostle's absence, the assembly having therefore itself to maintain the conflict. It had to overcome, instead of enjoying the victory gained over the enemy's power by the apostle when he was with them and could make himself weak with all who were weak.

The assembly cast more immediately on God

And, thirdly, the important truth, already mentioned, is set forth, that the assembly, in these circumstances, was cast more immediately on God—the inexhaustible source for it of grace and strength, of which it was to avail itself in an immediate way by faith—a resource which could never fail it.[2]

---

[2] We shall find the whole tenor of a life which was the expression of the power of the Spirit of God brought out in it. It marks this, that sin, or the flesh as working evilly in us, is not mentioned in the epistle. It gives the forms and features of the life of Christ; for if we live in the Spirit, we should walk in the Spirit. We shall find the graciousness of Christian life (chap. 2), the energy of Christian life (chap. 3), and its superiority to all circumstances (chap 4). The first more opens the apostle's heart as to his actual circumstances and feelings, as was

Paul's imprisonment and the jealousy of others overruled by the One who orders all things

I resume the consideration of the text with verse 12, which begins the epistle after the introductory portion. Paul was a prisoner at Rome. The enemy appeared to have gained a great victory in thus restraining his activity; but by the power of God, who orders all things and who acted in the apostle, even the devices of the adversary were turned to the furtherance of the gospel. In the first place, the imprisonment of the apostle made the gospel known, where it would not otherwise have been preached, in high places at Rome; and many other brethren, reassured as to the apostle's position,[3] became more bold to preach the gospel without fear. But there was another way in which this absence of the apostle had an effect. Many—who, in the presence of his power and his gifts, were necessarily powerless and insignificant persons—could make themselves of some importance, when, in the unsearchable but perfect ways of God, this mighty instrument of His grace was set aside. They could hope to shine and attract attention when the rays of this resplendent light were intercepted by the walls of a prison. Jealous but hidden when he was present, they availed themselves of his absence to bestir themselves; whether false brethren or jealous Christians, they sought in his absence to impair his authority in the assembly, and his happiness. They only added to both. God was with His servant; and, instead of the self-seeking which instigated these sorry preachers of the truth, there was found in Paul the pure desire for the proclamation of the good news of Christ,

natural. Exhortation begins with chapter 2. Still even in chapter 1 we find the apostle entirely superior to circumstances in the power of spiritual life.

[3] In the first edition I had taken this as the effect of the apostle's imprisonment in arousing the faith of those inactive when he was active. And this would be the sense of the English translation and is a true principle. But it seems that the force of the words is "rather got confidence as to my bonds." They were in danger of being ashamed of him, as if he were a malefactor.

the whole value of which he deeply felt, and which he desired above all, be it in what way it might.

The normal condition of the assembly, as presented in Ephesians, and its partial failure and the Spirit's restoring energy, given in Corinthians and Galatians

Already the apostle finds his resource for his own case, in God's operating independently of the spiritual order of His house with regard to the means that He uses. The normal condition of the assembly is that the Spirit of God acts in the members of the Body, each one in its place, for the manifestation of the unity of the Body and of the reciprocal energy of its members. Christ, having overcome Satan, fills with His own Spirit those whom He has delivered out of the hand of that enemy, in order that they may exhibit at the same time the power of God and the truth of their deliverance from the power of the enemy, and exhibit them in a walk, which, being an expression of the mind and energy of God Himself, leaves no room for those of the enemy. They constituted the army and the testimony of God in this world against the enemy. But then, each member, from an apostle down to the weakest, acts efficaciously in his own place. The power of Satan is excluded. The exterior answers to the interior, and to the work of Christ. He who is in them is greater than he who is in the world. But everywhere power is needed for this, and the single eye. There is another state of things, in which, although all is not in activity in its place, according to the measure of the gift of Christ, yet the restoring energy of the Spirit in an instrument like the apostle defends the assembly, or brings it back into its normal condition, when it has partially failed. The Epistle to the Ephesians, on the one side, and those to the Corinthians and Galatians, on the other, present these two phases of the history of the assembly.

The assembly deprived of normal energies, but not of God: the reason it was allowed

The Epistle to the Philippians treats—but with the pen of a divinely inspired apostle—of a state of things in which this last resource was wanting. The apostle could not labor now in the same manner as before, but he could give us the Spirit's view of the state of the assembly, when, according to the wisdom of God, it was deprived of these normal energies. It could not be deprived of God. Doubtless the assembly had not then departed so far from its normal condition as it has now done, but the evil was already springing up. "All seek their own," says the apostle, "not the things of Jesus Christ;" and God allowed it to be so during the life of the apostles, in order that we might have the revelation of His thoughts respecting it, and that we might be directed to the true resources of His grace in these circumstances.

Man's inability to maintain God's work: what faith brings out

Paul himself had to experience this truth in the first place. The bonds that united him to the assembly and to the work of the gospel were the strongest that exist on earth; but he was obliged to resign the gospel and the assembly to the God to whom they belonged. This was painful; but its effect was to perfect obedience, trust, singleness of eye, and self-renunciation, in the heart, that is, to perfect them according to the measure of the operation of faith. Nevertheless the pain caused by such an effort betrays the inability of man to maintain the work of God at its own height. But all this happens in order that God may have the whole glory of the work; and it is needed, in order that the creature may be manifested in every respect according to the truth. And it is most blessed to see how, both here and in 2 Timothy, the decay of individual life and ecclesiastical energy brings out a fuller development of personal grace on one hand and ministerial energy on the other, where there is faith, than is found anywhere else. Indeed, it is always so. The Moseses, and Davids, and Elijahs are found in the time of the Pharaohs, and Sauls, and Ahabs.

Christ and souls more precious to Paul than his own part in God's work

The apostle could do nothing: he had to see the gospel preached without him—by some through envy and in a spirit of contention, by others through love; encouraged as regards the apostle's bonds, these desired to alleviate 'them by continuing his work. Every way Christ was preached, and the apostle's mind rose above the motives which animated the preachers in the contemplation of the immense fact, that a Saviour, the deliverer sent of God, was preached to the world. Christ and even souls were more precious to Paul than the work's being carried on by himself. God was carrying it on; and therefore it would be for the triumph of Paul, who linked himself with the purposes of God.[4] He understood the great conflict which was going on between Christ (in His members) and the enemy; and if the latter appeared to have gained a victory by putting Paul in prison, God was using this event for the advancement of the work of Christ by the gospel, and thus in reality for the gaining of fresh victories over Satan—victories with which Paul was associated, since he was set for the defence of that gospel. Therefore all this turned to his salvation, his faith being confirmed by these ways of a faithful God, who directed the eyes of his faithful servant more entirely upon Himself. Sustained by the prayers of others and by the supply of the Spirit of Jesus Christ, instead of being cast down

---

[4] There is blessed faith in this. But then a man must have made the work his life. "To me to live is Christ." If so, if the work prospers, he prospers; if Christ is glorified, he is content, even if the Lord has laid him aside.

and terrified by the enemy, he gloried more and more in the sure victory of Christ in which he shared.

Christ glorified by Paul's life or death: to live—Christ; to die was gain

Accordingly he expresses his unchangeable conviction, that in nothing should he be made ashamed, but that it would be given him to use all boldness, and that Christ would be glorified in him, whether by his life or his death; and he had death before his eyes. Called to appear before Cæsar, his life might be taken from him by the emperor's judgment; humanly speaking the issue was quite uncertain.

He alludes to this, chapter 1: 22, 30; 2: 17; 3: 10. But, living or dying, his eye was now more fixed on Christ than even on the work, high placed as that work might have been in the mind of one whose life could be expressed in this one word—"Christ." To live was for him—not the work in itself, nor only that the faithful should stand fast in the gospel, although this could not be separated from the thought of Christ, because they were members of His Body—Christ; to die was gain, for he should be with Christ.

Work for the Lord or the Lord Himself: Christ holding the first place

Such was the purifying effect of the ways of God, who had made him pass through the ordeal, so terrible to him, of being separated for years, perhaps four, from his work for the Lord. The Lord Himself had taken the place of the work—so far at least as it was connected with Paul individually; and the work was committed to the Lord Himself. Possibly the fact that he was so engrossed with the work had contributed to that which led to his imprisonment; for the thought of Christ alone keeps the soul in equilibrium, and gives everything its right place. God caused this imprisonment to be the means through which

Christ became his all. Not that he lost his interest in the
work, but that Christ alone held the first place; and he
saw everything, and even the work, in Christ.

What consolation it is, when we are perhaps conscious
that our weakness has been manifested, and that we have
failed in acting according to the power of God, to feel that
He, who alone has a right to be glorified, never fails!

Christ and His will everything: the peace that is given by looking to Jesus

Now, since Christ was everything to Paul, it was evident gain to die, for he would be with Him. Nevertheless
it was worth while to live (for this is the force of the first
part of verse 21), because it was Christ and His service:
and he did not know which to choose. Dying, he gained
Christ for himself: it was far better. Living, he served
Christ; he had more, as to the work, since to live was
Christ, and death of course would put a stop to that.
Thus he was in a strait between the two. But he had
learnt to forget himself in Christ; and he saw Christ entirely occupied with the assembly according to His perfect
wisdom. And this decided the question; for being thus
taught of God, and not knowing for himself which to
choose, Paul lost sight of himself, and thought only of the
need of the assembly according to the mind of Christ. It
was good for the assembly that he should remain—for one
assembly even: thus he should remain. And see what
peace this looking to Jesus, which destroyed selfishness in
the work, gives to the servant of God. After all, Christ
has all power in heaven and earth, and He orders all
things according to His will. Thus, when His will is
known—and His will is love for the assembly—one can
say that it will be done. Paul decides as to his own fate,
without troubling himself as to either what the emperor
would do, or the circumstances of the time. Christ loved
the assembly. It was good for the assembly that Paul

should remain; Paul shall then remain. How entirely Christ is everything here! What light, what rest, from a single eye, from a heart versed in the Lord's love! How blessed to see self so totally gone, and Christ's love to the assembly seen thus to be the ground on which all is ordered!

What the assembly should be for Christ: the precious portion given to suffer with Him as well as to believe in Him

Now if Christ is all this for Paul and for the assembly, Paul desires that the assembly should be that which it ought to be for Christ, and thereby for his own heart to which Christ was everything. To the assembly therefore the apostle's heart turns. The joy of the Philippians would be abundant through his return to them; only let their conduct, whether he came or not, be worthy of the. gospel of Christ. Two thoughts possessed his mind, whether he should see them or hear tidings of them, that they might have constancy and firmness in unity of heart and mind among themselves; and be devoid of fear with regard to the enemy, in the conflict they had to maintain against him, with the strength that this unity would give them. This is the testimony of the presence and operation of the Spirit in the assembly, when the apostle is absent. He keeps Christians together by His presence; they have but one heart and one object. They act in common by the Spirit. And, since God is there, the fear with which the evil spirit and their enemies might inspire them (and it is what he ever seeks to do; compare 1 Peter 5: 8) is not there. They walk in the spirit of love and power and of a sound mind. Their condition is thus an evident testimony of salvation—entire and final deliverance—since in their warfare with the enemy they feel no fear, the presence of God inspiring them with other thoughts. With regard to their adversaries, the discovery of the impotence

of all their efforts produces the sense of the insufficiency
of their resources. Although they had the whole power of
the world and of its prince, they had met with a power
superior to their own—the power of God, and they were
its adversaries. A terrible conviction on the one side; profound joy on the other, where not only there was thus the
assurance of deliverance and salvation, but they were
proved to be salvation and deliverance from the hand of
God Himself. Thus, that the assembly should be in conflict, and the apostle absent (himself wrestling with all
the power of the enemy), was a *gift*. Joyful thought!
Unto them it was *given* to suffer for Christ, as well as to
believe in Him. They had a further and a precious portion in suffering with Christ, and even for Christ; and
communion with His faithful servant in suffering for His
sake united them more closely in Him.

A life above the flesh a glorious testimony to the power and working of God's Spirit

Note, here, how thus far we have the testimony of the
Spirit to a life above the flesh, not of it. In nothing he
had been ashamed, and fully trusted he never should be,
but Christ magnified in his body, were his lot life or death,
as He ever had been. He does not know whether to choose
life or death, both were so blessed; to live, Christ; to die,
gain, though then labor was over; such confidence in
Christ's love to the assembly that he decides his case before
Nero by what that love would produce. Envy and strife
against himself leading to preach Christ would only turn
to victorious results for himself: he was content if Christ
was preached. The superiority to the flesh, living above
it so completely, was not that it was not there or its nature
changed. He had, as we learn elsewhere, a thorn in the
flesh, a messenger of Satan to buffet him. But it is a
glorious testimony to the power and working of the Spirit
of God.

Chapter 2

The apostle's desire for the happiness of his beloved Philippians

BUT this, too, produced its effects. The apostle desired that their joy should be full, and that unity among the Philippians should be perfect; for his absence had allowed some seeds of disunion and disaffection to germinate. Love had been sweetly and powerfully demonstrated by the gift they had sent to the apostle. Consolation in Christ, comfort of love, fellowship of the Spirit, tender mercies were displayed in it, giving him great joy. Let them then make this joy perfect by the full establishment of this same bond of love among themselves, by being of one accord, of one mind, having the same love for each other, being all like-minded, allowing no rivalship or vain-glory to display itself in any way. Such was the apostle's desire. Appreciating their love towards himself, he wished their happiness to be complete through the perfecting of that love among themselves: thus would his own joy be perfect. Beautiful and touching affection! It was love in him which, sensible to their love, thought only of them. How delicate the way in which a kindness, which precluded reproof, made a way for what really was one, and which a heart that added charity to brotherly love could not leave unuttered!

"He humbled Himself": God has "highly exalted Him" in His just judgment and righteousness

Now the means of this union, of the maintenance of this love, was found in the abnegation of self, in humility, in the spirit that humbles itself in order to serve. It was this which perfectly displayed itself in Christ, in contrast with the first Adam. The latter sought to make himself like God by robbery, when he was in the form of a man, and strove to exalt himself at God's expense (being at the same time disobedient unto death). Christ, on the contrary, when He was in the form of God, emptied Himself, through love, of all His outward glory, of the form of God, and took the form of a Man; and, even when He was in the form of a Man, still humbled Himself. It was a second thing which He did in humbling Himself. As God, He emptied Himself; as Man, He humbled Himself, and became obedient unto death, even to the death of the cross. God has highly exalted Him; for he who exalts himself shall be humbled, but he who humbles himself shall be exalted. Perfect love, glorious truth, precious obedience! A Man by the just judgment and act of God is exalted to the right hand of the throne of the divine Majesty. What a truth is the Person of Christ! What a truth is this descent and ascension by which He fills all things as Redeemer and Lord of glory! God come down in love, Man ascended in righteousness; entire love in coming down, entire obedience by love also. Worthy from all eternity as to His Person to be there, He is now as Man exalted by God to His right hand. It is an act of righteousness on God's part that He is there; and our hearts can take part in it, rejoicing in His glory—rejoicing also that by grace we have part in it as to our own place.

The Lord's humiliation a proof that He is God: His highest place and supremely glorious Name

His humiliation is a proof that He is God. God only could leave His first estate in the sovereign rights of His love; it is sin for any creature to do so. It is also a perfect love. But this proof is given, this love accomplished, in the fact that He is Man. What a place has He acquired for us in Himself! But it is of Him, not of us who are its fruits, that the apostle thinks. He rejoices in the thought of Christ's exaltation. God has exalted Him to the highest place, and given Him a name which is above every name, so that everything in heaven and earth, and even in infernal regions, must bow before this exalted Man, and every tongue confess that Jesus Christ is Lord to the glory of God the Father.

Jesus owned as Lord of all throughout the whole creation

It will be remarked here, that it is the Lordship of Christ that is presented in this passage, not His divinity in itself. His divinity is indeed the primary point of departure. All in fact has its origin there—the love, the self-renunciation, the humiliation, the marvellous condescension. Nothing of all this could have been, or would have its value, without the former; but it is of the Lord, complete in His Person in the position which He took as Man —it is of Him who humbled Himself, who when He had gone down to the lowest possible place, was exalted by God; it is of Jesus, who could, without exalting Himself, be equal with God, but who emptied Himself, who went down even into death, that the apostle speaks: of Jesus, Lord of all, and who, thus exalted as Man, shall be owned as Lord throughout the whole creation to the glory of God the Father.[5]

The obedience of Christ applied for instruction: engaged with the enemy without Paul's aid but not deprived of God and His work in them

The apostle's heart enlarges whenever he speaks of the

[5] Observe also, that it is not with regard to that which He suffered, as the effect of His submission to the will of God in the position which He took, that Christ is here presented as our pattern. It is in His voluntary humiliation, the fact that in love he took the last—the lowest—place, that we are called to follow Him. Love serves, love humbles itself—readily takes the meanest position (meanest according to the pride of man) in order to serve, and delights in it. Christ acted from love; He chose to serve. Christ chose to take the low place—He who was able to humble Himself—and we?

Lord Jesus; but he turns to the objects of his solicitude; and as he had spoken of the self-renunciation and the humiliation of Christ, as a means of union, which would take all occasion from carnal rivalship, he had also been led to speak of the obedience of Christ in contrast with the first Adam and the flesh. He now applies this principle, also, for the instruction of the Philippians: "Wherefore," he says, "my beloved, as ye have always obeyed." And here the effect of his absence and removal from the work is introduced—"not as in my presence only, but now much more in my absence, work out your own salvation with fear and trembling; for," he adds, "it is God which worketh in you, both to will and to do." That is to say, while he was among them he had labored; now they were themselves engaged with the enemy, without the aid of Paul's presence and spiritual energy; but God Himself wrought in them, and they ought to work so much the more earnestly in that they found themselves in such a warfare, God Himself being engaged for them as acting in them for this conflict, and they themselves striving in their own persons, directly with the power of the enemy. This was not the moment to boast in their little gifts, on account of the absence of that which had thrown them into the shade, nor to be at strife among themselves. On the other hand, if they were deprived of Paul, they were not deprived of God. God Himself wrought in them. This is the great principle, and the great consolation of the epistle. The Christians, deprived of the important aid of the apostle, are cast more immediately on God. The apostle himself, separated from the assembly, finds his own consolation in God; and commits the assembly in its lack of his personal care, to God Himself, in whom he had himself found this consolation.

Exhortation to work because God wrought in them: two views of the Christian—"in Christ," a complete, perfect, present state, and yet also a pilgrim having to attain the goal

It is to be carefully remarked here, that it is the very opposite of an exhortation to our own working in contrast with God's effectual power. "Your own" is in contrast with Paul in his absence, who had labored for them, because God did work in them to will and to do. They were to work, because, if Paul was absent, God wrought in them. I have noticed already that salvation, every blessing, is looked at everywhere in this epistle as at the end of the Christian's course, even the manifestation of their righteousness (chap. 3: 9). This passage is an example. There are two ways the Christian is seen in the New Testament. In Christ—here is no progress, no question: he is accepted in Him—a complete, perfect, present state. But he is also a pilgrim upon earth, having to attain the goal: so always in Philippians. This gives occasion to every kind of exhortation, warning and "if." Thus he learns obedience and dependence—the two characteristics of the new man. But with this he is led to the sure infallible faithfulness of God to bring him through to the end, and bound to reckon on it. See 1 Corinthians 1: 8, which I cite because they were going on very badly; but passages abound.

Diligence and earnestness ought to characterize the walk of Christians in these circumstances, in which immediate connection with God and personal conflict with the enemy have to be realized.

Unity of spirit and godly walk: heavenly lights amid the world's moral darkness—what Christ was

The apostle returns to the spirit of meekness and peace, in which the fruits of righteousness are sown. "Do all

things," he says, "without murmurings and disputings,
that ye may be blameless and harmless, the sons of God
in the midst of a crooked and perverse generation, among
whom ye shine as lights in the world, holding forth the
Word of life:" a very striking passage, because it will be
found that in every member of the sentence it is an exact
statement of what Christ was. Whatever may be the circumstances in which the assembly is found, such, as respects itself, should ever be its state and its walk. Grace
sufficient for this is ever there in Christ.

The apostle's work and reward and the assembly's blessing

Unity of spirit among themselves by grace, and a walk
according to God, in order that they may be as heavenly
lights amid the moral darkness of this world—always
carrying, and thus holding forth, the Word of life: such
was the apostle's desire. They would thus give proof by
the constancy and practical effect of their faith, that the
apostle had not run or labored in vain; and they would
themselves be his glory in the day of Christ. Oh, if the
assembly had continued such! Be that as it may, Christ
will be glorified. The apostle thus unites his work and the
reward in the day of Christ with the blessing of the
assembly. He would not be separated from it in his
death. This union of heart and faith is very touching.
He presents himself as capable of being poured out (that
is to say, his life) upon the sacrifice and service of the
Philippians' faith. They had shown their devotedness to
Christ in thinking even of His servant; and he looks upon
all their faith as an offering to the Saviour and to God;
looking at them, Christ's people, as the substance of the
offering, the great thing, himself only as a libation—his
life poured out upon the offering. Perhaps his life would
be poured out in the service of the gospel, to which they
consecrated themselves on their part, and be a seal to

this offering of theirs, which was dedicated to God by this sacred bond with the apostle. He rejoiced, if it were so, that his life was poured out: it would crown his work for the Gentiles. He desires too that they also in the same spirit should rejoice in the same thing. It was all one thing, their faith and his, and their common service, offered to God, and well-pleasing to Him; and the most exalted proof of it should be the source of the most sacred joy. This world was not the real scene of that which was going on: what we behold here in connection with the divine work is but the outside. The apostle speaks this language of faith, which ever sees things as before God.

Timotheus to be sent to the Philippians

Nevertheless his watchful care did not cease, although he committed the Philippians to God. It is always thus. The love and the faith which commit everything to God do not cease to think according to God of that which is dear to Him. Thus in 1 John, chapter 2, the apostle, while saying that the little children in Christ needed not that any one should teach them, yet instructs them with all tenderness and foresight. Here also the apostle, full of holy solicitude for these souls who were dear to Christ, hopes soon to send Timotheus that he may know their state. But the condition of things is evident. He sends Timotheus because he had no one else in whose heart the same feelings towards them flowed forth from the same spring of love. All sought their own interests, not those of Jesus Christ. What an exercise for faith! But what an occasion for its exercise!

Still, with regard to Timotheus, these beloved Philippians should receive him with a heart that responded to the apostle's confidence. They knew how he had served Paul in the gospel. The bonds of love in the gospel are but the stronger—God be praised—when all grows cold.

And observe, that God carried on His work, when as to the common testimony of the assembly, everything failed through a coldness which oppressed the apostle's heart; for God does not weary in His work. This bond however does not fail here with the Philippians either. As soon as Paul knew how it would go with himself, he would send Timotheus to them; but, as he had said, he had confidence in the Lord that he himself should come shortly.

Epaphroditus and his service: a testimony of Christian love

But there was also Epaphroditus, who had come from the Philippians to carry their testimonial of affection to the apostle; and who, the faithful instrument and expression of their love, had risked his own life and suffered from dangerous sickness, in order to accomplish their service. This fine testimony of Christian love breaks out here on every side. Epaphroditus so counts upon the love of the Philippians, that he is much troubled, because they had heard he was sick. He reckons on the feeling they had towards him—the place he had in their affections. Would it not be thus with an affectionate son, who knew that his mother had heard such tidings of him? He would hasten to inform her of his recovery, in order to tranquillize a heart whose love he knew. Such is Christian affection, tender and simple, confiding, because pure and unsuspicious, and walking in the light of God—walking with Him and in the affections which Christ had consecrated as Man. Divine love, no doubt, goes higher; but brotherly love, which acts before men and as the fruit among men of that divine love, displays itself thus in grace.

The apostle responds to this affection of the Philippians for him who taught them and labored in the Lord for them (the Holy Ghost also remembers it here), and he sends back Epaphroditus, encouraging and seeking to sustain

this feeling in the heart of the Philippians. He takes part
in it himself, and brings into it God's own tender love.
Paul would have had sorrow upon sorrow (and he had
much already), if the Philippians had lost their beloved
servant and messenger by means of the services he had
rendered them; but God had spared Epaphroditus and
the apostle himself. He would however have them assured
of it by the presence of Epaphroditus again among them;
and thus the apostle's own heart freed from all anxiety,
would be also relieved. What a picture of mutual love and
kind solicitude!

Compassions and affections for God's laborers: a precious chain of love

And observe the ways in which God, according to the
apostle, takes part in it. What are presented to us here
are His compassions, not the counsels of His love, but
compassions worthy of God, and affections of which He
approves among men. These affections and this value for
laborers are sometimes feared; and so much the more so,
because the assembly has in fact to disentangle itself from
all false dependence on man. But it is in the entire failure
of manifested strength and outward organized bond,
through the apostle's absence, that the Spirit of God develops the play of these inward affections and bonds for
the instruction of the assembly; as he acknowledges all
that remains of the ruins of its primitive position and its
outward bonds. He does not create these anew; but he
acknowledges that which still exists. It is only the first
verse of the epistle which speaks of this—no more was
needed; but the inward bonds he develops largely, not as
doctrine, but as fact. God Himself, the apostle, his faithful Timotheus, the valued servant of the Philippians, who
was so dear to them, and the fellow-laborer of Paul, the
servant of the Lord, the Philippians themselves, all have
their part in this precious and beautiful chain of love. The

graciousness of the Christian life is thus developed in every part of this chapter; the delicacy of his reproof of the spirit of division; his sending Timothy when he can let them know how it went with him, but Epaphroditus at once because they had heard he had been sick. This graciousness, and consideration of others, note, connects itself with a Christ who humbles Himself. A lowly Christ humbling Himself from Godhead-form down to death, is the spring of lowly graciousness; an exalted One sought in glory, the spring of energy which counts all to be dross and dung to win Him.

Chapter 3

Full enjoyment: its prevention and preservation in Christian experience

AFTER all it was in the Lord Himself that they had to rejoice, and the apostle now puts them on their guard against that which had eaten away the life of the assembly, and produced the painful fruits that filled his heart with anguish, and the deplorable consequences of which we see at this day, even as he foretold—consequences which will yet ripen for the judgment of God. Be this as it may, the Lord does not change. "Rejoice," he says, "in the Lord." There all is sure.

That which might prevent their thus rejoicing is developed, as well as the true knowledge of Christ, which preserves us from it: not here according to the doctrine and the practice that belong to the high position of the assembly's union with a glorified Christ as His Body, nor according to the unity which flows from it. This is the subject of the Ephesians. Neither is it according to the urgent necessity of cleaving to the Head, because all fulness is in Him. This is the instruction of the Epistle to the Colossians. But, in accordance with the general character of the epistle, the subject is here treated in connection with the personal experiences of the Christian, and, in particular, of the apostle. Accordingly—as was seen in his personal combats and sorrow—he finds himself on the road to the full enjoyment of this object whom he has learnt to know, and the state which his heart desires. This ought to be the Christian's experience, for, if I am united by the Spirit to the Head as a member of the Body of Christ, and if by faith I apprehend this union, it is none the less true that my personal experience (although this faith is its basis) is necessarily in connection with the paths which I follow in order to reach the glory this entitles me to. Not that the sentiments awakened by that which I encounter on this path either falsify or contradict my position in Christ, or destroy the certainty of my starting-point. But, while possessing this certainty, and because I possess it, I know that I have not in fact reached the result of this position in glory. Now, in this epistle, we are on the road, we are individualized in our relations with God; for experience is always individual, although our union with each other as members of Christ forms a part of this experience.

Warnings and instructions against leaving a known and glorified Christ to return to Judaism

In chapter 3 Paul resumes his exhortation; but it was not burdensome to him, and it was safe for them (danger being present and his tender love watchful), to renew his warnings and instructions respecting the admixture of Judaizing principles with the doctrine of a glorified Christ. It was in fact to destroy the latter and to reinstate the flesh (that is, sin and alienation from God) in its place. It was the first man, already rejected and condemned, and not the Second Man. Yet it is not in the shape of sin that the flesh appears here, but in that of righteousness, of all that is respectable and religious, of ordinances which had the venerable weight of antiquity attached to them, and as to their origin, if all had not been done away in Christ, the authority of God Himself.

To the apostle, who knew Christ in heaven, all this was but a bait to draw the Christian away from Christ, and throw him back again into the ruin out of which Christ had drawn him. And this would be so much the worse, because it would be to abandon a known and glorified Christ, and to return to that which had been proved to be of no value through the flesh. The apostle therefore spares neither the doctrine nor those who taught it.

Concision or circumcision: real love to Christ gives evil its true character

The glory which he had seen, his contests with these false teachers, the state into which they had thrown the assembly, Jerusalem and Rome, his liberty and his prison —all, had gained him the experience of what Judaism was worth as to the assembly of God. They were dogs, evil workers, that is, workers of malice and wickedness. It was not the circumcision. He treats it with profound contempt, and uses language, the harshness of which is justified by his love for the assembly (for love is severe towards those who, devoid of conscience, corrupt the object of that love). It was the concision.

When evil without shame, and laboring to produce evil under a disgraceful veil of religion, is manifested in its true character, mildness is a crime against the objects of the love of Christ. If we love Him, we shall in our intercourse with the assembly give the evil its true character, which it seeks to hide. This is real love and faithfulness to Christ. The apostle had certainly not failed in condescension to the weak in this respect. He had carried it far; his prison testified it. And now the assembly, deprived of his energy and that spiritual decision which was full of love to all which is good, was more in danger than ever. The experience of a whole life of activity, of the greatest patience, of four years' reflection in prison, led to these forcible and urgent words, "Beware of dogs, beware of evil workers, beware of the concision." The doctrine of the Epistle to the Ephesians, the exhortation of that to the Colossians, the affection of that to these Philippians, with the denunciation contained in chapter 3: 2, date from the same epoch, and are marked with the same love.

But it sufficed to denounce them. Elsewhere, where they were not well known, he gave details, as in the case of Timotheus, who had still to watch over the assembly. It was sufficient now to point out their well-known character. Whatever Judaized, whatever sought to mingle law and gospel, trusting in ordinances and the Spirit, was shameless, malicious, and contemptible. But the apostle will rather occupy himself with the power that delivers from it. We are the circumcision (that which is really separate from the evil, that which is dead to sin and to the flesh), we who worship God not in the false pretension of ordinances but spiritually by the power of the Holy Ghost, who rejoice in Christ the Saviour and not in the flesh, but on the contrary have no confidence in it. We see here Christ and the Spirit in contrast with the flesh and self.

Paul's righteousness of the flesh and the excellency of the knowledge of Christ Jesus eclipsing everything

Paul might indeed boast, if needful, in that which belonged to the flesh. As to all Jewish privileges, he possessed them in the highest degree. He had outstript every one in holy zeal against innovators. One thing alone had changed it all—he had seen a glorified Christ. All that he had according to the flesh was thenceforth loss to him. It would place something between him and the Christ of his faith and of his desire—the Christ whom he knew. And, observe, that here it is not the sins of the flesh which Christ expiates and abolishes that he rejects; it is its righteousness. It has none, we may say; but even if the apostle had possessed any righteousness of the flesh—as, in fact, he did possess it outwardly—he would not have it, because he had seen a better. In Christ, who had appeared to him on the way to Damascus, he had seen divine righteousness for man, and divine glory in man. He had seen a glorified Christ, who acknowledged the poor feeble members of the assembly as a part of Himself. He would have nothing else. The excellency of the knowledge of Christ Jesus his Lord had eclipsed everything—changed everything which was not that into loss. The stars, as well as the darkness of night, disappear before the sun. The righteousness of the law, the righteousness of Paul, all that distinguished him among men, disappeared before the righteousness of God and the glory of Christ.

Gain turned to loss and Christ become all

It was a thorough change in his whole moral being. His gain was now loss to him. Christ was become all. It was not evil which disappeared—everything that belonged to Paul as advantage to the flesh disappeared. It was Another who was now precious to him. What a deep and radical change in the whole moral being of man, when he ceases to be the centre of his own importance; and Another, worthy of being so, becomes the centre of his moral existence!—a divine Person, a Man who had glorified God, a Man in whom the glory of God shone out, to the eye of faith; in whom His righteousness was realized, His love, His tender mercy, perfectly revealed towards men and known by men. This was He whom Paul desired to win, to possess—for here we are still in the paths of the wilderness—he desired to be found in Him: "That I may win Christ, and be found in Him." Two things were present to his faith in this desire: to have the righteousness of God Himself as his (in Christ he should possess it); and then, to know Him and the power of His resurrection—for he only knew Him as risen—and, according to that power working in him now, to have part in the sufferings of Christ, and be made conformable to His death.

The death of Christ and the power of His resurrection

It was in His death that perfect love had been demonstrated, that the perfect ground of divine and eternal righteousness had been laid, that self-renunciation was practically, entirely, perfectly, manifested in Christ, the perfect object to the apostle of a faith that apprehended it and desired it according to the new man. Christ had passed through death in the perfection of that life, the power of which was manifested in resurrection.

Paul's desire to follow his Lord in His sufferings having seen Him in the glory

Paul, having seen this perfection in glory, and being united (weak as he was in himself) to Christ the source of this power, desired to know the power of His resurrection, that he might follow Him in His sufferings. Circumstances held this as a reality before his eyes. His heart only saw, or wished to see, Christ, that he might follow Him there. If death was on the way, he was only so much the more like Christ. He did not mind what it cost, if by any means he might attain. This gave undivided energy of purpose. This is indeed to know Him, as completely put to the test, and thus to know all that He was, His perfection—of love, of obedience, of devotedness—fully manifested; but the object is to win Him as He is.

Having seen Him in the glory, the apostle understood the path which had led Him there, and the perfection of Christ in that path. Participating in His life, he desired to realize its power according to His glory, that he might follow Him, in order to be where Jesus was, and in the glory with Him. This is what the Lord said in John 12: 23-26. Who had apprehended Him like Paul by the grace of God? Observe here the difference between him and Peter. Peter calls himself "a witness of the sufferings of Christ and a partaker of the glory that shall be revealed;" Paul, a witness of the glory as it is in heaven ("as He is," as John says), desires to share His suffering. It is the special foundation of the assembly's place, of walking in the Spirit, according to the revelation of the glory of Christ. It is this, I doubt not, which makes Peter say, that in all Paul's epistles—which he acknowledges moreover as a part of the scriptures—there are some things hard to be understood. It took man clean out of the whole ancient order of things.

The righteousness of God in Christ and the knowledge of Christ

Having then seen Christ in glory, there were two things for Paul—the righteousness of God in Christ, and the knowledge of Christ. The first entirely eclipsed everything of which the flesh could boast. This was "mine own," the righteousness of man according to the law. The other was the righteousness *of God*, which is by faith; that is, man is nothing in it. It is God's righteousness: man has part in it by believing, that is to say by faith in Christ Jesus. The believer has his place before God in Christ, in the righteousness of God Himself, which He had manifested in glorifying Christ, having glorified Himself in Him. What a position! Not only sin, but human righteousness, all that is of self, excluded; our place being according to the perfection in which Christ, as Man, has perfectly glorified God. But this place is necessarily the place of Him who has accomplished this glorious work. Christ in His Person and in His present position,[6] is the

[6] Not, of course, as to being at the right hand of God—this was personal.

expression of our place: to know Him is to know it. He is there according to divine righteousness. To be there, as He is, is that into which divine righteousness freely, but necessarily, introduces man—introduces us—in Christ. Thenceforth, having seen the righteousness of God in that Christ is there, I desire myself to know what it is to *be* there: and I desire to know Christ. But in truth this embraces all that He was in accomplishing it. The glory reveals the power and the result. That which He suffered is the work in which He glorified God; so that divine righteousness has been fulfilled in His exaltation, as Man, to divine glory. And here divine love, perfect devotedness to His Father's glory, constant and perfect obedience, the endurance of all things in order to give testimony of His Father's love for men, perfect patience, unfathomable sufferings, in order that love might be both possible and perfect for sinners—all in short that Christ was, being connected with His Person, makes Him an object which commands, possesses, delivers, and strengthens the heart, by the power of His grace acting in the new life, in which we are united to Him by the all-powerful link of the Spirit, and causes Him to be the alone object before our eyes.

Paul's desire for Christ's cup and His baptism: his practical personal experience and his own resurrection

Accordingly Paul desires to have that which Christ can give, His cup, and His baptism; and to leave to the Father, that which Christ left to Him, the disposal of places in the kingdom. He does not desire, like John and James, the right and left hand, that is, a good place for *himself*. He desires Christ, he would win Christ. He does not follow tremblingly, as the disciples did in that chapter (Mark 10); he desires to suffer—not, that is, for the sake of suffering, but to have part in the sufferings of

Christ. Instead therefore of going away like the young man in the same chapter, because he had much that could profit the flesh, instead of clinging like him to the law for his righteousness, he renounces that righteousness which he had in common with the young man; and all that he had he counted but as dung.

Here then we have the practical personal experience of the operation of this great principle, which the apostle has set forth in other epistles, that we have part with a glorified Christ. Also, in telling of the result as to himself, he speaks of his own resurrection according to the character of Christ's. It is not that of which Peter speaks, as we have seen, the simply participating in the glory that was to be revealed. It is that which precedes. Having seen Christ in the glory, according to the power of His resurrection, he desires to participate in that: and this is the force of his word, "if by any means." He desired to have part in the resurrection from among the dead. If, in order to reach it, it was needful to pass through death (as Christ had done), he would go through it, cost what it might, be it in ever so painful a way—and death was at that time before his eyes with its human terror: he desired fully to take part with Christ.

The resurrection from among the dead: Christ the example and pattern

Now it is the character of this resurrection that it is *from among* the dead; it is not simply the resurrection of the dead. It is to come out, by the favor and the power of God (as it regards Christ, and indeed us too by Him, by the righteousness of God), from the condition of evil into which sin had plunged men—to come out, after having been dead in sins, and now to sin, through the favor and power and righteousness of God. What grace! And what a difference! By following Christ according to the will of God, in the place where He has set us (and to be content with the lowest place, if God has given it us, is the same renunciation of self as to labor in the highest—the secret of each, is that Christ is everything and ourselves nothing), we participate in His resurrection—a thought full of peace and joy, and which fills the heart with love to Christ. Joyful and glorious hope, which shines before our eyes in Christ, and in that blessed Saviour glorified! The objects of divine favor in Him, we come forth—because the eye of God is upon us, because we are His—from the house of death, which cannot detain those who are His because the glory and the love of God are concerned in them. Christ is the example and the pattern of our resurrection; the principle (Rom. 8) and the assurance of our resurrection is in Him. The road to it is that which the apostle here traces.

Forgetting and pressing on: an undivided heart and mind

But since resurrection and likeness to Christ in glory were the objects of his hope, it is very evident that he had not attained it. If that was his perfection, he could not be yet perfect. He was, as has been said, on the road; but Christ had apprehended him for it, and he still pressed onward to lay hold of the prize, for the enjoyment of which Christ had laid hold of him. No, he repeats to his brethren, I count not myself to have attained. But one thing at least he could say—he forgot all that was behind him, and pressed on ever towards the goal, keeping it always in sight to obtain the prize of the calling of God, which is found in heaven. Happy Christian! It is a great thing never to lose sight of it, *never* to have a divided heart, to think but of one thing; to act, to think, always according to the positive energy wrought by the Holy Ghost in the new man, directing him to this only and heavenly object. It is not his sins properly which he here says he forgot—it was his progress that he forgot, his advantages, all that was already behind. And this was not merely the energy that showed itself at the first impulse; he *still* counted everything but as dung, because he had still Christ in view. This is true Christian life. What a sad moment would it have been for Rebecca, if, in the midst of the desert with Eliezer, she had forgotten Isaac, and begun to think again of Bethuel and her father's house! What had she then in the desert with Eliezer?

Such is the true life and position of the Christian; even as the Israelites, although preserved by the blood from the messenger of judgment, were not in their true place till they were on the other side of the Red Sea, a freed people. Then he is on the road to Canaan, as belonging to God.

The walk of Christ on earth

The Christian, until he understands this new position which Christ has taken as risen from the dead, is not spiritually in his true place, is not perfect or full-grown in Christ. But when he has attained this, it is not assuredly that he is to despise others. "If," says the apostle, "they were otherwise minded, God would reveal" to them the fulness of His truth; and all were to walk together with one mind in the things to which they had attained. Where the eye was single, it would be so: there were many with whom this was not the case; but the apostle was their example. This was saying much. While Jesus lived, the peculiar power of this resurrection-life could not be revealed in the same way; and moreover while on earth Christ walked in the consciousness of that which He was with His Father before the world existed, so that, although He endured for the joy that was set before Him, although His life was the perfect pattern of the heavenly man, there was in Him a repose, a communion, which had quite a peculiar character; instructive nevertheless to us, because the Father loves us as He loved Jesus, and Jesus also loves us as the Father loved Him. With Him it was not the energy of one who must run the race in order to attain that which he has never yet possessed; He spoke of that which He knew, and bore witness of that which He had seen, of that which He had forsaken from love to us, the Son of Man who was in heaven.

The various viewpoints of John, Peter and Paul

John enters farther into this character of Christ: in his epistle therefore we find more of that which He is in His nature and character, than of what we shall be with Him in the glory. Peter, building on the same foundation as the others, waits however for that which shall be revealed. His pilgrimage was indeed towards heaven, to obtain a treasure which was preserved there, which shall be revealed in the last time; but it is more connected with that which had been already revealed. From his point of view, the morning star on which Paul lived appeared only on the extreme horizon. For him practical life was that of Jesus among the Jews. He could not say with Paul, "Be ye followers of me." The effect of the revelation of the heavenly glory of Christ, between His going away and His reappearance, and that of the union of all Christians to Him in heaven, was fully realized in him only who received it. Faithful through grace to this revelation, having no other object which guided his steps, or to divide his heart, he gives himself as an example. He truly followed Christ, but the form of his life was peculiar, on account of the way in which God had called him; and it is thus that Christians possessing this revelation ought to walk.

Accordingly Paul speaks of a dispensation committed to him.

Constantly looking to Jesus as the heavenly, glorified Christ

It was not to turn their eyes from Christ; it is on having the eyes constantly fixed upon Him that he insists. It was this which characterized the apostle, and in this he gives himself as an example. But the character of this looking to Jesus was special. It was not a Christ known on earth who was its object, but a Christ glorified whom he had seen in heaven. To press ever forward to this end formed the character of his life; even as this same glory of Christ, as a testimony to the bringing in divine righteousness and to the assembly's position, formed the basis of his teaching. Therefore he can say, "Be followers of me." His gaze was ever fixed on the heavenly Christ, who had shone before his eyes and still shone before his faith.

Enemies of the cross of Christ without life walking among Christians: a low tone of Christianity allowing this: the divine grave and solemn judgment

The Philippians were thus to walk together, and to mark those who followed the apostle's example; because (for evidently it was a period in which the assembly as a whole had much departed from her first love and her normal condition) there were many who, while bearing the name of Christ and having once given good hope, so that the apostle speaks of them with tears, were enemies of the cross of Christ. For the cross on earth, in our life, answers to the heavenly glory on high. It is not the assembly at Philippi which is the subject here, but the condition of the outward universal assembly. Many were already calling themselves Christians, who joined to that great name a life which had the earth and earthly things for its object. The apostle did not acknowledge them. They were there; it was not a matter of local discipline, but a condition of Christianity, in which even all were seeking their own interest; and, spirituality being thus lowered, the Christ of glory little realized, many who had no life at all might walk among them without being detected, by those who had so little life themselves and scarcely walked better than they did. For it does not appear that they who were minding earthly things committed any evil that required public discipline. The general low tone of spirituality among the real Christians left the others free to walk with them; and the presence of the latter debased still more the standard of godliness of life.

But this state of things did not escape the spiritual eye of the apostle, which fixed on the glory, discerned readily and clearly all that had not that glory for its motive; and the Spirit has given us the divine judgment, most grave and solemn, with regard to this state of things. No doubt it has grown enormously worse since then, and its elements have developed and established themselves in a manner and in proportions that are very differently characterized; but the moral principles with regard to walk remain ever the same for the assembly. The same evil is present to be avoided, and the same efficacious means for avoiding it. There is the same blessed example to follow, the same heavenly Saviour to be the glorious object of our faith, the same life to live if we desire to be Christians indeed.

The two ends—of those whose hearts were set on earthly things and of the true Christian: our bodies of humiliation conformed to Christ's glorious body

That which characterized these persons who professed the name of Christ was, that their hearts were set upon earthly things. Thus the cross had not its practical power —it would have been a contradiction. Their end therefore was destruction. The true Christian was not such;

his conversation was in heaven and not on the earth; his moral life was spent in heaven, his true relationships were there. From thence he expected Christ as a Saviour, that is to say, to deliver him from the earth, from this earthly system far from God here below. For salvation is always viewed in this epistle as the final result of the conflict, the result due to the almighty power of the Lord. Then, when Christ shall come to take the assembly to Himself—Christians, truly heavenly, shall be like Him in His heavenly glory, a likeness which is the object of their pursuit at all times. (Compare 1 John 3: 2.) Christ will accomplish it in them, conforming their bodies of humiliation to His glorious body according to the power whereby He is able to subdue all things to Himself. Then the apostle and all Christians will have attained the end, the resurrection from among the dead.

Christ as the spring of energy of the Christian life and of its graciousness of walk: the thing at which Paul aimed

Such is the tenor of this chapter. Christ, seen in glory, is the spring of energy to Christian life, to win Christ, so that all else is loss; as Christ making Himself of no reputation is the spring of Christian graciousness of walk: the two parts of Christian life which we are too apt to sacrifice one to another, or at least to pursue one forgetful of the other. In both Paul singularly shines. In the following chapter we have superiority to circumstances. This also is Paul's experience and state; for it will be remarked that it is the personal experience of Paul which runs all through his (humanly speaking) faultless experience—not perfection. Likeness to Christ in glory is the only standard of that. As to this third chapter, many have inquired whether the thing aimed at was a spiritual assimilation to Christ here, or a complete assimilation to Him in the glory. This is rather to forget the import of what the apostle says, namely, that the sight and the desire of the heavenly glory, the desire of possessing Christ Himself thus glorified, was that which formed the heart here below. An object here below to be attained in oneself could not be found, since Christ is on high; it would be to separate the heart from the object which forms it to its own likeness. But although we never reach the mark here below, since it is a glorified Christ and resurrection from among the dead, yet its pursuit assimilates us more and more to Him. The object in the glory forms the life which answers to it here below. Were a light at the end of a long straight alley, I never have the light itself till I am arrived there; but I have ever-increasing light in proportion as I go forward; I know it better; I am more in the light myself. Thus it is with a glorified Christ, and such is Christian life. (Compare 2 Cor. 3.)

Chapter 4

The value of "standing fast in the Lord"

THE Philippians were therefore to stand fast in the Lord. This is difficult when the general tone is lowered; painful also, for one's walk becomes much more solitary, and the hearts of others are straitened. But the Spirit has very plainly given us the example, the principle, the character, and the strength of this walk. With the eye on Christ all is easy; and communion with Him gives light and certainty; and is worth all the rest which perhaps we lose.

The apostle nevertheless spoke gently of those persons. They were not like the false judaizing teachers who corrupted the sources of life, and stopped up the path of communion with God in love. They had lost this life of communion, or had never had more than the appearance of it. He wept for them.

The writer and bearer of the Epistle

I think that the apostle sent his letter by Epaphroditus, who probably also wrote it from the apostle's dictation; as was done with regard to all the epistles, except that to the Galatians, which, as he tells us, he wrote with his own hand. When therefore he says (chap. 4: 3), "true [or faithful] yokefellow," he speaks as I think, of Epaphroditus, and addresses him.

The Lord's grace in remembering and beseeching those at variance as well as others who were fellow-laborers

But he notices also two sisters even, who were not of one mind in resisting the enemy. In every way he desired unity of heart and mind. He entreats Epaphroditus (if indeed it be he) as the Lord's servant to help those faithful women who had labored in concert with Paul to spread the gospel. Euodias and Syntyche were perhaps of the number—the connection of thought makes it probable. Their activity, having gone beyond the measure of their spiritual life, betrayed them into an exercise of self-will which set them at variance. Nevertheless they were not forgotten, together with Clement and others, who were fellow-laborers with the apostle himself, whose names were in the book of life. For love for the Lord remembers all that His grace does; and this grace has a place for each of His own.

Practical exhortations to the faithful to walk according to their heavenly calling: the pure, untroubled spring of joy

The apostle returns to the practical exhortations addressed to the faithful, with regard to their ordinary life, that they might walk according to their heavenly calling. "Rejoice in the Lord." If he even weeps over many who call themselves Christians, he rejoices always in the Lord; in Him is that which nothing can alter. This is not an indifference to sorrow which hinders weeping, but it is a spring of joy which enlarges when there is distress, because of its immutability, and which becomes even more pure in the heart the more it becomes the only one; and it is in itself the only spring that is infinitely pure. When it is our only spring, we thereby love others. If we love them *besides Him,* we lose something of Him. When through exercise of heart we are weaned from all other springs, His joy remains in all its purity, and our concern for others partakes of this same purity. Nothing moreover troubles this joy, because Christ never changes. The better we know Him, the better are we able to enjoy that which is ever enlarging through knowing Him. But he exhorts Christians to rejoice: it is a testimony to the worth of Christ, it is their true portion. Four years in prison chained to a soldier had not hindered his doing it, nor being able to exhort others more at ease than he.

Moderation and meekness in view of Christ's presence

Now this same thing will make them moderate and meek; their passions will not be excited by other things if Christ is enjoyed. Moreover He is at hand. A little while, and all for which men strive will give place to Him whose presence bridles the will (or rather puts it aside) and fills the heart. We are not to be moved by things here below until He shall come. When He comes, we shall be fully occupied with other things.

Anxieties and disquiet silenced: encouragement to go to God with our requests: His peace promised

Not only are the will and the passions to be bridled and silenced, but anxieties also. We are in relationship with God; in all things He is our refuge; and events do not disturb Him. He knows the end from the beginning. He knows everything, He knows it beforehand; events shake neither His throne, nor His heart; they always accomplish His purposes. But to us He is love; we are through grace the objects of His tender care. He listens to us and bows down His ear to hear us. In all things therefore, instead of disquieting ourselves and weighing everything in our own hearts, we ought to present our requests to God with prayer, with supplication, with a heart that makes itself known (for we are human beings) but with the knowledge of the heart of God (for He loves us perfectly); so that, even while making our petition to Him, we can already give thanks, because we are sure of the answer of His grace, be it what it may; and it is *our* requests that we are to present to Him. Nor is it a cold commandment to find out His will and then come: we are to go with our requests. Hence it does not say, you will have what you ask; but God's peace will keep your hearts. This is trust; and His peace, the peace of God Himself, shall keep our hearts. It does not say that our hearts shall keep the peace of God; but, having cast our burden on Him whose peace nothing can disturb, His peace keeps our hearts. Our trouble is before Him, and the constant peace of the God of love, who takes charge of everything and knows all beforehand, quiets our disburdened hearts, and imparts to us the peace which is in Himself and which is above all understanding (or at least keeps our hearts by it), even as He Himself is above all the circumstances that can disquiet us, and above the poor human heart that is troubled by them. Oh, what grace, that even our anxieties are a means of our being filled with this marvellous peace, if we know how to bring them to God, and true He is! May we learn indeed how to maintain this intercourse with God and its reality, in order that we may converse with Him and understand His ways with believers!

A command to the Christian to occupy himself with good, to be where the God of peace is found

Moreover, the Christian, although walking (as we have seen) in the midst of evil and of trial, is to occupy himself with all that is good, and is able to do it when thus at peace, to live in this atmosphere, so that it shall pervade his heart, that he shall be habitually where God is to be found.   This is an all-important command.   We may be occupied with evil in order to condemn it; we may be right, but this is not communion with God in that which is good.   But if occupied through His grace with that which is good, with that which comes from Himself, the God of peace is with us.   In trouble we shall have the peace of God; in our ordinary life, if it be of this nature, we shall have the God of peace. Paul was the practical example of this; with regard to their walk, by following him in that which they had learnt and heard from him and seen in him, they should find that God was with them.

The apostle's need: his practical experience in learning to trust in Christ who strengthened him: the Philippians' gift acknowledged

Nevertheless, although such was his experience, he rejoiced greatly that their loving care of him had flourished again. He could indeed take refuge in God; but it was sweet to him in the Lord to have this testimony on their part. It is evident that he had been in need; but it was the occasion of more entire trust in God. We can easily gather this from his language; but, he delicately adds, he would not, by saying that their care of him had now at last flourished again, imply that they had forgotten him. The care for him was in their hearts; but they had not had the opportunity of giving expression to their love. Neither did he speak in regard of want; he had learnt— for it is practical experience and its blessed result we find here—to be content under all circumstances, and thus to depend on no one. He knew how to be abased; he knew how to abound; in every way he was instructed both to be full and to be hungry, to be in abundance and to suffer want. He could do all things through Him who strengthened him. Sweet and precious experience, not only because it gives ability to meet all circumstances, which is of great price, but because the Lord is known, the constant, faithful, mighty friend of the heart. It is not "I can do all things," but "I can do all through Him who strengtheneth me." It is a strength which continually flows from a relationship with Christ, a connection with Him maintained in the heart. Neither is it only "one can do all things." This is true; but Paul had learnt it practically. He knew what he could be assured of and reckon on—what ground he stood on. Christ had always been faithful to him, had brought him through so many difficulties and through so many seasons of prosperity, that he had learnt to trust in Him, and not in circumstances. And Christ was the same ever. Still the Philippians had done well, and it was not forgotten. From the first God had bestowed this grace upon them, and they had supplied the apostle's need, even when he was not with them. He remembered it with affection, not that he desired a gift, but fruit to their own account. "But," he says, "I have all," his heart turning back to the simple expression of his love. He was in abundance, having received by Epaphroditus that which they had sent him, an acceptable sacrifice of sweet odor, well-pleasing to God.

The God whom Paul had learned to know: His sure goodness and faithfulness applied to the Philippians

His heart rested in God; his assurance with regard to the Philippians expresses it. "My God," he says, "shall richly supply all your need." He does not express *a wish* that God may do so. He had learnt what his God was by his own experience. "*My* God," he says, He whom I have learnt to know in all the circumstances through' which I have passed, shall fill you with all good things. And here he returns to His character as he had known Him. God would do it according to His riches in glory in Christ Jesus. There he had learnt to know Him at the beginning; and such he had known Him all along his varied path, so full of trials here and of joys from above. Accordingly he thus concludes: "Now unto our God and Father"—for such He was to the Philippians also—"be glory for ever and ever." He applies his own experience of that which God was to him, and his experience of the faithfulness of Christ, to the Philippians. This satisfied his love, and gave him rest with regard to them. It is a comfort when we think of the assembly of God.

Paul's greetings from himself and others and his special salutation

He sends the greeting of the brethren who were with him, and of the saints in general, especially those of Cæsar's household; for even there God had found some who through grace had listened to His voice of love.

He ends with the salutation which was a token in all his epistles that they were from himself.

The present state of the Church adding increased value to the Epistle as giving proper Christian experience, that of a heart which trusted God alone, while having a thorn in the flesh

The present state of the assembly, of the children of God, dispersed anew, and often as sheep without shepherd, is a very different condition of ruin from that in which the apostle wrote; but this only adds more value to the experience of the apostle which God has been pleased to give us; the experience of a heart which trusted in God alone, and which applies this experience to the condition of those who are deprived of the natural resources that belonged to the organized Body, to the Body of Christ as God had formed it on earth. As a whole, the epistle shows proper Christian experience, that is, superiority, as walking in the Spirit, to everything through which we have to pass. It is remarkable to see that sin is not mentioned in it, nor flesh, save to say he had no confidence in it.

He had at this time a thorn in the flesh himself, but the proper experience of the Christian is walking in the Spirit above and out of the reach of all that may bring the flesh into activity.

Special points in Chapters 3, 2 and 4

The reader will remark that chapter 3 sets the glory before the Christian and gives the energy of Christian life; chapter 2, the self-emptying and abasement of Christ, and founds thereon the graciousness of the Christian life, and thoughtfulness of others: while the last chapter gives a blessed superiority to all circumstances.

END OF VOL. 4.